INTERPERSONAL COMMUNICATION

Making Social Worlds

INTERPERSONAL COMMUNICATION
Making Social Worlds

W. Barnett Pearce

Loyola University of Chicago

HarperCollinsCollegePublishers

Tasha and Barry Daniel
"Live long, and prosper!"

Senior Acquisitions Editor: Daniel F. Pipp
Project Coordination and Text Design: York Production Services
Cover Design: Wendy Fredericks
Production Manager: Kewal Sharma
Compositor: York Production Services
Printer and Binder: RR Donnelley and Sons Company
Cover Printer: The Lehigh Press

Interpersonal Communication: Making Social Worlds

Library of Congress Cataloging-in-Publication Data

Pearce, W. Barnett.
    Interpersonal communication : making social worlds / W. Barnett Pearce.
      p. cm.
    Includes bibliographical references and index.
    ISBN 0-06-500288-1
    1. Interpersonal communication.   I. Title.
BF637.C45P347 1993
302.2—dc20   93-29384
                                      CIP

9 8 7 6 5 4 3 2 1

BRIEF CONTENTS

v

PART THREE
Recapitulation 337

CONTENTS

PART TWO
Motifs 101

CHAPTER 3 Speech Acts 102

CHAPTER 5 Relationships **200**

CHAPTER 7 Culture 296

PART THREE
Recapitulation   337

CHAPTER 8 Putting It All Together   338

PREFACE

Interpersonal Communication: Making Social Worlds is a textbook for college and university courses in interpersonal communication. These are very popular courses, but their popularity does not derive from a consensus on how they should be taught. Fifteen years ago, my survey of the field found three very different clusters of textbooks and related research programs. I called them the "objective scientific," "humanistic celebration," and "humane scientific" approaches (Pearce 1977). Although the field has developed in the intervening years, considerable diversity in the way this course is taught still remains. One index of the lack of consensus is found in bibliographies. Boynton-Trigg's (1991) survey of five leading textbooks in interpersonal communication found that although a total of 336 authors were cited, only two—Mark Knapp and Paul Watzlawick—were cited in all five textbooks.

I set my hand to the task of writing another textbook with the explicit understanding that it would not be "just another textbook." I wanted to make a contribution to the materials available for teaching interpersonal communication, and I had two choices: to write an integrative textbook including *all* the topics taught under the rubric of interpersonal communication, or to write a distinctive book that takes what I consider to be the most powerful concepts in the field and makes them available for students. I chose to do the latter; if I have succeeded, *Interpersonal Communication: Making Social Worlds* is conceptually distinctive, pedagogically rich *and* "user friendly."

The Conceptual Orientation

This book is written from the "social constructionist" approach to interpersonal communication. The body of work known as the "coordinated management of meaning" is the supportive infrastructure of this book, and is located in the larger context of systems theory (as articulated by Gregory Bateson and his intellectual heirs); language-game analysis (as developed from Ludwig Wittgenstein by Rom Harré, John Shotter, Ken Gergen, and others); the American Pragmatists (chiefly William James, John Dewey, and George Herbert Mead, as they have been interpreted by Richard Bernstein, Giles Gunn, and Richard Rorty); the symbolic analysis of Kenneth Burke (as it has influenced a generation of scholars); and contemporary ethnographic research (after the manner of Clifford Geertz, Harold Garfinkel, and Erving Goffman). My appropriation of all of these into a communication theory, particularly a theory of interpersonal communication, was done as part of a loosely bound group and in (sometimes intense) dialogue with communication theorists whose work focuses on interpersonal, intercultural, mass-mediated, and rhetorical communication.

The social constructionist approach thematizes interpersonal communication in a distinctive manner. The "process" of communication per se—an undulating, co-constructed activity of conversation—is emphasized; the various "products" of interpersonal communication are situated in that process. Traditional topics, such as intercultural communication, nonverbal communication, and self-disclosure are presented as part of an integrated analysis of conversation rather than as isolated variables or themes.

The Structure of the Book

Each chapter includes three parts: "Narrative," "Counterpoints," and "Praxis." These allow students to learn from complementary perspectives. "Narrative" sections provide information and concepts with which to think about interpersonal communication, "Counterpoints" provoke a playful peering around the corners of taken-for-granted assumptions, and "Praxis" sections structure activities in which students can learn from encountering the stuff of interpersonal communication. These sections do not duplicate each other. In fact, they are not always consistent: the tensions between exposition, provocation, and participation are the sites in which learning about interpersonal communication takes place.

The "Narrative" sections are the most familiar; they are straightforward expositions of information about interpersonal communication. This material is didactic, allowing students to learn by remembering what they read. Of the three types of material, this is the one about which I am most ambivalent. Straightforward expositions are the most effective way of teaching students who are highly motivated and who are appropriately focused. However, it is the least effective way of learning about interpersonal communication.

While Dean of the Annenberg School of Communication, George Gerbner noted that universities developed in a context best described as "informationally deprived." Students would leave their homes and go to colleges that were oases of information and intellection. Libraries and lecturers were appropriately seen as repositories of the accumulated information of the culture, and education was primarily a matter of access to those resources. This hardly describes the contemporary scene; Gerbner described ours as an "information-saturated" society. To avoid being swamped by information, our students have developed sophisticated skills in disattending to information; the college classroom often fares poorly in competition with the entertaining presentation of information in films, television, specialty magazines, and conventions of hobbyists or fans. The narrative description of interpersonal communication must be very good indeed to rival that provided in soap operas, serious films, *Nova* presentations, and an increasingly sophisticated street wisdom in which gangs, drugs, sex, and racial prejudice are a part of the overt consciousness of students. Because the "Narrative" sections must compare unfavorably with the production values of *MTV* and the marketing strategies of specialty magazines or narrowly cast electronic publications, the "Counterpoint" sections are included to exploit the potential of a printed textbook and the "Praxis" sections to exploit the resources of a college classroom.

"Counterpoints" comprise the second type of material in *Interpersonal Communication: Making Social Worlds*. Print remains the best medium for stimulating reflective, analytical thought. Inserted into the "Narratives" but distinguished from them by being enclosed in boxes, these materials include provocations, commentary, invitations to shift perspectives, metacommunication, and the literary equivalent to theatrical asides in which I "break character" as author and speak directly to the reader. Some are thought-provoking quotations or questions; some are simply bits of information or ideas that I want to call to students' attention; some are conundrums that perplex me; but all are intended to develop that serious but slightly irreverent attitude toward the "Narrative" that is the precondition for reflective, analytical thought.

The importance of an irreverent, playful mindset cannot be over stressed. Interpersonal communication is a fluid, contingent, unfinished process in which we participate from a perspective more like that of the paddler of a canoe on a whitewater river than that of a cartographer mapping the river's course; from a perspective more like that of a boxer whose chin has suddenly encountered the fist of his opponent than that of a celebrity television announcer. Our knowledge and participation in such a process from such a perspective requires a good bit of playfulness or at least intellectual athleticism. Much of the material in the "Counterpoints" consists of conceptual agility drills; limbering exercises for the mind that enable more flexible practice of interpersonal communication.

The "Praxis" sections comprise the third and most distinctive feature of the book. These are activities that I urge students to do, usually in groups and generally in class. I do not view these as a supplement to the text; to the contrary, these activities are the site where the most effective and valuable learning will take place. The activities are closely tied to the concepts presented in the "Narrative" and "Counterpoint" sections, but if one were forced to choose among them, I think that a student would learn more about interpersonal communication from participating in the praxis activities than from reading (and passing an examination on) the "narrative."

Differentiating Kinds of Knowledge

I am committed to "participatory learning" in interpersonal communication not because of personal preference but because that is what my analysis of interpersonal communication requires. In the *Nicomachean Ethics,* Aristotle differentiated *theoria* (spectator knowledge), *poesis* (knowledge of techniques), and *praxis* (good judgment, or practical wisdom). Each of these ways of knowing are appropriate for a particular category of events. *Theoria* is appropriate for eternal, immutable objects; *poesis,* for repetitive, rote performances; and *praxis,* for things that are contingent. Contingent things, in Aristotle's words, are those that could be other than what they are. Politics, public speaking, and household management, according to Aristotle, are included in the domain of *praxis* because they are contingent.

Interpersonal communication is clearly part of *praxis;* every conversation in which we participate *could* be (or has been) something other than it is (or was). If we had done *this* rather than *that,* then she would have done *that* rather than *this,* and our lives would have been different. This is the *form* of knowledge about interpersonal communication: it is contingent, uncertain, temporal, and from a first-person perspective. The next time we meet, so our knowledge goes, if I do *this* rather than what she expects me to do, then she may do *that,* which opens up a space in which we can do *that* . . . and so on.

The kind of knowledge illustrated in the preceding paragraph has little to do with "facts" and, although it presumes a mastery of technique, it goes far beyond it. Aristotle used the term *phronesis* for the kind of knowledge that is useful in *praxis*: it has more to do with the skilled judgment of a virtuoso artist than with a list of facts; more with the "instinctive" performance of a dancer or ballplayer than with an encyclopedia of information; it is better "coached" than taught.

Interpersonal Communication: Making Social Worlds is explicitly committed to facilitating the development of *phronesis* in the students who use it. For that reason, it invites participation rather than prescribes formula; it probes, suggests, playfully nudges, as well as didactically sets forth the received wisdom. It will frustrate those—teachers and students—who seek to utter the last word about interpersonal communication; it will reward those who seek to explore, open up possibilities, and enhance their ability to appreciate beauty and goodness in the social worlds in which they live.

Interpersonal Communication: Making Social Worlds provides a rich array of materials for the instructor. At the same time, it is a demanding text. The instructor must decide how much to emphasize the didactic material in the "Narratives," the metacommunication in the "Counterpoints," and the activities in the "Praxis." Some instructors will want to incorporate materials not covered in the textbook or to read further in social constructionist theory to lead critical discussions of the conceptual basis of the course. These topics, as well as suggestions for syllabus preparation and evaluation, are discussed in the *Instructors' Manual*.

Interpersonal Communication and "The Real World"

Just as our social worlds must, *Interpersonal Communication: Making Social Worlds* deals with real-life, tough problems such as race, gender, class, injustice, and ideological oppression as they relate to interpersonal communication. Embedded in the description of the process of interpersonal communication is a treatment of the human life cycle. The forms and functions of interpersonal communication change as we mature; the challenges and resources available to us are not always the same. *Interpersonal Communication: Making Social Worlds* attempts to enable students of all races, ages, and social classes to identify their own positions within the matrix of conversations in their lives, and to understand that others occupy other positions.

This leads me to a final confession. For twenty-something years I have labored as a minor academic, trying to develop communication theory. Any sufficiently self-aware person must occasionally ask, "Why?" What deep psychosis or purpose impels one to labor long into nights better suited for feasting or sleeping? What unconscious attraction drags the attention again and again to the same phenomena when one could look elsewhere for novelty? Why continue to wrestle with language, imprisoning legions of words on ranks of pages and struggling to find new ways of putting things?

These dark musings are in the spirit of e.e. cummings' observation that

> since feeling is first
> who pays any attention
> to the syntax of things
> will never wholly kiss you;
> . . .
> for life's not a paragraph
> and death i think is no parenthesis

Sometimes our students will ask, with fewer dark edges to their questions, "What will a course in interpersonal communication do for me?"

The answer that sustains me, and that I offer through this book to generations of students whom I will never see, is this. The study of interpersonal communication enhances our ability to appreciate beauty and goodness in the social worlds around us, it increases our ability to call into being patterns of social interaction that are good and beautiful, it empowers our ability to embrace the conditions of our lives playfully and thus transcend them, and in these ways, it enriches our lives and enhances our value as participants in our social worlds.

Because interpersonal communication is a form of *praxis,* it is best understood in terms of whether it is done well or poorly, and whether the patterns it produces are beautiful or ugly. There is far more than enough ugliness in the patterns of interpersonal communication that surround us, and the price that one pays for heightened ethical and aesthetic appreciation is a keener awareness of evil and ugliness. But if we are to avoid reproducing in our own lives variations of the same old reprehensible patterns we abhor, we must increase our *phronesis.*

The patterns of interpersonal communication in every social setting also contain beauty and goodness. Students who take seriously what is written here, and who engage with the questions and activities suggested in the text, will be better able to discern, appreciate, and create instances of such beauty.

Acknowledgments

Many people have contributed to the production of this book; some have contributed far more than they knew. (Confidentially, that's the risk you take when you are in the presence of social theorists who regularly plagiarize daily life!) Citing them in this preface reflects much more heartfelt gratitude than might appear to be conveyed in a list of names.

Vernon Cronen, University of Massachusetts, has been my partner for nearly two decades as we have tried to develop a coherent set of thoughts around the metaphor of "coordinated management of meaning." His influence on this book far exceeds the number of times his name is cited; of course, he will think—probably correctly—that the book would be better were his influence even greater!

My most valuable learning experience during this past decade has been working with an international group of therapists, consultants, and researchers who have been heavily influenced by the work of Gregory Bateson. Among many others, they include Peter Lang, Susan Lang, Martin Little, and Marjorie Henry of the Kensington Consultation Centre (London); Gianfranco Cecchin and Luigi Boscolo of the Centro Milanese di Terapia della Famiglia; Anna Castellucci of the Ospedale psichiatrico "F. Rancati" di Bologna; Laura Fruggeri of the Universita di Parma; Maurizo Marzari of the Universita di Bologna; Dora Schnitman of the Fundacion Interfas (Buenos Aires); Elspeth McAdam of Bethel Hospital (Norwich); and Eduardo Villar C. of the Fundacion de Psicoanalisis y Psicoterapis (Bogotá).

James Applegate, University of Kentucky, and Bob Craig, University of Colorado, made more contributions to this work than they probably realize; to them, a heartfelt thanks. The ideas in this book have been worked out in conversations over many years with Jim Averill, University of Massachusetts, Amherst; Art Bochner, University of South Florida; Bob Branham, Bates College; Donal Carbaugh, University of Massachusetts, Amherst; Victoria Chen, Denison University; Don Cushman, State University of New York at Albany; Sally Freeman, University of Massachusetts, Amherst; Ken Gergen, Swarthmore College; Rom Harré, Oxford University; Kang Kyung-wha, Office of the Speaker, National Assembly, Republic of Korea; Jack Lannamann, University of New Hampshire; Wendy Leeds-Hurwitz, University of Wisconsin, Parkside; Uma Narula, Indian Institute of Mass Communication, Delhi; Robyn Penman, Communication Research Institute of Australia; Gerry Philipsen, University of Washington; John Shotter, University of New Hampshire; Tim Stevens, Rensselaer Polytechnic Institute; Claudio Baraldi, University of Urbino; Jennings Bryant, University of Alabama, Tuskaloosa; Paulo Sacchetti, Forli; Stuart Sigman, University of New York, Albany; and Bob Saunders, University of New York, Albany.

I am particularly indebted to Diana Kincaid, North Central College, for many useful responses to early drafts of the manuscript. Melissa Rosati was the Communications Editor at Harper Collins who initially suggested this project; Anne Boynton-Trigg was the Development Editor who kept my feet to the fire; and Dan Pipp, the Editor who saw the project through: to them, thanks for allowing me the opportunity to break some of the conventions of textbook writing.

A number of anonymous reviewers sent often-conflicting messages about what was good and bad in various drafts of the manuscript; they comprised a goodly chorus of interlocutors to whom I am deeply indebted. When I discovered their identities, I found that three of these reviewers deserve my double thanks, both as reviewers and as continuing conversational partners over the years. So a special affirmation of gratitude for matters great and small to Stanley Deetz, Rutgers University; Stephen W. Littlejohn, Humboldt State University; and Sheila McNamee, University of New Hampshire. I appreciate the help offered by Joseph Folger, Temple University; Roger L. Garrett, Central Washington University; Beth A. LePoire, Texas A&M University, Jonathan Millen, Rider College; and George B. Ray, Cleveland State University.

Finally, my wife, Nur Intan Murtadza, accepted the intrusion of this project into our family gracefully. Her support and encouragement, particularly during the period when writing was a necessary obsession, is greatly appreciated.

References

Boynton-Trigg, Anne. Personal communication. 1991.

cummings, e.e., "since feeling is first." *The Norton Anthology of Poetry,* 3rd ed., 1042. New York: W.W. Norton, 1983.

Gerbner, George. "Liberal Education in the Information Age." *1983–84 Current Issues in Higher Education.* pp. 14–18.

Pearce, W. Barnett. "Teaching Interpersonal Communication as a Humane Science: A Comparative Analysis." *Communication Education,* 26 (1977): 104–112.

PART ONE

Overture

I use the word "conversation" metaphorically to refer not only to speech but to all techniques and technologies that permit people of a particular culture to exchange messages. In this sense, all culture is a conversation or, more precisely, a corporation of conversations, conducted in a variety of symbolic modes.

Neil Postman, Amusing Ourselves to Death. *New York:* Penguin, p. 6.

CHAPTER
1 *Understanding Conversations*

Suppose that a social scientist had observed a pair of friends sitting on a park bench having a conversation. . . . Suppose further that the social scientist approached the pair with the following: "Pardon me. I noticed that the two of you were having a conversation. As a scientist and a student of conversation, what I want to know is this: How did you do that?" Clearly the initial response to such a question would be utter befuddlement; the second would probably be "Do what?" Most of us regard conversation as *effortless*. . . . To suggest to its unreflecting practitioners that it might be appropriately regarded as an *accomplishment* would be to create doubt as to the number of oars, so to speak, that one had in the water.

Despite the fact that most people take the ability to carry on a conversation for granted, closer inspection reveals that [it] . . . is a highly complex activity that requires of those who would engage in it the ability to apply a staggering amount of knowledge . . .

McLaughlin 1984, pp. 13–14.

OBJECTIVES

After reading this chapter, you will be able to

- Analyze conversations from both first- and third-person perspectives

- Describe the moral orders of specific conversations

- Choose among alternative "readings" of conversations

- Compare the social constructionist perspective on communication with the transmission/representation model

KEY WORDS AND PHRASES

Some terms that will help you understand this chapter include

models and definitions of communication, common sense, first- and third-person perspectives, theoria and praxis, phronesis, and logics of meaning and action

Narrative

People have always participated in interpersonal communication, but only a few, and those only relatively recently, have ever *studied* it. Interpersonal communication is a relatively new addition (i.e., within the past fifty years) to the curriculum of most universities, and courses in interpersonal communication are still most commonly found in the United States. In most other countries, "communication" is virtually equated with "mass communication."

What have researchers found sufficiently interesting in interpersonal communication that we have invested our adult lifetime in studying it? Why have hard-nosed college administrators decided that the results of our work is important enough, even in an era of tight budgets, to include it in the curriculum? Much more importantly, what do *you* want to know about interpersonal communication? What do we mean by interpersonal communication anyway? What does "knowing" about interpersonal communication mean?

The Formal Study of a Familiar Process

Those who raise a quizzical eyebrow at the formal study of interpersonal communication have a point: there is nothing more "normal," central, or basic to what it means to be a human being than to be in interpersonal communication. Every one of us "knows" a lot about interpersonal communication, and we are all able to get along quite well in the conversations that comprise our daily lives.

When Common Sense Is Not Enough

If you are like most people, interpersonal communication is so much a part of your everyday life that you are unaware of it. Like walking or breathing, interpersonal communication is so normal that you only think about it when something goes wrong. But things do go wrong: if you have sprained your ankle, walking from your home to your car requires both thought and courage, or if you have asthma or infected sinuses, the very idea of an effortless breath of fresh air seems like an impossible ecstasy. A *sufficient* reason for taking a course in interpersonal communication as part of your higher education is that all of us will face situations for which our common-sense knowledge is insufficient.

What you learn from this book will probably not loom large in your consciousness while you are having a casual chat with your friends or enjoying a conversation during dinner with your family. However, life is not always so "normal." Think with me about some of the conversations that you will surely have at one time or another.

■ You are talking with a classmate about the careers you expect to have after graduation. To your surprise, your friend thinks that your assumption that hard work and personal contacts will lead to financial success is naive. She believes that God has a purpose for every life, and that this purpose may mean that you will live your life in poverty, regardless of your efforts. For the sake of your soul, she suggests, God might destroy your career and teach you the virtues of humility and poverty no matter how intelligent or diligent you are. A third classmate has overheard the conversation and disagrees with both of you. Citing the extent to which personal fortunes are dependent on political and economic factors far removed from the control of individuals, he cites economic determinism as the causal factor in your financial success. Your prosperity will rise or fall on the basis of decisions made by Japanese stockbrokers or Middle Eastern oil investors whom you will never meet. You have never really thought about these issues; how do you continue the conversation?

■ You are preparing for an important job interview. How do you make a good impression? How can you discern what the interviewer is looking for? How can you present yourself most favorably?

■ At another time, you are interviewing someone to work for you. What questions can you ask that will enable you to choose someone whose work will meet your needs rather than someone who just knows how to perform well in an interview?

■ A friend drops by your apartment late one night, deeply upset and needing to talk about some personal problems. What kinds of questions do you ask your friend? How do you answer your friend's questions? How is this conversation similar to and different from an employment interview?

■ Sooner or later, you will have a conversation with a medical doctor who will tell you bad news. These conversations often go badly; you find that you do not get the information you need to make some important decisions, such as whether to have surgery or to change some important part of your lifestyle. How can you do better in these conversations? How do you tell your spouse, your parents, or your children that you have a life-threatening physical condition? What do you say to a member of your family or a friend who has just learned that she or he has a sexually transmitted disease or a terminal illness?

■ There will be significant events in your relationships with your parents, your lover(s), your spouse, and your children. For example, you will discuss whether to live together, to get married, to get divorced, or to take that fateful first trip to meet your significant other's parents. You will decide whether to have children, how to apportion the tasks of raising the children, and whether the children should be encouraged to play contact sports in school. The meaning of these events will be constructed in conversations about them. Should these conversations have a special form? How should you speak and how should you listen in these conversations? Should you do anything differently than you normally do?

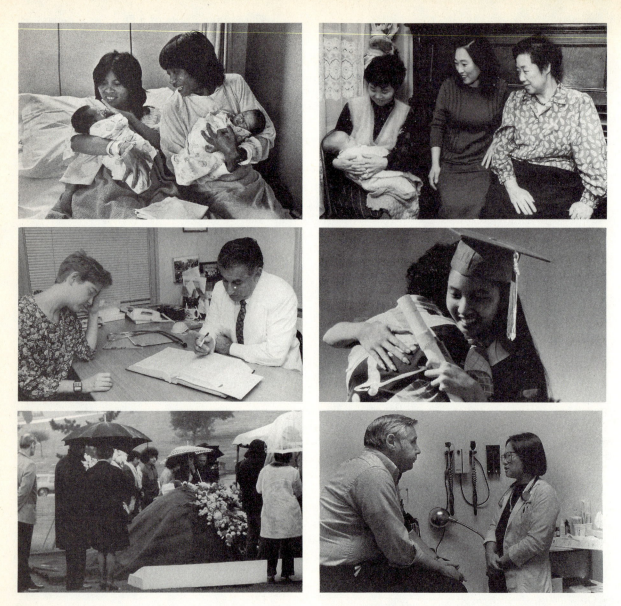

All of us will face situations for which our common-sense knowledge about interpersonal communication is insufficient.

Counterpoint 1.1

A sufficient reason for studying interpersonal communication is that all of us will participate, sooner or later, in unusual situations for which our common sense is not sufficient. This claim, however, depends on a particular notion of what is meant by *normal* situations and by *common sense*.

Anthropologist Clifford Geertz (1983, p. 75) defined common sense as "a relatively organized body of considered thought." That definition, of course, could apply to religion, science, or any political ideology. The distinguishing characteristic of "common sense," Geertz claimed, is that it *denies* that it is "a relatively organized body of considered thought." To the contrary, common sense presents itself as what anyone in his right mind knows, and its tenets as "immediate deliverances of experience, not deliberated reflections upon it." The power of common sense is exactly this pretense of immediacy, that everyone naturally knows what common sense means. As Geertz said, "Religion rests its case on revelation, science on method, ideology on moral passion; but common sense rests its on the assertion that it is not a case at all, just life in a nutshell. The world is its authority."

As a person who has lived in and studied many cultures, Geertz (1983, p. 80) noted the importance of common sense. "It is this conviction of the plain man [sic] that he is on top of things . . . that makes action possible for him at all, and which . . . must therefore be protected at all costs." Your ability to move through a day filled with complex conversations requires that you do *not* stop and make scientific or philosophical analyses every time someone asks you "How are you?" or encourages you to "have a nice day!"

However, the necessity for all of us to rely on common sense does not mean that the content of your common sense or mine is "right." Science is, among other things, a process for discovering that certain common-sense notions do not work out in real life, and anthropologists have shown that the common senses of various cultures differ significantly. For example, although the division of human beings into two genders is one of the most powerful dichotomies that we know, there are many people who have physical characteristics of both sexes. This is known as intersexuality or hermaphroditism. Geertz (1983, pp. 80–84) contrasted three cultures' common sense about hermaphroditism: contemporary Americans, Navaho, and Pokot (a culture in Kenya), and concluded (p. 84) that "Common sense is not what the mind cleared of cant spontaneously apprehends; it is what the mind filled with presuppositions . . . concludes. God may have made the intersexuals, but man has made the rest."

Our ability to carry on the many conversations that fill our days requires us to rely on our common sense. However, this common sense is a more or less well-organized body of (more or less) considered thought. One function of a liberal education is to call into question the common sense that you have acquired from your culture, permitting you to sift, test, rearrange, and finally to "own" your own common sense rather than relying on it unreflectively. This ownership of your common sense is valuable in two types of situations: those so unusual that your common sense provides an insufficient guide and those that strain your ability to act normally.

The concept of acting normally also requires some thought. The most common concept is that the *norm* is what most people do. That is, if a survey shows that most people between the ages of 18 and 22 have three romantic relationships, you are "normal" if you have three and "abnormal" if you have more or fewer.

Jack Bilmes (1986), among many others, argues that this concept of normal simply does not work. He came to this conclusion while doing research for his doctoral dissertation; the study "failed" (Bilmes 1986, p. 1) because people's talk does not represent how their minds work. He asked his subjects to explain how they came to community decisions, and found that their "talk was no longer useful to me as a description of the invisible motions of their minds—it was just talk. From their explanations of their decisions, I could not hope to learn how they had reached those decisions, but I could learn about how villagers explain their decisions, if I would be willing to settle for that."

Bilmes (1986, p. 161) suggested that norms are not statistical averages (e.g., "65 percent of 21–year-olds have had three romantic relationships") or moral imperatives (e.g., "21–year-olds *should* have had three romantic relationships"). Rather, they are "the idiom of negotiation." That is, they are bits of common sense that are cited in conversations to *make* what people say and do *normal.* We "orient to rules and . . . are capable of recognizing whether behavior conforms to the rules" (Bilmes 1986, p. 166). Twenty-one-year-olds are not abnormal if they have had more or fewer than the average number of romantic relationships as long as they know how to *normalize* their romantic history by orienting to the norm. "I'm saving my libido until later, when I can afford it," Emil said, normalizing his fewer-than-average relationships.

Normalizing your actions—that is, orienting them to some of the bits of information or value judgments embedded in common sense—is an important part of communication competence. However, there will be times when you need to examine the content of your common sense. Perhaps you want to be outrageous, acting in ways that are not normal; perhaps you need to expose and bring about change in some aspect of common sense. In these situations, you need to be able to put your common sense in the foreground and to choose whether and how to "normalize" your behavior.

■ You meet with your teacher to discuss an assignment for class. The quality of this conversation may determine whether you do well or poorly on the project, whether you understand when the assignment is due, and thus whether you do well in the course. How can you be sure that the conversation goes as well as possible?

■ Someone you know commits suicide, commits an unthinkable crime, or suddenly starts acting irrationally and has to be treated for mental illness. When this happens, you will ask yourself why you did not see it coming. What did they say or do that might have given you a sign of how distressed they were? You will find yourself thinking like a communication theorist, asking, If I had done *this,* would she have done *that?* or Was it inevitable?

Mundane Sites of Important Processes

When we examine these significant, abnormal conversations, we realize that many of the most important things that we do in our lives are done in conversations. From this realization, it is a simple step to realize that for most of us, *most* of our waking lives are spent in conversations. Interpersonal communication is not only normal, it is ubiquitous. When we stop taking conversations for granted and focus on them, we discover that even ordinary, mundane conversations are the sites of important processes.

For example, the way our parents treated us when we asked them to play with us in the park or if we could have a dog is more important than whether we went to the park or got the dog. These conversations taught us about who we are, what rights we have, and which ways of interacting with others are effective. Some of us learned that "asking politely" is both appropriate and effective; others of us learned that demands got better results than requests; still others learned that tears and tantrums worked best. Most of us have long since forgotten that we learned these lessons in conversations when we were very young, but they continue to give shape to our manner of relating to authority figures long after we have become adults.

A Distinctive Way of Understanding our Social Worlds

The best reason to study interpersonal communication is that it gives us a unique and incisive way of understanding ourselves, our relationships with others, and the situations in which we find ourselves—in short, our "social worlds." Of course, most of the departments in a university enhance your understanding of social worlds, but they do so in different (although frequently overlapping) ways. In this course, we will think about many of the same topics as you might explore in anthropology, psychology, sociology, economics, literature, political science, and history, but the *interpersonal communication perspective* is distinctive for three reasons.

First, it includes a first-person perspective, not only describing patterns of social interaction but also placing you within those patterns and helping you address the question, What should I do? That is, this course does not just tell you what generally happens or how you should critique what happens, it includes you and what you do *in* the process we are studying. Increasing your ability to sense openings, to envision a wider array of opportunities, and to intervene in ways that serve your purposes and those of the people around you—that is, your *competence* is an integral part of the course.

Second, the interpersonal communication perspective focuses on actions rather than on objects. That is, in addition to describing some of the wonderful and horrible events and objects in our social worlds, the study of interpersonal communication helps you deal with the question What should I *do* about it?

Third, the study of interpersonal communication is incomplete if all it does is to give you new facts about interpersonal communication (although

Counterpoint 1.2

The distinction between the first- and third-person perspective explains the difference between two wings of empirical research in the social sciences in the United States. About one hundred years ago, social theorists were just beginning to use empirical methods of research. J. B. Watson (1919; 1928) founded the school of behaviorism, which took an unremitting third-person orientation to the social world. In this view, the scientist cares only about data obtained by third-person observers in controlled, preferably laboratory, settings. On the other hand, William James and John Dewey, in somewhat different ways, offered versions of a first-person orientation to the social world. James (1967, originally published in 1912) used the term *radical empiricism* and Dewey (1929, originally published in 1925) *experience*. Both focused on the experiencing subject as the proper data for social theory.

Watson's ideas won the battle and dominated American social theory during the first half of the century. More recently, social scientists trained in this tradition have expended much energy learning how to think beyond it. "New paradigms" have been on the agenda for social theorists for the past twenty years.

The contest between these positions seldom focused on the perspective from which social activity was being analyzed. Perhaps it should have; in this book, we will carefully differentiate among the person-perspectives from which we understand interpersonal communication. A conversation is a very different thing, depending on whether it is understood from the first-person or the third-person perspective.

I suspect that you will learn quite a few). It is more important that you learn new tools for thinking about the process of interpersonal communication. That is, if you do well in this course, you may or may not increase your *knowledge* about interpersonal communication, but you will certainly increase your *sophistication* and *ability to make good judgments* in real situations. When someone asks you what you learned in this course, I hope that you will say something to the effect that you learned some new ways of thinking and acting.

To help achieve these goals, each chapter includes two sections. The first is "Narrative": these sections contain a straightforward presentation of information similar to any textbook. The second is "Praxis": these sections contain a series of discussions that require you to do things. I believe that the "Praxis" sections are the most important of the two; the "Narrative" sections provide you with information, but what you *learn* from this course will be achieved in the process of *doing* things with that information.

What Knowing About Interpersonal Communication Means

In the passage I quoted at the beginning of this chapter, McLaughlin (1984, p. 13–14) said that a "staggering amount of knowledge" is required to participate in a conversation. Clearly she is right, but questions remain. *What* knowledge? What *kind* of knowledge? Does this kind of knowledge come in measurable, quantifiable amounts? Is it more like the knowledge required to compute the radius of a circle or to run the weave pattern in a fast break in basketball? Is this knowledge something you learn by memorizing the results of research or by reflecting on your own experience?

A long-established prejudice in Western intellectual history makes us think that "knowing" means the ability to write sentences or answer multiple-choice questions, and that "knowledge" should take the form of the axioms in geometry or the equations in physics. This book about interpersonal communication offers a distinctive way of understanding your social worlds, in part because it opposes this prejudice. It envisions your knowledge as something more like a football running back who knows when to cut to his left than a diagram of a play in the playbook, more like an expert seamstress's knowledge of how to tie a thread than a textbook description of how the thread should be tied, and more like a public speaker who knows when to quit speaking and sit down than a rhetorical critic's checklist for a good speech.

If all goes well, what you will learn in this course will be more like getting the point of a joke than memorizing a list. Understanding interpersonal communication is, as Clifford Geertz (1983, p. 10) put it, "rather closer to what a critic does to illumine a poem than what an astronomer does to account for a star."

Fortunately, we can do more than cite similes to make distinctions among kinds of knowledge. The following paragraphs review some historical differentiations about things which are known and the form knowledge about them takes. In addition, they present some new models of the kind of knowledge that you should develop about interpersonal communication.

Interpersonal Communication as Contingent (Praxis)

The term *praxis* is a transliteration of a Greek word used by the philosopher Aristotle in his book, the *Nicomachean Ethics*. Aristotle was primarily a natural scientist; his studies of how eggs become chickens is a landmark in the development of science, and he spent much time categorizing the flora and fauna brought back by the armies of his student, Alexander the Great (Harré 1981). However, Aristotle also made important contributions to what we now know as the social sciences and humanities.

As Aristotle thought about these topics, he realized that it was important to distinguish different kinds of knowledge because, as he put it, in the physical world, things *have to be what they are,* but in the world of human activities, things *can be other than what they are.* That is, if you throw a rock, it has no choice but to travel in a trajectory governed by gravity, the resistance of the air, and the momentum that you gave it. If you know these things, you can compute (as Galileo did many years later) just where and when it will hit the ground. You need not ask the rock if it wants to hit the ground on that spot or what it thinks about being thrown. However, if you make an argument, the persons to whom you are speaking may or may not be persuaded, and you can *never* predict the extent and direction that they will be affected by your argument with the confidence that you can predict ballistic trajectories. Knowing that, you may decide not even to try to persuade them, or to use unusual techniques to persuade them—in short, your actions and theirs are *contingent* on each other and *both* may be, in Aristotle's terms, other than what they are.

Refrain 1.1

In the *Nicomachean Ethics,* Aristotle differentiated three parts of the world that humans know and said that the kinds of knowledge possible in each were different.

Domains	Types of events/objects	Types of knowledge	Expression
Theoria	Eternal and immutable; they must be what they are	Episteme (facts)	Syllogistic reasoning (induction, deduction)
Praxis	Things are contingent on each other; they may be other than what they are	Phronesis (practical wisdom; good judgment)	The practical syllogism; deontic logics*
Poesis	Things that are made	Techne (skill)	How-to-do-it manuals; training

Interpersonal communication is a part of the domain of praxis. What happens in any given conversation is *contingent* on everything else that happens; the conversation could have turned out differently if you had said "this" instead of "that." Knowledge about interpersonal communication takes the forms of *phronesis* or practical wisdom. The closest thing we have to a formal model of phronesis is the practical syllogism; the best metaphors are the ability of a virtuoso musician or the seemingly instinctive moves of a great athlete.

*Although formal deontic logics were developed only in this century, they are fully consistent with Aristotle's notions of *praxis* and *phronesis*. I think Aristotle would enjoy using modern modal logics.

Good Judgment or Practical Wisdom (Phronesis)

Being the great systemizer that he was, Aristotle developed formal descriptions of these domains of experience and the appropriate forms of knowledge for each. Aristotle believed that *theoria* (from which we get the term *theory*) was possible for things that must be what they are (e.g., the ballistic trajectories of a well-thrown rock), and *episteme* (from which we get the term *epistemology* or the study of how we know) is the corresponding means of knowledge. For this part of our experience, *syllogistic reasoning* is the valid form of thinking. For example, the following is a valid syllogism in that if the premises are true, then the conclusion must (without exception) be true:

> All men are mortal.
> Socrates is a man;
> therefore, Socrates is mortal.

Syllogisms do not tell us anything we did not already know; that is, the "conclusions" are already contained in the "premises." Their usefulness lies in providing patterns for our reasoning so that we can see just how we connect one thought to another. In the best instances, we can check to make sure that we are not making mistakes, such as believing what would be nice rather than what is true.

However, the syllogisms described above are not very useful for understanding interpersonal communication. Two features of interpersonal communication distinguish it from the class of statements like "All men are mortal." First, the connections among acts are contingent, not certain; that is, they deal with moral obligations rather than statistical probabilities or lawlike relationships. Second, interpersonal communication deals primarily with the question of What should I *do?* rather than the question What do I *know?*

To represent the logical structure of interpersonal communication, we have to deal with what people think they *must* or *ought* or *must not* do, and we need to deal with the fact that people do not always do what they think they should, and even when they do, things do not always work out as they expected.

For example, Kristina "knows" that if she *says,* "I want a puppy," her father will reply with a long list of reasons why a canine around the house is impractical, unnecessary, and expensive, and finally say "No!" However, she also "knows" that if she wants a puppy (i.e., for *X* to occur), she can bring one home and let her father play with it (i.e., she must do *Y*), and her father may bond with the puppy and agree to let her keep it. Therefore, she tries to find a puppy that she can bring home. Whether she gets to keep the puppy is clearly contingent: whatever happens does not *have* to happen, it could work out differently. The kind of knowledge that is useful for contingent relationships is not the sort that you write as "laws" or describe in formal syllogisms. Rather, it is the kind of knowledge that has conditional probabilities and first-person pronouns in it ("Maybe if I did this, then he would do that. . . .").

Praxis is the term Aristotle used for those aspects of human experience in which contingency and moral obligation provide the structure. He named politics, public speaking, and household management as examples. Certainly, interpersonal communication belongs on this list.

When dealing with things that are contingent, however, we strive for *phronesis* (practical wisdom and good judgment) rather than *truth* (i.e., intellectual certainty), and we must use a form of reasoning that differs from that syllogism described above. Fortunately, logicians have developed many useful logics.

When we begin to compare *types* of logic, the "covering law" syllogisms dealing with statements like "All men are mortal" are revealed as a particular form of logic, not the only one. Because the syllogistic reasoning structure deals with statements that are evaluated as "true" or "false," it is called an *alethic* (i.e., truth-oriented) logic. In interpersonal communication, we need a logical form in which the statements describe whether we should perform certain acts. Because it deals with moral obligation, this logic is called *deontic* logic.

For present purposes, it is not necessary for you to become an expert on various forms of logic. Just remember that the structure of interpersonal communication can be described in a logical form, and that the basis of that logic involves our perceptions of how we *ought to act*, rather than statements about how the world is.

Counterpoint 1.3

In its most general sense, *logic* refers to the way things relate to each other. If Jose cannot see the logic in what Carmine says, he cannot fit what she says into a pattern of other statements that she has made or that Jose thinks are relevant.

We use many patterns or logics when we think. Some involve rigorous reasoning, others, intuitive leaps. Kaplan (1964) made a useful distinction between "logic-in-use" and "reconstructed logic." *Logic-in-use* refers to the sometimes chaotic, fortuitous, serendipitous movement of our minds; *reconstructed logic* refers to the calm, orderly, formal patterns that we describe when we subsequently explain why we arrived at a conclusion. These patterns of reconstructed logic are useful for presenting ourselves as more logical than we really are, for stating our reasoning so that we can perhaps persuade others to agree with us, and for displaying the patterns of relations so that we can expose any unwanted leaps.

I included these formal patterns in the "Narrative" to make three points. First, the comparison of the different forms shows that there is a logic of *meaning and action,* not just a logic of propositions. The old adage is correct: "The heart has reasons of which the reason is unaware." Second, the formal patterns of deontic and practical reason show that it is possible to reconstruct the logic of meaning and action for what conversants do, even if they say that they do not know why they did what they did. Third, the presentation of the deontic and practical logics begin an argument that I extend throughout this book: the appropriate vocabulary for explaining my/your/our participation in conversations is comprised of terms of "oughtness" and "intentionality." That is, it is an inherently moral vocabulary.

The deontic logic of moral obligation resembles the alethic logic of truth in its syllogistic structure, but differs in the "logical operators" that comprise the verbs of the statements in the syllogism. Instead of using various forms of the verb "to be" (as alethic logic does), deontic logic uses various terms describing the moral obligation of an action. For example, Gerry Philipsen's (1975) studies of "teamsterville" (a suburb of Chicago) found that certain conversations follow this logical structure:

If another man insults your wife, you are obligated to fight him.
This man insulted your wife;
therefore, you must fight him.

This deontic syllogism reconstructs the logic in the following conversation (read it with a strong Irish accent):

Father O'Malley: Mike, I hear that you've been fighting in the bar again! What do you have to say for yourself?
Mike: Ah, Father! I had my mind set against it, just like you told me, but then he up an' said a word against my wife and I had no choice but to deck him. Sure and you can see that, can't you, Father?
Father O'Malley: A man's got to do what he's got to do, sure enough, Mike, but can I persuade you to do your drinking in another bar where such a word might not be said quite so frequently?

Communication theorist Vernon Cronen (in press) argues that two sets of deontic logics are necessary for understanding conversations. The first includes the operators "obligatory," "legitimate," "prohibited," and "undetermined." Using these terms, we can reconstruct the logic of meaning and action for things we do that we perceive as within our conscious choice as, for example, Mike's account of his fight. A darker form of human experience requires the operators "caused," "probable," "blocked," and "random." These terms express the felt moral obligation of action that we perform but do not think we can control. Outside conscious volition, they are actions that we just do, or do not do, or have happen to us. For example, our common sense tells us that we "fall" in love; it is something that happens to us rather than something that is in our conscious control (Averill 1992), and to reconstruct that logic, we would need the latter set of deontic operators.

If Father O'Malley asked Mike's friend Pat about Pat's participation in the barroom brawl (noticing that Pat's knuckles and nose are both a bit scraped up), Pat might reply, "I can't explain it, Father. When I'm talking to one of the fellows, sometimes something just comes over me and before I know it, I've hit him. One thing just leads to another, you know." Pat and Mike may get into the same number of fights and for what appears to a third-person observer (i.e., someone like Philipsen, who is doing a research project and is not from the culture) for the same reasons. However, they live in very different moral worlds. Both reconstruct their logic of meaning and action as deontic logic, but for Mike, there is a sense of consciousness of the relations within that logic. Pat, on the other hand, is always surprised by the course of events, no matter how frequently they occur because they just seem to happen.

Practical reasoning differs from alethic logic in both form and operators. A formal reconstruction of practical reasoning goes like this:

I want X to occur.
I believe that if X is to occur, I must do Y;
therefore, I set myself to do Y.

You probably have not seen this syllogism laid out just this way because it is a logician's nightmare. Even if both premises are true, I might be prevented from doing Y, I might do Y badly and thus fail to bring about X, or I might do Y perfectly and find out that X still does not occur for any of a dozen reasons (Pearce 1983).

At the end of this course, you will understand better where your "wants" come from, you will have some tools with which to analyze the process by which Xs and Ys are made, you will have a richer set of resources for your beliefs about what Ys bring about what Xs and for understanding how complicated that process is, and you will have an experiential knowledge of what "setting yourself" to do things in interpersonal communication is all about.

Conceptualizing Interpersonal Communication

The best way to define *interpersonal communication* would be for you and me to engage in a conversation and then stop it suddenly with the comment, *"This* is what this book is all about!"

The second-best way of defining it is to call your attention to the conversations occurring all around you: neighbors quarreling, students helping each other figure out registration procedures, teachers talking about a new study, Phil Donahue talking to the prominent or weird people on his show, and more. There is no dearth of conversations, and I hope that you will develop the knack of listening to those that go on around you using the concepts that you will learn in this book.

If we were in a conversation, we could work together to construct a satisfactory definition. Both of us would use practical reasoning ("Hmmm! If I say *this*, they will understand what I mean, but if I say *that*, it may be misleading"); and we would take turns directing the conversation ("Let interpersonal communication be defined as . . ." "Wait! Do you mean . . .?" "Exactly! And then . . ." "But what if . . .?" "Yes . . ." "No . . ." "I see!"). Such rapid give-and-take comprises the distinctive characteristic of interpersonal communication, and it clearly shows the difference between being *in* conversation and writing or reading *about* conversation. Because we are communicating in print, we are using the third-best way of defining interpersonal communication: to describe a conversation as an example that we can think through.

Sonia and Luis have just watched a movie. Luis is driving the car that is taking them home. They are riding in companionable silence when the following exchange occurs:

Sonia: Are you hungry?
Luis: No.
There is a brief pause.
Sonia: You are so selfish!
Luis: What? What are you talking about?
Sonia: I'm hungry and you don't even care!
Luis: Of course I care! If you wanted to stop for dinner, why didn't you say so?
Sonia: I did say so! Why don't you listen better?
Luis: There's a good Italian restaurant in the next block. I'll stop there.
Sonia: Don't bother! I'm not hungry anymore. Take me home.

This conversation is interesting in part because so many people find it familiar. I adapted it from Deborah Tannen's (1990, pp. 26–27) analysis of conversational styles in contemporary America, and the reception of her books shows that she is clearly onto something that strikes a chord with many people. I have used this example in lectures on three continents, and I find that men often laugh with rueful recognition of Luis's situation, and women often identify with Sonia's frustration.

Note that this conversation is not the stuff of great literature. No important aspect of human history hinges on whether Luis is clueless about what is going on; civilization as we know it is likely to continue regardless

Both Sonia and Luis think that they are misunderstood. This common conversation can be interpreted in a surprising variety of ways.

of whether Sonia gets dinner or not. This conversation is not "steamy" enough to be the basis of a popular romance novel or soap opera. However, this conversation—and the hundreds like it that we engage in every day—is important; these conversations are the ordinary, normal material out of which we fashion our lives, our personalities, and our relationships with others. Such apparently trivial interactions are the seemingly frail and imprecise processes in which we dream and make those dreams—and the attendant nightmares that are their shadows—into reality.

For many years, communication theorists have tried to develop a model of communication that would describe this process. A good model should serve as a heuristic (i.e., a device that facilitates discovery) to determine the factors that make communication sometimes succeed and at other times fail. Modeling communication has been an unexpectedly difficult process, requiring us to discover some embedded presuppositions in the structure of our language and work out some unconventional ways of thinking.

The concept of interpersonal communication used in this book is rather far from the first, or common-sense, idea of what communication is or how it works. To put it into context, let me give you a very brief description of some of the shoulders on which this idea stands.

What We Learned from the Failure of the Project of Developing a Model of Communication

If you were to ask the first ten people you meet on the street to define "communication," all ten would likely give some version of what we call the *transmission* theory. That is, they might identify communication with the media, by which messages are transmitted from one place to another (e.g., television, radio, or electronic mail) or offer some definition that describes a process of transmitting information or meaning from one mind to another.

These ten people you meet on the street are reflecting the dictionary definitions of communication, and they should, since dictionary definitions are based on popular use. However, the first notion that something might be wrong with the transmission concept comes from the etymology of the word "communication." There is an older concept of communication that identifies it with the process of "making common." What kinds of things are made "common"? Is the process by which things are "made" common limited to the transmission of messages?

As you will see, this book—and current communication theory—has a rich understanding of the process of "making common" that can easily be

---

Refrain 1.2

The transmission model of communication	**The social constructionist model of communication**
What communication is:	
One of many things that people do.	The webs of social interaction in which we find ourselves and in which we live, move, and have our being
How communication works:	
Messages are encoded/decoded so that they represent either the world of objects that exist outside the communication process or the intrapsychic world of meanings and emotions of people who communicate. These messages are transmitted from one place to another.	Patterns of social action are co-constructed in sequences of evocative and responsive acts; these patterns comprise an ecology that is our social worlds. This ecology includes systemic relations and is the site of co-evolutionary processes.
What work communication does:	
It moves information from one place to another with various degrees of accuracy and efficiency, it is encoded as a description of something else with more or less fidelity; and it is used in ways with greater or less persuasive effect and aesthetic value.	It calls into being and reproduces the events and objects of our social worlds; it is a process of making and doing.

distorted if the relatively simple process of transmitting messages is overemphasized. Let me show you how we got from the currently used definition of communication to an enriched sense of its etymological meaning.

From our current perspective, the earliest models of communication do not seem very helpful because they unquestioningly reproduced the "linearity" of the European languages in which they were framed. The Indo-European family of languages is built around a grammar of "subject-verb-object" and thus creates a picture of one thing (active, with powers) doing things to other things (inactive, without powers). As Ludwig Wittgenstein (1953) noted, whole clouds of philosophy are embedded in drops of grammar, and so it has been for communication theory.

The earliest models of communication were based on a unidirectional arrow, tracing the movement of a message from a source to a receiver. The Greek god Hermes (and his Roman imitator Mercury) is depicted (Figure 1.1) wearing boots with wings on them and carrying a messenger's staff. This symbol is still used by telegraph operators and florists who make deliveries.

In 1949, Claude Shannon and Warren Weaver introduced one of the most influential models of communication, which described the origin of a message in a "source" who "encoded" it, entrusted it to a "transmitter" that delivered it to a "receiver" who "decoded" it (Figure 1.2). They realized that messages go both ways on many transmitters, so they included a second unidirectional arrow that represented "feedback." David Berlo's (1960) communication model set the parameters of model-making in the 1960s. Working within the same paradigm or philosophy, Berlo's model was named by its acronym for "source," "message," "channel," and "receiver" (SMCR).

By the late 1960s, the limitations of this linear model for thinking about communication were becoming very obvious, even if the alternatives to it were not so apparent. It is hard to use English to express concepts that are contrary to the embedded linearity in its grammar, and some of the attempts to model communication were a bit bizarre. For example, Berlo's very influential book contained an excellent chapter on communication as a nonlinear process but then laid out a linear model. Frank E. X. Dance (1970) proposed a concept of communication as a "spiral," but generations of students looked at the picture he drew and called it the "bedspring model." Dean Barnlund (1968) drew a very complex model using curved arrows that captured some of the dynamism of the process of communication. Again, a generation of students looked at the picture and called it the whirlpool model.

The most influential and sophisticated attempt to get away from the transmission model was developed by Paul Watzlawick, Janet Beavin, and Don Jackson (1967), based on the systemic ideas of Gregory Bateson. This model did not use arrows at all; instead it took an *interactional view* that defined *the fit between sequences of messages,* not the movement of a message from one place to another, as the basic unit of analysis for communication theory. In 1970, Dance suggested that we adopt a "family" of models, each of which illuminated some portion of the process of communication and distorted some other, and most communication theorists agreed. After 1970,

Figure 1.1 *In the* Odyssey, *Hermes served as the messenger of the gods.*

Consider Hermes, the god of communication. In contemporary culture, Hermes is well-known as the Olympian being whose winged sandals whisk him from god to god, bearing messages of good and ill. Indeed, the predominant image of communication in the modern world concerns the transmission, rather than construction and interpretation, of symbols. . . .

Less well known is Hermes the god of invention, cunning, commerce, and thievery, the patron of both travelers and the rogues who may waylay them, the conductor of the dead to Hades, the prodigious liar and trickster, and the being who lends his name to hermeneutics. By making one being the god of communication, lying, invention and trickery, the ancient Greek recognized the family resemblance among the polymorphously perverse forms of human conduct: they are all the offspring of human artfulness. The Greeks saw that communication is not only a matter of conveying information; it is a matter of the construction of culture in the widest sense. Let us embrace the whole Hermes—not only the messenger of the gods but the clever fellow who displays the fruits and foibles of human creativity in all their glorious raucousness.

(Peters and Rothenbuhler 1989, pp. 25–26)

few people drew models of communication, and for those that did, unidirectional arrows were considered old-fashioned and unhelpful.

From these two decades of attempts to draw models of communication, we learned some important things. First, we learned that communication is processual and reflexive; that is, the sequence of events is important, and the

Figure 1.2 *The Shannon-Weaver model of communication. Note the linearity of the model, as evidenced by the unidirectional arrows.*

meaning of events is derived from their location within an ongoing sequence. The implicit linearity of our language was revealed in the collective stuttering that afflicted communication theorists as they tried to describe the process. We had to develop new ways of talking, new concepts, and new research methods. Our professional journals were filled with attempts to say *in English* things that went against the grain of English grammar. Much of the jargon that you encounter in this book is an attempt to say things in ways that stress the structure of the language in which it is written.

We learned to focus on patterns rather than on individual messages, and on interactions rather than on the movement of messages from one place to another. Specifically, we came to understand that the differentiation between "sources" and "receivers" distorts the extent to which all the participants in a conversation contribute to the meaning of any given aspect of the conversation. We now see sources and receivers as constructed in and by the shape of the conversation in which they participate.

We think of conversations themselves as fluid and systemic, metamorphosing from one configuration to another. The forces that give shape to clouds became our metaphors rather than the more mechanical structures of Newtonian physics. We are more attuned to "chaos theory" (Gleick 1987), ecological concepts, and evolutionary processes (Bateson 1979) than to Newton's "laws of motion." We spoke less of "things" and more of "relationships," less of "objects" and more of "patterns." Our language shifted from objects to energy, and then from energy to information, and then again from information to communication.

Second, we learned to think about communication as the "field" or "ecology" or "container" in which communicators act, not as one thing among many that communicators do. That is, as shown in Figure 1.3, conceptually we place the communicators "inside" the processes of communication in which they participate, not "outside," unaffected by the processes in which they are engaged. The technical name for this is *social constructionism;* it is a way of looking at communication as the site where the identities of the communicators are fashioned in interaction with other people, as the process in which purposes emerge, and as the means by which the events and objects of our social worlds are created.

This is the "learning" that breaks most dramatically from the implicit linearity of the Indo-European family of languages. The "drop of grammar"

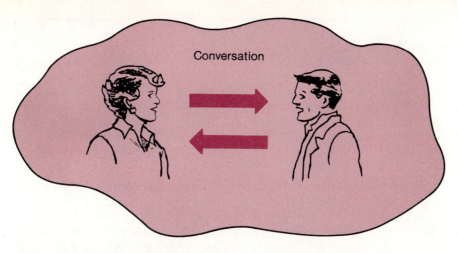

Figure 1.3   *Instead of thinking of conversations as the exchange of messages* between *conversants, the social constructionist perspective sees conversants as* within *an interlocking matrix of conversations. Each conversant is the* product *of previous conversations and the* producer *of the present and future conversations.*

> "From a communication standpoint we would have to say that each . . . presumed autonomous elements—an inner world, outer world, social relations, means of expression—are not only products of prior communicative processes, but require reproduction (enactment) to function in any particular context."
>
> (Deetz 1992, p. 14)

in English would lead us to see the verb (i.e., what people *do*) as something that happens between two independently existing entities, the subject and the object. The social constructionist way of thinking proposes a different *cloud of philosophy,* which is difficult to express in English without waving your hands or drawing strange pictures with brackets in funny places. In addition to making communication theorists stutter, there are three important implications of this way of thinking about communication.

First, this way of thinking treats *actions* as real, pivotal events, rather than simply as transitory states of, or between, preexisting entities. That is, the events and objects of the social world (subjects and objects) exist because of patterns of actions that have occurred previously and because actions are being performed now to bring them into being. Among other things, this social constructionist perspective portrays the events and objects of the social world as "achievements" rather than as "objective realities"; that is, the identities of persons and the reality of institutions are accomplished by patterns of interactions rather than being objects found to have the characteristics they possess.

Second, this social constructionist perspective on communication requires us to think in terms of interactive patterns, not atomistic units. That is,

Counterpoint 1.4

In this book, I am arguing against some deeply ingrained cultural prejudices. The first prejudice is that the study of social worlds is less important, less elegant, and less (can it be said?) "macho" than the study of the physical world. This prejudice was clearly exposed by the social theorist Giambittista Vico (1744/1968, #331) who opposed it over 250 years ago:

> *"the world of civil society has certainly been made by men [sic], and its principles are therefore to be found within the modifications of our human mind. Whoever reflects on this cannot but marvel that the philosophers should have bent all their energies to the study of the world of nature, which since God made it He alone knows; and that they should have neglected the study of the world of nations, or civil world, which, since men made it, men could come to know."*

No sooner is this prejudice overcome than we run afoul of the second prejudice: within the social world, *institutions* (e.g., churches, governments, banks, economies, and political ideologies) are more real than particular *actions* (e.g., speaking, standing, walking, pounding the streets, pounding a table, buying a pound of cheese).

For example, the statement "You can't fight City Hall!" is a part of common sense that explains why people do not protest injustice by taking specific actions. "City Hall" is believed to be real in a way that a demonstration in the streets or a petition is not. The (city) government is taken as a powerful entity while individual citizens are seen as powerless. While there is a sense in which this is true, there is another sense in which it is not. In many areas of our lives, our happiness and ability to function depend on our ability to find that sense in which institutions are ephemeral and the thoughtful acts of individuals, quite literally, change the world.

Historically, Western culture has respected abstract concepts (e.g., duty, honor, virtue, and truth) and social institutions (e.g., the British monarchy, the state, and the party) rather than particular actions (e.g., what Molly did yesterday). This preference has shaped our thought, society, and ethics. Many of us are engaged in attempting to reverse this perspective, suggesting that the actions in a particular conversation are what is real. Social institutions only *seem* more real because we act in ways that (re)construct them in that manner. Can you think of mottos or folk sayings that express the concept that the events and objects of your social worlds are made? For example, pacifists ask, "What if they gave a war, and nobody came?"

Some social theorists have referred to the *duality* of structure, insisting that social institutions cannot exist unless they are continually reproduced in actions, and that actions derive their meaning from occurring within continuous institutions. For example, Roy Bhaskar (1989, pp. 992–993) said

Society is both the ever-present condition *and the continually repro-*

duced outcome *of human agency: this is the duality of structure. And human agency is both work (generically conceived), that is, (normally conscious)* production *and (normally unconscious)* reproduction *of the conditions of production, including society: this is the duality of praxis. Thus agents reproduce,* non-teleologically *and* non-recursively, *in their substantive motivated productions, the unmotivated conditions necessary for—as a means of—those productions, and society is both the medium and the result of this activity.*

See how hard it is to say this in English!

---

we cannot follow the well-trod reductionistic path of identifying the smallest discernable units of what interests us and assuming that the properties of these smallest units tell us about the characteristics of the whole. Instead, we must treat conversations—and clusters of conversations—as systems in which the whole is different from the sum of the parts.

The organization of the elements in a conversation, not just the elements themselves, constitute the meanings of what is happening. To ask What did he say? is to request a quotation of a part of a conversation. Without seeing how that part fits into the rest—including what was said immediately before and after—is to guarantee that a verbatim quotation will distort the meaning of what was said.

Counterpoint 1.5

The traditional notion of analysis means to break something down into its component parts to determine its substance. This method works well as long as the thing being analyzed has a rather simple organization. When we start dealing with more complex entities, we have to see them as systems. To analyze a system is to trace the relationships between the parts, to learn what *emergent properties* characterize the system's organization that cannot be found in any of its parts. For example, stars have a complex, long evolution that cannot be determined from analyzing a sample of the star—you must know some of its systemic properties (such as the ratio of its heat to its mass) to predict whether it will become a red giant or a white dwarf.

Interpersonal communication is systemic—you cannot understand very much about a conversation by taking it apart. To understand a conversation, you must see it as a whole, with particular attention to the relationships among the parts and the emergent properties.

Gregory Bateson (1979) introduced systemic ideas to the analysis of interpersonal communication; more specifically, he applied evolutionary and ecological concepts to the understanding of social worlds. Bateson's writings are brilliant, filled with striking insights and lengthy digressions, mystical allusions and prophetic denunciations. In an attempt to tame Bateson's restless mind, philosopher Stephen Toulmin (1982, p. 207) summarized him as insisting on three notions: the necessity for multiple descriptions of all processes, a circular conception of causal interconnections, and the role of coevolutionary processes.

> *"A properly evolutionary way of dealing with experience obliges us to recognize that no event or process has any single unambiguous description: we describe any event in different terms, and view it as an element in a different network of relations, depending on the standpoint from which—and the purposes for which—we are considering it. Nor shall we usually be able to distinguish the "causes" among phenomena from their "effects" . . . in ecological and evolutionary processes . . . each of them is implicated in the causal fate of all the others.*
>
> *The best we can do in such a case is to understand all the interlinked chains within which our affairs are caught up, and consider how they might be modified so as to operate more advantageously as wholes; that is to say, in such a way that these entire systems become better adapted."*

Finally, because it focuses on actions rather than preexisting entities, the social constructionist perspective on communication foregrounds morality. That is, the social worlds in which we live are structured by complex, interlocking sets of perceived moral obligations. Our first question when we enter a situation is What should I *do*? Any increase in our sophistication about What should I do? must take into account these perceived moral obligations.

The project to develop a common, consensual model of communication failed. However, the project itself was very useful. It allowed us to learn that the very grammar of our language provided us with a picture of the process of communication that limited our understanding of it. By calling this picture into sharp relief, we have generated alternative ways of thinking about communication. In my opinion, the social constructionist perspective provides the richest way of formulating these insights for an understanding of interpersonal communication.

Definitions of Interpersonal Communication

Interpersonal communication is a term that marks off one form of communication ("interpersonal") from others, such as communication by means of a book, a videotape, a compact disk or an electronic database). Its distinctive feature is that we interact with other people in a pattern known as a conversation.

The *American Heritage Dictionary of the English Language* defines "conversation" as a noun with two meanings. The first meaning is "An informal spoken exchange of thoughts and feelings; a familiar talk." The second meaning is "social intercourse; close association."

I want to use more specific and descriptive definitions. To do so, it is important to identify the *perspectives* from which the definitions are offered. For present purposes, we will use only the first- and third-person perspectives.

A first-person definition.   If we approach interpersonal communication from a first-person perspective (i.e., using statements like "I feel . . ." or "I might do . . ."), we locate ourselves within a continuing process. From this perspective, what happens next is something that we might guess but cannot know, but it will have an impact on us. From this perspective, we see the conversation with an understandable asymmetry: we see our own actions from the inside and the actions of others from the outside. This perspective is particularly useful for developing competence in conversing with other people, particularly in abnormal or stressful situations.

From a first-person perspective, we can define conversations as *a process of coordinating actions within a working definition of a situation*. This definition indicates that persons in conversations (I will call them "conversants" or "interlocutors") have their attention focused in (at least) two different directions at once. These directions are indicated by the questions "What are we doing here?" (i.e., what is my working definition of the situation in which we find ourselves?) and "What should I do now?" (i.e., how should I act so that my actions will coordinate with those of the other person?).

The concept of a working definition of a situation refers to a sense of coherence, or an orientation to what is going on. As adults, we usually know

Refrain 1.3

Two definitions of interpersonal communication:

From a first-person perspective:
   A process of coordinating actions within a working definition of a situation.*

From a third-person perspective:
   A game-like pattern of social interaction comprised of a sequence of acts, each of which evokes and responds to the acts of other persons.

A person who participates in a conversation may be called a *conversant* or an *interlocutor*.

*Thanks to Jim Applegate for this definition.

what is going on in conversations, but there are instances in which we are not sure. At these times, we experience the opposite of coherence: vertigo.

Vertigo is the unpleasant sense of disorientation that occurs when you lose the sense of what is up and down. It can happen in an airplane or on a sailboat in fog; scuba divers can suffer from it, particularly if they are not getting sufficient oxygen.

There is also a social vertigo that occurs as "culture shock." If you are living in a strange culture, you may have an overpowering sense of disorientation; nothing seems to work as you expect it to, and everything is strange. You do not know whether to greet the strangers you meet or run from them; you cannot discern between what is for sale and what is free. Culture shock can make you physically ill. You can experience social vertigo if you have just joined a new group (perhaps the transition from high school to college), or if you have changed your role (e.g., by being elected team captain or president of your fraternity or changing from a single to a married state).

We avoid social vertigo by orienting to particular events, objects, and relations in our social worlds as if they were real. We construct working definitions of the situation that include a sense of who we are (our identities, discussed in Chapter 6), our relationships (see Chapter 5), the event in which we are participating (see Chapter 4), and the meaning of what is being said and done (see Chapter 3).

The question What do I do now? reminds us that from the first-person perspective, conversations have to be made by doing something in a temporal context *after* someone has done something and *before* they do something else. *From the perspective of the conversant,* these doings are not a free choice; they are enmeshed in a logic of meaning and action that makes some actions mandatory, optional, or prohibited.

This "logic of meaning and action" is generated by the conversant's perception of the moral obligations that link the sequence of actions. If Barry says "Go to dinner with me tomorrow night," Tasha may feel *obligated* to accept the invitation because she cherishes their relationship and has turned him down three times before; she may feel *prohibited* from accepting the invitation because she is a self-respecting feminist, and Barry presumes that she will drop everything when he asks her out for a date at the last minute; or she may feel that either accepting or rejecting the offer is *permissible*. The underscored terms represent the felt moral obligation to act in various ways as perceived by the conversant at each particular moment in the conversation.

While the term logic of meaning and action is awkward, it refers to a common experience. In a study of family violence (Harris et al. 1984), people who hit their brothers or sisters were asked why they were so aggressive. Their general response was not very helpful; the usual answer was something like "I don't know" or "s/he asked for it!" Treating the blow as a message within a conversation, the researchers then asked questions designed to elicit descriptions of the aggressors' "felt oughtness." They found that family members hit other family members when they feel that they *must* have some reaction and when all *symbolic* things that they might do are invalidated. The subjects in this study often said that they threw the punch because they had to; they could do nothing else.

From a third-person perspective, these descriptions of an overwhelming logical force are false. Of course, these people who abuse other members of their family could have done something else! They could have walked away, written a letter, phoned a friend, painted a fence, read a book—any of a thousand things that are obvious *if you are not in the first-person perspective*. However, I believe that these subjects gave a valid description of their logic of meaning and action in which it was true that they had no alternative that they could think of to throwing a punch.

You probably have a continuing, important relationship with someone, perhaps a friend or member of your family, in which there is an unwanted

Counterpoint 1.6

The term *logical force* is not in common use, but I cannot find a word in ordinary language that expresses what I mean. For example, take the first-person perspective on a conversation. You are in a restaurant having dinner. A man seated at the next table points his fork at you and shouts "What are you doing in here? Waiter, get *those people* out of here, they make me sick!" I suspect that you will feel a certain compulsion to do *something* in this situation: that compulsion is logical *force*. I suspect that you and I might differ in just *what* we feel compelled to do, but whatever acts are entailed by what this rude man just said is the *logic of meaning and action.*

Note that logical force is the force of an argument, not the force of mass in motion; it is the summation of the felt obligation to *act,* not a crude physical cause of mere motion. The notion of logical force simply says that people who are in conversations feel a sense of moral obligation about how they will respond to what was just said and what should be said next. For example:

Bill: "Hi! How are you?"
Henry: (nothing)
Bill: Well, go to hell, then!

In this conversation, I am not sure what logical force Henry felt, but clearly Bill felt that his first statement constructed a sufficiently strong and unambiguous logic that Henry was obligated to make some sort of friendly response. When he did not, Bill felt permitted, or perhaps obligated, to respond with a harsh comment. For a fuller description of logical force, see Cronen and Pearce (1981).

repetitive pattern of conversation. Perhaps the topic varies, but you recognize the pattern as one that 1) you can predict that it will occur and how it will go, 2) you dislike it, and 3) once it starts, you cannot avoid becoming deeply enmeshed in a logic of meaning and action that apparently requires you to act in ways that you know that you will regret.

- While she is away at school, phone calls between Barbara and her father take the same pattern. He asks how she is doing. No matter what she says, he replies by giving her a lecture on how she should be more careful, take better care of herself, study more and play less, and call him more often.
- Henry knows that every time politics is mentioned in a conversation with his father a bitter fight will follow. Both he and his father try to avoid mentioning anything having to do with current events for fear that they will lose control and become embroiled in a fight that neither can win and neither wants.
- Charlene and her mother have different ideas about when she should marry and have children. Charlene wants to establish herself in her career and besides has not met a man that she wants to marry; her mother is ready for grandchildren and is afraid that Charlene will never get married because she spends all her time working. There are a whole range of topics that they avoid mentioning, because any reference to Charlene's career, to her sister's family, or to her mother's daily activities invokes an inexorable logic of meaning and action in which her mother *must* advise Charlene and Charlene *must* defend her independence.

A study of college students found that virtually everyone has such unwanted repetitive patterns. When we asked our subjects why they responded in the conversation in ways that they knew full well would perpetuate an unwanted pattern, we were generally told "in that situation, the person that I am has no choice; I *had* to act that way even though I did not want to and I knew that it was counterproductive." Again, we interpreted this as a valid description from the first-person perspective of the logic of meaning and action in those conversations (Cronen, Pearce, and Snavely 1979).

A third-person definition.   If we take a third-person perspective, we use the grammatical form of the question What are they making? and How are they making it? We view conversations as if we were external to them, creating—through the power of our imagination and with the facilitation of a grammatical crutch—a neutral position outside the conversation. The existence of this position is a fiction, of course, because even observing a conversation is a form of participation in it. This perspective is particularly useful for discovering how various categories of people usually act. For example, this is the perspective from which we discover that men ask questions for different reasons and at different times than women do.

Refrain 1.4

Concepts for analyzing conversations:

From a first-person perspective:
   What are we doing here?—coherence/vertigo
   What should I do now?—logical force/enmeshment
From a third-person perspective:
   What are they making?—game-like patterns
   How are they making it?—the serpentine model
   How does it fit into patterns of other conversations?—the atomic model

From a third-person perspective (i.e., as if we were not a part of the conversation), we can understand a conversation as *a game-like pattern of social interaction comprised of a sequence of acts, each of which evokes and responds to the acts of other persons.*

This definition does not contradict the dictionary definition of conversation, but it calls attention to some particular features that are important. Focus on two aspects of this definition: *sequence of acts* and *evokes and responds.*

As a sequence of acts, conversations are extended through time. Conversations consist of what people actually do. A transcript of a conversation such as a court reporter might make of a witness's testimony is not a conversation; it is at best a record of a conversation. Conversations themselves exist in the real world of our lives, where we make and do things with each other.

As a sequence of acts, each of which *evokes and responds* to the acts of the other person, a conversation is not just a string of unrelated things but an interaction of interdependent events. As we will discuss in Chapter 3, no act in a conversation stands alone; its meaning is constituted by its place within an unfolding sequence of actions. There is a sense of back—and—forth in which what I say at each moment is "because of" what you just said and "in order that" you will say something else.

Two models represent the process of interpersonal communication from the third-person perspective: the *serpentine model* and the *atomic model.* Both models require a bit of conceptual agility on your part, and both are far removed from the linearity of early models of communication.

The boxes in the serpentine model in Figure 1.4 represent acts; the columns of boxes represent an unfinished sequence of acts. The interaction among conversants is indexed by the off-set rows; those in each column are understood as the actions performed by each of the conversants. The serpentine-like movement between the columns of boxes represents the connections between them, in which each action both responds to and evokes others.

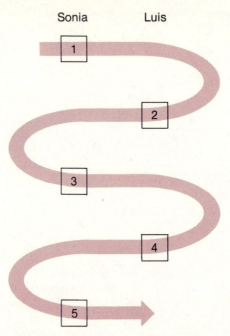

Sonia   Luis

Figure 1.4 *The serpentine model of conversation.*
Taking a third-person perspective, conversations are sequences of acts, each of which evokes and responds to the others. In this model, the boxes represent actions: the left column of boxes represents Sonia's actions, and the right, Luis' actions. The sinuous arrow shows how Sonia and Luis take turns producing actions, and how each act evokes and responds to the others. This is a bare-bones model, of course, that can be adapted to more complex situations.

To use this model from the third-person perspective, you first write as much as you can or need in each of the boxes. Sometimes this will simply be a series of notes to yourself; at other times, you will want a verbatim transcript; at still other times, you may want a full transcription of a conversation, including a verbatim transcript, codes for paralinguistic cues, such as hesitations, talk-overs, and the like, and codes for kinetic and vocalic messages. Record your best judgment of what the first-person participants thought they were doing. What did they say or do? What did they mean by what they said or did? What did they think the other first-person participant meant by what they said or did?

Next, look at the relationships between each pair of adjoining boxes. How does each communicative turn respond to the one preceding it? How does each communicative turn evoke particular responses to it? In this part of the analysis, you are looking at what is *between* the boxes.

One way of describing the connection between sequential acts is to assess the shape and strength of the logical forces felt by the participants. In the conversation between Sonia and Luis cited earlier, how did Luis feel that he *must* or *must not* respond to Sonia in particular ways? What was the logic of meaning and action in which Sonia was enmeshed?

You may find it useful to develop your own shorthand for the substance of the relationships between sequential acts. This shorthand might be as simple as a plus for a responsive act and a minus for an unresponsive act, or it might be much more complicated. Using whatever names you have for the relationships among sequential acts, take each pair in turn and pose a series of questions like these: Does Luis's statement "respond" to Sonia's? In what way? In what way does it fail to respond? How does Sonia respond to Luis's statement? Answers to questions like these give you a sense of the serpentine movement through the conversation.

Next, look at the conversation as a whole as a game-like pattern of social interaction. Conversations are game-like in several ways:

- They consist of mutually responsive acts performed by several people. From an observer's perspective, it seems as if the conversants know, and are following rules for, how they should act, similar to the rules for playing poker, hopscotch, or basketball.
- Each act may be seen as a move in a game; whatever else it might mean, it has the significance of moving the game along.

Ask yourself: What game is being played here? What are the rules for playing this game? How does the fact that this is the game that is being played affect the meaning of the participants' actions? Are all participants playing the same game? Do they understand the game in the same way?

The most interesting conversations are those in which it is difficult to say what game is being played. Certainly the conversation between Sonia and Luis is a "mixed-game" conversation which would have confused me, had I been riding in the back seat of the car listening to it unfold.

You will find that no analysis of a conversation is ever completed. There are always possible, even plausible, alternative ways of understanding any conversation. This persistent open-endedness is not simply the result of our methodology; it is a part of the nature of conversations.

Conversations do not stand alone; they are a part of "clusters" of conversations, some of which are alike and some different; they are a moment in a historical process in which what comes before and after affect what happens in the moving moment of "now" (Figure 1.5).

Communication researchers have become very cautious about giving interpretations of the meaning of conversations. In order to remind ourselves that there are literally an infinite number of interpretations of what is said and done in conversations, and that what is said and done in conversations is endless, we are careful to say that our interpretations are *a reading* (reflecting our own perceptions, reminding us all that others might read the same

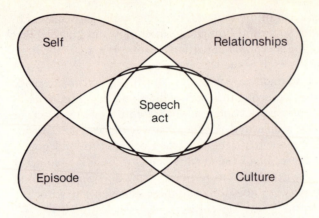

Figure 1.5   *A general form of the atomic model of conversation.*
Each action we perform is simultaneously a part of many conversations. In this model, four clusters of conversations are depicted: those comprising the conversant's sense of self, those comprising his or her relationships to others, those comprising the enactment of particular episodes, and those comprising his or her culture.

conversation differently) or *a gloss* (i.e., a story that lays upon another story as a coat of shellac lays upon polished wood). Good readings and useful glosses are much to be prized, however, because they reveal the various layers of meaning in the conversations they describe.

If Katherine describes a conversation between her brothers and herself to your class, she is taking a third-person perspective to the conversation with her brothers and a first-person perspective in a conversation with your class. Anything that she says, for example, "My brother does not understand me," is simultaneously a part of at least five conversations:

- With her professor (What game is being played? A request for family therapy? A demonstration of interest or ability in the class? Seizing an opportunity to pursue her curiosity?)
- With the other students in the class (She invites them to be open in describing their own important relationships? Is this a way of depicting herself as needing a strong masculine protector in the hopes of attracting the attention of a particular person in the class? Is it an attempt to cut through all the abstract talk and get to concrete matters?)
- With her brother (How does saying this in class fit into their ongoing relationship?)
- With her family (How does being misunderstood by her brother help define her relationship to her other siblings or parents?)

■ With her opposite-sex friends (I assume that working out one's relationship with an opposite-sex sibling has more than a little to do with relationships one can sustain with opposite-sex friends).

To get a grasp on these multiple conversations, the *atomic model* helps. This model is applied to each of the boxes in the serpentine model. That is, it is applied sequentially to each act in a conversation. It locates each act at the nexus of several ellipses, each of which represents another conversation. For example, Katherine's statement about her brother would be located at the overlap of conversations with her professor, classmates, family, and friends (Figure 1.6).

Not all of these conversations are of the same relevance, of course. One of the heuristic values of this model is that it requires us to address the question of which of these conversations is more relevant to a particular act than others. We might decide that Katherine's comments in class are really not to the class but are a very circuitous way of getting back at her father, or that they are a way of sending a message to the professor about why she did not complete her assignment on time. Interpersonal communication is filled with such oblique, subtle, and sometimes puzzling patterns that the atomic model helps us sort out.

Figure 1.6 *The* atomic model *of conversation applied to Katherine's discussion of her brother.*

We are never only in one conversation at a time. Each act we perform is at the nexus of many conversations, each with its own logic of meaning and action. In this illustration, Katherine's act of talking about her brother in class is part of at least four other conversations.

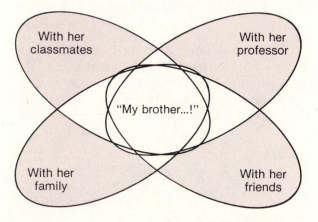

An Analysis of a Conversation from First- and Third-Person Perspectives

The conversation between Luis and Sonia (on page 17) is a recognizable part of social life in the 1990s in the urban industrialized countries. Let's use it as a conversation for analysis.

First-person Perspective

What do Sonia and Luis think they are making in this conversation? What game do they think they are playing? What does Luis think that Sonia means, and vice versa?

My reading of the conversation indicates that logical forces were strong for both Luis and Sonia and increased as the conversation went on. That is, when they started the conversation, each felt that they could do a wide variety of things. However, as the conversation developed, each felt more and more "forced" by what the other was saying to respond as they did.

Further, these logics of meaning and action drove their *working definitions of the situation* further and further apart until at the end, each of them was completely exasperated with the other.

Start with Sonia's first utterance. Lexically, it looks like a straightforward question about whether Luis is hungry; both we and Luis quickly learn that there is more to it than that, however.

Here is one reading of what is going on. When Sonia asks Luis if he is hungry, although her utterance takes the grammatical form of a question, it functions both as a statement and an invitation. It states that *she* is hungry; it invites a discussion about whether they should stop to eat. She intends to initiate a three-turn sequence something like this:

> *Sonia:* Are you hungry?
> *Luis:* No, but are you?
> *Sonia:* Now that you mention it, I am. Let's stop at a good restaurant—
> I'll treat!

On the other hand, Luis *heard* Sonia as asking a question, and interpreted this question to be an inquiry about a state of affairs—in this case, the state of his appetite. His response provided a factual description of what the question inquired about: his hunger or lack thereof. His answer was a coherent part of what he expected to be a two-turn pattern that would go something like this:

> *Sonia:* Are you hungry?
> *Luis:* No.

If Sonia was hungry, Luis would have expected her to have initiated a different two-turn sequence. Perhaps it might go like this:

Sonia: I'm hungry. Let's stop for dinner.
Luis: Sure. I know a good Italian restaurant just ahead. I'll stop there.

See, Luis is not such a bad guy! He will cheerfully accommodate Sonia's suggestion—even though he is not hungry at the moment—if he understands it. If the purpose of the conversation centers on a mutual decision about stopping for dinner, this can be accomplished if Sonia and Luis *coordinate* their activities sufficiently well to *initiate* either the three-turn sequence that Sonia had in mind or the last two-turn sequence that Luis envisioned. Either one could be performed graciously and effectively; their problem came from their bungled attempt to coordinate their enactment of either one.

The reading in the preceding paragraph assumed that the motives for both Sonia and Luis were clearly visible, and that the problem is really one of coordinating their actions within a shared definition of the situation. That is, they agree that what is going on is a collective decision about whether to stop at a restaurant, and the problem is Luis's literalness and Sonia's indirectness. But what if deeper levels of meaning were involved? Here is another reading of the same conversation.

Assume that Sonia is deeply enmeshed in the cultural norm that women should be thin, and that one implication of this is that no woman should, in the presence of male friends, appear to be a glutton. Men, on the other hand, are supposed to be hungry all the time. (This is sometimes referred to as the "Scarlet O'Hara Complex," referring to the practice of the heroine of *Gone With the Wind* of eating heartily before going to a dinner so that she could be seen as having a dainty appetite.)

If at least one level of Sonia's working definition of the situation involves her presentation of self as "thin" in this context, this has some important implications for understanding what is going on. In this definition of the situation, Luis's statement that he is not hungry is offensive, an attack on her self-concept, and a malicious refusal to cooperate in the co-construction of her definition of the situation. Luis's "No" is profoundly injurious, not just an expression of his insensitivity. It exposes Sonia as the person with the uncontrollable craving for food.

Her next statement, "You are so selfish," should be understood—in this reading—to refer to Luis's failure to help her protect her self-concept, not just his sensitivity to an indirect suggestion. Her accusation of selfishness attacks his ethics, not just his ability to coordinate a decision about whether to stop at a restaurant. Luis's response, "If you wanted to stop . . ." and his following suggestion, "There's a good Italian restaurant . . ." both compound his error. Imagine Sonia's horror at Luis's suggestion that he take her to a fancy restaurant where, in full view of the waiters and the other customers, she will consume a full meal, dirty dishes piling up in front of her, while her male companion ascetically sips a glass of water! In this reading, Sonia's final declaration that "I'm not hungry anymore" is a moral affirmation rather than a statement of frustration at their inability to coordinate, and certainly not a truthful description of her appetite.

Does it matter which reading is correct? Yes, of course. Given this latter reading, none of the alternative responses suggested for Luis would suffice; each would only make matters worse. In the first reading, the problem is simply one of coordination, and any of several subtle changes would improve the conversation; in the second reading, the problem stems from alternative working definitions of the situation. While it is relatively easy to explain "No, Luis, when I asked if *you* were hungry, I was really saying that *I* am," it is much more difficult to articulate differences in definitions of the situation. If Sonia really was acting out the "Scarlet O'Hara Complex," it is not likely that Sonia would explain to Luis the depth of the injury he inflicted on her, in part because her articulation of this norm would cause her to lose face. What would she say and how would she say it? "Luis, you are supposed to collaborate with me in the construction of an identity as a thin person; that means that you always make our dinners seem responsive to your appetite, not to mine . . ." That sort of talk is not likely, in part because saying just this would preclude the successful presentation of herself as someone who does not have to work at remaining thin.

Imagine Luis and Sonia talking about this conversation on the following day with their same-sex friends. Do you think it plausible that Sonia and her friends might resurrect the old stereotype of males as "clueless" about what is going on in conversations? Do you think it is plausible that Luis and his friends might reconstruct the old stereotype of women as illogical and unpredictable? If so, do you expect that conversations of this type are likely to occur between them again in the future? What could they do to minimize the frequency of such frustrations? What could they do to reduce the unwanted effects of such conversations when they do occur?

Third-person Perspective

Sonia and Luis have reproduced a pattern typical of male-female interactions in contemporary society. They have done so because the logics of meaning and action for each of them mesh in such a way as to require each to say and do things that render them opaque to each other. If we were to inscribe the conversation in the serpentine model and look at the sinuous arrow between each utterance, we would see that Sonia and Luis are pushing each other away (Figure 1.7). Each successive act is more divergent than the one before.

If we assume that the problem here is simply one of coordination, then we might turn our attention to typical conversational styles of men and women, noting how these differ and cause problems. We might envision some sort of training that teaches women how men speak and teaches men about the speaking patterns of women. Perhaps we could develop some sort of "phrase-book" for use in cross-gender communication, similar to the booklets that people who do not speak the local language take when they

Sonia   Luis

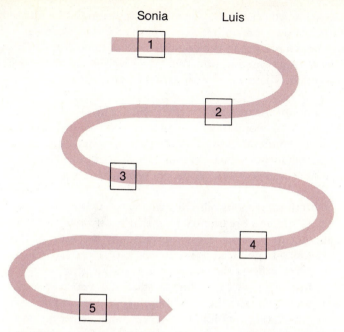

Figure 1.7 *Serpentine analysis of Sonia and Luis' conversation.*
*This is a way of describing the conversation that shows Sonia and Luis
becoming further and further apart in their working definitions of the situation
and thus having increasing difficulty coordinating their actions with each
other.*

travel to a foreign country. Imagine Luis thumbing the pages of this handbook
to the relevant page, noting that when a woman asks "Are you hungry?"
this may be her way of saying that *she* is hungry!

On the other hand, if we assume that the problem is one of the cultures
of men and women, or that the conversation in the car is only one aspect of
the real conversation, then it is not nearly so easy to figure out how to
improve the conversation. The atomic model shows one possibility: that the
prospect of being the only one eating was much more of a part of her
conversation with her girlfriends than it was part of her relationship with
Luis. In this reading, poor Luis did not have a chance; Sonia's real conversational partners were not in the car and nothing he said or did could outweigh
their evaluations of Sonia as she envisioned them.

A Final Word: Conversation and Moral Responsibility

Interpersonal communication becomes a legitimate topic for scholarly research and college-level courses when we focus on *actions* rather than on the

entities that act and are acted on. Throughout this discussion, I have urged you to think in terms of activities rather than objects, of the processes of making and doing things rather than the cognitive act of "knowing." This way of thinking assumes that the question What do I do? takes precedence over the questions What do I know? or What exists? or even What is it made of?

This shift from a noun-oriented technical vocabulary to a verb-oriented one moves us into a realm of moral obligation; ethics and responsibility are central to interpersonal communication. The question of what *should* I do take the place in a course in interpersonal communication that research methodology takes in a natural science course or proper brush-strokes in a course in art.

We bear no such ethical responsibility for the fact that we live on the third planet of a G-class star and breathe oxygen; that's just how we found things. We are beginning to bear some responsibility for the state of this planet, however, because our physical technologies have increased to the point that the ecology itself reflects the consequences of our actions.

How much responsibility do we bear for the state of our social worlds? Are the events and objects of our social worlds more like the "found things" in our physical environment (e.g., mountains, oceans, and air) or are they more like "made things" for which we bear responsibility? Are our actions simply in the context of existing patterns of race relations, economic disparities, opportunities for upward social mobility, and prospects for peace, or are our actions part of the process by which these patterns are reproduced?

Praxis

1. A Communication Analysis of Your Communication Class

In the quotation with which I introduced Part One of this book, Neil Postman referred to cultures as "corporations of conversations." I propose that we take this metaphor literally. We can treat any complex social event as a cluster of conversations, and not just conversations in general, but of specific conversations, the nature of which constitute the event.

For example, the class you are currently enrolled in is a cluster of conversations with the registrar, your professor, your classmates, and perhaps other people, such as your employer, your parents, and your athletic coach.

As a *cluster*, it includes some but not other conversations. What conversations comprise the class? Be careful: usually we underestimate the extent to which anything we do is connected to other people in our lives. There are conversations *in* class and *about* the class with other people. What do your parents or spouse think about your taking this course?

Do these conversations fall into subclusters? Can you give a descriptive label to the subclusters of conversations? For example, conversations about the class with your friends who are physics majors might be described as explaining that interpersonal communication is not a waste of time; with your friends who are psychology majors, that interpersonal communication focuses on the processes of communication, not variables or personality types; and those with your classmates, comparing notes about the projects your professor assigned. My examples will surely not be the ones that work for you, but your descriptions of the clusters of conversations is a powerful way of discerning what the course is for you.

Before coming to class. Make a list of the conversations you have that are related to this class. Organize that list by clustering together conversations that are alike. Write a word or phrase that indexes each conversation, and place the words that name conversations that resemble each other in clusters on a piece of paper. Draw a circle around each cluster and write a descriptive label for each. You should have a sheet of paper with two, three, or more circles, each of which contains the names of several conversations. Bring this sheet of paper to class.

In class. Form groups of three or four people and compare the number of clusters that you described on your paper. Also compare the names that you gave to those clusters. Discuss the following questions with the other members of your group:

In this project, are you taking a first- or third-person perspective on these conversations? As you look at the clusters you have developed, what catches your attention about the meaning of this class for you? Does it loom large or is it a small part of your life? Is it primarily positively evaluated or negatively? Would you be happier if you stopped talking about the class to certain people?

2. "What's Going On Here?" Giving a "Good Reading" of a Conversation

Practice analyzing a conversation, taking both the first- and third-person perspective. I suggest that you work in groups of two or three people, helping each other stay with the perspective you are working with and helping each other see alternatives to your first perception of what is going on.

Before class. Select a conversation that interests you. It can be a script from a play or a part of a novel; it can be a real-life conversation that you observed; it can even be a conversation in which you participated. Record the conversation—or some part of it—by writing down what the conversants said to each other. This might look something like the script for a play or film.

To start your analysis of the conversation, use the serpentine model. Pay particular attention to the way each utterance *responds* to what has gone before and *evokes* what is coming after.

Next, examine the connections between each sequential action from the first-person perspective of the conversants. That is, give answers, from their perspective, to these questions: How are they coordinating their actions with each other? What definition(s) of the situation are they working with?

Finally, take the third-person perspective and ask yourself, What are they making in this conversation? How are they making it? You might find it useful to use the serpentine model and identify the deontic logic that each conversant is following. That is, does each conversant feel that he or she "must" or "may" respond to the other in the way that he or she did? Also apply practical reasoning. That is, does each conversant feel that he or she should or must act in a particular way to evoke certain responses from the other?

I suspect that you will have some difficulty doing these analyses the first time you try. Do as much as you can and bring your work to class. In class, work in groups of two or three and help each other analyze the conversations that you selected.

Resist thinking that your interpretation is either obvious or final. Peter Lang, Director of the Kensington Consultation Centre in London, claims that he chose to analyze conversations the way he does because it allows him to be intellectually promiscuous. "Some say that you should not marry your hypotheses," he said. "Others warn that you should not even fall in love with them. I say that you should not even *date* your hypotheses! Be promiscuous!" Leaving aside the question of how one is to be promiscuous without dating, Lang's advice is good: be playful with your interpretations; look for alternative ways of accounting for what happened; build on the differing interpretations offered by members of your group.

As you go back and forth between the first- and third-person perspectives, you will find that you learn things. That is, you will notice details in the conversation that previously escaped your attention, you will notice connections among various parts of the conversation that have more or less meaning than you originally thought, and—I predict—you will simultaneously be more respectful of the conversants than you were when you began, and more aware of their shortcomings as conversants.

After your group has worked together. Prepare a brief report summarizing your findings. Use both the serpentine and the atomic models, and couch them in the best story you can generate.

Now, discuss among your group to whom this report should be made. In what conversations would your report in class be a part? What impact do you think it would have if you were to describe your findings to the conversants you observed? What impact would it have on the other members of your class? How should your professor critique it?

3. Learning the Moral Order of Conversations

Two arguments support the claim that the substance of social worlds is moral obligation. First, because conversations are activities in which each person's action is contingent on those of all the rest of us, our primary orienting question is What should I *do?* and this question is answered by locating the action within a complex web of intentions, anticipated responses, and justifications. The second argument simply notes the ubiquity of moral accounts in conversations. Every culture and every relationship develops sets of expectations for what will and should take place. If someone does not act as expected, they are challenged to account for their behavior. Why did you say that? What do you mean? Are you crazy?—all these are standard ways of demanding an explanation and presuppose that the other is accountable for their actions according to some shared set of norms.

The moral structure of conversation is seen by analyzing some of the responses given to such demand for accounts. "I don't know" is a very weak response because it denies the presupposition that the speaker is responsible for what he or she says and does. "I was angry" works better because we have, in this culture, defined anger as an emotion that "comes over" people, causing them to "lose control" and act in ways that they otherwise would not. "It seemed like a good thing to do at the time" accepts the implied criticism of what was done but asserts the actor's competence as a moral actor.

Communication theorist Richard Buttny (1987) has made an extensive study of "accounts"—statements that we give when called on to provide accounts of how our behaviors relate to the rights, responsibilities, and privileges that we have as interlocutors.

In a complex society like ours, it is clear that we do not all have the same understanding of the moral demands of conversations. Sometimes it is useful to bring our generally tacit understanding of this morality into full awareness: we can even write the rules for how particular persons in particular situations understand the structure of the game-like patterns of social interaction in which they participate.

Careful attention to accounts is one way of doing this. Listen carefully to a conversation and note the accounts given, the accounts demanded, and the accounts accepted.

1. Accounts *given* are those offered spontaneously, for example, "excuse me, but . . .", "I know this sounds silly, but . . .", "You'll probably resent my saying so, but . . .", and "I'm a communication major, and I noticed . . ." These accounts signal a very strong sense that what the speaker is saying or doing violates the moral structure of the conversation and must be shielded from the normal evaluative processes.

2. Accounts *demanded* are statements in which one person specifically asks the other for an account, for example, Who are you to tell me

that?, Did somebody ask your opinion?, Why do you say that?, and the ever-popular, Oh, yeah? These may be seen as one interlocutor's request for the other to provide a commentary on the relationship of his or her actions and the moral order of adult conversation.

3. Accounts *accepted* are those that when offered, are successful in explaining a person's unusual behavior. Accounts offered but not accepted indicate strong perceptions of the underlying moral orders.

Reconstruct the deontic and practical logics implied in these responses to a demand for an account:

- (Belligerent) "Who wants to know?" (This challenges the other's right to call the speaker's competence into question.)
- "What's wrong with what I did? Are *you* crazy?" (This response consists of a counterattack, asserting that the speaker's competence is unquestionable, and that anyone who questions it displays the insanity of their own moral system.)
- "Well, I'm a neo-Zoroastrianist, and we . . ." (This response claims a particular, nonstandard moral code, demanding that the other person respect it.)

Competent adult conversants recognize their status as moral agents. If they are about to do something that strains, if not violates, the normal rules for conversation, they will give an anticipatory justification. For example, in some societies, it is considered rude to interrupt another speaker, and one who interrupts might well say, "Excuse me, but the building has just caught on fire, and I wonder if we could move to another location?" This statement both denotes that the speaker is aware of—and takes responsibility for—violating the conversational conventions, and gives an explanation that the other person might reasonably find legitimate.

Consider some other anticipatory justifications and determine their implications for the moral performance of the speaker.

- "No offense intended, but . . ." (The speaker indicates that he or she is aware that what is about to be said might well be taken as offensive and asks for a temporary suspension of the rules on the grounds that the speaker is a moral agent and accepts responsibility for what is about to occur.)
- "I know this may sound crazy, but . . ." (Again, the speaker asks for an indulgence on the grounds of his or her moral rectitude, indicated by his or her ability to anticipate the other's response.)
- "I don't usually say this, but . . ." (The speaker asks that this situation be treated outside the normal rules.)
- "Well, since you asked . . ." (The speaker blames the other for the violation of the norms.)

■ "Will you still respect me if I . . . ." (A subtle ploy: this statement asks the other to act on a sufficiently flexible moral code to excuse what is about to happen.)

Before class. Over a period of several days, carry a notebook and record the accounts that you hear. Jot down enough information so that you can remember what account was offered and the contexts in which it was made. Differentiate among accounts offered, demanded, and accepted.

Organize your observations. Using the headings of accounts "offered," "demanded," and "accepted," list the types of accounts that you heard. This will give you a table with three columns.

In class. Bring this chart to class. Form a group of three or four people. Compare your observations. Do you see any patterns? What kinds of accounts are most rare? Which are most common? What accounts are most often demanded? Which accounts are *not* often accepted? Looking at these lists, draw up a description of the "moral orders" in which you and your classmates live. Compare your findings with those of other groups.

4. Judging the Actions of Other People

As part of the study of family violence, Dr. Linda Harris (1984) interviewed a man who physically abused his wife. Following the research protocol, she kept asking questions that elicited responses from his first-person perspective. He described a logic of meaning and action in which he simply could not control himself when he became angry. After beating his wife, he was very remorseful and begged her forgiveness, but in the heat of the moment, he said, he simply was not responsible for his actions. "It just happens," he said. "I can't control myself."

Usually, Dr. Harris would have interpreted this man's statements as the valid description of a logic of meaning and action in which he was deeply enmeshed and that compelled him to act in abusive ways. On this occasion, however, she interrupted the planned interview protocol and shouted, "Why don't you just kill her, then?" "Oh, I would never do that!" he replied.

His reply raises an interesting question about control and responsibility. Specifically, if he could not control himself when he beat his wife (i.e., he used a deontic logic of causality) then how could he control himself sufficiently that he would not injure her fatally (i.e., he used a deontic logic that allowed him conscious restraint)? Was he in control or not? To what extent are persons responsible for acting in ways that are prefigured by their logical force? To what extent are they responsible for *changing* or *transcending* their logical forces?

Form groups of five persons and constitute yourselves as a jury. Consider the evidence and questions presented in the paragraphs above and reach a verdict. Is he to be blamed or pitied for beating his wife? Is this man guilty of abusing his wife, or is he a victim of forces he cannot control? To what extent is "My logical force compelled me to do it; I could do nothing else" a valid excuse when he begs forgiveness from his wife? When he tries to explain his actions to a researcher? When he presents a defense at a trial in which he is accused of spouse abuse? Compare your verdict with those of other groups.

5. Comparing Readings of Conversations

I have never analyzed a conversation that permitted only one reading; every conversation that I have ever examined closely could be understood in at least two ways. What happens when you take a third-person perspective and feel confident of your reading of a conversation, and one of the conversants takes a first-person reading and disagrees with you? Who has the authority to say which reading is right or best?

In the example above, what reading do you give to Dr. Harris's outburst? Taking a third-person perspective, I say that she felt sympathetic to the abused wife and was expressing vicarious anger toward the husband. In my story, she felt contempt for the story he told of a recurring pattern in which he lost control, beat his wife, felt contrite, and begged for forgiveness. Harris did not believe that his abusive acts were out of control.

However, from her first-person perspective, Dr. Harris might say that she was aware that the planned interview protocol was not working; her questions were not eliciting interesting information. To probe his logic of meaning and action further without prejudging him or becoming emotionally involved in the family, she chose to ask a surprising, unplanned question. She offers as evidence for the quality of her deliberate decision the fact that the question "Why don't you just kill her, then?" elicited very interesting information.

Before class. Think through these issues. How would you decide which reading to believe: my third-person explanation or her first-person account? Under what conditions would you allow people to take authority for their own meanings in the conversations in which they are a conversant? In what situations would you *not* allow conversants to take authority for interpreting their own meanings? How do these conditions relate to the "moral order" you described in number 3, discussed earlier?

In class. Be prepared to discuss your interpretation of Harris's outburst.

References

Averill, James. *Voyages of the Heart: Living an Emotionally Creative Life.* New York: Free Press, 1992.

Barnlund, Dean. *Interpersonal Communication: Surveys and Studies.* Boston: Houghton Mifflin, 1968.

Bateson, Gregory. *Mind and Nature: A Necessary Unity.* New York: Bantam, 1979.

Berlo, David. *The Process of Communication.* New York: Holt, Rinehart and Winston, 1960.

Bhaskar, Roy. *Reclaiming Reality: A Critical Introduction to Contemporary Philosophy.* London: Verso, 1989.

Bilmes, Jack. *Discourse and Behavior.* New York: Plenum Press, 1986.

Buttny, Richard. "Sequence and Practical Reasoning in Accounts Episodes." *Communication Quarterly* 35 (1987), 67–83.

Cronen, Vernon. "Coordinated Management of Meaning: Practical Theory for the Complexities and Contradictions of Everday Life." In *The Status of Common Sense in Psychology,* edited by Jurg Siegfried. Norwood, N.J.: Ablex, in press.

Cronen, Vernon, Pearce, W. Barnett, and Lonna Snavely. "Unwanted Repetitive Patterns (URPs): A Study of Felt Enmeshment and a Theory of Episode Types." In *Communication Yearbook III,* edited by Dan Nimmo, 225–240. New Brunswick: Transaction Press, 1979.

Cronen, Vernon, and Pearce, W. Barnett. " 'Logical Force:' A New Concept of the 'Necessity' in Social Theory." *Communication* 6 (1981): 5–67.

Dance, Frank E. X. "The 'Concept' of Communication." *Journal of Communication,* 20 (1970): 201–210.

Deetz, Stanley. "Communication 2000: The Discipline, the Challenges, the Research, the Social Contribution." Rutgers University, unpublished paper, 1992.

Dewey, John. *Experience and Nature.* La Salle, IL: Open Court Publishing Company, 1929.

Geertz, Clifford. *Local Knowledge: Further Essays in Interpretive Anthropology.* New York: Basic, 1983.

Gleick, James. *Chaos: Making a New Science.* New York: Viking, 1987.

Harré, Rom. *Great Scientific Experiments: Twenty Experiments that Changed Our View of the World.* Oxford: Phaidon, 1981.

Harris, Linda, Alexander, Alison, McNamee, Sheila, Stanback, Marsha Houstin, and Kang, Kyung-wha. "Forced Cooperation: Violence as a Communicative Act." In *Communication Theory and Interpersonal Interaction,* edited by Sari Thomas. Norwood, N. J.: Ablex, 1984, pp. 20–32.

James, William. *Essays in Radical Empiricism and a Pluralistic Universe.* Gloucester: P. Smith, 1967.

Kaplan, Abraham. *The Conduct of Inquiry: Methodology for Behavioral Science.* San Francisco: Chandler, 1964.

McLaughlin, Margaret L. *Conversation: How Talk Is Organized.* Beverly Hills: Sage, 1984.

Pearce, W. Barnett. "The Practical Syllogism." In *The Encyclopaedic Dictionary of Psychology,* edited by Rom Harré and Roger Lamb, 484–486. Cambridge: MIT Press, 1983.

Peters, John Durham, and Rothenbuhler, Eric W. "The Reality of Construction." In *Rhetoric in the Human Sciences,* edited by Herbert W. Simons, pp. 11–27. London: Sage, 1989.

Philipsen, Gerry. "Speaking 'Like a Man' in Teamsterville: Culture Patterns of Role Enactment in an Urban Neighborhood." *Quarterly Journal of Speech,* 61 (1975): 13–22.

Shannon, Claude, and Weaver, Warren. *The Mathematical Model of Communication.* Urbana: University of Illinois Press, 1949.

Tannen, Deborah. *You Just Don't Understand: Women and Men in Conversation.* New York: Morrow, 1990.

Toulmin, Stephen. *The Return to Cosmology: Postmodern Science and the Theology of Nature.* Berkeley: University of California Press, 1982.

Vico, Giambattista. *The New Science of Giambattista Vico,* edited and translated by T. G. Bergin and M. H. Fisch. Ithaca, New York: Cornell University Press, 1744/1968.

Watson, John Broadus. *Psychology from the Standpoint of a Behaviorist.* Philadelphia: J. B. Lippincott, 1919.

Watson, John Broadus. *The Ways of Behaviorism.* New York: Harper and Brothers, 1928.

Watzlawick, Paul, Beavin, Janet, and Jackson, Don D. *Pragmatics of Human Communication.* New York: Norton, 1967.

Wittgenstein, Ludwig. *Philosophical Investigations.* Oxford: Blackwell, 1953.

2 *Competence in Making Social Worlds*

The limits of my language mean the limits of my world.

Wittgenstein 1922, p. 149 [#5.6]

Physical reality seems to recede in proportion as man's [sic] symbolic activity advances. Instead of dealing with the things themselves man is in a sense constantly conversing with himself. He has enveloped himself in linguistic forms, in artistic images, in mythical symbols or religious rites that he cannot see or know anything except by the interposition of [an] artificial medium.

Cassirer 1956, p. 43

Our conversations about nature and about ourselves are conducted in whatever "languages" we find it possible and convenient to employ. We do not see nature or intelligence or human motivation or ideology as "it" is but only as our languages are. And our languages are our media. Our media are our metaphors. Our metaphors create the content of our culture.

Postman 1986, p. 15

OUTLINE	OBJECTIVES	KEY WORDS AND PHRASES

Narrative

We Live in Multiple Social Worlds

Social Worlds Are Made

Social Worlds Are in a Continuous Process of Being Remade

Social Worlds Are Made with Other People in Joint Actions

Competence in Interpersonal Communication

After reading this chapter, you will be able to

- Analyze the process by which the events and objects in your social worlds are made
- Identify and resist *linguistic tyranny*
- Describe the shape and composition of your social worlds
- Differentiate two types of communication competence

Some terms that will help you understand this chapter include

language;
heteroglossia, polyphony, and polysemy;
joint action;
monologue and dialogue;
and competence

Praxis

1. Creating Events and Objects in Your Social Worlds

2. A Description of Your Social Worlds

3. Applying the "Heyerdahl Solution" to Interesting Conversations

4. Polyphony and How to Resist Linguistic Tyranny

5. Identifying the Scripts in Social Settings

6. Some Exercises in Conversational Competence

7. Competence in Ambiguous, Unstable Situations

Narrative

Chapter One, "Understanding Conversations," helped you understand *how conversations work;* this chapter directs your attention to *the work that conversations do.* Briefly put, conversations are the means by which the events and objects of our social worlds are produced; they are the processes by which identities, communities, relationships, emotions, moralities, ideologies, and all of the rest that comprises the human world are fabricated.

Of course, conversations could be treated in other ways. For example, they could be seen as art objects, the site of aesthetic performance. Or they could be treated as symptoms or manifestations of other, somehow more real, things, for example, as the site of clues about the conversants' "real" personalities or motives. Or conversations could be treated as tools to be used to persuade, mislead, ingratiate, or seduce other people.

However, the most radical and most useful way of treating conversations is as the processes by which people acting collectively make (and remake) their social worlds. In this way of thinking, there is no need to search for something "behind" conversations, and if we look *at* conversations (rather than through them or past them) we gain a unique and useful perspective on what Campbell (1972) identified as the basic questions that all human beings face: Who am I? (i.e., personal identity), Who are we? (i.e., relationships and community), What is the nature of the world around us? (i.e., cosmology), and What is the nature of the answers we get to questions like these?

The first part of the "Narrative" section of this chapter is written from the third-person perspective on *social worlds.* This section describes social worlds as made by—and in a continual process of being remade by—conversations and as a complex environment in which to live. Not only are there many social worlds that interpenetrate each other in sometimes surprising ways, but each point in these social worlds is a nexus of multiple conversations that do not always fit together without conflict. Because social worlds are so complex, all our actions are jointly produced with those of other people. Shifting to a first-person perspective, the second section of the "Narrative" focuses on *competence* in interpersonal communication.

Let the term *social worlds* denote the totality of all the conversations in which we participate and which go on around us. Your social worlds include compliments and insults; friends who take walks with you and business partners who walk out on you; having coffee with friends and dinner with your spouse's parents; playing basketball and waiting on tables; dieting and indulging yourself with a favorite food; making up after a fight, making do on your salary, and making the best of bad situations.

Your social worlds include yourself as a sexed entity, living within a world with predetermined gender roles. They include yourself as an aged individual, located at a particular moment in a developmental cycle that is inscribed in your culture by rules of politeness, privilege, and obligation.

Your social worlds identify yourself, perhaps in ways not of your choosing, as a member of a racial and economic group. Your opportunities, resources, and patterns of social interaction will be influenced by the shape of your eyes, the color of your skin, and the contours of your face.

Social worlds is an ecological concept in that it envisions all the conversations that occur in our society as interrelated, connected with each other in a complex system in which what happens at one place often affects—sometimes in surprising ways—what occurs in another. For example, a husband and wife have an argument; because of the argument, she arrives late at her job as a bus driver. Because she's late, a lawyer misses his meeting and a contract is not signed. Because the contract is not signed, the funding for a new building is lost, and ten men—including the bus driver's husband—are fired from a construction company.

We Live in Multiple Social Worlds

The plural social world*s* indicates that *your* world is not the same as those of other people. In terms of the social geography of these worlds, each of us lives in a different place; we find ourselves at each moment and throughout our lives at a unique nexus of conversations.

Differences between your social worlds and those of other people are easy to see if we take a third-person perspective on our own lives. For example, compare young adults in an urban, industrialized society with their contemporaries living in the Amazonian rain forest, the Kalahari Desert in Africa, or the outback in Australia. Of course, there are some similarities in these social worlds: all human beings experience much the same maturational sequence, all live in societies in which genders are differentiated, and all—so far—have lived their lives on the outside of a very large sphere in which "up" and "down" and "day" and "night" have particular meanings. However, these similarities should not obscure the very real differences between social worlds.

The cultures of Asia, the Americas, and Europe developed very different moralities, philosophies, and theories of personhood; they also developed very different patterns of communication. There is a connection here: different forms of interpersonal communication *cause and are caused by* different cultural patterns, social institutions, and ways of being a person.

The plural world*s* also denotes a particular characteristic of contemporary society: there are important differences *within* each of our social worlds. Not only are the worlds different, but they are also juxtaposed. Those of us who live in urban, industrialized societies participate in many different social worlds simultaneously, each with its own logic of meaning and action.

The continuity of our social worlds is not inextricably bound either to place or to personal identity. The same place may be the site for very different kinds of lives, and your own moral order may shift suddenly if you move from one place to another. For example, if you knock someone down while

All human beings have in common the facts that we make and are made by our social worlds. However, the social worlds that we make—and that make us—are very different. We experience sharply different forms of life because we are enmeshed in different patterns of communication.

Counterpoint 2.1

The study of communication has taken radically new forms in the past 30 years. At least one reason for this is that Western intellectual history has changed in some important ways. In fact, many current assessments of social thought refer to the "turns" taken in this century. Some describe this as the "linguistic turn," others as the "rhetorical turn," and still others as the development of a "postmodern" sensibility. (For an excellent discus-

sion of these developments, see Rorty 1979; Gergen 1982; and Bernstein 1971, 1978, 1983, and 1992).

At several times during this book, I claim that traditional prejudices must be set aside if you are to understand current thinking about communication. If you read these claims baldly (that's a term we will discuss at length in Chapter 6), they seem arrogant. In fact, I am claiming that the current understanding of communication is a part of a much broader shift in the sensibility of Western culture—a shift so great that it defies precise characterization. That's why some of the most articulate reporters wind up using such vague terms as "postmodern" (which does not say anything except that it is after something else) and referring to various "turns." However, these developments are revolutionary in that they require a patient reexamination of all our assumptions and a willingness to discard many of them.

Communication has a prominent place in late–twentieth-century Western intellectual history. In fact, it has not been seen as so central to what serious-minded thinkers in a dozen disciplines are doing since the classical Greek period of the 6th through 4th centuries B.C.E.

In this still-chaotic, rapidly changing constellation of perspectives in contemporary social theory, communication is seen as the material substance of the processes by which our forms of life are created. Do not read this as a cheery advertisement for communication. Many of the most profound contributors to the new sensibility, among them Derrida and Foucault, have shown us "that such ideas as authentic dialogue, community, communication, and communicative rationality *can* potentially—and indeed *have* in the past—become 'suffocating straitjackets' and 'enslaving conceptions' " (Bernstein 1992, p. 51). Those who decry the effects of communication outweigh those who, like Habermas, Rorty, and Bernstein, look to "a practical commitment to" some form of "authentic communication" or "dialogue" as "the basis—perhaps the only honest basis—for hope" (Bernstein 1992, p. 53). I agree; in another place I argued that "the material and social conditions of the contemporary world are profoundly disordered. Not for the first time, there is a discontinuity between the contemporary form of society and the ways of communication it institutionalizes. A new round in the coevolution of society and communication processes is in progress." (Pearce 1989, p. 91)

Our social worlds are multiple, complex, and contradictory.

wearing a football uniform during a game, you may be cheered and given the "most valuable player" award, but if you knock the same person down on a sidewalk, you may be arrested and taken to court. Does this seem strange?

Usually we handle such inconsistencies in our social worlds easily by making one logic of meaning and action more salient than the others at particular times. For example, the game of football is clearly marked off from the rest of life by its special stadiums, the referee's whistle, and the uniforms worn by the players. Usually we can differentiate among the various "hats" that we wear when relating to each other.

What are some of the ways in which you mark distinctions within your social worlds? If you take your meals in a cafeteria, watch the way people negotiate specific meanings by the way they place their books, jackets, or dining utensils on the table—these details define whether the person is merely eating or dining, whether the person is inviting others to join him or her (it is an "open" social event) or politely indicating a desire to remain alone. Observe the way that men and women signal each other about their relationships or their availability for the establishment of relationships. Notice the signals given at parties that define some people as a couple. For example, reciprocated glances across the crowded room, the use of the pronoun "we" to talk about plans, or a proprietorial straightening of the partner's clothing are bits of language used to say something like "We're together; intruders beware!" What language do people use to define themselves as "single"? Some people are very skilled at giving complex signals—for example, letting one person know that more attention would be welcome while letting others know that they should look elsewhere for social partners.

Sometimes, however, we run into problems. Young married couples find that the logic of meaning and action that was appropriate for them as lovers does not function as well when they are handling the family finances—cooing and caresses, however wonderful, do not help them decide whether to buy a new car or pay tuition for graduate school.

Sometimes the boundaries among these social worlds is blurred, such that we are not sure just what logic is in place. Using myself as an example, I am at once husband, father, son, and brother—each with a different, sometimes conflicting, set of rights, privileges, and responsibilities. I am at the same time student, professor, and Department Chair: sometimes I (the Department Chair) have to write myself (the Professor) a memo informing me (who?) about the rules for processing final grades or noting the results of the latest round of student evaluations. I am also a citizen, taxpayer, automobile operator, sometime sailor, and, in memory and imagination at least, martial artist.

The Complexities and Contradictions of Everyday Life

As social scientists have turned their attention to the accomplishment of the apparently routine events of everyday life, such as a person making a decision, a group arriving at an interpretation of an unusual event, or a family coordinating its actions well enough to get through the day, they have discovered that our social worlds are not homogeneous. Bilmes' (1986) study of group decision making showed that common sense contains contradictory moral precepts. Often our discussions consist of negotiations about which of these is the most relevant within our working definitions of the situation. Billig and his colleagues (1988) were impressed by the frequency with which people in ordinary jobs encountered and coped with what he called "ideological dilemmas." Cronen's (in press) study of family therapists revealed that the overlap of conversations in each client's life presented a unique set of conflicts and implications for each act that they would take. For example, he noted that a middle-class professional woman who is abused by her husband found severing her relationship with him difficult but conscionable; in fact, the logic of her self-concept "required" it. On the other hand, a working-class woman whose self-concept was defined by her marital relationship found severing her relationship with her abusive husband virtually impossible; that is, her deontic logic blocked her from divorce or separation and caused her to remain in an abusive relationship.

The implication of these findings is that everyday life is not a particularly orderly place in which reasonable solutions to problems can be found. Rather, it is a fluid, complex place in which each action is at the intersection of multiple logics, and these logics may reinforce, be irrelevant to, or contradict each other. Sometimes we are "compelled" by these logics of meaning and action to take mutually exclusive actions simultaneously; sometimes we are left confused by oddly intersecting logics.

Counterpoint 2.2

The conflicts between the various logics of meaning and action were first taken to be a "problem." Gregory Bateson and his colleagues coined the phrase "double bind" to describe a situation in which a person was simultaneously required to act in mutually exclusive ways, prohibited from leaving the situation, and prohibited from talking about it. They claimed that double binds caused major psychological problems, such as schizophrenia. This idea was a rich source of insight into certain forms of interpersonal communication, particularly family communication patterns (Watzlawick et al. 1967; Sluzki 1976).

The neat linear hypothesis ("double binds cause schizophrenia") did not stand up well to tests, however. Although proponents of the idea were able to show that there were double binds in the families of schizophrenics, other researchers found just as many double binds in the families of people who were healthy. One result of this was to accept double binds as a natural part of social worlds and to explore farther the patterns of conflicting logics.

Some interesting ideas were developed. A group of family therapists in Italy began using "paradoxes" as therapeutic interventions (Selvini Palazolli et al. 1978). A group of communication theorists reconceptualized the double bind and offered a much more rigorous understanding of "charmed" and "strange loops" and other forms of "paradoxical" relationships within logics of meaning and action (Cronen et al. 1982).

At present, communication theorists seldom treat a conflicted logic of meaning and action as if it were a problem, not even if the conflict is paradoxical. Rather, paradoxes and inconsistencies are seen as normal and are typically dealt with successfully by conversants. This benign treatment of paradox has improved the practice of therapists as well as facilitated the development of communication theory.

Heteroglossia, Polyphony, and Polysemy

If you were to make a map of your social worlds, it could not be as simple as the two-dimensional road maps that you use to find your way to another city or to a strange street in a large city. As shown in Figure 1.6, each point in your social worlds is the nexus of several simultaneous conversations; each act that you and others perform continue several conversations.

The geometry of such space presents an interesting challenge and would drive the Rand-McNally cartographers crazy. If you have a mathematical mind, you might find the work done by Forgas (1985) and Woelfel and Fink (1980) very interesting. They used the notion of multidimensional space as ways of mapping the shape of our social worlds. They found that the social worlds of different people have different shapes and that the complexity of these social worlds is not constant.

People who are more oriented to language than to mathematics have coined Latin or Greek neologisms to describe the plurality of our social worlds. Each of the three terms presented here focuses on a slightly different aspect of our social worlds.

Polysemy (literally, many meanings) focuses on each point within our social worlds. It refers to the fact that any single word or action is simultaneously a part of many conversations, each with a history and a future. For example, any word that "I" speak has many meanings because it has a history in which it has been used in various ways by myself and others, and it has a future, in which it will be used in various ways by myself and others. I am never in complete control of the meaning of what I say; once it is said, it enters into the public world, where you will hear it within the contexts of your social worlds which cannot be exactly the same as mine and which may differ substantially.

Refrain 2.1

Heteroglossia:
Literally: "many tongues." Many sublanguages are present within a language; "families" of language games resemble each other but have different logics of meaning and action

Polysemy:
Literally: "Many meanings." Words and phrases have multiple meanings; various sublanguages use the same words, but for different purposes; no utterance or action ever has only one meaning; meaning depends on the context in which it occurs and the perspective from which it is interpreted

Polyphony:
Literally: "many sounds." We are always involved in many conversations simultaneously; each utterance or action we perform is a voice in several conversations, and we may be saying very different things in them

From a third-person perspective, *polyphony* (literally, many voices) refers to the fact that none of us is alone in our social worlds. The same words spoken by someone else mean something quite different. Think of the injunction "Stop!" spoken by your 3-year-old nephew whose stomach you are tickling; Salvadoran Archbishop Romero, outraged at the violence of the civil war, addressing the death squads in a nationally broadcast sermon; and a proctor announcing the end of the time allotted for taking a standardized achievement examination. I am rather glad that the conversations that comprise our social worlds are not all in any one voice! The term polyphony reminds you that your social worlds include a wide variety of others who are not only *not* you but also not necessarily very much *like* you.

Also from a third-person perspective, *heteroglossia* (literally, different tongues) refers to the fact that the languages we use are differentiated into clusters, and these clusters permit us to do some different things. English (or any other language) is not just one language. It is better described as a family of languages, most of which are mutually comprehensible but each of which facilitate some things and impede others. You are familiar with this: if you are an expert in anything, you know how difficult it is to explain what you know to someone who does not know your technical language. I play chess but not bridge; I find discussions of chess strategy in the newspapers interesting and helpful but cannot make sense of the columns on bridge.

Although I know—and, in other contexts, have used!—every word in Charles Goren's commentaries, I have no idea what he is talking about.

Linguist Michael Bakhtin (1986) forcefully called our attention to heteroglossia. Writing during the Stalinist era in the Soviet Union, Bakhtin—and everyone else in his society—knew that there were several very different sublanguages, and that these served very different purposes. Sometimes one had to use the official sublanguage of official Marxism; at other times (perhaps taking care not to be overheard), one could speak in the languages of religion, individualism, or capitalism. Further, they knew that the choice of what language to use was not a politically neutral act. According to many reports, citizens of the Soviet Union became expert in code switching and in using the conventions of one sublanguage to perform the functions of another; that is, by deliberately playing with the polysemy of their vocabulary, they recognized the polyphony of their society. This was a subversive political act, of course: by their forms of conversation they were preventing the authoritarian government from silencing their voices. Polysemy gave them the opportunity to seem to speak in the politically correct manner while at the same time carrying on conversations that were independent or subversive to the party line.

At about the same time that Bakhtin was writing, the American linguist Benjamin Whorf was working out similar ideas but in a very different social context. The freedoms of speech, press, and assembly are guaranteed in the U.S. Constitution, and the popular myth in this country is of a free marketplace of ideas in which words are neutral tools of expression. Words are supposed to mean just what they say and nothing else, regardless of who says them. The commitment to an open society in the United States, for all of its many virtues, had the unexpected consequence of denying the heteroglossia, polyphony, and polysemy of our social worlds (Schultz 1990). Whorf worked within a society that embraced the notions of a conversational melting pot, or "level field," in which all could speak the same language, in which every voice sounds alike, and actions mean only what they are intended to mean. It turns out that this implicit theory of how communication works is simply not correct. The citizens of this country do not all speak English as their first language. Even those who do speak English do not speak it the same way.

■ There are regional dialects: as a southern male, I know that when I begin to speak, a well-developed set of not-very-favorable stereotypes slide into place. Other stereotypes are associated with the tonal and pronunciation characteristics of people from Brooklyn or the Bronx, Texas, Vermont, Boston, and other places not fully assimilated into the generic "American" accent.
■ Americans who have brought some of their national heritages with them have developed particular forms of English. You probably are aware of the controversy about whether these are alternative forms of English or just "bad" English. If you enjoy arguments like this, you are in for a good time: recent waves of immigrants to this country will present us with rich new forms of expression and communication.

■ There are technical languages used by the experts in every activity from knitting to sailing to computer programming. The language used by experts and teachers in these arcane arts is often completely unintelligible to outsiders.

■ Different discourses are used to discuss various topics. For example, since 1947, foreign policy in the United States has been framed within a particular use of language referred to as the "national security" discourse (Morales 1989). This discourse—like any other—has hidden presuppositions about what is important, what is equivalent, and what is dissimilar. Once you start to speak in a discourse, some things are easy to say, some seem necessary, others are difficult, and still others seem silly. In the same way, discussions with your parents or friends of what you should select as your major might be in any of several discourses, some of which focus on your lifetime earning power, others on your interests and personal development, and others on the amount of time you will need to spend studying.

Counterpoint 2.3

The polysemy of our social worlds is what makes wit, word games, and creativity possible. The humor in a pun stems from the recognition that a particular utterance simultaneously references two different meanings. For example, what do you call a woman who pretends to be a tailor? (A seems-tress.) What do you call an adult who makes puns? (A groan-up.)

Ambiguities in the words we use can cause real troubles. Benjamin Whorf was an insurance inspector who noted that fires kept starting in presumably empty gasoline containers. Of course, these containers were not empty at all; they contained highly volatile gasoline fumes but not liquid gasoline. Whorf is remembered for his contribution to the "linguistic relativism" hypothesis that claims that the structure of our language determines (or at least is correlated with) the structure of our thoughts and perceptions. If Eskimos, so goes the classic illustration, have many words for what we who speak English call by the one word "snow," then they will perceive differences where we do not. As Whorf (1956, p. 252) put it:

> Every language is a vast pattern system, different from others, in which are culturally ordained the forms and categories by which the personality not only communicates, but also analyzes nature, notices or neglects types of relationship and phenomena, channels his [sic] reasoning, and builds the house of his consciousness.

Given the sensibilities of modernity, it is a short step from the recognition of the polysemy and heteroglossia of language to a moral commitment to "fix" it. Among the attempts to purify language so that things mean only what they say are the movement called "General Semantics" (Korzybski 1958; Hayakawa 1964) and "analytical philosophy" (Whitehead and Russell 1962; Rapoport 1953).

This puritanical attempt to fix our language is not well advised. Some things that we prize greatly would be lost if language were so determinedly prosaic that there were no polysemy or heteroglossia. For example, Parry (1968) warned that

> *We must not assume that the whole purpose of communication is to ensure full understanding by every hearer. Such an ideal would entail the banishment of wit and vivacity from human discourse and the anaesthetization of keener instincts by laborious explanation. In these matters, the speaker must at times take calculated risks; sometimes his remarks will fall on strong ground and he will have lost the gamble.*

In addition, the polysemy and heteroglossia of our social worlds is a vital resource for speakers. Assume that you want to say something new, or that you want to say something that will escape the notice of the censors or thought-police; where do you find the resources to do it?

> *Speakers have far more resources at their disposal than the single set of forms and stylistic conventions of a single "language." In fact, every national language is teeming with sublanguages, each with its own conventions. Wherever significant social differentiation occurs in life, there too will begin to form a new sublanguage. In any society of any complexity, therefore, numerous such sublanguages always coexist, challenge one another, and become grist for the verbal mill of those who master their conventions. What we are describing, of course, is the state of* heteroglossia, *which Bakhtin takes to be the primordial linguistic state for human beings in society. (Schultz 1990, pp. 34–35)*

Heteroglossia and polysemy provide the opportunities for us to speak in our own voice, even if that voice is something different from the Establishment voice, and thus we can participate in a polyphonous society. How boring and tyrannical a monophony (one-voiced society) would be! Aldous Huxley, in *Brave New World,* and George Orwell, in *1984,* imagined the worst that our contemporary societies might become. In somewhat different ways, both envisioned a society in which only one voice was allowed.

An Inherent Tension Between "Stories Lived" and "Stories Told"

The comparison of "stories told" and "lived" evokes a recognition of the two sides of human experience. We write of the stars with hands genetically shaped for grasping a branch or crude tools, we dream of universal peace with minds that are affected by the enzymes secreted by our livers, our souls soar with aesthetic ecstacy while our bodies struggle against a maturational cycle that makes hair grey, skin wrinkle, and tendons tear instead of stretch.

We can come to grips with the tension between these two aspects of our experience by contrasting *stories told* and *stories lived*. On the one hand, our experience is the stuff of dreams: in the stories we *tell*, we can be like Superman, leaping over tall buildings in a single bound and feeling more powerful than a speeding locomotive. (If such stories do not have so much appeal, why did the James Bond and Rocky movies earn so much money?) However, our experience is also the stuff of the physical world. In the stories we *live*, our attempts to leap too far produce personal injury and public humiliation, and speeding locomotives, in the form of our personal mortality, the whims of the boss, and the routinized practices of the Internal Revenue Service, flatten us where we stand.

The stories we *tell* are subject only to the limits of our imaginations; however, the stories we *live* are performed in concert with other people. In the stories we tell, we have access to every resource that we can imagine—we can imagine ourselves with superhuman strength, surrounded by admiring and capable assistants, and with an unlimited supply of money; in the stories we live, we can only put into play resources that we can access.

Any attempt to reduce our lives to either the stories we live or tell is a mistake. Although inextricably interrelated, they are distinguishable. One expresses our enmeshment in a world of imagination, including both logic and fantasy. The other expresses our simultaneous enmeshment in a world of movement, including the coordination of our movements with those of the objective world and other people.

Conversations are a fluid result of the interpenetrations of these two worlds. They include both the dream-stuff of the stories we tell and the physical-stuff of the stories we live. Neither is complete without the other; neither is reducible to the other. That is, while we are in fact the "authors" of our experience, we are at best, "co authors." As any journalist or textbook writer can tell you, the stories we live (or publish) are co–constructed by authors, editors, reviewers, publishers, and distributors. Contemporary American culture celebrates individual autonomy; however, far more than we usually realize, we have to share authorship with others in the stories we live.

Even the resources we have for the stories we tell are derived from other people. We are born into clusters of conversations already in progress. The main themes have already been selected, the lines of discussion determined, and the major roles defined.

As human beings, we have a biologically implanted ability to join in ongoing patterns of activities—we do not have to be taught how to play games, just given the opportunity. We "internalize" the games we are playing; to do well becomes important for us. When we are born into a cluster of conversations comprising gender, race, economic processes and classes, religion, and identity, we find our place in these conversations by understanding their terms. We act in ways prefigured by the logics of meaning and action of these conversations, and we come to know who we are, what we want, and how to get it from the perspective of being inside these games. Our dreams, religions, and philosophies are composed of the terms of the conversations into which we are born. Muslims seldom have visions of the Madonna (the Virgin Mary, not the singer), and Christians seldom call upon the compassionate Buddha.

Counterpoint 2.4

Being deliberately provocative, Nigel Calder (1976) argued that there is a "human conspiracy" to take newly born infants and turn them into copies of the adults who care for them. Calder notes that a newborn *homo sapiens* is far more helpless than the infants of, for example, the great apes or other mammals. He claims that a member of our species is not a human being at birth but has the capacity to become one.

Put with slightly less sensationalism, it is clear that newborn babies are absorbed into ongoing game-like patterns of social interaction not of their choosing or making, and that they have tremendous abilities to find places in these games in which they can act as first persons. We do not have to teach children how to engage in game-like patterns of action, but the specific games they find teach them many things about who they are and about the possible and appropriate array of relationships with others. Researchers who have studied the social worlds of infants have repeatedly revised their opinions of the significance of early social experiences. These experiences are far more important than they first thought, and they occur at a far earlier age.

What seems like free play or purely social interactions between parent and infant during the first six months of the infant's life are the site of important developments.

> The infant has developed schemas of the human face, voice, and touch, and within those categories he knows the specific face, voice, touch, and movements of his primary caregiver. He [sic] has acquired schemas of the various changes they undergo to form different human emotional expressions and signals. He has "got" the temporal patterning of human behavior and the meaning of different changes and variations in tempo and rhythm. He has learned the social cues and conventions that are mutually effective in initiating, maintaining, terminating, and avoiding interactions with his mother. He has learned different discursive or dialogic modes, such as turn taking. And now he has the foundation of some internal composite picture of his mother so that, a few months after this phase is over, we can speak of his having established object permanence—or an enduring representation of mother that he carries around with him with or without her presence. (Stern 1977, pp. 5–6)

Curiously, the way adults converse with infants has some striking similarities, even in very different cultures and language groups. "Baby talk" uses a simplified syntax, short utterances, many nonsense sounds, and certain transformations of sounds. Even more conspicuous is the variation in adults' prosody (i.e., the vocal, facial, bodily manner in which they engage in conversation). The pitch of the voice is raised, long utterances in falsetto are common, sometimes interspersed with deep bass rumbling. Variations in loudness or intensity, from whispering to loud "pretend scary," are exaggerated. Facial expressions and body movements are simplified and exaggerated. A sing-song quality is achieved by exaggerating the stress on syllables, elongating vowels, and pausing between utterances (Stern 1977).

This cross-cultural similarity seems unusual. What else might be going on in these patterns of baby talk? How and when do human beings learn the array of human emotions? How do personalities get formed? What happens if an infant or child is invited to participate in a broader-than-usual array of conversations? Do they become confused, or do they develop unusual abilities? What happens if an infant or child is limited to a smaller-than-usual array of conversations? Do they fail to develop some of the normal human emotions? Are there crucial game-like patterns of social interaction for the development of prosocial emotions, such as empathy, altruism, courage, and responsibility?

Social Worlds Are Made

In the experience of each person, the events and objects of the social world seem solid, objective, and monolithic. However, just a moment of reflection reminds us that there was a time when none of the "facts of life" in your social worlds existed and that there will be a time when they have vanished. In the present moment, there are other families and other cultures in which very different facts of life are believed as fervently and for the same reasons as you believe your own. At the very least, the events and objects of the social world are transitory; I want to make the further claim that they are fabricated or made in conversations.

Common sense treats the events and objects of the social world as "found" things, fully formed and finished. Families, the CIA, mass murderers, weddings, political parties, IBM, the film industry and the like all seem like physical entities that exist whether we do anything about them or not. However, I suggest that we see them as events and objects that are made in conversations by human beings. That is, let's focus on the *process* by which the events and objects in the social world are made.

The claim that the events and objects of our social worlds are *made* stands opposed to a historic prejudice. This prejudice was most forcefully stated by the French philosopher René Descartes and is known as *dualism*.

In this way of thinking, there are two separate types of things: subjective (i.e, cognitive processes like thoughts, doubts, and beliefs) and objective (i.e., the uninterpreted things outside our consciousness). This Cartesian dualism created the epistemological problem that has entertained philosophers for hundreds of years. This problem can be stated very simply: how can what is outside be represented accurately by what is inside our heads? That is, How can we know (i.e., construct accurate representations in our heads using subjective materials) the real world?

From Descartes to Kant, the history of philosophy consists of various ways of wrestling with the epistemological problem. In his book *Beyond Objectivism and Relativism,* Richard Bernstein (1983) declares the problem a conundrum; that is, Descartes' question itself is based on a misleading set of assumptions (dualism) such that no matter how you answer it, the answer is not very useful. It is like asking Which way shall we go, left or right? when your purpose is to remain right where you are. No matter how well someone argues for "left" rather than "right," it does not help you stand firm.

Bernstein said that we should not even try to answer the dualists' question of How can we cognitively represent external reality? Rather, we should set the question aside in favor of a more useful perspective. Three sources converge, in what Bernstein (1992) called *The New Constellation,* to produce a more useful perspective. These include Wittgenstein's analysis of language; contemporary hermeneutics (particularly the work of Gadamer); and the American Pragmatists, including William James, John Dewey, George Herbert Mead, Richard Rorty, Clifford Geertz, and Bernstein himself.

Instead of dualism and its question about How can we cognitively represent external reality? this new constellation of approaches assumes that we have experience, that this experience includes *both* us (i.e., our subjective perceptions) *and* what is known (i.e., objective reality). Further, it identifies experience as a form of *acting* in the world of which we are a part. When this prejudice replaces that of dualism, the problem that interests us is How do we (collectively) act in the world to create our experience? or, more prosaically, How do we make our social worlds? At least part of the answer to that question is "in conversations."

The "Heyerdahl Solution"

To understand a process in which things are continuously being created, we need to ask the question How is it made? We do best if we develop a certain kind of curiosity, the kind that takes things apart and looks for the patterns that connect some things with others.

An excellent example of this kind of curiosity was displayed by the Norwegian explorer Thor Heyerdahl (1960). It is so simple, so unusual in its context, and so clearly successful that I call it the "Heyerdahl solution" and nominate it as the model for us to use in understanding the events and objects of the social worlds in which we live.

These giant stone carvings baffled scientists for many years. Instead of asking Who made them? or Why were they made? Thor Heyerdahl asked the islanders if they could make another one and was able to watch as it was carved and set into place. Applied to the events and objects of our social worlds, the Heyerdahl solution focuses our attention on how they are made.

Perplexed like many others by the giant stone carvings on Easter Island, Heyerdahl resisted the temptation to treat the figures as "found things" and speculate about who might have made them. Instead, as he reveals in his book *Aku Aku,* he focused on the activities by which the heads were brought into being. As a bet, he challenged the mayor of the community on Easter Island to duplicate the feats of whoever was responsible for the carvings.

As Heyerdahl told the story, he asked the mayor, Petro Atan, if he knew how the giant stone carvings on Easter Island had been raised into place.

Atan: Yes, Señor, I do know. There's nothing to it.

Heyerdahl: Nothing to it? It's one of the greatest mysteries of Easter Island! [One Western investigator suggested that the ancient Egyptians had somehow found their way to this remote south Pacific Ocean island to practice their well-known expertise with large stones; another claimed that aliens from outer space had visited the earth and left these stones as a symbol of their visit— perhaps to inform us that they, like the stones, were red-headed.]

Atan: But I know it. I can raise a *moai.*

Heyerdahl: Who taught you?

The mayor grew solemn and drew himself up in front of me.

Atan: Señor, when I was a very little boy I had to sit on the floor, bolt upright, and my grandfather and his old brother-in-law Porotu sat on the floor in front of me. They taught me many things, just as in school nowadays. I know a lot. I had to repeat and repeat it until it was quite right, every single word. I learned the songs, too. (Heyerdahl 1960)

Heyerdahl was able to watch as the Easter Islanders repeated the forms of action that had been passed down from father to son for many generations, and 18 days later, a new stone head was standing, facing the sea as did all the others.

Note what the Heyerdahl solution does to the question of how the events and the objects of social worlds come to be. Instead of asking *why* or even *by whom,* he asked *how* they were made. I suggest that we apply the Heyerdahl solution to the events and objects of social worlds. Rather than treating sexism, racism, the university, or even textbooks as found things, or asking *why* or *for what purpose* or *whose fault is it,* let's ask *how they are made.*

Counterpoint 2.5

The *Heyerdahl solution* consists of looking at *how something is made.* It stands in contrast to asking What is it? or Why did it come to be? As such, the Heyerdahl solution is particularly useful for thinking about how the events and objects of our social worlds are made in conversations.

My selection of Thor Heyerdahl's work is an appropriate tribute to this resourceful explorer, but his solution is really just an application of the *pragmatic method* developed at the beginning of the twentieth century by the American philosophers William James and John Dewey. This pragmatic method consists of looking at how things work out in practice. That is, "truth is what works." As James (1907/1975, p. 97) put it, "The truth of an idea is not a stagnant property inherent in it. Truth *happens* to an idea. It *becomes* true, is *made* true by events. Its verity *is* in fact an event, a process: the process namely of its verifying itself, its veri-*fication.* Its validity is the process of its valid-*ation.*"

In the minds of self-centered people who see themselves as individuals acting on or against other people (i.e., in what I call *monologic* communication later in this chapter), this seems a vulgar excuse for making up any story that will get them what they want. James and Dewey had quite a different view. Because they looked at the ecology of conversations as a whole and saw these conversations continuing into the future (i.e., what I call *dialogic* communication later in this chapter), they defined "what works" in terms of its implications for all of the people involved. In this way of thinking, "truth" is what stands the test of being put into practice; those practices create the future in which we live, and the self-centered individualism embedded in monologic communication is one of those things that do not "work" very well.

Counterpoint 2.6

How far should we push the Heyerdahl solution as a way of understanding our social worlds? Should we treat *all* the events and objects of our social worlds as existing solely because they are made in conversations, or should we take a less extreme position? This is an issue about which many people have thought carefully, and they do not agree. Here are some questions that will help you think through the issue. Be warned, there are no simple answers to these questions.

- If you grant that *some* of the events, objects, and relations in our social worlds are made, by what criteria do we judge which are socially constructed and which are not?
- What kinds of conversations can—and should—occur when we disagree about which events are socially constructed and which are not?
- What events, objects, and relations are made by the conversations that occur when we disagree about whether specific things are socially constructed?

The issue is whether the social worlds in which we live have some permanent, objective landmarks or whether it is all fluid and shifting. If we use the similies "clouds" and "clocks," the question is how "cloudlike" and how "clocklike" our social worlds are.

On one hand, if we see the events and objects of our social worlds as socially constructed, we risk a rootless relativism. The folk maxim from the 1960s, "Different strokes for different folks," is not a particularly strong basis for choosing a President, devising national strategy, or addressing the ethical questions surrounding racial prejudice, prevention of sexually transmitted disease, and protection of human rights.

On the other hand, if we treat the events and objects of our social worlds as found things, we prepare ourselves to be prisoners of the conversations into which we were born and tyrants who enforce our perceptions onto others. That is, instead of saying "That's the way I see it," we insist "That's the way it is!"

The issue is both real and important. It may be expressed as the question of whether the polyphony of our social worlds is superficial or deep seated. That is, is there a single reality somewhere out there that is obscured by the many voices that describe it, or is reality itself polyphonic, called into being by the voices that speak? The implication of this decision is summarized in the prayer offered by Alcoholics Anonymous: "Lord, grant me serenity to accept the things that I cannot change, courage to change those that I can, and wisdom to know which is which."

Language

Language is the single most powerful tool that humans have ever invented for the creation of social worlds. In fact, it is so powerful a tool that some thoughtful analysts have suggested that language created us! Do we speak language or does language speak us? Which came first, the thought or the word?

There is much about the origin of language that we will never know. There is evidence that one million years ago our ancestors were engaging in activities requiring some degree of cooperation and foresight, including organized hunting of large animals and the controlled use of fire. Whatever language they spoke was surely far simpler than any modern language because the anatomy of the vocal tracts of our distant ancestors could produce far fewer distinguishable sounds than our own. However, as long as 50,000 years ago, our ancestors had fully modern vocal tracts and were capable of producing the full range of sounds in today's languages (Claiborne 1983, pp. 22–23).

However, we can be absolutely sure that the first instance of human communication was a conversation—language was originally spoken (not written) in the physical presence of another person with the keen anticipation of a response by that other person. That is, Ug the Caveman said/signed/grunted something that indicated to Uk, who lived in the next cave, that it would be nice if they went hunting together tomorrow, and found Uk ready and waiting to go the next day.

Counterpoint 2.7

The relationship between the media and the process of communication has caused considerable confusion.

Entranced by the potentials of telegraph, telephone, television, audio- and videotape recording, and other technical means of getting a message from one place to another, some people have focused on the media and neglected the process of communication. Those who use the late, unlamented *transmission* model of communication discussed in Chapter 1 are particularly susceptible to this temptation, of which Ong (1972, p. 176) remarks, "This model obviously has something to do with human communication, but, on close inspection, very little, and it distorts the act of communication beyond recognition."

On the other hand, those who are entranced by the process of communication have sometimes treated the media as if they were merely different technical means by which the same process occurs. For example, Berlo (1960) put "media" as one of the variables ("channels") within the process of communication in his "source → message → channels → receiver" (SMCR) model.

We now have sufficient reason to believe that the medium in which communication occurs is far more important than we believed, but that its effects are far more subtle than early analysts imagined. In brief: media are the enabling infrastructures of the process of communication; they shape what is possible, what is usual, and what is difficult. In doing so, they constrain the development of communication processes (including the forms of consciousness of the communicators, the patterns of social interaction, and thus the events and objects of social worlds) in much the same way as the course of rivers affected the development of cities and trade in Canada (Innis 1951) and railroads determined the place of cities in the American west (Cronon 1991).

Oral speech is the primary medium of communication. Every language used by human beings (with the exception of computer "languages," if they be included) was first spoken without having a written form.

> "Wherever human beings exist they have a language, and in every
> instance a language that exists basically as spoken and heard, in
> the world of sound . . . Indeed, language is so overwhelmingly oral
> that of all the many thousands of languages—possibly tens of thousands—
> spoken in the course of human history only around 106 have ever been
> committed to writing to a degree sufficient to have produced litera-
> ture, and most have never been written at all." (Ong 1982, p. 7)

Every society has, at one time or another, relied on speech for its most important social functions. Ong calls these "primary oral societies." Some societies have become "primary literate societies" in that they regularly entrust their most important social functions (or at least some of them, perhaps the most "public" of them) to printed materials using written language. We now know that this is not just an exchange of one medium for another; it is an exchange of one form of consciousness and society for another (Ong 1982).

We find ourselves at a most interesting moment in social evolution. The United States (and many other industrialized nations) are moving from a literate society to one that uses the electronic media for many of its most important functions. Although we are not sure exactly what effects this shift will have, there is reason to believe that they will be significant, rivaling the change from oral to literate society in impact. For example, Postman (1985) argues that television has trivialized our ability to engage in public discourse about the public's business, and Meyerwitz (1985) argues that the structure of society's boundaries have been changed by the electronic media. At the same time, many of the nations of the world that did not become so deeply literate are moving from what Ong calls a "manuscript" society (they have a written language, but manuscripts are used to back up—not replace—oral speech) directly to an electronic society. We really do not know what kinds of effects this shift will have: the best discussion is by Tehranian (1990), who offered four possibilities and said—in the best pragmatic tradition—that subsequent events will determine which one is true.

The development of other media of communication (e.g., print or elec-tronic) enables us to see more clearly the characteristics of oral speech, the medium of interpersonal communication. Speech involves the whole person; it includes both verbal and nonverbal elements, such as the quality of the voice, facial expressions, body posture and movements, and use of the space between conversants. These non-verbal aspects of interpersonal communication are so important that some books and college courses focus specifically on them (Knapp and Hall, 1992). In addition, speech includes a give-and-take between speakers, in physical proximity to each other, and in a specific setting. Unlike print, which can be anonymous, taken from one setting to another, and read and written in private, speech disappears as it is said and is intensely personal.

Once language was developed, it permitted our ancestors—and us—to go far beyond what is possible without language. "Language creates a domain which has no counterpart in the animal world—an elaborate set of rules and norms, rights and duties without which it is impossible to visualise, let alone describe, the realities of human existence. It is only inside this framework that concepts such as shame, pride, honour, embarrassment and humiliation have any meaning" (Miller 1983, p. 156). Symbols have the power to conceal as well as reveal. When we call a certain person "uncle," this symbol illuminates certain aspects of his identity but at the price of ignoring other aspects. Your uncle is many things in addition to being your uncle—taxpayer, Vietnam veteran, forward on his over-40 basketball team—and calling him "uncle" directs your attention away from these things and toward your relationship with him.

Language and human beings have grown up together. Philosopher Ludwig Wittgenstein demonstrated that words do not have *meanings,* they have *uses.* We use them to signal others, to express our moods or emotions, to refer to events and objects, and to write textbooks. These uses change from one context to another and over time. Linguist Richard Lederer (1989, pp. 177, 187–188) captured this relationship between conversations and language with this observation.

> *Has it ever struck you how human words are? Like people, words are born, grow up, get married, have children, and even die . . . The family resemblances between words and people should come as no surprise. After all, language is not something that cave people discovered in the woods or turned up under a rock. Language is a human invention, and humanness is the invention of language. The birth of language is the dawn of humanity, and each is as old as the other. It is people who make up words and it is people who decide what words shall mean . . . From a creature who is a little lower than the angels and a little above the apes, who embraces tiger and lamb, Apollo and Dionysus, the Oedipus Cycle and the Three Stooges, we can expect nothing less or more than a language in which people drive in a parkway and park in a driveway and play at a recital*

and recite at a play, a language in which a slim chance and a fat chance are the same but a wise man and a wise guy are opposites. From such a changeful and inconstant being we can expect nothing more or less than an outpouring of words that are brightly rational, wonderfully serviceable, maddeningly random, frenetically creative, and, of course, completely crazy.

Communication theorists sometimes differentiate language from nonverbal cues. That is, words are separated from voice quality and tone, facial expressions, posture, and bodily movements. However, in interpersonal communication, these are artificial distinctions. Conversations are oral, and in oral speech, there can be no words without all of these nonverbal cues. For us, language is not separate from its embodiment in a speaker.

The invention of the phonetic alphabet led to the differentiation of language and nonverbal communication. This one-time event in human history allows us to freeze words on a page, thus stripping them of voice, face, body, interpersonal relationship, and situational context in which they occurred. Like butterflies in a museum, words in print are killed, impaled, and held up for display in an artificial setting (Ong 1982). Because we are interested in conversation, I will not treat verbal and nonverbal cues as separate; but because I am writing about interpersonal communication in a printed book, I will often give you a transcript of a conversation. Please understand that you should reincarnate these transcripts as you read them, investing them with sound and movement. All of this is part of language.

Social Worlds Are in a Continuous Process of Being Remade

Clarifying the nondualistic assumptions of the social constructionist understanding of interpersonal communication is important because the concepts that are presented here simply do not make sense if they are stuffed into the categories of Cartesian dualism. Conversations are neither objective (in Descartes' sense) nor subjective; they are a form of action and they are, in themselves, the real substance of our social worlds. Participating in conversations by speaking, listening, laughing, grimacing, frowning, answering, not answering, embracing, and shrugging calls into being something that never existed before that will always be a part of your social worlds from this time on.

Physicists are undecided about the nature of the physical world. Some believe that the universe began in the "Big Bang," and everything that now exists was created at that moment. Others believe in "continuous creation," that there is an ongoing interaction between matter and antimatter such that new material is being created in the universe all the time.

There is no such ambiguity about the social world. Clearly, the social world is in a process of continual creation. The actions that you perform in this moment add to the sum total of human experience; the future of the human race is not fixed, it is still being developed through our actions.

I get very excited about this. When we communicate, we are not just talking *about* the world, we are literally participating in the creation of the social universe. What will be will grow out of what was, but it will take on the form of the actions that you and I perform in this particular moment.

If I tell you that it is snowing heavily and that you should not come to my office today, part of what I have done is to refer to a meteorological condition. However, this is just a component of performing a particular act. Depending on the rest of our conversation, that act might be understood as warning, advising, giving permission (for you to turn in your paper a day late), or explaining (my absence from my office).

Social Worlds Are Made with Other People in Joint Actions

Conversation cannot be done by one person alone. You can *simulate* a conversation by talking to yourself but only by shifting from one role to another. To be involved in a fight, a love affair, or an intellectual discussion, you have to find someone with whom you can coordinate the appropriate actions. You co–construct the conversation when each of you cooperate in shaping a logic of meaning and action that calls into being something like your working definition of the situation.

Communication theorist John Shotter (1994, p. 9) coined the term *joint-action* to describe "the contingent flow of continuous communicative interaction between human beings." Joint-action is a category of events "lying in a zone of uncertainty somewhere between . . . human *actions* (what 'I' as an individual agent do, explained by me giving my reasons), [and] . . . natural *events* (what merely 'happens' to, in, or around me, outside of my agency as an individual to control, explained by their causes)" (Shotter, 1994, p. 3). That is, joint-actions are those that *we* do that are produced by the intermeshing of your acts *and* mine.

To understand the nature of joint actions, consider the first person plural pronoun we. The grammar of Indo-European languages makes it easy for us to think of "we" as an *aggregate* of autonomous individuals, such that the phrase "we construct our social worlds" is heard as "we" (each one of us, acting autonomously, each like the other) "construct" (invent) "our social worlds." However, Shotter is right in saying that conversation is a form of joint action, which means that we must strain our language a bit and hear the statement this way: "we" (acting collectively) "construct" (our actions intermesh in such as way to produce) "our social worlds." That is, we need to think of the first person pronoun as a *collective* term.

Counterpoint 2.8

If Bill and Mary have a fight, the fight itself is often treated as if one or both of them intended it. However, the events and objects of our social worlds—fights as well as helping episodes—are often the aggregate of actions that were not intended to produce them; in fact, sometimes joint-actions produce things quite the opposite of what we intended.

The difference between each act taken singly and their aggregate was captured in an old Roman saying that translates something like "Every Senator is a prince, but the Senate is a beast." Closer to home, as people select their seats in an auditorium, they want to sit close to other people but not too close, and they do not want to sit in the first row that has people in it. As a result, the front of the auditorium is empty and the back over-crowded. No one set out to produce this pattern, it is simply the result of the aggregate of a particular style of individual choices. Several new areas of study have opened up that look at the properties of aggregates produced by iterations (repeated instances) of individual behaviors (Schelling 1978; Gleick 1987).

Shotter (in press) suggests that we (individually) act *into* situations that are unfinished and underdetermined by our individual actions. Their meanings are determined by the way they intermesh with others. As a result, we should not necessarily assume that the *result* of our actions will be consistent with our intentions, and we should not assume that those who participate in the creation of a particular event or object intended to do so.

Thus understood, joint-action is at the same time the product of what we do but not solely the product of what any one of us does; it is better understood as the combination or intermeshed product of the collective "we" who act. This means that we affect but do not individually control the conversations in which we participate. Shotter (1994, p. 3) says that the key characteristic of joint action is "its very lack of specificity, its lack of any pre-determined final form, and thus its openness to being specified as determined by those involved in it."

Monologue and Dialogue

Communication theorists have long recognized that there are qualitative differences in conversations. One way of distinguishing them is to contrast *monologic* and *dialogic* conversations. In *monologue*, one conversant treats the others as if they were third-person objects to be manipulated; in *dialogue*, one conversant treats the others as if they were second-person subjects to be in relation with.

Depending on what person-perspective you take and on how you treat other persons, very different moral orders are invoked. Acting as a first person, you are a performer or an agent who does and makes things. If you act as a first person and treat someone else as a second person, you are one who understands, and you are the recipient of the actions of another first person. However, if you act as first person and treat someone else as a third person, you are the judge, critic, or "object" of that other person's actions.

Second persons are personified; that is, they are expected and allowed to engage in the distinguishing acts of persons, such as having purposes, acting as agents of their own motives, and owning their own feelings and meanings. The difference between second and first person occurs in a courtroom, in which defendants (treated as third persons) are told at the end of a trial whether they are innocent or guilty, regardless of what they claimed (when treated as second persons) at the beginning of the trial.

Elaine had worked for Harry until an incident occurred at an office party. From Elaine's perspective, Harry had sexually harassed her; Harry did not agree. A few days later, Elaine quit her job. A few days after that, the two accidentally met on the street. "Hi!" Elaine said, "I'm glad to sue you— I mean, see you!"

How should Harry reply, and what should he think about this slip-of-the-lip? If he treats Elaine as a second person, he will allow her to specify what she means and read nothing else into what she says. Shotter (1984, p. 16) explains

> *As second-persons in everyday life, we do not have the right to step out of our "personal involvement" with other people, and attend to*

Refrain 2.2

In *monologue,* you treat other people as if they were "third persons" or "objects." You take the role of observer, critic, "cause" of certain effects," an "agent" who acts intentionally. In monologue, it is easy to treat other people as if they had no value except to the extent that they serve your purposes.

In *dialogue,* you treat other people as if they were "second persons" or "moral entities." You take the role of one who understands, acts with, is a participant in the experience of the other. In dialogue, it is easy to treat other people as if their intentions are as valid as your own, and to seek ways of braiding together your fortune and theirs. You feel a strong interdependence with others such that their feelings and meanings are part of your own experience.

> *aspects of their person to which they do not intend us to attend—*
> *and to ask them to account for matters for which they do not deem*
> *themselves responsible. In the ecology of daily social life, there seems*
> *to be a moral sanction against such a shifting of roles; unless, that*
> *is, one is a physician or psychotherapist, hairdresser or dentist, or*
> *suchlike, and then people do intend you to examine the unintended*
> *aspects of their behaviour and appearance.*

On the other hand, if Harry treated Elaine as a third person, he would likely interpret her misstatement as a "slip" that indicates that she intends to press charges against him based on the incident at the office party. In his thoughts and in his report of this meeting to his lawyer, he will probably use the third-person pronoun (and maybe some vivid descriptive adjectives) when referring to Elaine and offer explanations about her actions that differ from the ones she herself gave. Again Shotter (1984, p. 14) explains,

> *. . . third persons need not be personified (they can be "its"); nor*
> *are they "present" in themselves, so to speak, to other beings or entities;*
> *nor are they necessarily "in a situation." Indeed, the category is so*
> *non-specific that it may be used to refer to absolutely anything so*
> *long as it is external to, or outside of, the agency or situation of first*
> *as well as second persons.*

Counterpoint 2.9

The distinction between monologue and dialogue marks incommensurate ways of communicating. Not only do monologists read the definitions of interpersonal communication offered in Chapter 1 differently from the way dialogists do, but they coordinate their actions with those of other people in a very different way. In my judgment, monologists are usually genuinely oblivious to aspects that are of primary concern to dialogists and hence do not understand what dialogue is all about. On the other hand, dialogists sense what is missing in the monologists perspective but often have a hard time expressing it. For this reason, I review two of the most articulate descriptions of the differences between the two forms of communication.

Martin Buber (1967, p. 113) distinguished "genuine dialogue" from two counterfeits. In genuine dialogue, "each of the participants really has in mind the other or others in their present and particular being and turns to them with the intention of establishing a living mutual relation between himself and them." *Technical dialogue* makes "objective understanding" the sole goal, not the establishing of a continuing relationship. *Monologue disguised as dialogue* is a "strangely tortuous and circuitous way" in which people imagine that they have "escaped the torment of being thrown back on their own resources" by giving the appearance of establishing an I-Thou relationship when it is in reality an I-It.

Anatol Rapoport (1967, pp. 90–91) made a similar distinction between people who approach others strategically (i.e., in monologue) and those who approach others based on conscience (i.e., in dialogue).

> *The basic question in the strategist's mind is this: "In a conflict how can I gain an advantage over him?" The critic cannot disregard the question, "If I gain an advantage over him, what sort of person will I become?" For example, he might ask what kind of a nation the United States might become if we succeeded in crushing all revolutions as easily as in Guatemala. With regard to deterrence, the critic might ask not, "What if deterrence fails?" (everyone worries about that) but, on the contrary, "What if deterrence works?"*

Rapoport's example is all the more powerful because it was offered during the Cold War. Subsequent events have shown that the United States was unprepared for the "victory" for which it fought so hard. According to Rapoport, there are three distinctions between the forms of thinking characteristic of monologue and dialogue.

First, "strategists" conceive action in terms of its effects on objects or other people, whereas dialogists think of action in terms of its reflexive effects on themselves as well as on others. Second, monologue presumes that values are already established; for dialogists, determining values is a principal preoccupation. Third, in monologue, conversants assume that objective facts are there to be ascertained, whereas dialogists take into consideration their perspectives and the forms of action that they take to determine what the facts might be.

Think of a conversation from the first-person perspective. You are acting in ways that respond to and evoke actions from another person. There are *qualitative* differences in the kinds of conversations you produce, depending on whether you treat the other person as a second or third person. These differences start with who *you* are. Martin Buber (1988) captured this difference in his famous aphorism, "The 'I' of 'I-thou' is not the same 'I' as the 'I' of 'I-it.'" Specifically, in monologue, you treat the other as an "it" and you treat yourself as if you were an autonomous individual acting in ways that affect the other. On the other hand, in dialogue, you treat the other as "you" and you treat yourself as if you were part of a relationship, engaged in joint action with another "I" whose motives and meanings are a part of the conversation in which you live.

Coordinating Actions

The distinction between monologue and dialogue gives distinctively different readings to the definitions of interpersonal communication offered in Chapter 1.

From a monologic first-person perspective, the issue is how "I" (as an autonomous individual) can coordinate my actions with those of the other person whose cooperation is necessary for me to achieve my goals. That is, how can I work through this joint action to accomplish my purposes? This gives rise to questions about how I can achieve my goals, secure the other person's compliance, and perhaps induce the other person to act in ways that I can use against him or her.

From a dialogic first-person perspective, the issue is how "we" can coordinate our actions so that we can realize our goals. The most important difference in the dialogic perspective is that "I" see myself *within* the conversation rather than outside it, using it for purposes of my own. With this comes an identification with the other persons in the conversation such that their well-being and purposes and meanings are a part of the whole to which I attend. This perspective gives rise to questions about what kind of person I will become if we produce this or that form of conversation. What goals are constructed in the conversation, and how do they relate to the form of the conversation? What resources are available to us to improve our coordination?

Game-like Patterns of Social Interaction

The definition of interpersonal communication from the third-person perspective also differs depending on whether one takes a monologic or dialogic stance.

If I treat the other as a third person, then the "game-like pattern of social interaction" is a means of doing something *to* the other person. It is this sense of "game-playing" that has acquired a negative connotation. For example, Donna acts hurt every time Ronald works late: she is playing a game in which he is forced to take the role of penitent, begging her forgiveness, and she gets to play the role that she wanted, of judging his behavior. Psychologist Eric Berne (1964) compiled a book full of examples of these games people play in order to take advantage of others.

On the other hand, if I treat the other as a second person, then the "game-like pattern of social interaction" is a means of doing something *with* the other person. (Berne, 1976). In this sense, "game-like" means only that there are complex clusters of reciprocal expectations in which each action does not stand alone but is a "move" that initiates a logic of meaning and action. For example, when Ronald comes home after working late, he notices that a single candle is lit on the dining table. Because he and Donna have worked out a game-like pattern of social interaction, he knows that the candle is a "move" rather than just a single act. That is, it does not indicate that the electricity has been shut off or make the statement "candles are pretty"; rather, it invites him to respond with the next act in a sequence that comprise the episode "romantic evening home alone."

The ability to participate *with* others (treating them as second persons) enriches human life by an incredible amount. The existence of such game-like patterns makes complicated patterns of coordination possible that could not be achieved without them. Think of the difference between the artistry demonstrated by a pair of ice skaters who have practiced game-like patterns for years in contrast to what two skaters of equal ability would be able to do spontaneously the first time they ever skated with each other. In addition, the existence of such game-like patterns makes wit and eloquence possible. The eloquence of the single candle burning when Ronald arrives home is far greater than Donna's explicit statement that she would like a romantic evening home alone.

It is not too far-fetched to say that participation in such game-like patterns of social interaction *as second persons* is the way that we become human beings. Philosopher/psychologist Rom Harré noted that "When mothers talk to babies they continually embed their babies in a conversation in which the baby is treated as if it had a full complement of moral and intellectual qualities." (in Miller 1983, p. 168) In baby talk, the infant is treated as if he or she possessed the characteristics of moral agents that he or she will need but does not now have. "It really is a vastly complex psychology and moral sensibility that they are ascribing to their infants. They do not talk *about* their infants' intentions; they provide them with them, and then they react to the infant as if it had them." (in Miller 1983, p. 168).

Of course, adults do the same thing with their pets, and children with their dolls, toys, and imaginary friends. The difference is that the animals with which we live and the inanimate objects with which we play do not have the human infant's capacity to appropriate the moral world in which they are enmeshed; they do not have the human infant's ability to discern spaces in ongoing game-like patterns of social interaction in which they can insert themselves as a first–person participant. This process of becoming a participant in the game is what differentiates a human child from, for example, a gorilla or chimpanzee raised identically in a human home. The human child begins to use the language surrounding it, sometimes making up sentences, grammar, and vocabulary that it has not heard; it begins to act out of a position of moral responsibility; it is started on a path in which it will eventually pick out certain features in the social environment as "me" and reproduce those features as "who I am." This is so momentous a process that we treat the child as if it were no longer an object but a subject, no longer an "it" but a person: a "he" or "she" with the rights, responsibilities, and obligations of an interlocutor, a full participant in our social worlds.

Competence in Interpersonal Communication

The dialogic perspective on the simile that conversations are "game-like" provides us with a way of talking about competence that does not reduce it to a static list of things that you know or can do. Competence is found in the relationship between what each communicator can do and the game-like

Counterpoint 2.10

The topic of communication competence is of great interest; it is equally relevant to a little boy caught with his hand in the forbidden cookie jar and to the candidates for elected office in democratic nations. Not surprisingly, it has been the subject of serious inquiry for thousands of years. Spitzberg and Cupach (1984) offer a comprehensive survey of issues, ideas, and research about competence in interpersonal communication.

Many concepts of interpersonal communication competence focus on an individual's ability to align his or her own interests with the demands of the situation in such a way as to maintain the cooperation of the other people involved. For example, John Weimann (1977, p. 198) defined "the competent communicator [as] the person who can have his way in the relationship while maintaining a mutually acceptable definition of that relationship." In his introduction to the Spitzberg and Cupach (1984, p. 7) book, series editor Mark Knapp praised their emphasis on "communicator interdependence."

> *This issue strikes at the very heart of* where competence resides. *Virtually all prior accounts of communicative competence have conceived of competence as something exhibited or possessed by a single individual. To say that competent interaction is rooted in the configuration of behavior manifested by both interactants is a radical departure from previous ways of thinking about this issue—although it seems more in line with current communication theory. By taking into account the responses of one's interaction partner, our whole previous understanding of what is competent, normal, and problematic seems subject to revision.*

My discussion of competence in this chapter is far from comprehensive. In one sense, using Spitzberg and Cupach's terms, the concept offered here is a radical contextualist one because the acts that are considered "competent" derive from the characteristics of the situation. In another sense, however, it focuses on the individual, making the distinction between game playing and game mastery. The combination is a relational model, in which competence is determined by the "fit" between the situation and the mode of acting by the communicator.

pattern of social interaction in which he or she acts. Let us focus on two characteristics: one of the game, the other of the communicator.

Types of Game-like Patterns of Social Interaction

For these purposes, the game-like patterns of conversation may be described along a continuum from *stable and clear* to *ambiguous and unstable*. Stable and clear conversations are fully scripted. When you enter an elegant restaurant, you are seldom surprised by the sequence of events. First, you will be asked the size of your party, about your seating preferences ("Smoking or nonsmoking?"), then you will be offered a place at the bar to wait until your table is ready and encouraged to purchase a greatly overpriced beverage ("May I get you started with something to drink?"). When finally seated, you will be offered another expensive beverage, followed by a confrontation with the specials of the day. Your order will be taken, you will be asked if you want anything more, perhaps enticed with a tray of tempting desserts, and presented a bill that you are expected to pay in addition to leaving a sizable tip.

Of course, this is a carefully scripted sequence of action. The staff of the restaurant have been trained (in a process in which customers are treated as anonymous third persons) just how to proceed. Very skillful waitpersons can perform this script as if it were spontaneous and make it seem as if they were treating specific customers as second-persons. They are the ones who get large tips.

Most of the social situations you confront during a normal day are sufficiently stable and clear that you need not think very much about them; in theater terms, you are part of a cast of a long-running play, doing daily performances with matinees on Wednesdays and Saturdays.

Other conversations are ambiguous and unstable. These are less frequent in your social worlds, they tend to be traumatic, and they capture your attention in dramatic fashion. For some of these situations, you do not know the rules; if there is a "script," you do not know it. Others are situations in which there are many rules, but they contradict; you know two or more scripts for how to proceed but cannot follow them all.

"The first time" for any important activity is usually somewhat ambiguous and unstable. Watzlawick et al. (1967) told a sorrowful story of a couple whose marital problems started on their honeymoon, simply because they had different scripts for how to be a married couple. He expected them to spend all of their time together, shutting the rest of the world out. Specifically, he expected to be the sole object of her attention. She was excited about being married and wanted to show off her husband and their new relationship to everybody they met, so she invited other people to their table at dinner and spent time talking with other couples. He perceived her as . . . well, you can fill in the rest, but this is an example of an ambiguous and unstable game-like pattern of social interaction.

Every time there is a change in a relationship, there is some degree of ambiguity—which is the source of revitalization and excitement as well as uncertainty and problems. For example, during some transitional stage, dating couples change from separate people who are dating to a "couple"; at another point, from being a couple to being married; at another point, to being parents of an infant; at another point, to being parents of a teenager; at another, to being parents of grown children who are parents themselves; and, often, one member of this couple will survive the other and have to adjust

Figure 2.1
Competence in interpersonal communication.

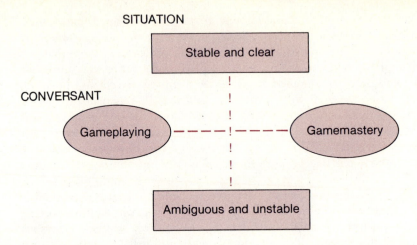

SITUATION

CONVERSANT

Stable and clear

Gameplaying

Gamemastery

Ambiguous and unstable

to being a widow or widower. Each of these transitions introduces a great deal of ambiguity and uncertainty.

Game Playing and Game Mastery

Competence in interpersonal communication is clearly different in stable and clear situations than it is in ambiguous and unstable ones (Figure 2.1). Again staying with the games metaphor, there is a distinction between game playing and game mastery.

The basic move in game playing is to follow the rules, to perform as expected, and perhaps to move within the rules in unusually effective ways. For example, a person who dresses in a conservative business suit while interviewing for a job at IBM is playing the game; a salesman who uses the "pitch" taught to him in the company training program is game playing. If you do not know the rules, or if you are somehow incapable of performing them adequately, you have not performed competently. The best form of game playing consists of following the rules and doing so with just a bit of style, wit, or cleverness.

As a form of communication competence, game playing is relatively easy to develop. All of us have great skill in discerning the rules of the games in which we are caught up. There are many self-help books that will give you some additional information on how to play the games of your social worlds. They deal with everything from how to fight productively with your spouse to how to find a spouse, from how to lose weight (yes, that is a conversational as well as nutritional process) to how to cope with the loss of a job, a leg, or a loved one.

Game mastery refers to ways of moving within or among games for purposes not comprehended by the games themselves. Game mastery may take several forms. For example, you might participate in a game while locating it in a larger context. However, sometimes you may not want to play the game even if you know how. Game mastery in stable and clear situations may consist of breaking the rules on purpose and deliberately forfeiting one objective within the game to achieve another outside the game. I have the image of two people seated at a table on which are the objects for many games: cards, dice, several types of boards, chess figures, dominoes, and checkers. One person picks up the deck of cards and deals five cards to each player; the second ignores the cards and moves kings' pawn to K-4. This is an act of game mastery. In conversation, one person may attempt to initiate a sequence of events that will culminate in the other's spending money for a product; the other person may deliberately choose not to play that game by selecting another—for example, by analyzing the strategy of the first.

In ambiguous and unstable situations, game playing is a losing strategy. There are many poignant instances of people trying their favorite or most familiar patterns of social interaction in situations in which the rules have changed or in which there is simply too much ambiguity. For example, tourists in exotic cultures often find themselves—after the novelty wears off—reproducing the familiar patterns of their native culture and getting irritated when the "locals" do not cooperate sufficiently. (When this happens, it is time to go home!)

Game mastery in ambiguous and unstable situations consists of creating order where there is none, of calling into being forms of social coordination under the most difficult circumstances. This is often accomplished by giving a description of the situation: that is, one conversant will say admit that there is no single way to act. Sometimes the person uses the ritualistic formula, "I just don't know what to say . . ." or "I just can't tell you . . ." and sometimes it consists of full-blown analyses of the lack of, or conflict between, various scripts.

Another form of game mastery in ambiguous and unstable situations is to perform a creative act that generates clarity and stability. Rather than be caught between the demands of adolescence and adulthood, at some point most of us will take decisive actions to clarify that we are no longer children (that is, as St. Paul said, "to put aside childish things") and in that moment of clarifying action, initiate a new set of conversations with those around us.

By its very nature, game mastery cannot be codified into a skill to be learned as you would the multiplication table. Rather, it consists of an ability to perform in unique ways that are responsive to the demands of specific situations. One major purpose of this book is to increase your ability to act competently as game masters in both clear and stable and ambiguous and unstable situations.

Adult conversations are structured on a vast set of performance skills and moral obligations. To perform in this complex, game-like pattern of social interaction requires years of practice, and even then, mistakes will occur. Subtle nuances of timing, expression, or prosody—to say nothing of speech itself—can make the difference between making a friend or an enemy, getting a job or losing one, or finding out what one wants to know or being misled.

These first two chapters have introduced many themes that will be discussed in greater length later in the book. They function as an "overture"; Chapters 3 through 7 develop particular "motifs" at greater length.

The organization of Chapters 3 through 7 is shown in the general atomic model of communication (Figure 1.5). Each chapter focuses on one of the aspects of our social worlds that simultaneously envelop each act that we perform.

Praxis

1. Creating Events and Objects in Your Social Worlds

To demonstrate how the events and objects of the social world are made, let's examine one particular object: contemporary standards of feminine attractiveness, specifically the criterion of "thinness." If you look at the women who are selected as models for clothing or just to adorn advertisements for all sorts of things, you notice that they are much thinner than the norm.

A first step in showing that this standard is *made,* not a fact of nature, consists of making comparisons. That is, we can illumine the social processes of making the events and objects of our social worlds by showing that the *products* of these processes are different in various times and places. Specifically, thinness has not always or everywhere been associated with attractiveness. Take a look at the nudes painted by Renaissance artists and you will see figures that would today be used as the "Before!" part of an advertisement for a health club or diet food. However, these physiques were the standard of beauty in their own society.

A second step consists of looking at who is involved in the conversations in which this particular aspect of our social worlds is made. For example, we might ask who stands to profit most from the contemporary concept of feminine beauty? The proprietors of exercise clubs, the makers of diet products, the purveyors of motivational or exercise videotapes, and fashion designers, among others, come to mind.

Third, identify the particular conversations in which this event or object is made. How are you informed of this standard of feminine beauty? In what conversations is the physical attractiveness of women important? Who initiates these conversations? Women might ask: To whom do you show the weight that you have lost or gained? Who is the first to notice a change in your figure? Which of your relationships would be most affected if you suddenly gained or lost inches from your waist? Men might ask: How do you know which women your friends think are attractive? How do you tell a woman that you find her attractive?

You should answer these questions for yourself, but I suspect that the answers are straightforward. Women talk a lot with each other about their weight and figures; I have overheard many conversations about such topics as diets and exercise programs. In addition, there are organized groups deliberately attempting to induct women into conversations in which "thinness" is equated with beauty. These groups include fashion magazines, advertisements in every medium from television to magazines, and the selection of models and actresses featured as the examples of femininity. Might there be a more sinister political and economic movement to equate thinness with health in the medical and pharmacological professions?

Anorexia nervosa and bulimia are two major medical problems confronting primarily young women in Western societies. Which came first, the societal norm that thinness equals attractiveness or the behaviors that we call anorexia nervosa and bulimia? I do not want to suggest simple causal relationships, but do you think that there is some more complex relationship between the quest for thinness and these eating disorders?

In this example, I am first asking you to see standards of feminine beauty as socially constructed rather than fixed. That seems easy enough. We could even invent some new objects of lusty fascination. Let's try it.

As far as I know, the line from earlobe to neck vertebrae has never been featured as the most alluring body part—we have not even given that line a name as we have "lap," "forearm," and "ankle." But we could name it. Because this is a line perpendicular to the nape of the neck, I suggest we call it the apne—an anagram of "nape." Now that it is named, it can enter into our conversations.

- "You are so beautiful! Your eyes . . . your lips . . . your apne!"
- "Doctor, I want to have cosmetic surgery. My self esteem is low because I have such an ugly apne. Do you have some photographs so that I can choose a more attractive shape?"
- "Do a few more military presses, buddy. That'll build up your apne."

Now we can develop a keen sense of aesthetic appreciation for apnes, making them the subject of romantic poetry and songs, a site for reconstructive surgery and cosmetics, and a special feature challenging the skills of those who design clothing. Perhaps a pornographic industry would develop showing photographs of particularly attractive apnes. All of this activity would socially construct a new object and locate it within our logics of meaning and action. Those who did not cover (or uncover) their apne would be considered vulgar or rude.

In class. Form groups of four or five. Create an event or object in your social worlds following a process similar to that in which apnes were created.

Make the event or object real by making comparisons with other events and objects, by identifying who else is involved, and by locating particular conversations in which this event or object exists. Compare your creation to those of other groups.

2. A Description of Your Social Worlds

For several days, keep a running record of all the conversations in which you participate. Use an appointment book or something that will allow you to note what you are doing at specific times of the day.

In your description, note the duration of the conversation, the participants, and the topic. Think of verbs, not nouns. For example, you may write "having lunch with Bill" or "doing physics homework with Elise."

For your own use, put a few descriptive words about each conversation. Think of adverbs and adjectives: "dull," "useful," "painful," or "vacuous."

After completing these diaries, get a pack of index cards and transfer what you have written about each conversation to the cards, one card per conversation. Include a descriptive label that answers the question What were you doing with whom?, the time, and the date of each conversation.

If you compare these conversations, you will find that some of them seem more similar than others. Put those that are pretty much alike in a stack and make a series of stacks—at least two, perhaps as many as five or six—in which the conversations in each stack resemble each other in ways that those in different stacks do not.

The number of stacks give you a rough description of the complexity of your social worlds. How many stacks do you have? Do these translate into the different worlds in which you participate in a normal day?

The size of each stack gives you a rough description of the array of conversations in each of your social worlds. Without pushing this too far, these conversations are substitutable for each other—at least, you have perceived them as similar in some sort of way. If you were prevented from participating in one of these conversations—for instance, your interlocutor moved away—one of the other conversations in this stack would allow your social world to remain pretty much intact. However, if something happened that eliminated *all* of the conversations in one of the stacks, this would be much more traumatic; you would have to restructure your social world in some important way.

Now compare the stacks. What is the characteristic that all of the conversations in one stack possess that differentiate them from those in the other stacks? This is a way of answering for yourself how you structure your social worlds. Perhaps the difference is by persons; one stack includes all the conversations with a specific person and the other stacks, with other persons. Perhaps you differentiate on the basis of purpose: some stacks have to do with your job, some with your schooling, some with your family, and some with your

your best friend. Perhaps you have several different criteria on which you base these distinctions.

Finally, look at the adverbs and adjectives you provided as descriptions of each conversation. Do they cluster? That is, do all the positive descriptions fall into a particular stack and all the negative ones in another? If so, what does this tell you about your social worlds? Or do you have more complex structures, in that a single stack contains both the most positively and most negatively described conversations? If so, what does this tell you about your social worlds?

The information you have gained is your own, and you should indeed feel that you own it. However, it would be interesting to compare with your classmates the number of stacks, the number of conversations in each stack, and the criteria for differentiating among them.

3. Applying the Heyerdahl Solution to Interesting Conversations

Look at the stacks of index cards you made. If you treat them as a rough map of your social worlds, there are probably some conversations that are particularly interesting. Perhaps there is one that stands out from the others in its stack—it is the only positively described conversation in a stack of negatively described conversations, or it is the one in which you feel most constrained in a stack where you generally feel quite free and spontaneous.

Select one or two conversations that interest you and apply the Heyerdahl solution. That is, observe it in the process of being made. One way of doing this is to write a script that records the conversation; use all the conventions of script writing that the authors of plays have developed. Describe the setting and the characters; write the dialogue, with stage directions for how the actors—that is, you and your interlocutors—moved, spoke, and expressed emotion. Keep developing the characters—what was she thinking when she said what she did? How did you feel when you replied? Continue until you feel that you have written everything that an actor playing the part would need to know to experience this conversation in the same way that you did. You might find the *serpentine model* from Chapter 1 a useful way of structuring your dialogue.

Now shift your perspective from *author* to *critic*. Do you find this believable? Are the characters well developed? Are they equally developed? Would it make an effective play? Who should be praised or blamed? How do each of the characters participate in the co-construction of what happened?

What surprised you as you were writing the script? Did you have to change your mind about the meaning of what was said and done? Write some new dialogue—this time not trying to reproduce what was really said but taking this opportunity to have all conversants say what you would have liked them to have said.

What surprised you as you were critiquing the script? Are your evaluations more or less certain than they were before? Do you praise or blame one person more than the others?

4. Polyphony and How to Resist Linguistic Tyranny

Every communication event is polyphonous; even when you talk to yourself, there are multiple voices that support or contradict each other. But what is the relationship among these voices?

Bakhtin (1986, pp. 88–89) introduced two useful terms. *Canonization* is the development of a standard form of speech that serves as the norm against which every other voice is heard. For example, in Medieval Europe, Christianity was the norm for expressing religious experience; any other form of expression was defined as deviant. Even if they were tolerated, Muslims and Jews knew that when they used the words of their religious heritage, they set themselves apart by doing so. In the contemporary United States, the whole "political correctness" controversy is about what, and to what extent, certain forms of communication will be canonized.

The opposite of canonization is *reaccentuation,* the process by which our voices can use words that have been used by many others to express just our meanings. For example, Bakhtin noted how authoritative utterances can be undermined by repeating them word-for-word in a mocking, ironic tone of voice. Bakhtin urged us to understand the genres of speech in our society to achieve freedom of speech; that is, by assimilating, reworking, and reaccentuating them, we can express our own individuality.

These terms describe our social worlds as a dynamic place in which we must deal with the tensions between pressures to conform to the standards (canonization) and the need to speak our own individual voices (reaccentuation). I propose the term *linguistic tyranny* for a category of communication situations in which the polyphony of our social worlds is suppressed. That is, by whatever means, you are required to speak in the canonical form; any attempt to speak freely in your own (reaccentuated) voice will be punished if detected.

Whether benevolent, benign, or despotic, linguistic tyranny consists of a local suppression of polyphony and polysemy. It treats what you say as if it had only one set of possible contexts and thus meanings, and as if you were participating in only one conversation. Although this standard is sometimes a useful fiction, allowing us to coordinate lines of action within reasonably stable definitions of the situation, it remains a fiction. If you are to achieve the freedom of speech we prize so highly, you need to be alert to the efforts of others to restrict you to a particular sublanguage or to limit your social world to a particular set of objects and relations.

The linguistic tyranny that I have in mind occurs when someone insists that their language is the only language and requires you to answer in it. This happens in legal proceedings: the judge will require you and your attorney to speak in a strange language with very specific meanings. There are precise differences between an adult and a minor, between a misdemeanor and a felony, between civil and criminal courts, and between manslaughter and murder—and these differences are very important to the defendant.

Linguistic tyranny also occurs in academic settings. "Without using any big words," I was once charged, "tell me the result of your study." "I can't," I replied honestly. On another occasion, one of my colleagues demanded that I explain my theory of communication (that features stories and interpretations) in his language (which is limited to descriptions of physical movements). Again, "I can't," I replied honestly. Neither person believed me, and both were displeased.

Linguistic tyranny occurs when you are forced to put your experience into a language in which it does not fit. Perhaps you need to make a distinction that the language does not allow or suggest an additional explanation:

> Did you screw up on purpose, or is it just your ignorance that enabled you to make such a mess? Don't try to squirm out of it! Which was it?

One way to escape linguistic tyranny is to remember that no answer might be better than a wrong answer to some questions. My response "I can't" was honest, but it was also not very eloquent. Here's one way of doing better. If someone tries to make you the victim of linguistic tyranny, reply with a question:

In what language would you like for me to respond?

For example, if asked the question about "screwing up" you might say,

> In what language would you like for me to respond? Shall I limit myself to the simplistic moral dichotomy between purposive and ignorant action? Or may I use a more realistic set of explanations of what occurred?

In class. Working in groups of two, practice escaping from linguistic tyranny. Take turns interviewing each other, but instead of answering the questions, 1) identify the assumptions presumed in the question, 2) identify the language-game in which that presumption occurs, and 3) respond in a way that calls into question that language-game. For example:

> *Tom:* Why did you choose to take a course in interpersonal communication?

The *assumption* is that Mary "chose" to take the course. Perhaps it was a requirement for her major; perhaps she found herself in the course by accident having made a mistake in registration or wandering into the wrong room; perhaps it was the only course that she could take because of her work schedule. Let her say:

Mary: You assume that I chose to take the course.

In what language-game does this assumption fit comfortably? It presumes that Mary is a free moral agent, that she has the ability to choose among various courses, and that she knew something about this course so that she could choose. Is this necessarily correct? No, perhaps Mary is a full-time employee at a research center on campus and has only this time period open; perhaps she is on scholarship, the terms of which require this course; etc. But how should she respond?

The question prefigures an answer using the vocabulary of individual motivation: "I wanted . . ." or "I chose . . ." or "it will help me to . . ." or even "Bob told me that it would be a good course for me." What other vocabularies are available? One has to do with causes—"because it was required," or "because I had no choice."

Let's assume that Mary wants to escape the linguistic tyranny imposed by the assumption presumed in the question. She might say:

Mary: Just lucky, I guess.

This is a surprising answer that rejects the vocabulary of individual intention and perhaps opens the conversation up to new vocabularies of accounts for how she came to be in the class. Or she might say,

Mary: It is my fate. I must have done something terribly wrong in my previous life.

If this does not end the conversation, it will open it up to all sorts of interesting possibilities.

Another form of linguistic tyranny is the claim that anything can be said, and that if you cannot say (or write) it, then you are being evasive or are not thinking very well. For example, philosopher John Searle (1969, p. 17) proposed the principle of expressibility, by which he meant that "whatever can be meant can be said. A given language may not have a syntax or a vocabulary rich enough for me to say what I mean in that language but there are no barriers in principle to supplementing the impoverished language or saying what I mean in a richer one." Literary critic George Steiner (1967, p. 12) claimed that Western culture has always believed "that all truth and realness—with the exception of a small, queer margin at the very top—can be housed inside the walls of language."

Are Searle and Steiner practicing linguistic tyranny? There are persistent reports from some of the most articulate speakers and writers that any verbal description they give of experience trivializes it. Someone once lamented that our fate (what "our" was he referring to, I wonder?) was to touch the pure lyrics of experience and, unless by a million-to-one chance we happen to be Shakespeare, to reduce them to the verbal equivalents of tripe and hogwash. A remark by Joseph Campbell (1976, p. 84) has haunted me for years: "The best things cannot be told, the second best are misunderstood. After that comes civilized conversation . . ."

The artist M. C. Escher found ways to do marvelous things with woodcuts, expressing impossible realities, and yet he said, "If only you knew the things I have seen in the darkness of the night . . . at times I have been nearly demented with a wretchedness at being unable to express these things in visual terms. In comparison with these thoughts, every single print is a failure, and reflects not even a fraction of what might have been" (quoted by Falletta 1983, p. 43).

In direct contradiction to Steiner and Searle, Shands (1971, pp. 19–20) urged us to transcend words:

> *The problem is words. Only with words can man become conscious; only with words learned from another can man learn how to talk to himself. Only through getting the better of words does it become possible for some, a little of the time, to transcend the verbal context and to become, for brief instants, free.*

In class. Stage a debate, with some people defending the Searle/Steiner *principle of expressibility* and others the Shands/Campbell/Escher *principle of ineffability.* As you debate, explore what Steiner might have meant about the "small, queer margin at the top" and what Shands might mean by becoming, briefly, "free." Use this debate as a way of testing what *you* think about the issue.

Now simulate a conversation between Searle or Steiner as one conversant and Shands, Campbell, or Escher as the other. Start the conversation with Shands/Campbell/Escher claiming to have had an experience that cannot be expressed verbally; let Searle/Steiner reply next by denying the claim. Then play out the conversations in several ways. After several simulations, decide whether Searle/Steiner are cutting through the murk of obscure expressions or whether they are practicing linguistic tyranny.

5. Identifying the Scripts in Social Settings

The extent to which our social worlds are stable and clear often escapes us; we are not mindful of the repetitiousness of much of what we do. Some people say that we put the same shoe on first every day and go through the same sequences of brushing our teeth and our hair. It is clear that we develop patterns of who to greet and how to greet our friends, classmates, and coworkers. A psychologist once confided his greatest problem listening to his clients: he was tempted to lip-synch what they told him! After awhile, he said, there was a great predictability in the problems that people brought to him. (Hmm . . . I wonder to what extent the predictability was in the stories they *told* him and what stemmed from the way he *heard* them? That is, were his clients boring him, or was he bored?)

As an exercise, pay attention to these "fully scripted" parts of your social worlds. The "sales pitch" used in commercials and by salespersons are usually carefully patterned.

Stable and clear game-like patterns of social interaction are deliberately used by those who want to get their hands into your wallet. Salesmen learn to initiate conversations in which your "place" is as a paying customer; if you interact with a sales person on his or her terms, you will find yourself "forced" to a point where you should sign an agreement or pay for goods and services. Note that the persuasion in these conversations does not necessarily have anything to do with the product you are purchasing; it has much to do with the role you have taken in the conversation initiated by the sales person.

Although there are some "intuitive" salesmen, most are trained to initiate specific forms of conversation. For example, one simple trick is for them to ask you a series of questions to which you will answer affirmatively, "Yes." (Do you want your parents taken care of in their old age? Would you like to have financial independence?) Then they will confront you with another question that relates far more directly to the cash in your wallet: "Then you want to subscribe to our new magazine, *Financial Tips for the Homeless*!" The conversation has steered you to a point where it is logical for you to say, "Yes! Sign me up!"

As a way of increasing your competence in dealing with these situations, see if you can infer the conversational structure that sales persons try to initiate. Observe or participate in a sales interview or watch or read some commercials. However, instead of acting spontaneously, think about what the sales person is trying to *do* by saying what he or she says. How is the customer being maneuvered in the conversation into a position to send money?

Before class. Write the underlying scripts of some of these sales pitches.

In class. Compare the scripts you wrote with those written by other people. What common features stand out? What are some of the unique features?

6. Some Exercises in Conversational Competence

There are many self-help books that advise you how to be competent in monologic games. For example, Stephen Potter's (1970) *The Complete Upmanship* contains advice on how to win games without *actually* cheating. One specific set of advice shows you how to "win" at chess even if you do not know anything about the game. You begin by making a series of very ordinary moves but spending an increasing amount of time between moves, giving the impression that you are laboring hard. After the sixth move, you concede the game, saying "Well done! You have me checkmated on the ninety-third move. Thank you for the game." As you walk away, you suddenly stop and say "Unless, on the seventy-sixth move . . . after sacrificing your Queen, you . . . but, no, you are far too skilled a player to make such a foolish move. Thanks again." As you walk away, you have lost the game of chess but established your reputation as a chess expert. For more active gameplayers, Lardner's (1968) *The Underhanded Serve: Or How to Play Dirty Tennis* will be interesting.

Are these "tricks" best understood as examples of game playing or game mastery? Compare the structure of Potter's examples with the advice in a good book on training dogs, such as Siegal and Margolis (1973). Dogs are prefigured by their genetics to act in particular ways; if you want to train a dog, you must accept these prefigurations as part of the scripts and find ways to insert yourself so that you and your dog can coordinate in the ways that you want. For example, a dog will "heel" if you fit that behavior into its scripts.

Is training a dog best understood as game playing or game mastery? What are the similarities and differences between what Potter's chess player did and what Siegal and Margolis urge you to do?

Now, take the descriptions of stable and clear scripts that you developed in Praxis #5, and think of how you would engage in game playing and game mastery in them. Use the scripts as a way of structuring improvisational skits in which you practice the skills of competence. If these scripts do not work, use the scenarios sketched below:

■ Bill has just been hired as a reporter for a major newspaper. Because he impressed his editor when he interviewed for the position, he was assigned to cover the governor's press conference. When he arrived, he realized that there was a very powerful logic of meaning and action governing who asks what kinds of questions in what sequence at these press conferences, and that he did not know how to fit into it. What should Bill do? How long will it take and by what means can he learn to fit into the logic of gubernatorial press conferences?

■ Elsa is a member of a student government committee. Unfortunately, the committee has developed a very powerful logic of meaning and action that assigns her a role that is not respected. When she makes suggestions, they are dismissed because she is a "foreigner" and a "newcomer" to the committee. She knows the logic of meaning and action all too well but finds that it does not permit her to act in the ways that she cares to. What should Elsa do? Is it possible for her to act in such a way to change the logical force? Should she resign from the committee? Should she try to reform it? Should she give in?

■ Eduardo has a friend whose life is out of control. His friend is abusing drugs, is committing misdemeanors, is in danger of losing his job, and has alienated his family. Eduardo wants to help his friend but is not sure what to do. His friend's life is so confused that there does not seem to be a sufficiently strong logical force such that anything Eduardo does would have a helpful effect. What should Eduardo do? Can he do anything? If he tries, is he likely to make things worse rather than better?

In class. Form groups of three or four people. Simulate conversations that follow some of the scripts that you have identified (or the ones provided here). Practice using game playing and game mastery. Note the range of things that you can do and the kinds of effects they have.

7. Competence in Ambiguous, Unstable Situations

It is easier, I think, to act competently in stable and clear situations than in the opposite. Think of some unstable and ambiguous situations, for example, when you go through a major life transition (wedding, first child, or leaving home), when you have suffered a traumatic experience (bereavement, diagnosed with a major illness, loss of sight or hearing), or when your whole social world falls apart (midlife crisis, successful political revolution, invasion from outer space, ecological crisis, or culture shock).

Work in groups and select one unstable and ambiguous situation in which you are interested. First, work together to give a rich description of the situation, remembering to resist the temptation to make it too neat and orderly. Next, talk through what game playing and game mastery would look like in such a situation. Next, prepare a list of possible things you could do and evaluate them as a group in terms of the competence they demonstrate or require. Finally, discuss the practicality of doing these things. How difficult would they be—if you were really in the situation—to think of and to implement?

References

Bakhtin, Mikhail. *Speech Genres and Other Late Essays,* translated by Vern W. McGee, and edited by C. Emerson and M. Holquist. Austin: University of Texas Press, 1986.

Berlo, David. *The Process of Communication.* New York: Holt, Rinehart and Winston, 1960.

Berne, Eric. *Games People Play: The Psychology of Human Relationships.* New York: Grove, 1964.

Berne, Eric. *Beyond Games and Scripts.* New York: Grove, 1976.

Bernstein, Richard J. *Praxis and Action: Contemporary Philosophies of Human Activity.* Philadelphia: University of Pennsylvania Press, 1971.

Bernstein, Richard J. *The Restructuring of Social and Political Theory.* Philadelphia: University of Pennsylvania Press, 1978.

Bernstein, Richard J. *Beyond Objectivism and Relativism: Science, Hermeneutics, and Praxis.* Philadelphia: University of Pennsylvania Press, 1983.

Bernstein, Richard J. *The New Constellation: The Ethical-Political Horizons of Modernity/Postmodernity.* Cambridge: MIT Press, 1992.

Billig, Michael, Condor, Susan, Edwards, Derek, Gane, Mike, Middleton, David, and Radley, Allan. *Ideological Dilemmas: A Social Psychology of Everyday Thinking.* London: Sage, 1988.

Bilmes, Jack. *Discourse and Behavior.* New York: Plenum Press, 1986.

Buber, Martin. "Between Man and Man: The Realms." In *The Human Dialogue: Perspectives on Communication,* edited by Floyd Matson and Ashley Montagu, 113–118. New York: Free Press, 1967.

Buber, Martin. *I and Thou,* translated by Walter Kaufmann. New York: Macmillan, 1970/1988.

Calder, Nigel. *The Human Conspiracy.* New York: Viking, 1976.

Campbell, Joseph. *Myths to Live By.* New York: Viking, 1972.

Campbell, Joseph. *The Masks of God: Creative Mythology.* New York: Penguin, 1976.

Cassirer, Ernst. *An Essay on Man.* Garden City: Doubleday Anchor, 1956.

Claiborne, Robert. *The Life and Times of the English Language: The History of our Marvelous Native Tongue.* London: Bloomsbury, 1983.

Cronen, Vernon E., Johnson, Kenneth, and Lannamann, John W. "Paradoxes, Double-binds, and Reflexive Loops: An Alternative Theoretical Perspective." *Family Process.* 20 (1982):91–112.

Cronen, Vernon E. "Coordinated Management of Meaning: Practical Theory for the Complexities and Contradictions of Everyday Life." In *The Status of Common Sense in Psychology,* edited by Jurg Siegfried. Norwood: Ablex, in press.

Cronon, William. *Nature's Metropolis: Chicago and the Great West.* New York: Norton, 1991.

Falletta, Nicholas. *The Paradoxicon.* Garden City: Doubleday and Company, 1983.

Forgas, Joseph P. *Interpersonal Behaviour: The Psychology of Social Interaction.* New York: Pergamon Press, 1985.

Gergen, Kenneth J. *Toward Transformation in Social Knowledge.* New York: Springer-Verlag, 1982.

Gleick, James. *Chaos: Making a New Science.* New York: Viking, 1987.

Hayakawa, Samuel I. *Language in Thought and Action,* 2nd ed. New York: Harcourt, Brace, and World, 1964.

Heyerdahl, Thor. *Aku-Aku: The Secret of Easter Island.* New York: Pocket Books, 1960.

Innis, Harold. *The Bias of Communication.* Toronto: University of Toronto Press, 1951.

James, William. *Pragmatism and The Meaning of Truth.* Cambridge: Harvard University Press, 1975.

Knapp, Mark L., and Hall, Judith A. *Nonverbal Communication in Human Interaction,* 3rd ed. Orlando: Holt, Rinehart and Winston, 1992.

Koryzbski, Alfred. *Science and Sanity: An Introduction to Non-Aristotelian Systems and General Semantics,* 4th ed. Lakeville: International Non-Aristotelian Library Publishing Company, 1958.

Lardner, Rex. *The Underhanded Serve: Or How to Play Dirty Tennis.* New York: Hawthorne, 1968.

Lederer, Richard. *Crazy English.* New York: Pocket Books, 1989.

Meyerwitz, Joshua. *No Sense of Place: The Impact of Electronic Media on Social Behavior.* Oxford: Oxford University Press, 1985.

Miller, Jonathan. *States of Mind.* New York: Pantheon, 1983.

Morales, Waltraud Queiser. "The War on Drugs: A New US National Security Doctrine?" *Third World Quarterly* 11 (July 1989):147–169.

Ong, Walter J. *Orality and Literacy: The Technologizing of the Word.* London: Routledge, 1982.

Parry, John B. *The Psychology of Human Communication.* New York: American Elsevier Publishing Company, 1968.

Pearce, W. Barnett. *Communication and the Human Condition.* Carbondale: Southern Illinois University Press, 1989.

Postman, Neil. *Amusing Ourselves to Death: Public Discourse in the Age of Show Business.* New York: Penguin, 1985.

Potter, Stephen. *The Complete Upmanship.* New York: Holt, Rinehart and Winston, 1970.

Rapoport, Anatol. *Operational Philosophy: Integrating Knowledge and Action.* New York: Harper and Brothers, 1953.

Rapoport, Anatol. "Strategy and Conscience." In *The Human Dialogue: Perspectives on Communication,* edited by Floyd Matson and Ashley Montagu, 79–96. New York: Free Press, 1967.

Rorty, Richard. *Philosophy and the Mirror of Nature.* Princeton: Princeton University Press, 1979.

Schelling, Thomas C. *Micromotives and Macrobehavior.* New York: Norton, 1978.

Schultz, Emily A. *Dialogue at the Margins: Whorf, Bakhtin, and Linguistic Relativity.* Madison: University of Wisconsin Press, 1990.

Searle, John. *Speech Acts: An Essay in the Philosophy of Language.* London: Cambridge University Press, 1969.

Selvini Palazolli, Mara, Boscolo, Luigi, Cecchin, Gianfranco, and Prata, Giuliana. *Paradox and Counterparadox: A New Model in the Therapy of the Family in Schizophrenic Transaction.* New York: Jason Aronson, 1978.

Shands, Harvey Cecil. *The War with Words: Structure and Transcendence.* The Hague: Mouton, 1971.

Shotter, John. *Social Accountability and Selfhood.* Oxford: Blackwell, 1984.

Shotter, John. *Cultural Politics of Everyday Life: Social Constructionism, Rhetoric, and Knowing of the Third Kind,* 1994.

Siegal, Mordecai, and Margolis, Matthew. *Good Dog, Bad Dog.* New York: New American Library, 1973.

Sluzki, Carlos. *Double-Bind: The Foundation of the Communicational Approach to the Family.* New York: Grune and Stratton, 1976.

Spitzberg, Brian H., and Cupach, William R. *Interpersonal Communication Competence.* Beverly Hills: Sage, 1984.

Steiner, George. *Language and Silence: Essays 1958–1966.* New York: Atheneum, 1967.

Stern, Daniel. *The First Relationship: Mother and Infant.* Cambridge: Harvard University Press, 1977.

Tehranian, Majid. *Technologies of Power: Information Machines and Democratic Prospects.* Norwood: Ablex, 1990.

Watzlawick, Paul, Beavin, Janet, and Jackson, Don D. *Pragmatics of Human Communication.* New York: Norton, 1967.

Wiemann, John. "Explication and Test of a Model of Communicative Competence." *Human Communication Research* 3 (1977):195–213.

Whitehead, Alfred North, and Russell, Bertrand. *Principia Mathematica*. New York: Cambridge University Press, 1962.

Wittgenstein, Ludwig. *Tractatus Logico-Philosophicus*, translated by C. K. Ogden. London: Routledge & Kegan Paul, 1922.

Woelfel, Joseph, and Fink, Edward L. *The Measurement of Communication Processes: Galileo Theory and Method*. New York: Academic Press: 1980.

Whorf, Benjamin Lee. *Language, Thought, and Reality: Selected Writings of Benjamin Lee Whorf,* edited by John B. Carroll. Cambridge: MIT Press, 1956.

PART TWO

Motifs

[An understanding of how our social worlds are made produces] a rather paradoxical phenomenon . . . an oppressive sense of bondage . . . and a liberating feeling that the social world is far more tenuous than had previously seemed to be the case. This paradox is only a superficial one. The liberating feeling comes from the valid insight that the social world is an artificial universe, whose laws are conventions, rules of the game that have been agreed upon but that can also be broken and against which one can cheat. The sense of bondage comes from the equally valid insight that society not only encompasses us about but penetrates within us, that we are ourselves products and playthings of society, irrevocably social in our innermost being. The one insight uncovers the fictitiousness of society, the other its oppression.

Peter L. Berger, The Precarious Vision. *Garden City: Doubleday, 1961, p. 16.*

CHAPTER
3 *Speech Acts*

. . . in everyday life, words do not in themselves have a meaning, but a *use,* and furthermore, a *use only in a context;* they are best thought of, not as having already determined meanings, but as *means,* as tools, or as instruments for us in the "making" of meanings. . . . For, like tools in a tool-box, the significance of our words remains open, vague, ambiguous, until they are used in different particular ways in different particular circumstances.

Shotter 1991, p. 200

After reading this chapter, you should be able to

- Exercise greater choice in making and blocking the performance of speech acts

- Identify and use nonverbal cues in making speech acts

- Identify structures and sources of power in the process of making speech acts

Some terms that will help you understand this chapter include

the conversational triplet, speech, nonverbal communication, logics of message design, active listening, conversational implicature, and empowerment

Narrative

> *Carl:* Turn left at the next light.
>
> *Tom:* O.K.
>
> *Carl:* Be sure to stay in your lane. Many accidents happen on this corner.
>
> *Tom:* O.K.
>
> *Carl:* Get ready, the light is about to change.
>
> *Tom:* (turns left; pulls over to the side of the road and stops) Get out.
>
> *Carl:* What!?
>
> *Tom:* I said, Get out! You are my brother, not my driving instructor! I won't have you constantly nagging me about my driving.
>
> *Carl:* I was not nagging, I was just trying to be helpful. What's the matter with you!

Are Carl and Tom communicating well? At one level, they certainly are. Neither has any trouble understanding the *content* of what the other is saying. The terms "left," "the light," and even "get out" are fully comprehended. However, at another level, they are having great difficulty coordinating their actions within a working definition of the situation. The problem focuses on their strikingly different ideas about what is being *done* in this conversation. The fight that is about to take place can be seen as a form of negotiation about the *speech acts* that Carl performed. Were they "providing help" or were they "nagging"?

Other than a brotherly brawl, how might Carl and Tom determine who is right about what speech acts were performed? Whose fault is this communication problem, anyway: is it Carl's, Tom's, or both?

This chapter focuses on the social construction of speech acts. Although the term *speech acts* is not often used in ordinary conversation, it is very familiar to social theorists in several fields, and you will find it useful in understanding interpersonal communication.

The concept is not at all mysterious. Speech acts are actions that we perform by speaking. They include compliments, insults, promises, threats, assertions, and questions.

Suppose that you were asked to describe a conversation that you overheard. If you were a trained court stenographer or a journalist, you might quote, word-for-word, what the conversants said. More likely, however, you would give a paraphrase (putting what they said in your own words) or describe what they *did* by what they said. For example, you might describe a very long argument by saying that she *insulted* him, he *threatened* her, she *argued* her case, he *apologized,* and she *complimented* him on his ability to back down from an untenable position, he *offered* to take her to dinner as a way of making reparations, and she *accepted.*

The thought experiment in the preceding paragraph was designed to show you that you already know a great deal about speech acts. If pressed, you could generate a long list of speech acts; without thinking much about it, you can perceive the speech acts in the conversations in which you communicate. You naturally modulate your voice, your face, your word choice, and particularly, the direction of your gaze to participate in the construction of certain speech acts (paying attention, challenging, politely deferring) and to avoid performing others. It matters greatly to you whether the conversation in which you are participating produced the speech act "insult" or "compliment"; you are keenly alert to subtle cues that differentiate "criticism" from "helpfulness."

This chapter will move you beyond the ability to recognize and perform speech acts and beyond the common-sense understanding of what they are. By asking how speech acts are *made* (that is, applying the "Heyerdahl solution"), you will discover that speech acts are far more complex than they appear, and that this complexity contains opportunities for increasing our communication competence.

What Are Speech Acts?

Social theorists have two ways of thinking about speech acts. One may be characterized as the *basic building blocks approach;* the other as the *unfinished creative process approach.*

The difference starts in the grammatical ambiguity of the term speech acts itself. Some theorists read the phrase as a brief but complete sentence in which "speech" is a noun and "acts" is the verb. That is, it portrays speech as a way of making and doing things. Speech *acts* in the same way that bees fly and bells ring.

Other theorists read "speech acts" as a name for the smallest unit of analysis in communication. *Speech* acts are the component parts of larger communication patterns. These theorists read the phrase as a noun ("acts") modified by the adjective "speech." For example, they identify compliments, insults, promises, assertions, and questions as a few of the many speech acts that comprise the events and objects of our social worlds.

The difference between these approaches can be illustrated by an analogy. Think of a white-water river cascading down a steep slope with furious rapids and foaming shoals. There are two types of things in the river that can be confused because their names have the same grammatical form. On one hand, there are rocks, water, and banks. These are *objects* that have the same chemical properties whether they are in the river or not. On the other hand, there are eddies, whirlpools, and currents. These are *configurations* or *patterns.* They have no chemical properties; if the river were to dry up, they would cease to exist.

There are two kinds of things in this picture: objects and configurations. Objects include water, rocks, and banks; configurations include eddies, whirlpools, and currents. Speech acts are not things; they are configurations.

Are speech acts more like rocks or eddies? Are they objects or configurations? Or is this a false dichotomy? Should we distinguish among them for different purposes, just as we remember whether we are taking a first- or third-person perspective on conversation? Let's start by taking a brief look at the intellectual traditions that look at speech acts as one or the other.

The "Basic Building Block" Approach to Speech Acts

J. L. Austin (1965) popularized the study of speech acts when he noted an important difference among the various utterances that we make. Some utterances (he called them "constatives") are usefully treated as "true" or "false." For example, if I say, "it is snowing outside," you might look out the window and conclude that my utterance is factually correct or not. Other utterances (Austin called them "performatives"), are largely irrelevant to the criterion of "true" or "false." Rather, they are ways of *doing* things. If a minister says, "I pronounce you husband and wife," or if a judge says, "I sentence you to 50 days in the County Jail," it makes little sense to say, "That's true" or "That's false." The minister and the judge *make things happen* by saying what they did. Instead of true or false, we say that the act occurred or did not occur. We might add the evaluation of whether they did the act well or not.

Austin noted that simply saying something does not make it happen; it has to happen in a certain context (he said that certain "felicity conditions" must be met). If your best friend (who is neither a judge nor a minister) says, "I pronounce you husband and wife," the act does not happen (at least in the eyes of the legal profession); only people with appropriate credentials can "bring off" certain speech acts.

Austin's work was extended by John Searle (1969, p. 4), who started out to say some philosophically interesting things about language and has developed this into a "philosophy of mind," based on an analysis of all possible forms of speech acts. He argued that

> *. . . there are five and only five basic things we can do with propositions: We tell people how things are (assertives), we try to get them to do things (directives), we commit ourselves to doing things (commissives), we express our feelings and attitudes (expressives), and we bring about changes in the world so that the world matches the proposition just in virtue of the utterance (declarations). This is a strong claim in the sense that it is not just an empirical sociolinguistic claim about this or that speech community, but is intended to delimit the possibilities of human communication in speech acts. (Searle, 1990, p. 410)*

By identifying all possible speech acts, Searle thinks that he has discovered the basic building blocks of our social worlds.

Although it is not his analogy, Searle's way of dealing with speech acts might be compared to a chemist who has identified all the elements in the universe and has each stored in a sealed container. The periodic table of the elements summarizes all their properties. If I read him correctly, I imagine that Searle would be delighted if his analyses progressed to the point where he could construct something like the periodic table of the elements for speech acts.

If you extend this analogy to the point of absurdity, we could say that your ability as a communicator depended on such factors as the array of speech acts that you know how to produce, your knowledge of the various ways they can be performed, and your sense of how various speech acts fit when put into sequences of other speech acts. That is, a good day is when you perform three "assertives" and two "commissives" without making a mistake.

Certainly, this view of speech acts as the basic building blocks of social interaction seems to underlie some very common conversational patterns. For example:

Harry: Why did you do that?
Rhonda: Do what?
Harry: Put me down in front of your parents!

If speech acts are the basic building blocks of conversations, we ought to be able to construct something like the periodic table of the elements. Such a table would summarize the characteristics of each speech act as well as indicate how various speech acts fit together.

REPRESENTATION ELEMENTS

I	II											III	IV	V	VI	VII	VIII
1 H Hydrogen 1.008																	2 He Helium 4.003
3 Li Lithium 6.94	4 Be Beryllium 9.012											5 B Boron 10.81	6 C Carbon 12.011	7 N Nitrogen 14.007	8 O Oxygen 15.999	9 F Fluorine 18.998	10 Ne Neon 20.17
11 Na Sodium 22.990	12 Mg Magnesium 24.305											13 Al Aluminum 26.98	14 Si Silicon 28.09	15 P Phosphorus 30.974	16 S Sulfur 32.06	17 Cl Chlorine 35.453	18 Ar Argon 39.948
19 K Potassium 39.098	20 Ca Calcium 40.08	21 Sc Scandium 44.956	22 Ti Titanium 47.90	23 V Vanadium 50.942	24 Cr Chromium 51.996	25 Mn Manganese 54.938	26 Fe Iron 55.847	27 Co Cobalt 58.933	28 Ni Nickel 58.71	29 Cu Copper 63.546	30 Zn Zinc 65.38	31 Ga Gallium 69.735	32 Ge Germanium 72.59	33 As Arsenic 74.922	34 Se Selenium 78.96	35 Br Bromine 79.904	36 Kr Krypton 83.80
37 Rb Rubidium 85.467	38 Sr Strontium 87.62	39 Y Yttrium 88.906	40 Zr Zirconium 91.22	41 Nb Niobium 92.906	42 Mo Molybdenum 95.94	43 Tc Technetium 98.906	44 Ru Ruthenium 101.07	45 Rh Rhodium 102.91	46 Pd Palladium 106.4	47 Ag Silver 107.868	48 Cd Cadmium 112.41	49 In Indium 114.82	50 Sn Tin 118.69	51 Sb Antimony 121.75	52 Te Tellurium 127.60	53 I Iodine 126.904	54 Xe Xenon 131.30
55 Cs Cesium 132.905	56 Ba Barium 137.33	57–71 * Rare Earths	72 Hf Hafnium 178.49	73 Ta Tantalum 180.947	74 W Wolfram 183.85	75 Re Rhenium 186.207	76 Os Osmium 190.2	77 Ir Iridium 192.22	78 Pt Platinum 195.09	79 Au Gold 196.967	80 Hg Mercury 200.59	81 Tl Thallium 204.37	82 Pb Lead 207.2	83 Bi Bismuth 208.98	84 Po Polonium (209)	85 At Astatine (210)	86 Rn Radon (222)
87 Fr Francium (223)	88 Ra Radium 226.03	89–103 † Actinides	104 Unq Unilquadium (261)	105 Unp Unilpentium (262)	106 Unh Unilhexium (263)	107 Uns Unilseptium (262)	108 Uno Uniloctium (265)	109 Une Unilennium (266)									

TRANSITION ELEMENTS

57 La Lanthanum 138.91	58 Ce Cerium 140.12	59 Pr Praseodymium 140.91	60 Nd Neodymium 144.24	61 Pm Promethium (145)	62 Sm Samarium 150.36	63 Eu Europium 151.96	64 Gd Gadolinium 157.25	65 Tb Terbium 158.93	66 Dy Dysprosium 162.50	67 Ho Holmium 164.93	68 Er Erbium 167.26	69 Tm Thulium 168.93	70 Yb Ytterbium 173.04	71 Lu Lutetium 174.967
89 Ac Actinium 227.028	90 Th Thorium 232.038	91 Pa Proactinium 231.036	92 U Uranium 238.029	93 Np Neptunium 237.048	94 Pu Plutonium (244)	95 Am Americium (243)	96 Cm Curium (247)	97 Bk Berkelium (247)	98 Cf Californium (251)	99 Es Einsteinium (254)	100 Fm Fermium (257)	101 Md Mendelevium (258)	102 No Nobelium (259)	103 Lr Lawrencium (260)

* Rare earths (Lanthanide series)

† Actinide series

A *group* is a vertical column of elements that have similar physical and chemical properties. The groups are identified by numbers that go across the top of the periodic table. The elements on the periodic table are divided into eight (I–VIII) "A" groups of *representation elements* and the *transition elements.*

Metals

Nonmetals

Upper number is *atomic number,* the positive charge of the nucleus in multiples of the unit charge *e.* Lower number is *atomic mass* averaged by isotopic abundance in the earth's surface, expressed in atomic mass units (amu). Atomic masses for radioactive elements shown in parentheses are the whole number nearest the most stable isotope of that element.

Rhonda is producing some very specific non-verbal cues. Do they comprise the speech act "putting Harry down"? What else would you need to know to determine what speech act is being performed?

Rhonda: I did no such thing! What's the matter with you?
Harry: You did too! You rolled your eyes and made faces when I was telling them about my plans for getting a job after graduation.
Rhonda: You're seeing things that just are not there!

Did Rhonda "put Harry down"? Perhaps so; Harry is certainly treating certain movements that she made as if they constituted one of Searle's speech acts, probably an "assertive." If speech acts are the basic building blocks of the social world, the act of "putting Harry down" either happened or it did not, and Harry and Rhonda ought to be able to decide whether it did. On the other hand, if speech acts are an unfinished creative process, then the meaning of what Rhonda did is inherently negotiable and still open; in addition to arguing about what actually happened in a specific, completed instant of time, Rhonda and Harry can participate in the continuing construction of the meaning of what is still in the process of happening.

The "Unfinished Creative Process" Approach to Speech Acts

Wittgenstein used the term "language games" (or, more precisely, he used a German phrase that might more accurately be translated as "speech playing") rather than "speech acts" as part of his project of clarifying the ways that our language gets us into muddles. Although he was particularly interested in helping philosophers avoid repeating the mistakes built into the grammar they used, his insights are very useful for understanding interpersonal communication wherever it occurs.

Wittgenstein was frustrated because successive generations of philosophers seemed trapped within the same problems.

> *People say again and again that philosophy doesn't really progress, that we are still occupied with the same philosophical problems as were the Greeks. But the people who say this don't understand why it has to be so. It is because our language has remained the same and keeps seducing us into asking the same questions. As long as there continues to be a verb "to be" that looks as if it functions in the same way as "to eat" and "to drink," as long as we still have the adjectives "identical," "true," "false," "possible," as long as we continue to talk of a river of time or an expanse of space, etc. etc., people will keep stumbling over the same puzzling difficulties and find themselves staring at something which no explanation seems capable of clearing up. (Wittgenstein 1984, p. 15e)*

Wittgenstein accepted the task of developing a method for exposing the clouds of philosophy that are inherent in drops of grammar. Part of this method consists of treating utterances in terms of their uses rather than assuming that they have any inherent meaning.

> *We do the most various things with our sentences. Think of exclamations alone, with their completely different functions.*
> > *Water!*
> > *Away!*
> > *Ow!*
> > *Help!*
> > *Fine!*
> > *No!*
> *Are you inclined still to call these words "names of objects"? (Wittgenstein 1958, p. 12e)*

Wittgenstein noted that we use language in various contexts (that is, in "language games") in which the meaning of what we say is determined by how it fits into the game. Consider the statement "I do." You can identify a language game in which saying this joins you in holy matrimony for better or for worse, in sickness and in health, and so on. But there is another language game that you can readily identify in which saying "I do" makes you subject to the penalties for perjury if you tell a lie. In yet another language game, to say "I do" means that you are the one who has the key to the house in your pocket, that you know the answer to a teacher's question, or that you know how to play the saxophone.

So what is the meaning of the phrase, "I do"? Well, it depends. Specifically, it depends on what language game you are playing when you utter it. The phrase is not tied to some objective event or object in the world such that every time you use it, you point to that object; rather, it is tied to the way it is used in particular instances.

A Comparison of the Two Approaches

To this point, the differences between Austin/Searle's and Wittgenstein's approaches do not seem very great. Both refer to utterances as ways of doing things rather than talking about them. However, certain features in the way they approach speech acts have very different implications for interpersonal communication. Depending on which approach you take, you will treat speech acts as if they were substances (like rocks or water) or configurations of a process (like eddies or currents).

How many speech acts are there?   Austin (1965, p. 150) was a bit daunted by this question and guessed that there might be between 1 and 10,000, grouped in a rather smaller set of "families." For Searle, this is an important question and he argues very cleverly to defend his claim that there are only five and can be no more (Searle 1990).

For Wittgenstein, this is not an important question, and Searle's answer is clearly wrong, because our social worlds are much more fluid than Searle thinks. Wittgenstein (1958, p. 11e) said that there are "*countless* kinds. . . . And this multiplicity is not something fixed, given once for all; but new types of language, new language-games, as we may say, come into existence, and others become obsolete and get forgotten."

Counterpoint 3.1

Are new speech acts invented? Do old ones die? Do different cultures have different speech acts?

I think some important things hang on the answers we give to these questions. If there is a finite set of speech acts and they have all been invented, then our lives consist of various ways of performing the same acts, or perhaps of working our way into one array of speech acts and out of another. On the other hand, if the set of possible speech acts is "open," then we might find ourselves living very different lives than anyone else ever has.

If the set of possible speech acts is relatively small and all cultures simply enact the same acts in different manners, then all human cultures are—at the level of speech acts if not at the level of their performance—interchangeable. We should expect to understand other cultures if we can see past the surface level of how they perform speech acts, and we should not worry too much if some cultures disappear because they really did not have anything substantially different from all other cultures.

On the other hand, if the set of possible speech acts is larger than can be performed by any single culture, or if different cultures invent and practice speech acts unknown (and unknowable?) by other cultures, then the array of human cultures is a tremendous resource for human creativity. We should prize exotic cultures because they show us alternative ways of being human.

But how shall we answer these questions?

Raymond Gozzi Jr. (1990/1991) selected an interesting source of data that sheds some light on these questions. Twelve thousand new words were introduced to the English language in the 26 years between 1961 and 1986. (i.e., the folks who publish the Merriam-Webster listed these 12,000 as a supplement to their *Webster's Third, Unabridged Dictionary* published in 1961.) Of these, 75 were "new speech act verbs."

Noting that these 25 years were times of "turmoil and ferment in the United States," Gozzi suggested that changes in our language are a "cultural indicator" of what is going on in society. These 12,000 words are those that have "caught on" well enough "to find their way into print, more than once, over a period of time. . . . The very fact of its presence in a dictionary certifies, to some extent, that the new word has been more than a passing fancy, and many people have paid attention to it—enough to remember it, use it, and perpetuate it" (Gozzi 1990/1991, pp. 449–450).

Gozzi (1990/1991, p. 450) coded 40 of the new terms of speech acts as "negative." These terms "implied that deceptive or inaccurate communication was occurring, information was decreasing, and/or negative emotions occurred." Further, he divided them into six categories:

1. Deception-mystification, including "come on," "do a number on," "downplay," "hype," and "stonewall"
2. Combat-war, including "blow away," "overrespond," and "trash"
3. Social pressure, including "blow one's cool," "hassle," "lean on," and "put the make on"
4. Competition, including "bad-mouth," "choke," "blindside," and "put down"
5. Drug experiences, including "blow one's mind," and "freak out"
6. Unfaithfulness, including "fink out" and "cop out"

He found 25 words that seemed to him to be "positive"; that is, "they implied that open communication was occurring, information was increasing, and/or positive emotions occurred" (Gozzi 1990/1991, p. 450). The largest category was "psychobabble," including "hang loose," "let it all hang out," "pick up on," and "psych up." Other categories included

1. Terms deriving from drug experiences, including "groove" and "turn on"

2. Terms coming from ethnic and social minorities, including "rap," "come out," and "play the dozens"
3. Terms coming from technology, including "hook up," "interface," and "plug into"
4. Terms coming from competition, such as "shoot from the hip"
5. Terms coming from social pressure, such as "go public"

How seriously should we take the appearance of new words for speech acts? Are they just new labels for old acts, or does our culture really invent new things to do as well as new names for things? How should we think about the number of new acts? Is 75 new acts in 25 years a lot? (Hmm . . . That translates into three new speech acts per year.) Is 75 out of 12,000 surprisingly few? (Hmm . . . That means that speech acts comprise only six tenths of one per cent of the linguistic creativity of our culture.)

Michelle Rosaldo (1980; 1990) approached the topic in a different way. An ethnographer, she studied the culture of the Ilongot, a head-hunting tribe in a remote part of Southeast Asia. She claimed that the Ilongot practiced speech acts not known in European/North American culture. Communication theorist Donal Carbaugh (1990) published a symposium in which John Searle (1990) strongly contested Rosaldo's claim, and Del Hymes (1990) commented on the controversy.

Marga Kreckel (1981) started with the question Where do speech acts come from, anyway? She studied family communication patterns to see how infants learned speech acts by insinuating themselves into the game-like patterns of social interactions in which they found themselves. Her data showed that families differ in the ways various speech acts are performed; what would be recognized as a successful accomplishment of, for example, "warning" in one family simply would not be heard the same way in another. Further, she found that there are differences among the members of the same family in what actions comprise what speech acts.

At the very least, Kreckel's data locate speech acts within the actual practices of social life rather than an abstract list. Even if we do not create new speech acts, we are always involved in the negotiation of how we will perform the speech acts in which we live.

What is the relation between speech acts and contexts? For Austin and Searle, speech acts are made when utterances occur that fit into the existing contexts in appropriate ways. Much of their work consists of identifying the "felicity conditions" that must be met if speech acts such as "promise" are to be performed.

For Wittgenstein, the contexts themselves are fluid. Language games come and go; they are created, modified, and eliminated as life goes on. As a consequence, an utterance that meets all the criteria for performing a speech act today might not have done so at another point in the past and may not at some point in the future. As a result, Wittgenstein's ideas focused social theorists' attention on the continuous, reflexive process by which speech acts make the contexts that give them meaning *and* contexts make the speech acts that occur in them.

Counterpoint 3.2

You are familiar with the notion that the meaning of any act depends on the context in which it occurs. But where do contexts come from?

If we accept the notion that contexts are made, then the answer to the question is clear: contexts are made by specific actions. At the same time, specific actions derive their meaning from the contexts in which they occur.

In my description of Wittgenstein's theory of speech acts, I described a fully reflexive relationship between contexts and the acts that occur in them. The circular causal link that relates actions and contexts is neither paradoxical nor simple minded. Rather, it depicts a temporal process of coevolution, in which acts occur that simultaneously are in existing contexts and call into being the contexts that exist subsequently.

This coevolutionary process is the site of human agency or power to bring about changes in our social worlds. If contexts were fixed, unaffected by our actions, then our social worlds would be unresponsive to our actions. At best, we might move around within our social worlds, but we could not change them. However, if contexts coevolve, then our actions do not simply have to fit into predetermined molds, they can be creative, calling into being contexts that did not exist previously into which we can act.

This creative, empowering ability can be illustrated by a true story. Chicago is a violent city; almost 1,000 homicides occurred in the city during 1992. Most of the victims were young African-American men, many were killed in gang-related violence, and many of these were by-standers not involved in the gangs.

After one particularly awful event in which an elementary school student was shot while walking to school, the leaders of several of the gangs in Chicago announced that they were declaring a "truce." Immediately, there were calls on the Mayor to respond appropriately, but opinions differed about what that response should be. The discussion focused around the question of what the gang leaders meant when they announced the truce. Specifically, people heatedly debated whether the gangs were sincere.

"It does not matter," one rather radical voice claimed. "What matters is what the collective 'we' *do* about the truce. The gang leaders do not get to decide all by themselves what their 'truce' means. We can help to make it mean whatever it will mean."

This suggestion reflects the creative power of speech acts. Rather than focusing on the intrapsychic states of the gang leaders (i.e., what they meant), this approach looks for ways of positioning their behavior within co-constructed speech acts that serve what may be better purposes than the gang leaders intended.

In the conversation given earlier, did Rhonda "put down" Harry? Who gets to decide if that is what she did or not? How can she plausibly argue that Harry should not feel "put down"? One way that she can deny having "put him down" is to describe a context in which her actions mean something else. For example, she might say, "Harry! Quit jumping to conclusions. You know that I have been having trouble with my contact lenses!"

Recall the argument between Carl and Tom. Which came first, the *relationship* in which Carl's comments counted as the speech acts "nagging" or the *speech acts* of nagging that constructed this relationship? The Austin/ Searle approach would not pose the question this way, and their ways of working focus on the context as the pre-existing reality in which utterances occur. This is a very appropriate way of posing the question from a Wittgensteinian perspective, and the answer is that there is no a priori answer; it could be either, and you would have to investigate each particular instance to see what was going on.

When are speech acts completed?   Again, this is not the way the question would be proposed from the Austin/Searle perspective, but their way of working indicates a kind of "yes/no" orientation to speech acts. That is, it either occurs or it does not. For example, Taylor and Cameron (1987, p. 43) suggested that conversations can be analyzed "as a series of discrete acts, sequentially organized." In this task, "our main preoccupation will be with matters of taxonomy and identification of acts in conversation" (p. 43), that is, with making lists of all possible forms of speech acts and defining how to identify them.

From the Wittgensteinian approach, speech acts are never completed. Rather, they are part of an ongoing process in which they both fit into contexts and create the contexts in which they fit, and in which they are a part of a continuing sequence of actions, each of which has the potential to reinterpret those that came before them.

Among other things, the "incompleteness" of speech acts implies that the meanings of our social worlds are not fully determined. A certain openness in the meanings of what we say and do is not just the result of our lack of precision but because of the nature of speech acts themselves. As Shotter (1991, p. 202) said

Everyday human activities do not just appear *vague and indefinite because we are still as yet ignorant of their true underlying nature, but they are really vague . . . the fact is, there is no order, no already determined order, just . . . an order of possible orderings which it is up to us to make as we see fit. And this, of course . . . is exactly what we require of language as a means of communication: we require the words of our language to give rise to vague, but not wholly unspecified "tendencies" which permit a degree of further specification according to the circumstances of their use, thus to allow the "making" of precise and particular meanings appropriate to those circumstances.*

This is the most striking and important difference between the two approaches, and the nature of the difference can be shown by an analogy. The sports section of most newspapers carry box scores of baseball and football games. These box scores present a summary of what happened by categories. For example, a baseball game will be summarized in terms of how many runs each team scored, how many hits they got, and how many errors were committed by each team.

The information you get from a box score differs very much from a play-by-play broadcast of the game or, better, what it feels like to be *in* the game as a participant. The box score cannot be computed until the game is over, but when you are standing at the plate, waiting on the two and two pitch, you do not know whether you will knock in the winning run, strike out, or be knocked down by a wild pitch. The meaning of the two and two pitch in the sixth inning is determined by what happens next, and in the next inning, and even by games later in the season.

The Wittgensteinian approach takes the play-by-play perspective; it locates us in the actual process of producing speech acts rather than an after-the-fact process of summarizing what was and was not done. As such, it is far more useful for our understanding of interpersonal communication.

How Speech Acts Are Made

Traffic in London is really terrible, particularly during the weekend. A group of therapists and social workers had gathered on a Saturday for an all-day workshop on communication theory; I was the guest "expert" charged with planning the activities of the day. We were taking a break for lunch, and one of the participants asked another

> *Anne:* Would anyone mind if I left early so I can miss the traffic?
> *Tom:* When did you first decide that you needed to ask permission to leave this class?
> *Anne:* Right.

What speech act was Anne performing when she said, "Would anyone mind . . ."? Was it a request for information? Was it an announcement of

If speech acts are discrete, complete units of the social world, as Searle thinks, then an analysis of a conversation can resemble a "box-score" summary of a baseball game. On the other hand, if, as Wittgenstein believes, speech acts are inherently unfinished and co-constructed, then an analysis of a conversation must include the perspective of a player while the game is still going on. That is, it is not clear to the batter in the sixth inning with two on and two out how the game will turn out. In fact, the outcome of the game depends on what the pitcher does . . . and how the batter responds to the pitch . . . and how the fielder responds to the ball that he hits . . . and so on in an ongoing sequence.

her intention? Was it an account offered to make her subsequent early departure less rude than it might otherwise have seemed? Was she subtly suggesting that Tom leave with her? Was she asking Tom for a ride?

Her action alone provides too little information for you to decide. In fact, any such action is incomplete; it provides an opening for any number of subsequent acts, each of which adds to the meaning of the act.

What else might Tom have said? Note how each of his potential responses helps "make" the meaning of Anne's statement. He might have said, "Yes, we would all be very offended." This response would have "made" her question a request for information. He might have said, "Now that you mention it, I need to leave early as well. May I ride with you?"

His actual answer was even more interesting. How do you interpret what he said? My own understanding is that he did something very like the exercise in escaping linguistic tyranny. That is, he recognized that Anne's question was based on an underlying assumption: "My behavior depends on the evaluations of other people." He was confronted by a paradox: he wanted (I suppose) to challenge that assumption, but if he said, "You should not decide what to do based on what other people tell you," he would have told her what to do! Anne could not "obey" this instruction without "disobeying" it. As a way of achieving his objective without placing Anne in a paradox, he posed a question about *when* she decided to let others make her decisions for her. This is, I believe, a remarkably sophisticated way for Tom to call into question her original assumption and to say, "Anne, make up your own mind and accept the responsibility for your decision." (Of course, he might *also* be saying, "No, Anne, I will not go away with you for the weekend.")

Note that Anne's answer had nothing to do with the semantic content of the question; that is, she did not cite a time or date when she first decided to let other people's opinions control her actions. Rather, she acknowledged what he *did* rather than pay any attention to what he *said*. (By the way, she stayed until the very end of the workshop.)

Counterpoint 3.3

The meaning of any utterance is never completed, but each subsequent act becomes part of the context from which its meaning derives. In the conversation between Anne and Tom, Anne's initial utterance (like most utterances) was sufficiently polysemic that it could mean many things, depending on how Tom responded. For example:

Anne said	Tom might have said
"Would anyone mind if I left early?"	"May I ride with you?"
	"Of course, not."
	"It would be very rude . . ."
	"When did you start asking for permission?"

What speech act would *Anne's* utterance become depending on *Tom's* response? Assume that Anne had a very particular speech act in mind, how could she "control" the meaning of her utterance?

Of course, neither you nor I really know what act was performed in this conversation. Was it "therapy" successfully accomplished? An unsuccessful attempt to lure Tom away for carnal purposes? A bungled attempt to ask for a ride home? An exchange of national security secrets in a private code known only to Tom and Anne? Of such complexities are all our conversations made!

The Co-Construction of Speech Acts

No speech act consists of a single action. You simply cannot perform a speech act alone. The act you perform is as much given by the responses of other people as it is taken by your own acts.

Speech acts are not things; they are configurations in the logic of meaning and action of conversations, and these configurations are co-constructed. You cannot be a "victim" unless there is a "victimizer." Perhaps this explains why so many people seem to enjoy the role of being a victim: it is a passive-aggressive way of accusing others of acting in a brutish manner. You cannot be an expert unless there are people who are less knowledgeable than you, or a leader unless there are people to be led. Perhaps this is why so many people resent those who offer themselves as experts or leaders: they do not want to do what is necessary to "complete" the speech acts of "expertise" or "leadership."

The term *co-construction* is a bit awkward; when you say it, you sound like you are stuttering. However, some social theorists have taken to using it as a way of reminding themselves that the events and objects of our social worlds are made by the collective us, working together. As noted in Chapter 2, the speech acts that we co-construct do not necessarily resemble any of the individual actions that we perform and may be something that we did not intend to produce, but whatever they are comes from the connections or combinations of *your* act followed by *my* act followed by *your* act yet again. That is, speech acts are configurations in the logic of meaning and action, something like a whirlpool or eddie is a configuration in the movement of a river.

The co-construction of speech acts is the point of an activity that I enjoy when I teach interpersonal communication. After giving an arid lecture on the co-constructed nature of speech acts, I make an erroneous and ridiculous claim to the effect that *I* can control *their* speech acts. Specifically, I tell them that they *cannot* insult me. "Do you know how to do the speech act 'insult'?" I ask. Of course they do. "How good are you at insulting other people?" Usually someone brags about his or her expertise or is identified by other members of the class as particularly good at insulting people. "O.K., Try to insult me. You can't do it!" Getting into the spirit of the game, "Come on," I urge, "take your best shot! This is your one chance to insult a tenured full professor and get away with it!" After a few moments of hesitation ("Is he serious?"), there are plenty of highly motivated volunteers.

- "Your mother dresses you funny!" One will say.
  I reply, "Thank you! That's a good one, because college professors are notorious for being poorly dressed. Next?"
- "That's the ugliest, most out-of-fashion tie I have ever seen."
  "My wife gave it to me for Christmas. I'll relay your comments to her. Next?"
- "Your book is boring!"
  "Oh, good!" I answer, "you've read it! I wondered if anyone had!"
- "You scum-sucking worm!"
  "What?"
  "I said, you scum-sucking worm!"
  "That sounds disgusting, but I don't know what it means. Can anyone do better?"

And so on. After a while, the class gets frustrated because the things they are saying—which meet all of Austin's "felicity conditions" for being an insult—are not working as insults. Clearly something unusual is going on here, but what?

To challenge and provoke my students, I interpret this exercise as showing that *I* can control the meaning of what *they* say. In fact, that is precisely what it does *not* demonstrate. Again, this exercise does *not* demonstrate that one of us controls the process by which both or all of us co-construct speech acts!

There's a trick in what I did, and the structure of the trick illustrates the point I want to make. The exercise really shows that speech acts are co-constructed; they are the result of the interaction of two or more actions. No single person—neither *I* nor *they*—exerts absolute control over what occurs. However, the *sequence* of acts is important.

The trick in the "You Can't Insult Me" exercise depends on who starts the sequence of actions (i.e., it is like the strategy in playing the game "tic-tac-toe" or "naughts and crosses": if the person who makes the first move does it correctly, she or he will win or tie but never lose.) The conversation does not start with the insult; it starts with my *request* that they insult me, and this makes an important difference. Given the request, any ostensibly insulting phrase, no matter how grotesque or vile, is in fact *complying with* what I asked them to do. All their efforts to think of something to say or do that would offend me has been co-opted into a collaboration with me in the conjoint production of a classroom exercise. The conversations go like this:

Prof: I request that my students insult me.
Students: They make statements that in other contexts would be insulting.
Prof: I thank them for complying with my request.

Note that for this sequence to work as a demonstration, I must "complete" it by treating their "insult" as if it were "compliance with my request" rather than an "insult." If I say or do something that makes them think that I have been insulted, the exercise fails—and we co-construct an insult rather than a class exercise.

As they grasp the point of the game, my students scrutinize my performance with disconcerting intensity. If my voice quivers, my face gets red, I hesitate in making my customary snappy reply, or in any other way I fail to treat their "insult" as "compliance," they *know* that they have successfully performed the speech act insult. Nothing that I can say or do will convince them otherwise.

I am, of course, insultable, but *in this context* the most grievous insult is for a student to say, simply, "no," that is, to refuse to participate in the activity. Anything else can be, if I keep my wits about me, incorporated into the exercise—that is, I can "complete" their actions in such a manner that it becomes the speech act "classroom demonstration" rather than "insult."

The Conversational Triplet

Communication theorist Changsheng Xi (1991) proposed the notion of a *conversational triplet* as the basic structure for the performance of a speech act. The triplet consists of at least three actions in which the speech act to be identified is the second, or middle action. It can be modeled like this:

> *Anne says:* ——
>
>   *Tom says:* ——
>
> *Anne says:* ——

If you want to know what act Tom performed, you must look at it in the context of what was done before and after.

Counterpoint 3.4

The structure of the "conversational triplet" is closely related to the serpentine model of conversation shown in Figure 1.4. Speech acts are configurations in the logic of meaning and action of a conversation. To identify what speech acts in any given conversation, in somewhat the same way as you would identify the currents or eddies in a white-water river, you can take these steps:

1. Record the whole conversation, using the structure of the serpentine model.

2. Now superimpose the conversational triplet on the first three acts: this is the structure of the first speech act.
3. Now superimpose the conversational triplet on the second, third, and fourth acts; this is the structure of the second speech act.

■ Note: as you move through the conversation, the "triplet" alternates from a shape with two left- and one right-column acts to a shape with one left- and two right-column acts. This is of no matter because "left" and "right" are purely arbitrary ways of representing an oral (in which there is no "left" or "right") conversation visually (in which you *must* use the left-right dimension).

■ Note: the fluidity of conversations is indicated by the fact that each statement participates in more than one speech act. Note the third statement in the conversation: it will be in the last place in the first conversational triplet; the middle place in the second triplet; and the first place in the third triplet. This is one of the reasons why it is impossible to say what this statement means in a simple, declarative sentence; except in the most unusual circumstances, our social worlds are just too complicated for such clarity.

Continue the process of identifying speech acts by moving the triplet structure along the serpentine model. This will give you the kind of "action description" of a conversation that we often want to understand what occurred in a conversation. For example:

"What did she say?"
"She said, 'O.K.' "
"Yes, but did she *promise* to do it?"
"Her exact words were 'I don't mind doing that.' "
"But is that a *promise* to do it?"

The conversational triplet is the *minimal* structure in the performance of speech acts, of course. Like any analytical device, the conversational triplet conceals as well as reveals what it is designed to illuminate. In real life, speech acts can be much more complex than the examples I can give in a few lines ripped from the fabric of people's lives. For example, we are seldom so simple-minded as to refer only to the immediately preceding statement.

1. "Where is Billy?"
   2. "Who wants to know?"
3. "This is his mother. His father is sick and we need him to come home right away."
   4. "He's away from the office. I expect him back in about an hour."

Statement #2 combines with #1 to make a challenge. Statement #3 combines with #2 to discredit that speech act. Statement #4 responds to #1 in a standard question-and-answer pattern.

In principle, speech acts are never completed; they are always evolving, open to reconstruction based on what you or other people do, and not necessarily in the immediately following event.

The unfinished creative nature of speech acts seems easy enough to defend, but what implications does it have for how you communicate? Communication theorist John Shotter and I were talking about this issue once, and he offered some very interesting advice that I propose calling the "Shotter strategy."

Assume that you are talking about something important to you, and someone asks, "What does that mean?" Shotter suggested that you should reply, "I'm not completely sure yet; we have not finished our conversation."

The Shotter strategy will draw curious comments from your interlocutors, but think it through. If the meaning of whatever we do *now* is incomplete, and if our action is moved toward completion by being joined to the actions of other people, then you or I *really cannot know* what our statement meant until we know how our interlocutors respond to it.

In the common sense of contemporary American society, the question What does that mean? normally elicits a description of the speaker's cognitive state. It is a way of asking, What were you thinking of or What did you have in mind? Such descriptions are notoriously self-serving and unreliable; your reconstruction of your cognitive state in *this* moment is affected by the subsequent history of the conversation, including the challenge to explain yourself. In *this* moment, you have a first-person perspective on what you are saying now, but a third-person perspective on what you said then. In effect, your description of your cognitive state *then* is a fabrication (literally, "something made") in the present from a different person perspective and within a different context than whatever happened then. No wonder these reports are so unreliable.

The Shotter strategy is a deliberate attempt to transcend common sense and act within a more informed understanding of how interpersonal communication works. Like the American pragmatists and Wittgenstein, it focuses attention on what is *done* in ongoing, co-constructed conversations rather than what is *thought* by one of the conversants at a particular moment in the process.

As Shotter worded his advice, it works well as a reminder of the co-constructed nature of speech acts for those of us who have already thought about these things and need to be prevented from slipping back into the comfortable patterns of common sense. As a formula that might be used for people who have not been emancipated from common-sense notions of communication, it needs a bit of work. Try these as ways of answering the question What does that mean?

- "I intended that you would respond by doing . . . ."

- "What I hoped you would hear me say is . . ."
- "It seemed like a good idea at the time."

Are these consistent with the principle that speech acts are unfinished and with the emphasis on the co-construction of speech acts? (I think the first two are; the third is not).

Counterpoint 3.5

Have you ever been in a conversation where the meaning of what you said changed because of something that happened ten minutes, ten days, or ten years later?

The unfinished nature of speech acts is particularly apparent in the speech acts "promises" and "predictions." These are overtly open-ended. Consider the traditional wedding vows: "to have and to hold, in sickness and in health, for richer or poorer, so long as you both shall live." What speech act are you performing when you say—right there in front of God and everybody—these words? How long will it take for this speech act to be completed?

Not only promises and predictions cast shadows into the future. Sometimes the meaning of what you do is "completed" by events that seem to be, but were not in fact, responses to what you do. Let me tell you a true story of a speech act that *almost* happened and would have been tragic if it had.

A professor in a major state university was appalled by what he perceived as the political apathy of his students. Rather than just complain about the sorry state of affairs, he decided to do something about it—something sufficiently spectacular that it would at least put the question of political activism on the agenda of classroom and coffee-house conversation.

He wrote a sensationalistic call for political action. Deliberately in the style of Thomas Paine's writings that encouraged the American Revolution, he urged students to take to the streets, to act both within and outside of conventional political structures to oppose injustice, to make government responsive to the people, and so on.

He printed thousands of leaflets containing this "Activist Manifesto." Since he was a pilot who owned his own airplane he planned to strafe the campus on a particular Friday and drop the pamphlets on the students as they were going from one class to another.

Confiding his plans to some friends, he was distressed to learn that they did not share his opinion that this was a totally good idea. After several beers and a good bit of talk, he decided not to distribute the leaflets, and they remained bundled in his garage.

Competely unrelated to this professor's plans, a nationally publicized event occurred over the weekend that excited political passions. On

Saturday—the day after he planned to bomb the campus with leaflets urging students to rise against "the establishment"—a group of students organized a demonstration on campus protesting the government's actions in the event that was dominating the headlines. The campus police, followed by the state police, over-reacted; the demonstration spilled off campus, and before it was over, many people had been arrested, some had been injured, many downtown businesses had been vandalized, and a full-scale investigation was launched to determine who was at fault for instigating what was being officially called a riot.

The professor who did *not* bomb the campus with radical calls for students to rise in protest against the system was, of course, not a target of the investigation. (And, I suspect, the bundles of pamphlets in his garage were kept safely locked away!) But what if he had gone ahead with his plans? Would his spectacular distribution of incendiary pamphlets have caused the riot? Of course not; the riot happened anyway. But *if* he had distributed them and *then* the riot had occurred, would the investigating committee have concluded that he performed the speech act "incitement to riot"? Yep!

Imagine the conversation as he was brought before the University President and the Circuit Judge, accused of inciting to riot.

Prosecutor: Did you distribute these pamphlets on Friday?
Defendent: Yes, but . . .
Prosecutor: Just answer the questions I ask. Did a riot occur on Saturday?
Defendent: Yes, but . . .
Prosecutor: Your Honor, whatever the defendent *intended* to do when he illegally littered the campus with these salacious pamphlets, when combined with the actions of the students this weekend, it is clear that the defendent is guilty of inciting to riot. The prosecution rests its case.

Quite shaken by the turn of events, the professor vividly imagined something like the conversation above. "No jury in the country would have believed me," he said. "I would have spent the rest of my life as a janitor at Cowpasture State College!"

Oral Speech Is the Medium for Interpersonal Communication

Have you wondered why common sense seems to be such a poor source for understanding interpersonal communication? I think that there are two reasons.

The first is that we are in the middle of a series of cultural revolutions. By its very nature, common sense does not fare well in revolutionary times, and we have had such a series of profound revisions in our forms of life and ways of thinking that common sense simply has not been able to keep up.

These revolutions have converged from many directions, including science and technology, philosophy, social science, literature and art, and the media of communication. The impact of communication media on the continuing series of revolutions that have comprised the twentieth century is hard to exaggerate. For example, the telegraph changed the relationship of distance to community. In the 1800s, Americans were busily trying to conquer the distance that separated them. Until the 1840s, information as well as raw materials and manufactured products, "could move only as fast as a human being could carry it; to be precise, only as fast as a train could travel, which, to be even more precise, meant about 35 miles per hour" (Postman 1985, p. 64). In the middle of the nineteenth century, America was more a composite of regions, each with its own interests, loosely linked by relatively inefficient means of communication and transportation than it was, in the proud words of the "Pledge of Allegiance to the Flag," "one nation, under God, indivisible, and with liberty and justice for all."

Samuel F. B. Morse's invention of the telegraph eliminated distance as a practical barrier to (a certain form of) communication. Morse prophesied that the telegraph would make "one neighborhood of the whole country." In his book *Walden,* Henry David Thoreau (1957, p. 36) wondered if Texas and Maine had much to say to each other.

> *We are in great haste to construct a magnetic telegraph from Maine to Texas, but Maine and Texas, it may be, have nothing important to communicate. . . . We are eager to tunnel under the Atlantic and bring the old world some weeks nearer to the new; but perchance the first news that will leak through into the broad flapping American ear will be that Princess Adelaide has the whooping cough.*

Thoreau was right: the telegraph—and each new medium of communication that has been developed since—has not only permitted but insisted on the development of conversations among previously isolated groups of people, and at the same time, it has altered the structure of that conversation because of its properties as a medium of communication.

Communication media are the enabling infrastructures of the game-like patterns of communication. They do not *determine* what kinds of communication occur, but at the same time they are far from neutral. They have the same relationship to patterns of communication that the chessboard does to the game of chess, the gridiron to the game of football, and the court to the game of tennis. The chessboard, gridiron, and court, do not determine what game will be played or who will win, but they define what movements are significant and what strategies will be effective, and they shape the actions that are possible to perform. If the football field is made wider or more narrow, the game itself will change; if a tennis court is made longer or wider, or if the net is raised by an additional three feet, whole new strategies for play will develop, previously champion players will become mediocre, and

Counterpoint 3.6

Who first thought about the relationship between patterns of social interaction and the medium in which communication occurs? We tend to think
that "media studies" are very recent developments, and that the so-called
mass media are the only ones to have a major impact on society. Not so,
on both accounts.

Walter Ong's (1982) study of the development and use of writing, particularly in print, shows that this was the first "communication revolution." As
I read his work, I get the impression the effect of print was greater—at
least so far—than that of the current communication revolution
brought on by the development of electronic media.

By the same token, the idea that "forms of media favor particular kinds
of content and therefore are capable of taking command of a culture"
is not a new one. Neil Postman (1985, p. 9) said that the earliest record
of this idea is in the Decalogue, or "Ten Commandments." The second commandment says: "Thou shalt not make unto thee any graven image, any
likeness of any thing that is in heaven above, or that is in the earth
beneath, or that is in the water beneath the earth."

Why all the fuss about pictures and statues? Postman says that it is a
strange injunction "unless its author assumed a connection between
forms of human communication and the quality of a culture." The God
of the Hebrews, Postman observes, was different in kind from the
gods of those in neighboring cultures. Specifically, the worship of their
God required "the highest order of abstract thinking. Iconography thus became blasphemy so that a new kind of God could enter a culture" (Postman 1985, p. 9).

Perhaps Postman is guilty of reading too much into the second commandment, but if so, then why the ban on icons? What difference, if any,
does it make that most forms of the Christian Church have quietly ex-
empted themselves from this commandment, while Muslims have
submitted to it with commendable integrity? Is the quality of religious
experience different? Is the form of worship or theology affected by the
medium in which it occurs?

Walter Ong (1982, p. 179) notes that the orality-literacy polarity is particularly acute in Christianity.

> For in Christian teaching the Second Person of the One Godhead, who
> redeemed mankind from sin, is known not only as the Son but also as the
> Word of God. In this teaching, God the Father utters or speaks His
> Word, his Son. He does not inscribe him. The very Person of the
> Son is constituted as the Word of the Father. Yet Christian teaching
> also presents at its core the written word of God, the Bible, which,
> back of its human authors, has God as author as no other writing does.
> In what way are the two senses of God's "word" related to one
> another and to human beings in history?

vice versa. In the same way, the media of communication structure the game-like patterns of communication.

The second reason why common sense is such a poor guide to interpersonal communication is specific to the media of communication. Common sense is always grounded in the past, and the recent past in the United States was framed by the medium of print. From its beginning to sometime in the twentieth century, the United States was distinguished among the nations of the world by its literacy. In this sense, literacy means not only the percent of its population that can read but also the percent that does in fact read and the extent to which the public discourse is structured by print as the medium of communication (Postman 1985, Chapter 3).

The common sense we inherited is a poor guide for understanding interpersonal communication because conversations are oral, and common sense, that of my generation at least, reflects a mentality structured around print.

In his analysis of the famous debates between Abraham Lincoln and Stephen Douglas in 1858, Postman (1985, pp. 44–49) noted that both spoke for hours at a time, used complex sentences, convoluted arguments, and sophisticated vocabulary.

> *For all of the hoopla and socializing surrounding the event, the speakers had little to offer, and audiences little to expect, but language. And the language that was offered was clearly modeled on the style of the written word. . . . [Their] language was pure print. That the occasion required it to be spoken aloud cannot obscure that fact. And that the audience was able to process it through the ear is remarkable only to people whose culture no longer resonates powerfully with the printed word. (Postman 1985, pp. 48, 49).*

To the extent that our common sense is based on print, it creates a particular set of habits of mind that Postman (1985, p. 63) called "exposition."

> *Exposition is a mode of thought, a method of learning, and a means of expression. Almost all of the characteristics we associate with mature discourse were amplified by typography, which has the strongest possible bias toward exposition: a sophisticated ability to think conceptually, deductively and sequentially; a high valuation of reason and order; an abhorrence of contradiction; a large capacity for delayed response.*

All of these features are quite different from the bias of oral speech.

In his analysis of orality, Walter Ong (1982, pp. 8–9) noted that people in nonliterate cultures think and converse differently than do literates. Further, he argued that they think differently *because* they converse differently. Finally, people who are primarily oral learn differently than literates; in fact they do not "study" at all!

> *All thought . . . is to some degree analytic: it breaks its materials into various components. But abstractly sequential, classificatory, explanatory examination of phenomena or of stated truths is impossible without writing and reading. Human beings in primary oral cultures, those untouched by writing in any form, learn a great deal and possess and practice great wisdom, but they do not "study."*
>
> *They learn by apprenticeship—hunting with experienced hunters, for example—by discipleship, which is a kind of apprenticeship, by listening, by repeating what they hear, by mastering proverbs and ways of combining and recombining them, by assimilating other formulatory materials, by participating in a kind of corporate retrospection—not by study in the strict sense.*

To understand interpersonal communication, and particularly to understand speech acts, we need to understand the characteristics of oral speech as the medium of conversation. That is not always easy; our literateness (or our orientation to the electronic media) is so deeply engrained that we see *through* it rather than seeing it. "We—readers of books such as this—are so literate that it is very difficult for us to conceive of an oral universe of communication or thought except as a variant of a literate universe" (Ong 1982, p. 4).

Do you know people who speak print? Or who re-enact films in their conversations? Or whose conversations are oral translations of a computer electronic mail? These translations from one medium into another are curious and perhaps important objects in our social worlds, but let's look now at the characteristic of the oral medium of communication as such.

Presentness

Oral communication is characterized by *presentness*. A word disappears even as it is spoken. The first part of a word or utterance must become silent so that the second can be heard. A written page captures words, preserves them, and displays them, much like butterflies are mounted in a museum. You can turn back a page to reread what you missed when your attention lapsed, or you can turn forward a few pages to see "who done it" or where the argument is going. You cannot do that in oral speech; you must hear what is said *now;* the speaker controls the pace of the conversation; and you must attend to it as it happens.

Counterpoint 3.7

In the "Narrative" section, I said: "The common sense we inherited is a poor guide to understanding interpersonal communication because conversations are oral and that common sense, that of my generation, at least, reflects a mentality structured around print."

I think that I can argue convincingly that a common sense based on print is a poor guide for understanding interpersonal communication. For example, the Austin/Searle approach to speech acts is a careful articulation of a thoroughly literate, or print-based way of understanding speech acts. Their literateness goes far beyond the examples they use, of course, but it is evidenced by the fact that Austin and Searle seldom distinguish between a printed sentence on a page and a spoken utterance in a conversation. In fact, in Searle's later work, he seems to focus on sentences far more than speech.

But is it accurate to characterize contemporary common sense as literate? Common sense changes (although it does not usually represent itself as changing), and the series of revolutions in which we live are having a major impact on what seems "normal" to us—that is, to our common sense.

With incredible rapidity, contemporary United States society is changing from one that uses print as its medium of choice for a broad range of communication events to one that uses a cluster of electronic media, including television, audio and video tape, computers, and new technologies not yet on the shelf, even in the specialty stores. My generation was clearly literate (in the sense of having its consciousness shaped by print media). I believe that the current generation of 18- to 25-year-olds is mixed: while some are "literate" (in this specific sense), an increasing percentage are not. I do not mean that this group cannot read; I mean that their consciousness is shaped by film, television, audio recordings, electronic bulletin boards, ham radio, photography, and virtual reality rather than by print. Even the use of written language is different now than it was 50 years ago. Is word processing on a computer the same as writing by hand or printing a pamphlet or book? Is your ability to do desk-top publishing for a club newsletter or your term paper the same activity as what HarperCollins does when it publishes a book? I think they are clearly different and that no one knows just what is the extent and significance of the differences.

As far as I know, there is no good way to measure oral, literate, and (shall we say) electronically shaped consciousness, and thus I cannot offer empirical proof that common sense is changing. What I can do is note that I perceive myself more and more in intercultural communication when I talk with people 25 years younger than I am. This does not mean that we cannot understand each other or have a good time; it does mean that we have to recognize that our consciousnesses are differently shaped.

If any of this is true, then it creates a truely amusing spectacle. Here I am, a literate person, writing (!) for people, many of whose consciousness have been shaped by the electronic media, about oral communication! Such is life in periods of cultural revolution.

Even if common sense is changing because it is based on electronic media of communication rather than print, this does not invalidate my original claim. I'm not sure just what might be the content of a common sense fashioned on the enabling infrastructure of the electronic media, but it will surely be different than that based on oral speech. For that reason, it will continue to be a poor guide to understanding interpersonal communication, although perhaps for different reasons than those that make a print-based common sense is a poor guide.

Personalness

Oral communication is characterized by *personalness.* That is, the whole self of the conversants is involved. When I write this book, all you have of me are the words I used. You do not hear the sound of my voice, see the expressions on my face, watch the changes in my posture—you do not even see my handwriting because all of this is set in very clear typeface by people neither of us know. When you read this book, you can do so alone in your room with your feet propped up, chewing gum, and listening to radio—a form of behavior that I would find rude if you and I were engaged in oral conversation. Interpersonal communication involves far more of us as persons than any other form of communication.

Responsiveness

Oral communication is characterized by *responsiveness.* One of my chief frustrations in writing this book is that it consists of an incredibly long communicative "turn" that is unbroken by your response. This book would be very different if you could say or show that you did not understand the discussion on polysemy (I would then try to clarify) or that you immediately grasped the structure of the "Serpentine model" of conversation (I would then have moved on more quickly) or that you have an experience that enriches the discussion of "scripts" (I might even shut up and listen).

Walter Ong (1982) noted that the development of the printing press made possible a significant social change. When manuscripts were rare and expensive and not very many people could read, the repositories of knowledge and information in any society were specific people—the elders or priests. If you wanted to learn what your society knew, you had to consult them. Further, you had to do so in a personal, responsive, real-time conversation with them. Notice how this social structure fosters conservatism: the elders not only controlled what information was disseminated by choosing what to tell whom but they were also necessarily involved in the conversations in which would-be radicals, innovators, and change agents learned what they needed to know. When literacy became common and books relatively cheap, libraries and bookstores became the repositories of our culture's knowledge. You can take a book to a private place and there learn from, argue with, or even make fun of authors without having to engage in conversational triplets with them. This greatly increases your freedom to think independently.

Multichannelled

Oral communication is *multichannelled*. The human voice is a marvelous instrument. When you speak, you do far more than simply pronounce words. The quality of your voice, the rate of your speech, the accent with which you pronounce words, and the inflections of your voice all comprise messages that constitute interpersonal communication. In addition, your facial expressions, body posture, gestures, even the extent to which you touch or do not touch your interlocutor is part of the conversation. Communication theorists Mark Knapp and Judith Hall (1992, p. 4) noted that "(1) while we are in the presence of another person, we are constantly giving signals about our attitudes, feelings, and personality; and (2) others may become particularly adept at sensing and interpreting these signals."

A great deal of research has been done on nonverbal communication, most of which exploits a thoroughly literate form of consciousness that first divides words or verbal communication from nonverbal channels or cues of communication. For example, Judy Burgoon (1980, p. 184) first separated verbal and nonverbal channels of communication and then differentiated visual and vocal cues in the nonverbal channels. Reviewing the research, she concluded that "the nonverbal channels carry more information and are believed more than the verbal band, and that visual cues generally carry more weight than vocal ones."

Such separations can be done using various research procedures, such as band-pass filters of aural recordings, and they function to demonstrate the importance of voice, face, posture, and the like, but are these *separate* from verbal communication? Well, on a printed page, perhaps so. The words are all in a neat row and figures and margins surround them. But in oral speech, there can be no words without voice, and voice is not separated from the face, posture, and gesture of the speaker. Knapp and Hall (1992, p. 38) advised, "Nonverbal communication should not be studied as an isolated phenomenon, but as an inseparable part of the total communication process." They repeated a comment attributed to Ray Birdwhistell, a pioneer in this research tradition: "studying *nonverbal* communication is like studying *non-cardiac* physiology" (Knapp and Hall 1992, p. 5).

The multiple channels of oral speech include at least six distinguishable aspects. These include 1) the communication environment or setting, including the use of objects; 2) the communicators' physical appearance, including clothing, make-up, scars, and insignia; 3) the use of social and personal space (technically, proxemics); 4) body movements or gestures (technically, kinesics); 5) nonverbal properties of the voice (technically, paralanguage); and 6) the use of time, including turn taking in conversation and punctuality and tardiness in keeping appointments.

British social psychologist Michael Argyle (1988) said that nonverbal communication serves four functions: expressing emotion, conveying interpersonal attitudes (like/dislike, dominance/submission), presenting one's personality to others, and accompanying speech for the purposes of managing such elements as turn taking, feedback, and attention.

Nonverbal communication is particularly important in evoking and responding to definitions of identity and relationship. The eyes, someone once said, are the windows of the soul. If so, then the voice is, ah, so to speak, the voice of the soul and the face is the face of the soul. Because interpersonal communication is oral, one of its distinctive features is the importance of vocal and facial cues. A glance, a tone of voice or an inflection can completely change the meaning of what is said.

Hundreds of studies have been done that describe particular aspects of nonverbal communication. For example, middle-class white Americans generally do not look each other in the eyes when they converse; instead, they look at each other's face somewhere near the eyes. Direct eye-to-eye gaze occurs in highly intimate relationships, in episodes in which dominance is being asserted, and in episodes in which one or both is being aggressive (Scheflen 1973, p. 65). But we also know that almost all of these nonverbal patterns varies across cultures and that there are many exceptions to each generalization that is offered.

Rather than memorize long lists of what generally happens, your ability as a communicator is better served if you develop a keen sensitivity to the multiple channels of communication in interpersonal communication. Do some people watching and single out each of the five categories of nonverbal communication listed above. Practice focusing on each of them in turn until you get to the point where you can look at them as they fit together into patterns.

Interactive

More so than any other medium, oral communication is *interactive*. In conversation, the interlocutors exchange the roles of speaker and listener. Ong (1982, p. 176) said

> *To speak, you have to address another or others. People in their right minds do not stray through the woods just talking at random to nobody. Even to talk to yourself you have to pretend that you are two people. The reason is that what I say depends on what reality or fancy I feel I am talking into, that is, on what possible responses I might anticipate. . . . To speak, I have to be somehow already in*

communication with the mind I am to address before I start speaking. . . . Human communication is never one-way. Always, it not only calls for response but is shaped in its very form and content by anticipated response.

Even in more one-sided oral communication situations, such as public speaking, the very presence and activity of the audience affects all but the most stilted speakers. In public events, the restlessness of the audience (expressed in the buzz of conversation, the frequency and pattern of coughing, and the shuffling of feet and shifting of position) creates a continual feedback channel that becomes part of the speaker's consciousness and shapes the speech. Conversants are never silent; even when they are not talking, they are producing messages that are part of the conversation. Research has shown that we make very subtle facial expressions without being aware of doing so, and that we respond to those facial expressions made by others, again without being aware that we have done so, and on this basis, we judge that the other is fascinated or bored by what we are saying, that the other understands or is confused, that the other is listening or daydreaming—judgments which greatly affect the way the conversation continues.

Competence in Making Speech Acts

Speech acts are co-constructed. That means that we are always involved as a participant in constructing the speech acts in which we live. The most exciting implication of this is that we always have some power to shape, change, or direct the development of those speech acts. To be sure, we cannot control them unilaterally, but neither are we helpless. In this section, I hope to help you discover openings in the conversations in which you participate; by acting into these openings, you can exercise power in the shaping of the events and objects of your social worlds.

In Chapter 2, you learned to distingish two forms of competence: game playing and game mastery. Using this distinction, we can identify the skills we need to discern the logics of meaning and action in the process by which speech acts are co-constructed. Some of these are the skills required to move effectively *within* the game-like patterns of social interaction in which you find yourself. However, sometimes you encounter a stacked deck, a rigged game, a logic of meaning and action in which you cannot "win." In these situations, you need to exercise game mastery.

Game Playing: Co-Constructing Speech Acts within Logics of Meaning and Action

It is important to remember that there is no final list of all the speech acts that can be performed, and no authoritative list of how to perform them.

Competence in performing speech acts is more a matter of negotiating or dancing with your interlocutors than it is looking up a definition in a dictionary for how to spell a word, or consulting a rule book to see how to play baseball.

All people who engage in conversations participate in the performance of speech acts. They differ, however, in many ways.

- People vary in the range of speech acts that they can, or normally do, perform. Some people just do not know how to perform "apology"; some people cannot allow themselves to be "complimented."
- People vary in the gracefulness and variety with which they perform particular speech acts. Some people know how to say "I love you" in a thousand ways, each more delicate and subtle than the single way that others have of blurting out a profession of affection.
- People vary in their sensitivity to other's initiatives and resistences in the performance of particular speech acts. A skillful therapist or negotiator senses the act that a conversant wants to avoid performing; successful salespersons learn to maneuver their interlocutors into positions where they want to perform precisely the speech act that enhances the salesperson's commission. Other people seem resolutely oblivious to the possibilities in particular interactions, or to the intentions of those with whom they communicate.
- People vary in the specific "rules" they know for how to perform particular speech acts. That is, some people would perform a "promise" by swearing by a diety; others would find such an oath evidence that the other is insincere.
- People differ in their openness to new information and to variation in the ways in which specific speech acts can be performed. For some people, there is one way to do an apology and nothing else counts; others are far more adaptable.

Awareness of language.   A certain kind of mindfulness or awareness of the uses of language increases your competence in performing speech acts. Reflecting the old adage that fish are the last to discover the existence of water because they are always surrounded by it, children are nurtured in a social womb of conversation, and must learn to be mindful of it. In her book, *Children's Minds,* Margaret Donaldson (1988, p. 90) said

> . . . *the normal child comes to school with well-established skills as a thinker. But his thinking is* directed outwards *on to the real, meaningful, shifting, distracting world. What is going to be required for success in our educational system is that he should learn to turn language and thought in upon themselves. . . . He must become able not just to talk but to choose what he will say, not just to interpret but to weigh possible interpretations. . . . Now the principal symbolic system to which the preschool child has access is oral language. So the first step is the step of conceptualizing language—becoming aware of it as a separate structure, freeing it from its embeddedness in events.*

This awareness of language can be accomplished in many ways, including playing word games with children or by teaching them to read. However acquired, "It is clear that being aware of language as a distinct system is relevant to the business of separating what is *said* from what is done or from what is somehow salient in a situation" (Donaldson, 1988, p. 95).

Awareness of the *uses* of language as a distinct system for doing things is the first step in increasing one's competence in performing speech acts. The second step is to develop a sensitivity to the multiple layers of each speech act. Every action in a speech act has multiple potential meanings; as the communication triplet is completed, many of these meanings are eliminated, and others are made real by the interaction. The most skilled conversationalists are sensitive to the array of potential meanings they create by performing specific actions and how that array differs from that created by other actions that they chose not to perform.

Logics of message design. Barbara O'Keefe (1988) differentiated three ways in which people invent the next message in the co-construction of a speech act. She called them "logics of message design" and labeled them "expressive," "conventional," and "rhetorical."

Assume that you are participating in a conversation. It is your turn to speak, and you have a conflict between saying one thing that will satisfy your personal goals and saying another that will be considerate and polite to others.

- If you are following an *expressive* system of designing your messages, the appropriate maxim is "be tactful." You will say what will get what you want while at the same time editing your message a bit or distorting the truth somewhat so as to avoid unnecessary rudeness.
- If you are following a *conventional* system, the appropriate maxim is "be polite." You will likely use apologies, compliments, hedges, or excuses in the statement you make so as to avoid rudeness.
- If you are following a *rhetorical* system, the appropriate maxim is "be someone else." You may change your sense of what you wanted, you may cast yourself in a different role in which there is no conflict between your wants and the other's feelings, or you may urge the other people to change their definitions of the situation so that you don't hurt their feelings.

O'Keefe believes that these three logics of message design comprise a natural developmental progression, at least in contemporary society. That is, she believes that children are naturally *expressive*. As they grow older and learn more about communication and about other people, they shift into a *conventional* mode of relating to other people and participating in the construction of speech acts. Finally, if they learn still more, they change again into *rhetorical* logics. However, she allows for the fact that not everyone goes through this sequence.

Refrain 3.1

O'Keefe's theory of three "logics of message design:"

The *expressive* logic of message design:

- Views communication as only a way to express one's thoughts
- Values clarity of expression
- Is oriented to the past
- Focuses on editing what is said as the way of making the message more effective

The *conventional* logic of message design:

- Views communication as a cooperative, rule-governed game
- Values "fitting-in" and doing what is appropriate
- Is oriented to the present
- Focuses on the management of personal relations as the means of making the message more effective

The *rhetorical* logic of message design:

- Views communication as a creative process in which selves and situations are negotiated
- Values flexibility and sophistication
- Is oriented to the future
- Focuses on redefining the context as a way of making messages more effective

Adapted from O'Keefe (1988, p. 85)

Because "social environments can differ systematically in their representation of particular message design logics, and this will have consequences for individual development . . . communication is not necessarily a uniform process" (O'Keefe 1988, p. 89). That is, in some social groups, the rhetorical logic of message design will appear slippery and unethical, whereas in others it will appear sophisticated and functional. In groups of college-aged adults, all three logics can be found in conversations. It is likely that individual communicators shift among these logics as they move from one situation to another.

Conversational implicature and indirect speech acts.   Participating in the co-construction of speech acts requires the ability to hear what is not said and to take note of what is not done. Conversants seldom say all that they expect to be heard as having said, and they sometimes say something quite different from what they expect to be heard as having said. The remark-

Counterpoint 3.8

O'Keefe (1988) found that college-aged adults differ in the logic of message design that they use in conversations. She believes that the social worlds into which children are enmeshed are not all alike, and that some social worlds favor the development of expressive, some conventional, and some rhetorical logics of message design.

In a study of 97 students in an introductory speech communication course at a large midwestern state university, she found that women were more likely than men to use rhetorical message design. Does this suggest that the social worlds of midwestern Americans are gender inflected in such a way that men are taught, encouraged, or allowed to be more expressive or conventional and women taught, encouraged, or allowed to be more rhetorical in their conversational styles? Two important recent books have documented differences in the cognitive and communicative styles of adult men and women: Carol Gilligan's (1982) *In a Different Voice* and Deborah Tannen's (1990) *You Just Don't Understand*. If we link O'Keefe's description of these logics of message design to the Heyerdahl solution, has she given us a plausible account of the process by which these differences are made?

O'Keefe also found that these college-aged students differed in "cognitive complexity," or the number of categories that they use in their perception of their social worlds. (Recall the activity in the Praxis section of Chapter 2, in which you divided your social worlds into stacks of index cards, each naming a conversation. "Cognitive complexity" is something like the number of different stacks of cards needed to sort out these conversations.) She found that both men and women who were highest on her measure of cognitive complexity were more likely to use the rhetorical logic of message design; those who scored lower were more likely to use expressive and conventional logics.

What conclusion should we draw from this finding? O'Keefe suggested that young adults who live in more complex social worlds tend to use the rhetorical logic more than those whose social worlds are less complex. But what implications does this have? If we assume that a highly industrialized, urban, media-saturated social environment is more complex than a bucolic, rural, less informationally saturated environment, is the rhetorical logic of message design correlated with a particular social structure? Does it mean that changing social structures imply changes in the forms of conversations? Are some patterns of social prejudice and difficulty in understanding each other the result of conversants who use (and appreciate) different logics of message design, and are those differences the appropriate result of social structures? Or is this line of reasoning getting too close to a social determinism? Is it the individual's responsibility to develop his or her own logics of message design regardless of the social context in which he or she lives?

able thing about all of this is that the conversations usually turn out all right because we know how to perform some speech acts indirectly and how to hear what is *implied* (i.e., the conversational implicature) but not *stated* in a conversation.

> *Bill:* Are you going to the party tonight?
> *Jane:* Is the Pope Catholic?
> *Bill:* I'll pick you up about 8.

What has the Pope's religion to do with the party? You probably have no difficulty in discerning that the speech act Jane (and Bill) performed was an *answer* (although it has the grammatical form of a question), and that it was a strongly affirmative answer.

Indirect speech acts are those performed by doing something other than what we say we are doing. We understand them because we engage in *conversational implicature*. The speech act answer is performed indirectly in the conversational excerpt above by what has the grammatical form of a question. The question "Is the Pope Catholic?" is such an inquiry that it signals that something special is going on; specifically, the answer to the question is such an obvious "Yes! Of course!" that the question itself is heard as an emphatic answer to the inquiry about Jane and the party.

If I ask you for directions to the store, you will probably give me as much information as I need, but no more. You will make judgments about how much background information I have and rely on me to combine that information with what you tell me. For example, you might say, "It's at Wabash and Chicago, one block east of State," leaving me to figure out that to get there, I have to go north, then west; that Wabash and Chicago are streets; that they intersect at right angles; and that Wabash Street is the East/West divider in Chicago. You also leave me to figure out on which corner of Wabash and Chicago Loyola University's new library is located. You do this because you assume that both of us are trying to be cooperative, and that I am reasonably knowledgeable about Chicago and normally competent to find my way around. My task is to perform conversational implicature by adding all the necessary information that you did not present. If all this goes well, we have successfully enacted the speech act "giving directions."

However, you can perform some other kind of speech act if you present me with too little information. "What is 'Wabash and Chicago?' " I might ask, telling you that I cannot perform the necessary conversational implicature. We might call this speech act "mystification"; perhaps it is a subtle form of putting me down by displaying my ignorance. By forcing me to ask the question "What is 'Wabash and Chicago?' " you reveal me as an outsider.

Another kind of speech act can be performed indirectly if you give me too much information. For example, if you begin your directions like this, "Well, 'Wabash' and 'Chicago' are streets in Chicago. They run perpendicular to each other . . ." I am likely to be offended. By *not* expecting that I will do normal conversational implicature, I take it that you are treating me as ignorant, needing the verbal equivalent of someone holding my hand while crossing the street.

Conversations can also go astray if you supply the wrong information. In her book, *The Kitchen God's Wife,* Amy Tan (1991) describes a scene in which a Chinese-American woman brought her Anglo-American boyfriend to her parents' house for dinner. Her mother, who prided herself for her cooking ability, prepared her "special" dish. Following the family custom, however, when she served the food she complained that the dish was not well cooked. This was the cue for the family to taste and exclaim how wonderful it was, persuading the mother that she had actually excelled even her own high standards. Unfortunately, Rich did not understand this ritual. When his girlfriend's mother apologized for her poor cooking, he tasted it and graciously suggested that it would not be too bad if liberally seasoned with soy sauce—which he proceeded to pour onto his serving. Although well-intended, the speech act that he actually performed was a tremendous insult.

Active listening.   Sometimes we think that listening is passive, that all we have to do to listen is to pay attention. It is more useful to distinguish mere hearing from listening, and to view listening as a very active process.

Conversational implicature is one form of the activity involved in listening. Because speakers seldom say everything they expect to be heard as having said, we have to supply the missing information. We can do this by conversational implicature, cognitively "completing" or supplementing what we heard; we can also do it conversationally, asking for the relevant information that we need. The fact that listening is inherently active, however, means that if we want to, we can misunderstand any speaker, no matter how hard he or she tries to be clear.

Here are three forms of active listening that produce misunderstanding.

1. We can simply be too frugal with our conversational implicature. That is, we do not work hard enough to supply missing information. When told where the store is, we do not ask for or supply the information that would make what the speaker said an adequate instruction.
2. We can obsfucate. That is, we can supply the wrong information, or we can ask questions that lead to information unrelated to what we need to know in order to follow the instructions given us.
3. We can filter what we hear through a defensive perceptual climate. If we have already decided that the other person is "out to get us" somehow, then we will perceive threats no matter what is said. If we distrust the other, anything they say or do—including promises to be trustworthy—will appear sinister and insincere. There is a self-fulfilling prophecy in this, of course, because by responding to the other as untrustworthy or hostile, we can *make* them into what we

perceive them to be. Paranoids are often correct: other people don't like them and are hostile toward them. The question is whether the paranoid correctly *perceived* a state of affairs or *called it into being*.

Part of active listening consists of asking questions that lead the speaker to supply the information that you want or need. Such questions are not always easily framed; it takes a certain skill in posing questions that are precisely targeted to get the information you want and encourage the other person to speak openly. For example, "Huh?" is not a very sophisticated way of saying, "I do not understand; could you repeat what you said?" "Where's that?" is less precise than "I know where Wabash Street is; is Chicago north or south of the river?" "That's interesting! Is it near the Water Tower?" is more likely to invite fuller descriptions than "Can't you be more precise than that?"

Another aspect of active listening consists of calling your own perceptions into question. To what extent are you *projecting* rather than *perceiving* what is being said? To what extent are you involved in the co-construction of what you hear? Simply by posing these questions, you open yourself up to a healthy curiosity that will improve your ability to listen.

Game Mastery: Going Outside the Logics of Meaning and Action in the Co-Construction of Speech Acts

As a conversation goes on, the logic of meaning and action often seems to become more restrictive. You often feel that you *must* act in a particular way, even if you do not want to and doing so will frustrate accomplishing your goals.

Refrain 3.2

Communication theorists say that speech acts are "intentional"; that is, they refer to something "beyond" themselves. More precisely, each act within a conversational triplet occurs in the context of the triplet as a whole.

Or so it seems. In fact, the "first" act in the triplet assumes, more or less explicitly, what the second and third will be and thus acts into a context that does not (yet) exist. In the same way, the "second" act in the triplet charts a trajectory of intentions between the first and the second and presumes that the "third" act will "complete" this trajectory.

Shifting to the first person perspective, competence of the "game playing" sort consists of being able to identify the logic that connects the three acts and the ability to perform the appropriate act appropriately. This sort of competence is usually easiest when performing the "third" act in a sequence, because you have two other acts on which to base your perception of what is happening. It is more difficult in the "second" place, and, paradoxically, most difficult in the "first" act of the sequence. When you are performing the "first" act, you have too many degrees of freedom; you have to act in such a way that your interlocutor can discern the pattern and respond appropriately.

Competence of the "game mastery" sort consists of being able to identify the logic that connects the three acts and the ability to perform an inappropriate act (that is, one that does *not* "fit into" this logic) appropriately (that is, so that it makes sense, but a different kind of sense).

The ability to discern this logic of meaning and action is part of the skill necessary for the kind of competence described as *game playing*. If you cannot discern and follow the rules, then you cannot participate in the coherent production of normal conversations.

However, there are times when you should select or change the games being played, not just act as others expect you to. In these situations, you need the ability to engage in game mastery.

In the co-construction of speech acts, game mastery means performing an action that fits into the emerging logic of meaning and action well enough that it is treated as a part of what is being done, but sufficiently different from that logic so that it transforms the act from one thing to another. If the act that you do is too different, it will stop the conversation and bewilder the other conversants. On the other hand, if the act is not different enough, it will be subsumed into the logic, perpetuating what you were trying to change.

Two concepts that you are already familiar with help in the discussion of game mastery: the conversational triplet (page 121) and the atomic model of communication (Figure 1.5). If we put them together, we get a schematic for thinking about the possible connections among the actions in a speech act. That is, the first act in the conversational triplet is simultaneously a statement about the speaker and a request for the other conversant to take complimentary positions on each of the elements of the atomic model: the episode they are enacting, their relationship, their identities, and their cultures. The rule of thumb for game mastery is to take the complimentary position on at least one of these elements and to take noncomplimentary positions on at least one other. Following this rule of thumb, the competent communicator will make a statement in the second position in the conversational triplet that for example, responds within the logic of meaning and action with respect to their relationship but sharply breaks that logic with respect to the episode that they are enacting.

Bill says, "Jane, you don't understand physics; let me help you with your homework." This action simultaneously

- Comprises the *speech act* "offer to help"
- Defines *Bill's identity* as responsible and competent
- Defines *Jane's identity* as incompetent, needing help
- Defines the *episode* as one of helping
- Defines their *relationship* as asymmetrical, with Bill as the caretaker and Jane as the cared for
- Defines the *task* as preparing for a physics exam

This action is not complete until it is joined by Jane's response. She may need the help but not want to accept the definition of herself or of their relationship that Bill offered. As a result, she may

- Swallow her pride and say, "Thanks. I really do need the help," thus participating in the co-construction of an unwanted identity and relationship
- Stiffen her resolve and say, "No way, buddy. I am not your inferior. I will take responsibility for my own performance in physics."
- Use a more sophisticated technique that allows her to accept some but not all of his definition of the conversation, such as saying "Thanks, I do need help in physics, but I will let you help me only if you will let me help you in your history assignment, where you need a lot of assistance."

Here is another example of game mastery in co-constructing speech acts.

Juan: Would you like to buy a beautiful present for your wife?
Carlos: No! If I did, she would think that I had done something wrong and was trying to apologize.
Juan: But I have these beautiful pearl necklaces at a great price.
Carlos: Yeah, I wish I could help you out, buddy, but it would ruin my marriage if I did. You understand, huh? Better luck next time.

In this conversation, Carlos successfully avoids participating in the performance of a sales presentation. Carlos' "trick"—or game mastery—is very obvious, but let us use it as an example for thinking through the ways Carlos discerns what is going on and selects his response.

Using Figure 3.1, imagine a series of lines connecting Juan's first statement to Carlos's response. Each line represents one of the many meanings of the utterance "Would you like to buy . . ." This utterance is located in the context of the *episode* that Juan and Carlos are engaged in; in the *relationship between Juan and Carlos* (Are they strangers on the street, old friends, business associates?); in the *relationships between Juan and everyone else he knows* (does he have a wife? If so, has he bought a necklace for her? Why is he trying to sell them instead of giving them to his wife?); in *Juan's identity*

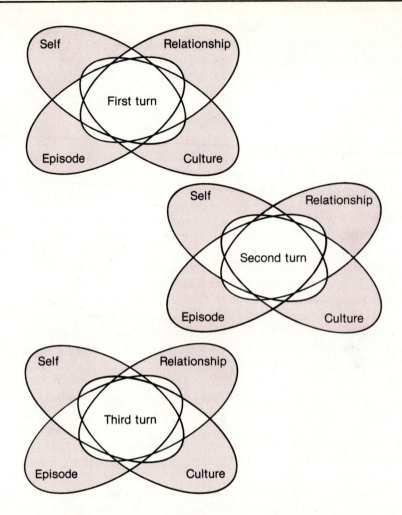

Figure 3.1
An integration of the conversational triplet and the atomic model.

(Is he normally a salesperson?); in *Juan's perception of Carlos' identity;* and in the *social/cultural context* (and perhaps in other conversations as well—this is an open-ended list). Each of these multiple meanings presents an opening, or opportunity for game mastery.

■ Are all of these meanings consistent with each other? If not, Carlos might exploit the conflicts among them. For example, he might choose to misunderstand what he is being asked to do—perhaps he might take the question to be a philosophical inquiry ("Ah, that is the question, is it not? How more beautiful to give than to receive . . .") or an insult ("What do you think I am, a brute? Of course . . .").

■ Not all of these meanings are of equal importance. Carlos might guess which are most salient to Juan and deliberately respond to one of the least important.

Juan may have defined his relationship to Carlos as "salesmen-client." In the context of this relationship, he disguised his motive of separating Carlos from his money by cloaking it in the appearance of a friend being helpful. Carlos thwarted Juan's attempt by selecting the (pretended) friendship and treating it as if it were the most important context. Within this context, Carlos argued, purchasing the expensive gift would be a terrible thing, one that his friend Juan would not like to see. Thus, Carlos claimed, he had to keep his money in his pocket in order to spare Juan the burden of seeing his friend Carlos's marriage destroyed.

A Final Word: Empowerment in Speech Acts

Throughout history, men and women have struggled for power. Usually, they have committed what I would like to call the *objectivist fallacy*. That is, they have confused power with the possession of various objects, such as money, guns, muscle, or votes. By stressing communication, we view these things in terms of the production of speech acts, and we are repeatedly brought back to the realization that speech acts are co-constructed. Money equals power only when other people allow it to sway them, guns can kill but not coerce people unafraid to die, and votes only count when people choose to count them.

The "reality" of power is not these external trappings of inequitable access to cultural resources, but the positions in the moral order into which we are cast. The mechanism by which power is exercised consists of our being excluded from participation in the speech acts that define our lives or of our being compelled to participate in speech acts that injure or offend us.

The fact that we are all involved in the co-construction of the speech acts that constitute our social worlds has far-reaching implications. For one, it means that we have sources of power that are often obscured. If we are competent enough to do game mastery, we can exert far more influence on the acts that involve us than we might expect. Another implication has to do with the attribution of praise or blame. We tend to identify individuals as the proper recipients of criticism or valorization. Instead, we should see that heroes as well as villains are a part of complicated social dances in which the speech acts they perform are co-constructed with others. Rather than making us incapable of praising or blaming, this insight should focus us on social systems and on patterns of interaction rather than on single individuals or single actions. Finally, aware of our involvement in co-constructing the speech acts within which we live, we should have heightened sensitivity to the moral orders that restrict or compel our participation in the performance of particular speech acts.

The net effect of these three implications is to suggest a source of empowerment. We are full-fledged participants in the creation of the universes in which we live. No one else has exactly the same position within these social worlds as we do, and that confers on us both power and opportunity.

Praxis

1. Making Speech Acts

Speech acts are made when the actions of two or more people combine in certain ways. It would be hard to exaggerate the importance of your ability to affect what speech acts are made in your conversations. Literally, the quality of your life consists of the speech acts in which you participate. The purpose of this exercise is to give you some practice in taking an active, assertive role in making speech acts.

You will experience crucial moments in your life when it is absolutely necessary that one speech act and not another is made. The activities suggested here deal with less stressful speech acts, but they should develop a sense of how to assert yourself that you can use in other occasions when more is at stake.

Doing the Same Thing in Different Ways

Many speech acts are routine; you and your conversant can coordinate your actions by following a cultural script. For example, the speech act "greeting" can be performed without much thought if two conversants enact this conversation:

> "Good morning!"
> > "Hi! How are you?"
> "Fine, and you?"
> > "Good, thanks."

(Note: there are *two* conversational triplets in this conversation.)

One of the nice things about these fully scripted, conventional routines for performing speech acts is that they permit artistic embellishments! That is, you can say things that are *not* part of the routine that will be *heard as* part of the routine with the *addition* of your own personality or a bit of cheery cleverness. For example,

> "Good morning."
> > "It is, and so am I!"
> "Well, how am I?"
> > "You are doing very well! Congratulations!"

Before class. Make a list of common, routine speech acts. You might start with promise, insult, compliment, warn, and inform.

In class. Form groups of two persons. With your partner, practice performing these speech acts. First perform them following the routine sequence of statements, then begin to embellish them with unconventional ways of doing the same thing. Have fun! Be inventive! Help each other out by responding to statements, no matter how outlandish, in ways that "make" them into the speech act you are intending to produce. Record or remember your best ways of doing these things and demonstrate them to other groups.

Making a Speech Act without Cooperation

Sometimes you will want to produce a speech act that is different from the one that someone else wants to make, or you will want to prevent someone from making a speech act in which you do not want to participate. A man is walking down a dark alley late at night. Well-dressed, he is carrying a briefcase and looks prosperous. Suddenly an unshaven thug with a gun jumps out of the shadows and says:

> "Your money or your life!"
>> "No, no, no! You are doing it all wrong! Look at you, hunched over and speaking in a pinched voice. You must relax and speak more authoritatively. Now, repeat what you said."
> "I said, your money or your life!"
>> "Right. You are putting the emphasis on the wrong syllable. Say it this way: 'your money *or* your life!' It sounds more menacing that way. And relax! Lower your shoulders and use that nice bass voice to full advantage. Now, back to the shadows and good luck!"

(Note: I offer as an example for classroom discussion, not as advice about how to handle this situation.) The well-dressed man successfully blocked the attempt to make the speech act "robbery" by transforming it into "instruction." When the would-be robber said "Your money or your life" the second time, it was a form of "practice."

In class. Work in groups of three or four people. Take the same list of speech acts that you used before, and practice performing them again. This time, however, instead of cooperating with each other, try to prevent each other from producing the speech act that your partner wants. Again, be playful and have fun. Here are some variations that you might want to use.

King of the Mountain

One conversant announces the speech act that she or he wants to produce and makes a statement; another conversant replies in a way that attempts to prevent that speech act from occurring; the first completes the conversational triplet with a statement that tries to bring the announced speech act into being. The other members of the group decide whether the speech act was brought off or not. (Do you find that there are some kinds of statements that are more powerful than others in blocking the successful accomplishment of a speech act? Are some speech acts more difficult to accomplish without cooperation than others? Does your experience confirm the old adage that it takes two to make peace but only one to make war?)

Head-to-Head Competition

One member of your group announces the speech act that she or he wants to produce; another member announces a different speech act. These two people have a conversation in which they compete to see which speech act they can make. Again, the other members of your group act as scorekeepers.

Vary the speech acts that you attempt to perform so that you can get a strategic sense of what kinds of speech acts are more robust than others; that is, in head-to-head competition, which is easier to make than the others? Make a list of the speech acts that tend to be winners and those that usually lose in the competition. Compare these lists with those of other groups. Does this suggest anything to you about the robustness of various speech acts? What conclusions, if any, do you draw?

Be observant about the kinds of statements that succeed or fail in producing the desired speech acts. Compare these and see if you note any similarities and differences. Give particular attention to "metacommunication"' that is, statements that describe the context in which they occur. For example, these are metacommunicative statements: "I know that you are trying to make me say . . . , but I won't," and "This is a hostile, aggressive response using obscene language that indicates my unwillingness to help you in any way."

Strangers in the Night

This variation is the same as number two above except that the conversants do not tell each other what language game they are trying to make. Each conversant selects a speech act, writes it on a card, and turns it face down. They have a conversation, and the other members of the group announce what speech acts they think have been made in the conversation. The conversants then display what they have written on their cards.

This variation creates the opportunity for misdirection. Give particular attention to the form of the first statements in the conversational triplets. What kinds of statements give an advantage to the speaker?

After playing this game several times, where do you think the greatest power lies in the conversational triplet? In the first, second, or third position?

2. Nonverbal Communication in Making Speech Acts

The first activity focused on the content of statements in making speech acts, although I suspect that you also took advantage of the multiple channels of oral communication, particularly in the "Strangers in the Night" variation, where you tried to conceal your motives or deceive your partner. In this second activity, focus more specifically on the nonverbal aspects of oral speech.

Actor Vincent Price once gave a demonstration of how to make a horror film; he said that the key to provoking "horror" was a matter of subtle inflections, timing, a raised eyebrow, and a slight brandishing of props. To prove his point, he and an actress played the same scene twice. The lines were identical, but the first portrayal was of a pleasant dinner party; the other was of an ominous, frightening dinner. As Price predicted, the culmination of hundreds of tiny, virtually unnoticeable nonverbal cues made the second scene somber and menacing. His line, "Have some more of this soup. I think you will find it . . . unusual" was delivered first as a warm act of courtesy and second as a sinister act of evil.

In the "Narrative" section of this chapter, I wrote the text for several conversations in which the conversants were not clear about just what speech acts had been made. Use them like Price used the dinner scene.

Working in groups of three or four people, take turns as performers and observers. Practice performing these conversations orally. When you read them aloud, you will find that you cannot be as neutral as a printed text; the medium of speech will not allow you that distance.

Can you perform the conversation between Carl and Tom so that Carl is clearly, beyond shadow of reasonable doubt, nagging? Can you perform it so that Carl is just as clearly being helpful? Do you find that you need help from the person who is reading Tom's lines to make these speech acts?

The conversation between Anne and Tom is delightfully ambiguous. Practice reading it aloud so that you can bring out several of the possible meanings.

Take turns being conversants in this activity. When you are not one of the conversants, pay close attention to what the conversants are doing. Make a list of the six categories of nonverbal cues described in the "Narrative" section, and note what each conversant is doing in each category. Between conversations, act as coaches, advising the next pair of conversants what they might do in each category of cues to bring off the desired speech act.

You will probably exhaust the conversations written in this chapter fairly soon. When you do, improvise new conversations or use cuttings from a play as the texts.

3. Power and Speech Acts

If power is defined as your ability to perform certain speech acts, then it is clear that none of us have absolute power, but that some of us have more power than others. Children, for example, are not allowed to perform certain speech acts; they are prevented from entering into legally binding financial contracts, from marrying, from holding jobs, and—in most cases—from making important career and other life-changing decisions, such as whether to move to another state. Convicted felons are not allowed to perform the speech acts of voting, having a driver's license, or, while incarcerated, going to a shopping mall.

The difference between citizens of democracies and subjects in monarchies has to do with what speech acts are permitted and enabled. The difference between a free press and a controlled press is determined by what speech acts journalists are allowed and enabled to do.

In recent years, politics in the United States has focused on the "rights" of various groups. To my knowledge, none of the political debates has used the language game of speech acts to discuss these rights. Perhaps they should, or at least, perhaps it is worth a try.

Form groups of four to seven people. Talk about the issue of human rights; specifically, identify categories of people you think have not been treated as if they had the full complement of human rights. These categories might include racial groups, genders, age groups, people with specific traits (handicaps or disabilities), or people with different economic resources (socioeconomic class). At this point, do not get into the question of whether these groups *should* have more or fewer rights, confine yourself to the question of *whether* they have more or fewer rights.

Now, identify some of the specific speech acts that members of this group are not allowed to perform. For example, someone from a low socioeconomic class is not able to perform the speech act "buying on credit."

Next, describe just how these people are prevented from performing these speech acts. For example, bankers and retail merchants require anyone buying on credit to show that they have adequate collateral.

Finally, using the skills that you developed in the first and second activities, describe how members of these groups could be empowered to participate in the speech acts that are currently denied them. Remembering that speech acts are co-constructed, you should direct your attention both to what they can do and to what their conversants can do.

References

Argyle, Michael. *Bodily Communication,* 2nd ed. London: Methuen, 1988.

Austin, J. L. *How to Do Things with Words.* New York: Oxford University Press, 1965.

Burgoon, Judy K. "Nonverbal Communication Research in the 1970s." In *Communication Yearbook 4,* edited by Dan Nimmo. New Brunswick: Transaction Press, 1980.

Carbaugh, Donal. *Cultural Communication and Intercultural Contact.* Hillsdale: Lawrence Erlbaum, 1990.

Donaldson, Margaret. *Children's Minds.* New York: Norton, 1988.

Gilligan, Carol. *In a Different Voice: Psychological Theory and Women's Development.* Cambridge: Harvard University Press, 1982.

Gozzi, Raymond, Jr. "New Speech Act Verbs in American English." *Research on Language and Social Interaction* 24 (1990/1991): 449–459.

Hymes, Del. "Epilogue to 'The Things We Do With Words.'" In *Cultural Communication and Intercultural Contact,* edited by Donal Carbaugh, 419–430. Hillsdale: Lawrence Erlbaum, 1990.

Knapp, Mark L., and Hall, Judith A. *Nonverbal Communication in Human Interaction,* 3rd ed. Orlando: Holt, Rinehart and Winston, 1992.

Kreckel, Marga. *Communicative Acts and Shared Knowledge in Natural Discourse.* New York: Academic Press, 1981.

O'Keefe, Barbara J. "The Logic of Message Design: Individual Differences in Reasoning About Communication." *Communication Monographs* 55 (1988): 80–103.

Ong, Walter. *Orality and Literacy: The Technologizing of the Word.* London: Routledge, 1982.

Postman, Neil. *Amusing Ourselves to Death: Public Discourse in the Age of Show Business.* New York: Penguin, 1985.

Rosaldo, Michelle. *Knowledge and Passion: Ilongot Notions of Self and Social Life.* New York: Cambridge University Press, 1980.

Rosaldo, Michelle. "The Things We Do With Words: Ilongot Speech Acts and Speech Act Theory in Philosophy." In *Cultural Communication and Intercultural Contact,* edited by Donal Carbaugh, 373–408. Hillsdale: Lawrence Erlbaum, 1990.

Scheflen, Albert E. *How Behavior Means.* New York: Gordon and Breach, 1973.

Searle, John. *Speech Acts: An Essay in the Philosophy of Language.* New York: Cambridge University Press, 1969.

Searle, John. "Epilogue to the Taxonomy of Illocutionary Acts." In *Cultural Communication and Intercultural Contact,* edited by Donal Carbaugh, 409–418. Hillsdale: Lawrence Erlbaum, 1990.

Shotter, John. "Wittgenstein and Psychology: On Our 'Hook Up' to Reality." In *The Wittgenstein Centenary Lectures,* edited by A. Phillips-Griffiths, 193–208. Cambridge: Cambridge University Press, 1991.

Tan, Amy. *The Kitchen God's Wife.* New York: Putnam, 1991.

Tannen, Deborah. *You Just Don't Understand! Women and Men in Conversation.* New York: Morrow, 1990.

Taylor, Talbot J., and Cameron, Deborah. *Analyzing Conversation: Rules and Units in the Structure of Talk.* New York: Pergamon, 1987.

Thoreau, Henry David. *Walden.* Boston: Houghton Mifflin, 1957.

Wittgenstein, Ludwig. *Philosophical Investigations,* translated by G.E.M. Anscombe. Oxford: Basil Blackwell, 1958.

Wittgenstein, Ludwig. *Culture and Value.* Translated by Peter Winch. Chicago: University of Chicago Press, 1984.

Xi, Changsheng. "Communication in China: A Case Study of Chinese Collectivist and Self-Interest Talk in Social Action from the CMM Perspective." Ph.D. dissertation, University of Massachusetts, Amherst, 1991.

. . . when individuals attend to any current situation, they face the question: "What is it that's going on here?" Whether asked explicitly, as in times of confusion and doubt, or tacitly, during occasions of usual certitude, the question is put and the answer to it is presumed by the way the individuals then proceed to get on with the affairs at hand.

Goffman 1974, p. 8

[Episodes are] communicative routines which [conversants] view as distinct wholes, separate from other types of discourse, characterized by special rules of speech and nonverbal behavior and often distinguished by clearly recognizable opening or closing sequences.

Gumperz 1972, p. 17

OBJECTIVES

After reading this chapter, you will be able to

- Perceive wider arrays of options in your punctuation of episodes

- Use disclaimers, excuses, and contextual reconstruction more skillfully

- Juggle scripts, goals, and interactional contingencies with greater facility

- Identify and perhaps avoid unwanted repetitive patterns in conversations

- Understand how conversations are co-constructed by the way actions mesh into patterns

KEY WORDS AND PHRASES

Some terms that will help you understand this chapter include

punctuation, frame analysis, interaction analysis, keying, scripts, goals, rules, metacommunication, accounts, and contexts

Narrative

Walking along the sidewalk, you hear a single statement.

> *Unidentified woman's voice:* . . . don't do that again.

What more do you need to know if you are to understand what is going on in the conversation onto which you have stumbled? Obviously, you need to know the context in which the statement was made.

But what context? The "atomic model" in Figure 1.5 names five types of contexts: speech acts, episodes, relationships, selves, and cultures. Further, the model depicts these as overlapping at the point of each action, but not necessarily aligning with each other. That is, this statement—like all others—is polysemic; it is simultaneously a part of many aspects of your social worlds.

Episodes are one answer we give to the questions What is going on here? or What are we doing to each other? The vocabulary for such answers includes "watching a movie with a friend," "having dinner with my family," "studying for a test," and "just goofing off."

The fragment of conversation you heard might be part of any number of episodes. You can fit it into any of these: a mother trying to teach her daughter not to run out into the street, a wife arguing with her husband, a doctor admonishing her patient to be more careful to take his medicine, or a friend describing the dialogue from a favorite movie or soap opera. Significantly, the *meaning* of what you heard depends on which of these contexts it occurred in and on its placement within that context.

Characteristics of Episodes

Formal definitions of the term *episode* can be misleading because episodes themselves are made and are constantly in the process of being made. The best way of defining them is as a category of events and objects in our social worlds. They function as *frames* that define some things as "inside and during" the episode and others as "outside and before or after" the episode. Episodes have an internal structure. Whether rigid or flexible, they are perceived as a pattern. Episodes are made by a process called *punctuation,* in which conversants impose a set of distinctions on the ongoing stream of events, thus setting some off as bounded wholes. These wholes are episodes.

It is useful to treat episodes as if they were organized in terms of time, boundaries, and structure. In this discussion, please note that episodes are made by being *punctuated* by conversants. Duration, boundaries, and structure are not "found things" but the result of the activity of conversants.

Counterpoint 4.1

When we are in conversations, we are always playing the guessing game What episode are we doing? We interpret the meaning of what people say in terms of the episode we *think* we are enacting. Often we guess correctly; sometimes we work hard to clarify and define just what the episode is, using props (e.g., desks, contracts, or wine and soft music) as well as explicit statements ("This isn't what it seems . . ."); and sometimes we misjudge, following the wrong scripts. For example:

Little Johnny interrupted his father's reading of the Sunday newspaper by asking, "Dad, where did I come from?" Having anticipated the question with considerable dread for a long time, his father launched into the standard lecture about the birds and bees, comparative anatomy of men and women, sexual practices and the circumstances under which they were desirable, a brief history of matrimony, and a discussion—complete with visual aids—of the practices of safe sex. Exhausted, he paused for a moment and noticed that his son looked more bored than enlightened. "Well, Johnny," he asked, "do you have any more questions?" "No," Johnny replied cautiously, "Billy said that he was from Toledo and I just wondered where I came from."

Whether we guess correctly or not, our behavior is powerfully influenced by what we perceive as the context in which we act. In fact, social scientists who followed J.B. Watson's advice to take an unremitting third-person orientation to their "subjects" were surprised to find just how important were those subjects' subjective perceptions of the situations in which they found themselves. Three classic studies make the point.

■ Psychologist Stanley Milgram (1974) found that 65% of randomly selected American citizens would give near-fatal electric shocks to another person if ordered to do so by a scientific researcher. They were persuaded, apparently against their best judgment, simply by being told that "this is a scientific experiment."

■ Psychologist P. G. Zimbardo (1973) assigned college students to play the roles of prisoners and prison guards. Those assigned to be guards acted in such a tyrannical way toward those assigned to be prisoners that the experiment had to be halted.

■ Michael Argyle and B. Beit-Hallahmi (1975) studied religious sects. They found that people who were quite normal in their social and business contexts engaged in quite extraordinary activities on their holy days. They spoke in unknown languages, held poisonous snakes as a way of proving their faith, and reported near-psychotic experiences. The story of Jim Jones, who led hundreds of people in mass suicide, emphasizes the extent to which people get caught up in the situation in which they are acting.

Time

Episodes are punctuated as having a beginning, a middle, and an end. There was a time before the episode started and will be a time after it is over. During the episode, the sequence of events is significant; it makes a difference, for example, whether you compliment the chef on the deliciousness of the meal before or after you taste it.

Let me call your attention to some of the things you already know about episodes. If you were invited to a friend's apartment for dinner, how much time do you expect to spend there? If you were invited to leave after 15 minutes, would this seem too soon? Would a 15-minute dinner be "a dinner" or would you call it something else?

Take the time span you think is appropriate for "dinner with a friend" and see what happens if you lengthen or shorten it. If it is 15 minutes more or less, does that change the nature of what is being done? If it is an hour more or less? Three hours?

Assume that you arrived late for an appointment to see your professor to talk about your exam scores. If you were one minute late, it probably would not require an apology, nor would it change the nature of the episode. At what point would you feel that you should make an apology? Five minutes? Ten? At what point would you feel that no apology would suffice to sustain the meaning of the episode?

Your sense that the flow of events is bracketed into meaningful spans of time is part of your knowledge about episodes. McHugh (1968, p. 3) noted that social situations or episodes are made when you transform physical space and chronological time into meaningful units of action, that is, "into social space and social time."

Boundaries

Episodes are punctuated so that they have boundaries between what is "inside" and thus a part of them and what is "outside" and thus not a part of them.

The existence of these boundaries is sometimes quite clear and other times less so. Scheflen (1973) noted that people who have identified themselves as together orient their bodies in such a way as to suggest the outlines of a closed shape that includes them but excludes other people. (Sheflen called this "quasi-courtship behavior" but noted that it occurs in a wide variety of social situations.) This physical orientation is a visual form of other, less tangible forms of marking boundaries around episodes.

Structure

Episodes have an internal structure or pattern such that the relationship among events that occur is significant. This is the aspect that most researchers

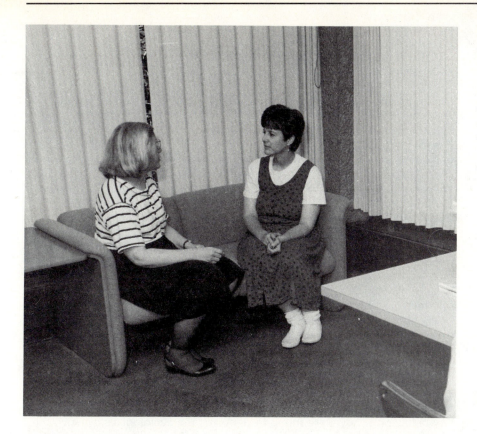

This illustrates a quasi-courtship. *Notice how the conversants mirror each other's posture. Further, they use their shoulders, arms, and legs to define boundaries that enclose a private, common space between them.*

have focused on. For example, Forgas (1979, p. 15) defined episodes solely in terms of "cognitive representations of stereotypical interaction sequences, which are representative of a given cultural environment."

The internal structure of episodes must be important. If the episode we are cocreating is "having dinner with your friend's family," there are certain acts that *must* occur (e.g., food must be served, and you must eat it); that *must not* occur (this is probably not the time for a wrestling match); and that must occur *in particular sequences*.

But we should not grow comfortable saying what must and must not occur because the logics of episodes are "local," or specific to particular families and friendships. There is no reason to assume that any such rule is universal; on the other hand, there is every reason to assume the universal existence of such rules, the content of which may vary enormously. Two stories indicate both the importance of internal structure and the way it varies in the way people from different cultures perform the "same" episode.

Edward T. Hall (1977) told of an event that got out of hand because the conversants had different notions of the appropriate sequence of acts in

Counterpoint 4.2

How rigid are the boundaries of an episode? How permeable are they?

You will rightly insist that what is "inside" and "outside" of a particular episode does not *have* to be where it is, that it could be other than it is. Right, but if the boundaries were moved, it would be a different episode. If you are having an important conversation with your best friend and a casual acquaintance joins the conversation, you and your friend are confronted with a decision about what boundaries to make. If you expand the boundaries to include the casual acquaintance, you will change the quality of the conversation; if you maintain the quality of the conversation, you will exclude the casual acquaintance one way or another.

In my judgment, many social scientists have tried to accomplish the impossible: they seek to discover (not "invent") *the* pattern (not *a* pattern or *many* patterns) underlying episodes (and the rest of our social worlds). Some have tried to write the rules for "games"; others focus on "roles"; still others on the material conditions (e.g., geography, climate, or economy) in which people live. For example, if you do not take his single-simple-explanation-for-everything too seriously, Marvin Harris's (1989) *Cows, Pigs, Wars, and Witches* is a delightful romp through cultural anthropology that reduces the rich array of human cultures to varied consequences of their economies. I am more in sympathy with Erving Goffman (1974, p. 5), who scoffed at those of his colleagues who thought they could find a finite set of "informing, constitutive rules of everyday behavior." They were trying to perform "the sociologist's alchemy," he chuckled: "the transmutation of any patch of ordinary social activity into an illuminating publication."

If we take seriously the claim that our social worlds are made in conversations, then we are free to discover and describe the many varied ways that episodes are structured. As a way of sensitizing ourselves to the possibilities, join me in listing some possible organizing structures:

1. A stochastic sequence of speech acts in which one act must follow another, which is followed by a third, and so on.
2. Harmony, in which the roles of the participants must stand in harmonious relationship at each point in the unfolding of the episode, no matter what speech act is performed.
3. Plot, in which different stages in the development of the episode have a particular relationship to each other; the specific speech acts do not matter as long as the structure of the plot is sustained.
4. Negotiation, in which the episode is less dependent on the product than on the process by which it is brought into being. That is, primary attention is given to the speech acts of negotiation, less to the identities, roles, and relationships arrived at as a result of the negotiations. For example, Lawrence Rosen (1984, p. 4) described the social worlds of the residents of Sefrou, Morocco, as "open texts." Struck

by "the astonishing malleability of social relations and the supple yet distinct shape of their conceptual surround," he suggested that "Reality for the Moroccan is the distribution of ties that he or she possesses to others. And that reality is achieved through a process of negotiating the meaning of the terms and relationships of which it is composed."

Are there other possible patterns of organization?

---

an episode. A young man had a grievance against the local government. He armed himself, went to the City Hall, took hostages, and threatened to harm them if the government did not comply with his demands. The local governor called out the troops and pledged that there would be no negotiations as long as the young man was threatening hostages. As Hall recounts the situation, the young man was in fact fully prepared to negotiate but envisioned a sequence in which he took dramatic actions that showed how serious he was and then participated in negotiations. The governor, on the other hand, envisioned a sequence in which negotiations come first and more dramatic actions are reserved until a last resort. When the young man took hostages, the governor interpreted him as desperate and not likely to be reasonable in negotiations; when the governor refused to negotiate, the young man interpreted him as unreasonable and unwilling to negotiate.

Paul Watzlawick (1974, pp. 63–64) described another situation in which communication problems occurred because of different notions of the proper sequences of events. Literally hundreds of thousands of American soldiers were stationed in Great Britain during World War II. Many of these young men met and courted British women. Interestingly enough, both the American men and British women accused each other of being sexually forward. Those who study such things concluded that the sequence of events in a courtship consists of about 30 steps, and that both American men and British women agreed quite closely on what those steps were. However, they differed in what they considered the appropriate sequence of events. For the American men, kissing is positioned relatively early in the sequence (say, about step 5). However, the British women interpreted kissing as highly erotic behavior that occurs quite late in the sequence (say, about step 25). Watzlawick recounts the experience, repeated thousands of times, in this way:

> *So when the U.S. soldier somehow felt that the time was right for a harmless kiss, not only did the girl feel cheated out of twenty steps of what for her would have been proper behavior on his part, she also felt she had to make a quick decision: break off the relationship and run, or get ready for intercourse. If she chose the latter, the soldier was confronted with behavior that according to his cultural*

rules could only be called shameless at this early stage of the relationship.

Goffman said that we are always confronted by the question of What is it that's going on here? and he is right *if* you remember that this is a question growing out of *praxis,* not *theoria.* When you are communicating, you are required to *act* in the *now* of each moment, not to think or give a report about what act might be (or might have been) appropriate. That is, you get your sense of bearings in your social world by interpreting what is going on, and your actions, of course, enter into the process by which that social world is continually being made.

Without such a sense of our place and orientation within the social world, we suffer from vertigo: we do not know *what* we should do; we do not know *how* to go on. As a result, we collectively work quite hard to create a social navigation system so that we do not get lost.

Punctuation

Communication researchers have found the term *punctuation* (and its verb form, *to punctuate*) useful in describing how episodes are made. The term refers to the act of imposing a set of distinctions on the stuff of your social worlds, perceiving *this* as "inside" and *that* as "outside" a particular episode.

In terms of the temporal dimension, punctuation is the act of deciding when an episode began and when it is over. In terms of boundaries, it is the act of deciding what is "inside" and what is "outside" the episode. In terms of structure, it is the act of deciding what fits the pattern of the episode and what does not.

In the preceding paragraph, I used the phrase "the act of deciding" almost as a mantra. I did this to emphasize the fact that episodes are made, and that their characteristics are the result of the act of punctuation. And, of course, the act of punctuation is co-constructed. All the participants in a conversation are involved in the act of punctuation; often, they manage to coordinate their acts into a consensual punctuation, but sometimes the punctuation itself is the object of the conversation.

When you and I converse, part of our task is to decide (collectively) what episode we are enacting. This process is sufficiently open to distortion, misunderstanding, and misrepresentation that it can be the site of some pretty ugly things. Sexual harrassment at work consists of an immoral and illegal blurring of the lines between the episodes of romantic relationships and employer-employee relationships. Television advertisers deliberately try to dull your sensitivities to the episode of watching a program they sponsor or watching their commercial. They distract you with entertainment in the hopes that you will purchase their product.

One instance of a faulty coordination about what episode we were in stands out in my memory. A salesman came by my office in the late morning.

Counterpoint 4.3

Just how much certainty do we want or need? How much ambiguity can we tolerate? How much ambiguity do we need? Informed opinion differs. For example, Rom Harré (1980, p. 194) writes as if we long for a completely structured social environment. He said,

> . . . *we create and maintain such structures and endow them with meaning as a kind of permanent or semi-permanent bill-board or hoarding upon which certain socially important messages can be 'written.' The very fact of order, when recognized by human beings, is,* in itself, *the source of a message that all is well. Orderliness of the physical environment broadcasts a kind of continuous social Musak whose message is reasssurance.*

On the other hand, Erving Goffman (1974, p. 2) seems to relish the openendedness of episodes—at least some of the time. "There are occasions," he wrote, "when we must wait until things are almost over before discovering what has been occurring and occasions of our own activity when we can considerably put off deciding what to claim we have been doing."

I discussed this topic with Harré, and he suggested that there is a cultural difference. He noted that British and continental social theorists (like himself) live in a different historical and social condition than American social theorists (like Goffman and myself). The preference for order, stability, and certainty, he said, is deeply rooted in European thought, while an affinity for disorder, ambiguity, and innovation are distinctively American.

I think that there is much to what Harré said, but there is an additional factor. The series of social and intellectual revolutions that are upon us have undercut the historical and theoretical rationales on which a preference for order is based. The current buzzword for these developments is "postmodernism," and *to the extent that we live in a "postmodern" world,* the willingness to impose order on the world (Harré's social "Musak") is pathological. At least, I think so. This is the subject of my book *Communication and the Human Condition* (Pearce 1989); you will encounter some of Harré's more recent thinking in Chapter 6, "Self."

I indicated that I was not interested in making a purchase. He relaxed and began telling me of the hard life of a traveling salesman, particularly, how lonesome it was to be on the road. I interpreted this as marking the end of the "sales" episode and the beginning of a "personal conversation" episode, and I could easily understand what it meant to be in a different, strange city every day. I invited him to join me for lunch and he accepted. As soon as we were settled and had order our lunch, he resumed his "salesman's" tone of voice and said, "Now, about our new line of products . . . ." I suspect that you have had similar experiences in which someone invites you to participate in one episode and then, when you have started the conversation, suddenly attempts to switch it to another.

To communicate effectively, we must be alert to what episodes we are participating in and we must be able to construct the episodes that we want and need. If we lose our place or err too often in the guessing game of What's this episode? we will suffer vertigo, but if we develop sufficient phronesis, we can use our ability to move in and out of episodes as a way of structuring our social worlds to our advantage.

The next section of this chapter, "The Episodic Structures of Social Worlds," reviews some of the things we have learned about episodes from researchers who take a third-person orientation. The following section, "How Episodes Are Made," looks at some of the work done by researchers who take a first-person perspective. The section after that, "Juggling Scripts, Goals, and Contingency," focuses directly on some of the ways in which you can move effectively among the episodes in your social worlds.

The Episodic Structure of Social Worlds

Your social worlds are too large and too complex to perceive as a whole; you think of them, describe them, and perceive them in smaller, more manageable chunks. This process of "chunking" is well known to researchers, who have discovered that most adults can deal only with about seven (plus or minus two) units of information at any one time (Miller 1967).

For example, telephone numbers are strings of seven digits, but most telephone directories punctuate them into two groups of three and four digits. Listen carefully when people tell you their telephone numbers: many times they will chunk them even further by saying "eight hundred" (one unit) rather than "eight-zero-zero" (three units) or "nineteen forty-nine" (two units) rather than "one-nine-four-nine" (four units). (There are other mnemonic devices, of course, including memorizing a singsong pattern or remembering the numerical progression of the digits).

If we focus only on the temporal dimension of our social worlds, life can be seen as an unpunctuated sequence of acts or as an incessant stream of behavior. The point is, of course, that we cannot and do not perceive it this way. We impose punctuations so that our social worlds are clusters of episodes.

From a third-person perspective, conversations are *game-like patterns of social interaction comprised of sequences of acts, each of which evokes and responds to the acts of other persons.* Taking this perspective, it makes sense to ask questions like these:

- What episodes exist in the social worlds of particular conversants?
- What are the relationships among these episodes? That is, are some episodes interchangeable with others? Are some episodes mutually exclusive?
- What are the patterns in episodes?

In this section of the chapter, I review three approaches that researchers have taken that cast light on episodes from a third-person perspective.

Interaction Analysis

The impetus for this line of research is belief that the sequence of statements or of speech acts is the most important feature in the structure of episodes. This belief was most poetically expressed by the novelist Ursula Le Guin (1972, 34–25), when she had her protagonist Sparrowhawk offer this advice to a younger man:

> *Try to choose carefully, Arren, when the great choices must be made. When I was young, I had to choose between the life of being and the life of doing. And I leapt at the latter like a trout to a fly. But each deed you do, each act, binds you to itself and to its consequences, and makes you act again and yet again. Then very seldom do you come upon a space, a time like this, between act and act, when you may stop and simply be. Or wonder who, after all, you are.*

But how do acts "bind you" to themselves and their consequences? How does one act make you act again (Figure 4.1)? Make a comment about this system. Into which category would you place that statement? Can you say or do anything that is *not* included in one of these categories? What is lost when the actual statement you made is discarded and treated only as an instance of one of these categories?

The strategy used by interaction analysts is straightforward. First they devised a set of categories so that they could reduce the infinite variety of statements people make to some manageable number. One of the most frequently used category systems is the "interpersonal process analysis" scheme devised by Bales (1950). This is a scheme that suggests that all statements that can be made in a conversation can be fitted into one of twelve categories (see Figure 4.1). That is, the "raw data" consist of what was actually said and done in a conversation (or a transcript of it). These raw data are translated into these categories, a process that reduces the complexity of what is said so that a researcher can deal with it.

The next phase in this research procedure depends on what the researchers are trying to do. In some instances, they will look to see if there are differences in the frequency of various types of statements between conversa-

Figure 4.1
Bales's categories for "interaction process analysis."

- Shows solidarity
- Shows tension release
- Agrees
- Gives suggestions
- Gives opinion
- Gives orientation
- Asks for orientation
- Asks for opinion
- Asks for suggestion
- Disagrees
- Shows tension
- Shows antagonism

tions; in others, they will look to see if there are differences between the kinds of statements made by the participants in a single conversation; and in yet others, they will look to see if there is a greater frequency of certain types of statements at different stages of the conversation.

For our purposes, let's focus on the research that seeks to determine the stochastic probability of particular sequences of statements. (*Stochastic probability* means the statistical probability that one thing follows another.) That is, these researchers ask, What is the statistical probability that one type of statement, for example, "shows solidarity," will be followed by other types of statements, for example, "shows solidarity," "shows tension release," or "agrees"? By computing the correlations between each set of adjacent statements in a conversation (actually, over many conversations), the researcher can develop a precise mathematical description of which sequences are most likely and which are most unlikely.

Not for the first time, this very rigorous research program is more useful for what it did not show rather than what it found. The researchers had great difficulty in coming up with category schemes for utterances in conversations, as you might expect, having read about the co-construction of speech acts in Chapter 3. Speech acts simply do not sit still overnight, waiting to be counted and measured by a communication researcher. In addition, their calculations produced very little of the only thing these researchers value: predictability. Based on the best of this research, you still could not predict what utterances were going to occur with much more accuracy than you would have gotten by chance. These negative results combine to provide a strong reason for believing that whatever is going on in conversation, it is far more complicated than what the stochastic modeling of sequences of observer-coded utterances can come to grips with, so let's look at some more complex, richer approaches.

Counterpoint 4.4

My description of the research protocol of "interaction analysis" is simplistic. I did not describe many of the sophisticated innovations in that research, including the use of more subtle categories for coding statements, rigorous procedures for testing the reliability and validity of the process for assigning statements into particular categories, and statistical processes for computing the stochastic relationships in sequences of statements.

This research tradition is one corner of a much larger project that attempts to model the way human beings think and act as if we were digital computers. That is, this research operates from the assumption (which the researchers may well not believe, but treat as an assumption) that conversants compute stochastic probabilities and thus "know" that if they "ask for opinion," there is a two-to-one chance that the next statement by the other conversant will be "gives opinion" rather than "shows antagonism."

Even if this statistical relationship is true (i.e., it occurs with sufficient generality in many conversations), does it tell us anything about how conversants actually perceive episodes? There is reason to believe that it does not. Gardner (1985) gives a very useful summary of the whole movement that tried to model human behavior on the digital computer and concludes that the primary "finding" of this project points to how *different* human beings are from computers.

I think Aristotle had it right when he differentiated the domains in which things have to be what they are from those in which things may be different from what they are. That is, I believe that conversants perceive episodes as a matter of *praxis,* not *theoria.* Let me make the point by means of a thought experiment and a story.

If I told you that *in my opinion* the stochastic probability of the sequence "gives opinion" followed by "agrees" was so high that it approached certainty (i.e., the correlation was 0.99), how would you respond? If you have anything of game mastery in your repertoire, you would recognize that what I had done was to "give an opinion" and you would respond with any kind of statement *other than* "agreement." That is, you might say, "I'm so relieved to hear that! I have been wondering about that for years! Thank you!"—which is "shows tension release," not "agreement." In that way, you have made a coherent speech act that *denies* my opinion without appearing to do so *because* you wanted to make something other than the usual episodic sequence. Although telling this little experience makes it seem academic and dry, were we to actually engage in it, we both could share a chuckle at your clever wordplay.

In his novel *Nice Work,* David Lodge (1988) subtly makes the point that writers (and presumably normal human beings) are not like computers.

Lodge tells of an author whose work has been analyzed by a computer. To the author's absolute amazement, there are some highly significant statistical patterns in his writing having to do with plural nouns, active verbs, and feminine pronouns. This information came as quite an illumination, but, unfortunately, after learning this, he was completely unable to write anything ever again. No computer would be so affected by learning of its tendencies.

The Factorial Structure of Episodes

Just as interaction analysis was a research tradition built around the statistics of correlation coefficients, studies of the structure of episodes were based on a cluster of statistical procedures called *factor analysis* and *multidimensional scaling*.

The basic idea is simple: if our social worlds are too complex for us to perceive them all at once, then we chunk them into smaller units called episodes. But how do we array those episodes? Is the geography of our social worlds one dimensional, like a string? Or is it two dimensional, like a map? Or three dimensional, like a globe? Or four dimensional, like space and time? Or does it have even more dimensions?

Researchers in this tradition have close affinities with their colleagues in the natural sciences and in mathematics, and they are very aware of the importance of specifying the dimensionality of the objects they study. The most amusing and intriguing treatment of this topic is Abbott's (1991) *Flatland,* in which a three-dimensional object (a sphere) suddenly appears in a two-dimensional world ("Flatland," of course). As the sphere moves up and down (these are dimensions invisible to the inhabitants of Flatland), it appears *to them* to change its size and shape, which is, of course, obscene. The Flatland police cannot apprehend the sphere because it disappears in a direction they cannot imagine, much less pursue, so they arrest the Flatlander who reported the disturbing event and throw him in jail where, in a fit of social vertigo, he writes the book!

In much the same way, if you perceive your social worlds in, say, three dimensions, and I am trying to understand you (as a researcher or as your friend, academic advisor, or therapist), I cannot use a one- or two-dimensional "map." If I do, I will find that your conversations often go in directions that I cannot anticipate or follow. Our attempts to coordinate our working definitions of the situation will have predictable problems because some of your episodes go at right angles to mine; from my perspective, they appear to change shape at awkward moments. Like the poor Flatlanders trying to comprehend a sphere, I might find your episodes disturbing or obscene simply because I have no way to place them in my map of your world.

The best research in this tradition uses a version of the statistical procedure called INDSCAL, which permits the researcher to describe the number of dimensions that a given individual or group uses in their perception of their social worlds (Forgas 1979). The research protocol is both simple and familiar to you because I used an approximation of it in the Praxis sections of Chapters 1 and 2. First, subjects keep a diary of the episodes in which they participate during a period of time. Second, subjects complete a questionnaire in which they describe each episode on the same list of bipolar scales. The scales ask for various perceptions, including how well you liked what you were doing, felt in control of what you were doing, and felt that what you were doing was important. Finally, the researcher uses INDSCAL (or some similar statistical procedure) to compute the *factors* or *dimensions* that account for most of the variance in your ratings. That is, by analyzing all the correlations, a series of lines are constructed in n-dimensional space that come the closest to fitting the ratings you gave. If only one line accounts for most of the variance in your ratings, then you have a one-dimensional structure of episodes in your social worlds; if two lines are necessary, then you have a two-dimensional structure, and so on. Figure 4.2 shows the results of one such study.

Figure 4.2 *Researchers "map" our social worlds. Most studies suggest four dimensions like those shown here (adapted from Forgas, 1983, p. 43). Imagine that each dimension is at right angles ("orthogonal") to all of the others. For example, the meaning of "dinner with your fiance's parents" is determined by its location in this four-dimensional space: it might be an unpleasant, highly involving, very serious event in which you feel low self-confidence.*

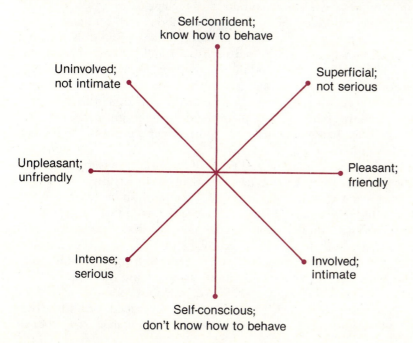

In a review of the research in this tradition, Michael Cody and Margaret McLaughlin (1985, p. 287) concluded that six factors recur in the study of how people structure their episodes. That is, some people use only one and very few use all six, and the following list names all of the dimensions of our social worlds that have been uncovered by this research project: the degree of 1) *intimacy* involved in the situation, 2) *friendliness*, 3) *pleasantness*, 4) *apprehension*, 5) *involvement*, and 6) *dominance*.

Frame Analysis

Something bothers me about Figure 4.2. Although I think the notion of dimensionality of our social worlds is important, I am uneasy with representations of episodes as a single point within multidimensional space. There is no wit, play, or poetry—to say nothing of polysemy—about episodes portrayed in this manner. At the very least, we need to supplement these descriptions with more complex approaches. The "frame analysis" of Gregory Bateson (1972) and Erving Goffman serves nicely.

Bateson suggested that we punctuate social episodes by placing what we are doing within "frames." As Bateson developed the concept, "frames" have some of the properties of picture frames and some of the properties of mathematical "sets." When we impose a frame, we stipulate not only that what is inside is set off from what is outside, but also that what is inside the frame derives is meaning from the frame itself. That is, to use another of Bateson's most helpful terms, the frame is a *metacommunication* about how we should interpret what we say and do "in" the episode.

The classic exposition of Bateson's ideas about metacommunication and frames for episodes comes from his observations of animals at play. Bateson noted that the more advanced animals, including human beings, do not react automatically to the mood signals of others. Rather, they recognize the behaviors of others as symbols that can be distrusted, falsified, denied, amplified, corrected, and so on. To determine some of these things we do with the symbols we exchange, Bateson distinguished the signals we exchange (e.g., grunts, calls, statements, scholarly tomes) from "metalanguage" and from "metacommunication."

In metalanguage, the subject of thought and discourse is the language of that discourse itself. In the sentence "Think of the word, 'cat'," the word "cat" is used in a metalanguage. Unlike the animal that it names, the word "cat" has no fur and cannot scratch, and unlike the word that names it, the animal does not have three letters. Bateson uses this distinction to call our attention to the fact that the words and things that we do in conversation are not all alike, and to warn us that we can get into trouble if we use the same language game for talking about both the word and the animal.

In metacommunication, the subject of discourse is the relationship among the speakers, the activity in which they are engaged, or both. That is, the vocabulary of metacommunication includes the names of episodes.

Refrain 4.1

Bateson differentiated between "language," "metalanguage," and "meta-communication." The difference is between actually *saying* something and saying something *about* what you are saying.

In *metalanguage,* the subject of thought and discourse is the language of that discourse itself.

In *metacommunication,* the subject of thought and discourse is the relationship between the speakers and/or the activity in which they are engaged.

If I say that I intended this Refrain to be helpful to you, I am engaging in *metacommunication.* If I told you that this Refrain is written in English, I am engaging in *metalanguage.*

Of course, many utterances are combinations of two or more of these types of communication. For example, the following statement contains language, metalanguage, *and* metacommunication: "in this Refrain, I am using very precise language because I am a teacher and you are a student."

When we answer the question What is it we are doing here? we are engaging in metacommunication.

Bateson said that he realized that we have to distinguish between language, metalanguage, and metacommunication while watching monkeys at the Fleishhacker Zoo in San Francisco. The monkeys were playing; that is, they were engaged in an episode in which the actions were those of combat. However, it was obvious from Bateson's third-person perspective that the combat-like acts were framed as "play." What he was seeing was *not* combat and, more, that the monkeys *knew* that it was not combat. "Now, this phenomenon, play, could only occur if the participant organisms were capable of some degree of metacommunication, i.e., of exchanging signals which would carry the message, 'this is play.' " (Bateson 1972, p. 179).

In the frame "play," a monkey bite means something other than it does in the frame "fight." Monkeys, like human beings, must play the game "Guess the Episode" if they are to know whether to interpret a growl as a warning or as an invitation to romp. Once an action is placed within a frame, its meaning derives from that frame.

Bateson believes that this ability to metacommunicate makes it possible for our social worlds to have multiple layers of meaning in each episode, not just multiple dimensions of meaning along which episodes are arrayed. Much of the humanness of our worlds includes such frames as mystery, fantasy, horror, irony, and play. For example, Bateson points out that the image of the monster in a horror film does not denote what it seems to; that is, it is not a documentary that says "monsters exist." Rather—if you can follow

Bateson's expression—the image denotes what would be denoted by the monster if the monster existed; that is, if the horror movie works, we are terrified even though we know that the monster is not real.

All of this is a bit more than "let's pretend." Bateson notes that human beings take this kind of multiple layers of frames very seriously.

> *In the dim region where art, magic, and religion meet and overlap, human beings have evolved the "metaphor that is meant," the flag which men will die to save, and the sacrament that is felt to be more than "an outward and stable sign, given unto us." (Bateson 1972, p. 183)*

Erving Goffman borrowed the concept of frames from Bateson. For Goffman, a frame is a "rendering." I think he uses the term *rendering* in the sense of the verb *to rend,* or *to tear apart, into pieces.* This is a very vivid notion of how we take the undivided whole of our social worlds and tear it into pieces, each of which is the frame for particular patterns of actions.

Frames function to make "what would otherwise be a meaningless aspect of the scene into something that is meaningful" (Goffman 1974, p. 21). The events within the frame are arrayed according to a framework that gives them a meaningful structure. These frameworks vary; some are rigid and explicit, others are flexible and "appear to have no apparent articulated shape, providing only a lore of understanding, an approach, a perspective." In any case, however, the framework "allows its user to locate, perceive, identify, and label a seemingly infinite number of concrete occurrences defined in its terms."

Goffman's concept of frames seems most useful in answering the question How do we recognize episodes when we see them again? Suppose you have had a disastrous romantic relationship, and some time later, you find yourself beginning another relationship. How do you know whether it is different this time? How accurately can you tell whether the pattern of your episodes are repetitions of what happened previously or whether they are something different?

The question is similar to the old playground joke. "Do you know what this is?" he asked, waving his hand in the air. "No, what is it?" came the reply. "I don't know either," he said gleefully, "but," waving his hand in the air again, "here it comes again!" If you will pardon the sophomoric humor, that joke captures our situation quite well. How do we know if *this* episode that we are enacting today with Tony has the same pattern as *that* episode we enacted last week or last year with Rudy?

Goffman suggests that there are many answers to the question of *how* we recognize episodes, but that they all have in common the phenomenon known as *pattern recognition.* He suggests that certain elements function as "keys" to our recognition of patterns. Like the key in music, this characteristic

Counterpoint 4.5

I'm struck by the differences between the ways Bateson and Forgas think about social worlds. Both believe that our social worlds are complex and that episodes (or "frames," in Bateson's vocabulary) are multidimensional. However, Forgas locates each episode as a single, unique point within multidimensional space, arguing that its meaning derives from (or can be expressed as) its coordinates within that space. Bateson, on the other hand, notes that each episode has multiple dimensions, including the signals themselves that are produced, the metalanguage in which some of these signals refer to themselves or to other signals, and metacommunication, in which some signals refer to the frame in which they occur.

Bateson's concept is much more consistent with the notions of heterglossia and polysemy. Compared to Forgas's, his is a much more complex model of our social worlds, filled with things that do not denote what they seem to denote and that refer to themselves. Such willful complexity disturbs some people.

Earlier in this century, C. P. Snow (1959) declared that he had discovered "two cultures" among his contemporaries, equivalent in education, income, and nationality, but virtually opaque to each other. These cultures were those of the scientists (with whom Snow worked during the day) and humanists (with whom Snow socialized at night). I suspect that the former would find Forgas's work compelling and the latter would find Bateson far more illuminating.

I suspect that the differences between these cultures are not nearly as sharp at century's end as they were in the middle. For one thing, we have come to understand the workings of fantasy much better than we did (see, for example, Le Guin's 1979 essay that addresses the question "Why are Americans Afraid of Dragons?"); for another, the discoveries in science have made mystics of many of us who thought of ourselves as hard-nosed realists. We now think of the physical universe as a much more dangerous and interesting, but less predictable, thing than was supposed only a few years ago.

If we take seriously Bateson's view of multilayered (as well as multidimensioned) social worlds, how can we put the concept to use? One suggestion is that we see each act as within multiple hierarchial layers of context, each of which functions as a frame, and each of which may or may not correspond to the others. That is, at one level we know that the monster in the movie is not real, but at another level we react as if it is, and our ability to move among these levels is a fact of our experience even if it would take ten pages of turgid prose to describe it.

The atomic model of communication in Figure 1.5 is one way of describing each act as multiply contexted, in which episodes are just one of the layers. For a more sustained attempt to work with this phenomenon, see Pearce et al. (1979) and Cronen et al. (1982; 1985).

of the pattern is a metacommunication about how to perceive itself and the episode of which it is a part (Goffman 1974, pp. 43–45).

Interactional "Ladders"

Social psychologists E. E. Jones and H. B. Gerard (1967) developed a very useful device for describing the extent to which conversants attend to the contingency of their interaction. Figure 4.3 starts with the familiar anatomy of a conversation: two persons produce a sequence of actions, each of which evokes and responds to the others. In Figure 4.3, lines connecting the communicative turns represent these "evocative and responsive" relationships. But does a particular act respond to the *other* conversant's acts, or to his or her *own* acts? That is, is the conversation a dialogue in which each conversant takes the other into account or is it a pseudoconversation, actually a monologue in which someone else speaks but is not taken into consideration?

This question is posed in Jones and Gerard's interactional ladders by having two sets of lines. One set of lines zig-zags between the sequential turns of both interlocutors; another set of lines moves vertically down the figure connecting the sequential turns of each interlocutor. In the figure, dark, solid lines indicate a close connection between sequential communication turns, and light, broken lines indicate a weak connection between turns.

These simple diagrams allow us to differentiate among conversations. Jones and Gerard suggest that what is said and done in conversation may be driven by some combination of three factors: 1) each conversant's own purposes and motives (indicated by heavy vertical lines in Fig. 4.3); 2) the evocative force of the other conversant's previous act (indicated by heavy oblique lines in Fig. 4.3); or 3) a combination of each conversant's motives and his or her responsiveness to each other. The possible combinations produce four types of conversations.

- *Pseudocontingency* is a conversation in which the interlocutors take turns in their roles as speakers but do not really respond to each other. If both are reading from a script or simply following cultural norms, they can give the appearance of conversing without listening to or responding to each other. Long-married couples sometimes carry on dual monologues while exchanging speaking turns.
- *Asymmetrical contingency* is a conversation in which one conversant follows the lead of the other, but the other does not reciprocate. When you apply for a loan or if you are audited by the Internal Revenue Service, you will find yourself in what might appear to be a conversation. In fact, the interviewer is reading a series of questions from a predetermined protocol and simply recording your answers. Your statements have to respond to the questions asked, but the next question comes from the interview schedule rather than being evoked by what you said.
- *Reactive contingency* is a conversation in which each person responds to

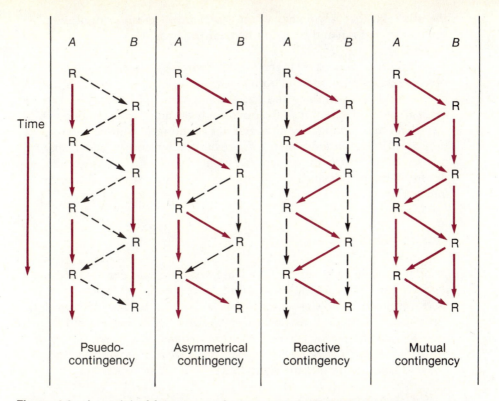

Figure 4.3 *A model of four types of conversation. The differences among these conversations derive from the manner in which each act is contingent on the ones preceding it. In the figure, solid lines indicate strong contingency and broken lines indicate weak contingency. In the pseudocontingent conversation, the conversants take turns speaking, but what they say is more related to their own previous statement than to what their interlocutor said. That is, they are both engaged in a monologue although they appear to be taking turns. In the reactive contingency conversation, there is little coherence to the sequence of things that each person says; both are responding to what the other just said in a kind of mutual free association. (Reprinted by permission of John Wiley and Sons.)*

the most recent comment made by the other. You and a friend are lying on a beach, tired from a long snorkling adventure, and you have nothing that you have to do for the rest of the day. He comments that the water was very warm; you reply by describing how thirsty you were when hiking in the desert; he tells you of his favorite desserts; and so on. There is no unifying theme to the conversation; both of you are responding to the other with a free association to some word or topic mentioned by the other.

■ Mutual contingency is a conversation in which each conversant is pursuing his or her own goals and simultaneously responding to the moves made by the other. Neither is "in charge" or "in control" of the conversation, but both affect its form and direction by their behavior.

These distinctions are useful for some purposes. For example, the definitions of communication from both first- and third-person perspectives apply best to *mutual contingency,* and *pseudocontingency* and *asymmetrical contingency* are good descriptions of various kinds of monologue. Dialogue must involve mutual contingency, although not all mutually contingent conversations are dialogic. In addition, the device of the interactional ladders sharpens our sensitivity to the differences between sequences of messages that are driven by the conversant's own purposes and those that are driven by the interaction between them.

How Episodes Are Made

The third-person perspective is useful for identifying episodes and for describing how they fit within the social worlds of conversants. However, they tell us very little about how episodes are made. For this, we have to turn to the first-person perspective, and here we find a rich array of research and theory.

From a first-person perspective, conversations are *a process of coordinating actions within a working definition of a situation.* Taking this perspective, it makes sense to ask questions like these:

- How do conversants coordinate their actions?
- How do conversants construct working definitions of the episodes in which they are communicating?
- What happens when conversants have different definitions of the episode that they are co-constructing?
- What happens when conversants realize that they are co-constructing an episode that they did not want or expect?
- What happens when conversants run into difficulties coordinating their actions?

Conversants employ three things as they put together smooth and rewarding enactments of episodes: scripts, goals, and interactional contingencies. I believe that all three parts are always involved in every performance of an episode, although not necessarily to the same extent.

- First, the conversants may focus on what are variously called the scripts for enacting particular episodes. If so, their task is to see to it that their actions conform to the expectations for the event. Here, the focus of attention is on the objective social world in general; what "everybody" knows or expects.
- Second, the conversants may focus on their purpose or goal for the episode.

In this case, their task is to do whatever is needed to bring about the outcome they desire. Here the focus of attention is on one's own purposes or goals in an imagined future.

■ Third, the conversants may focus on rules for the contingent interaction for what they and their interlocutors do. That is, they attend to how what they do evokes and responds to what their interlocutors do, and vice versa. Here, the focus of attention is on the unfolding pattern of a specific interaction with another person.

In this section, we will look at each of these—scripts, goals, and rules— in turn. In the following section, "Juggling Scripts, Goals, and Contingency," we will look at how conversants put them together in the co-construction of episodes.

Scripts

Scripts are standardized punctuations of episodes. They are what people think that other people think goes on in these episodes. As a performer in the theater has a script that tells him or her when to move, what to say, and how to dress, so these usually unwritten but widely known scripts provide instructions on what to say and do in specified social situations.

There are scripts for how to act at elegant restaurants and for how to queue up at McDonald's. Often, we have learned these scripts so well that we have forgotten that we learned them; we think that everybody already knows how to act and we are deeply offended if someone does not. However, to take just one example, when McDonald's opened its Moscow restaurant, the management found that they had to be far more explicit than they expected in teaching their staff to smile when serving customers (not a

---

Refrain 4.2

Communicators have three types of materials to use as they make episodes:

1. *Scripts* are standard sequences of actions; they are what "everybody knows" about how to do certain things, such as ordering a dinner at an elegant restaurant.
2. *Goals* are the imagination of what does not exist coupled with the determination to bring it into existence.
3. *Rules of interactional contingencies* are logics of "oughtness" that organize sequences of actions in terms of what should follow and precede what.

Moscow custom) and in teaching their customers that they could line up in front of any of the registers (also a novelty in Moscovian culture). That is, neither the Moscovite staff nor the customers knew the McDonald script.

Etiquette books and protocol officers in the State Department are textbook examples of scripts for the enactment of episodes and of those who enforce them. I have often been in situations in which my interlocutors have come from very different cultural, social, and religious backgrounds. There is a kind of excitement in noticing the cultural differences and in exploring personal idiosyncracies in such settings. However, sometimes—and often when your attention really needs to be on more pressing matters—it is a great comfort to have someone whisper in your ear the rules of etiquette. By following such rules, you can avoid being offensive unless you choose to be, and you spend your energy trying to figure out, for example, what plots these nice folk are hatching rather than worrying about whether to eat with your fingers or use chop sticks, or whether you should refrain from ordering pork, or beef, or meat of any kind.

Some institutions in our society are fully scripted. For example, courts of law have elaborate procedures for determining what speech by what persons in what order will be allowed to occur, and if you speak out of turn or in an inappropriate manner, you may be sent to jail for contempt of court. Churches have liturgies that guide the performance of the episode "worship."

Some social scientists have suggested that, far more than we commonly realize, there are unwritten scripts underlying what seems to be spontaneous conversations. Those who observe us closely can describe small rituals and major regularities in our behavior that we recognize but are not aware of performing.

O'Keefe et al. (1980, p. 27) described the "interpretive schemes" with which we perceive our social worlds as providing the scripts we follow in conversations. We *perceive* our interactions with others in ways that guide the way that we and they can coordinate our behavior.

In a certain law school, future trial attornies are taught that if they have the facts on their side, they should address the jury, and if they have legal technicalities on their side, they should address the judge. The expected question is always asked: What if I have neither the facts nor the law on my side? "Then pound on your desk and shout," they are told.

This tired joke describes three interpretive schemes: one is structured by the facts, one by the law, and the third by the speaker's ability to intimidate the jury. As Wittgenstein said about ways of doing speech acts (discussed in Chapter 2), there are a countless number of such schemes. However, in practice, individuals tend to use the same schemes over and over; families tend to "specialize" in particular schemes, and as a result have communication styles that differ from other families.

Do not push the concept of interpretive schemes too far; I think you strain language if you were to say that "Jack did what he did *because* he used

Counterpoint 4.6

The scripts that we follow are often invisible to us; they are just the natural things to do. But, as Robert Burns noted in his famous poem "To a Louse," if we could see ourselves as others see us, it would make a difference in our lives. Ethnographers make their living by inscribing such scripts and making them available to us.

Sometimes they do it for more doubtful motivations. For example, ethnographer Renato Rosaldo (1989, pp. 46–47) entertained the family of his fiancee by giving them a description of their ritualized behavior at the breakfast table.

After falling head over heels in love, I paid a ceremonial visit, during the summer of 1983, to the "family cottage" on the shores of Lake Huron in western Ontario. Much as one would expect (unless one was, as I was, too much in the thick of things), my prospective parents-in-law treated me, their prospective son-in-law, with reserve and suspicion. Such occasions are rarely easy, and this one was no exception. Not unlike other rites of passage, my mid-life courtship was a blend of conventional form and unique personal experience.

My peculiar position, literally surrounded by potential in-laws, nourished a project that unfolded over a two-week period in barely conscious daydreams. The family breakfast started turning in my mind into a ritual described in the distanced normalizing mode of a classic ethnography. On the morning of my departure, while we were eating breakfast, I revealed my feelings of tender malice by telling my potential in-laws the "true" ethnography of their family breakfast: "Every morning the reigning patriarch, as if just in from the hunt, shouts from the kitchen, 'How many people would like a poached egg?' Women and children take turns saying yes or no.

"In the meantime, the women talk among themselves and designate one among them the toast maker. As the eggs near readiness, the reigning patriarch calls out to the designated toast maker, 'The eggs are about ready. Is there enough toast?'

" 'Yes,' comes the deferential reply. 'The last two pieces are about to pop up.' The reigning patriarch then proudly enters bearing a plate of poached eggs before him.

Throughout the course of the meal, the women and children, including the designated toast maker, perform the obligatory ritual praise song, saying, 'These sure are great eggs, Dad.' "

According to Rosaldo's account, the family was greatly amused and even found his telling of their scripts useful. Perhaps, but I would think that this is a risky business for a prospective son-in-law.

this interpretive scheme." It is more accurate to use terms relating to *how* the episode was achieved. "Jack did this *by* using this interpretive scheme" is more consistent with the Heyerdahl solution and the emphasis on communication as a way of making social worlds.

That caution having been made, the notion of interpretive schemes is a very powerful tool for seeing how conversants respond to, and evoke responses from, others. It is as if conversants had models of the communication triplet in mind, as if they said, "hmm, she just did this, so if I respond in this way, she will reply by doing that. Good!," and then set themselves to act appropriately.

The most interesting account of underlying scripts is psychologist James Averill's (1982, 1992) theory of emotion. We usually think of emotion as a physiological or intrapsychic state that happens to us. Averill says that it is no accident that we think this because this theory of emotion is embedded in the grammar of our language games. However, he believes that emotions are in fact roles that we play. These roles do not last very long (he calls them *transitory* roles); they require supporting casts (i.e., they are transitory *social* roles); and they are enacted as episodes (i.e., they have beginnings and ends, internal patterns, and we know when and where to engage in them).

For example, we usually frame "anger" as a natural event. We think of ourselves as "overcome" by anger; it is something that happens *to* us, not something that we do; and when in a state of anger, we have diminished responsibility for what we do. All this, Averill argues, is prefigured in the grammar of our ordinary language about emotions.

Closer inspection shows that there are recognizable episodic sequences of actions that occur when we are angry, that these episodic sequences are at least in part volitional, that these episodic sequences are learned, not innate, that these episodic sequences differ among cultures, and that these sequences fulfill the social purposes of the angry person with suspicious regularity.

Counterpoint 4.7

The strongest support for Averill's theory that emotions are transitory social roles that we learn comes from the work of Randy Cornelius (1981) and Catherine Lutz (1988; 1990). Lutz studied a small (fewer than 500 people) community on an island in the south Pacific. The people distinguish at least five kinds of anger, one of which, *song* or "justifiable anger," is very different from the others. *Song* is morally approved, while the others are not; the others are thought to stem from selfish motives, while *song* is rooted in the public moral order: "The claim to be 'justifiably angry,' . . . is taken seriously as a moral assertion; by identifying *song* in oneself or in others, the speaker advertises himself or herself

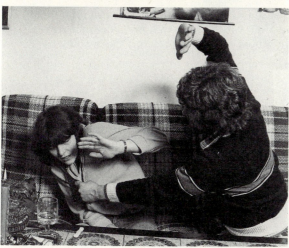

These are faces of angry people. Are these expressions natural or learned? Is anger something that "comes over us" or is it something that we learn to perform?

as someone with a finely tuned and mature sense of island values." (Lutz 1990, pp. 206–207)

To claim *song* is not to describe an internal state or emotional arousal; it is to initiate a specific episodic sequence in which 1) there is a rule or value violation, 2) it is pointed out by someone, 3) the person claiming *song* calls for the act to be condemned, 4) the perpetrator reacts in fear to the anger, and 5) amends his or her ways. Lutz (1990, p. 204) concludes that "this emotion does not simply occur as a form of reflection on experience, but emerges as people justify and negotiate both cultural values and the perogatives of power that some members of this society currently hold."

Cornelius studied weeping among men. In this sense, weeping involves shedding tears when in an intense emotional state; it is not the same as crying because of pain. He asked a large number of men to describe an episode in which they wept and to answer a series of questions about it. He found that the men followed the grammar of our language games about emotions when asked to give an account of their weeping. That is, they described weeping as something outside of their control, as something that happened to them, and certainly not something deliberate or intentional. However, when Cornelius asked the men to each act in sequence in the episode, he found—and most of them realized, to their surprise—that they knew full well what the result of their weeping would be in terms of their interlocutors' response, that the weeping occurred in the most strategic place possible in the development of the episode, and that they did not weep in other places in the episode, although their emotions were equally intense.

These studies indicate that there are probably far more scripts underlying our behavior than we are aware of, and that one way that we coordinate our actions with others is to orient toward these scripts.

Goals

Throughout this book, I have argued that *we* are *in* our social worlds, not somewhere outside them, acting *on* them to serve to purposes that emerge from somewhere else. Without retracting an inch from that position, I want to acknowledge that *we* are not simply the reflections of our social worlds. As Harré says, human beings are "powerful particulars" who act as agents within our social worlds. Among other things, "we create structures in thought, anticipating the forms we will realize in public social activity. We do not yet fully understand the principles which control our acts of creation. But we do know that our conceptions are only partly in imitation of the forms we experience in the world around us." (Harré, 1980, p. 6)

As human beings, we have the ability to imagine what does not exist, to set ourselves on a course of action designed to bring that state of affairs into existence, to monitor our progress toward those goals, and to decide when and whether to declare them accomplished, unobtainable, or deferred. The imagination of these goals is a magnet that drives our performance of episodes. We will sometimes deliberately invoke or violate a cultural script in order to increase our chances of accomplishing those objectives; we will sometimes deliberately act in a conformist or outrageous manner in order to reach our goals.

The language games of all societies include grammars of *agency*, such that we attribute our actions to our choices and make those choices on the basis of imagination of future states of affairs, some of which we desire and others we want to avoid. The practical syllogism, introduced in Chapter 1, is a formal reconstruction of these grammars.

"Why did you do that?" I might ask, referring on an episode in which you participated. "Because I wanted to," you reply, or perhaps, "because it suited my purposes to do so." *If I treat you as a competent moral agent,* I have to accept these statements as rational, legitimate reasons for doing what you did.

Rules

The third way that we coordinate our actions with others is to follow rules that prescribe patterns of contingent actions among conversants. But where do these rules come from? How do they have force? There are two sets of answers to these questions; call them *conversational principles* and *logics of meaning and action.*

Conversational principles.   This approach locates rules in the characteristics of conversation itself. That is, there are just some things that you have to do if you are to participate in the activity.

Starting with the observation that "our talk exchanges do not consist of a succession of disconnected remarks and would not be rational if they did," Grice (1975, p. 45) reasoned *from* the fact that rational coordination does occur to the *necessity* that rational coordination requires conversants who are committed to cooperate with each other. All conversants, he proclaimed, can and must follow the "cooperative principle."

The cooperative principle means that conversants act as if they were obeying this command: "Make your conversational contribution such as is required, at the stage at which it occurs, by the accepted purpose or direction of the task exchanges in which you are engaged." Grice said that the cooperative principle can be further elaborated into four "maxims":

- *Maxim of quantity.* Make your contribution as informative as is required, but give no more information than is required.
- *Maxim of quality.* Try to make your contribution one that is true. That is, do not say anything you believe to be false or lack adequate evidence for.
- *Maxim of relevance.* Make your contribution relevant to the aims of the ongoing conversation.
- *Maxim of manner.* Be clear. Try to avoid obscurity, ambiguity, wordiness, and disorderliness in your use of language.

If you follow these maxims, you will talk like an eminent British University Professor. Such people, of course, comprised the social worlds in which Grice lived and worked.

The rigor of these formal maxims have proved more useful than their specific content. Many people have used them as a standard against which to analyze specific conversations. The general opinion is that if you treat Grice's maxims as very abstract, they are correct but not very useful. For example, how much information is "required"? What are the standards for believing something is "true"? Who decides what is "relevant" to the conversation? If these criteria vary from one conversation to another, then of course Grice is right, but he has not provided the most interesting information.

However, enterprising researchers have taken advantage of this ambiguity and used it as the basis for studying particular cultures and language games. That is, they ask a particular speech community how much information is required when enacting a particular episode. These criteria differ significantly. For example, ethnographer Elaine Keenan (1975) studied the Malagasay and found that they treated information as a resource not to be given away. By the standards of Grice's social worlds, the Malagasay speak in circumlocutions; by their own standards, they give just as much information as is required.

In fact, the Malagasay differed from Grice's ideal in ways that go far beyond the quantity of information: Grice's maxims presume that the purpose of conversation is to accomplish a task as quickly and efficiently as possible. Keenan's studies showed that the Malagasay used oral speech for many purposes, and that they have aesthetic as well as functional criteria for evaluating speakers.

Logics of meaning and action.   One of the most vigorous areas of communication research in the last 20 years has been the study of communication rules (Shimanoff 1980). The concept of a "rule" was developed as an alternative to the notion that something "causes" conversants to act the way they do. As such, they focused on intentions, on what conversants know, and on mutable patterns (i.e., things that could be something other than what they are) of conversation.

McLaughlin (1984, p. 14) said that conversants know far more than they realize. Only in special cases do we "retrieve" the information that we normally use to guide our actions. But what is the nature of this information?

Much of the work of rules theorists has been to clarify the form of this knowledge. The general opinion is that rules are best "written" by researchers as contingent statements of deontic logic, something like, "in a formal job interview, if my potential employer asks if I can work late several times a week, I [must, may, may not] say 'yes,' so that I can get the job."

This formula serves the purposes of communication researchers, but does it have anything to do with the way normal people act? Many researchers believe that it does. Conversants act as if these descriptions have moral force; that is, the rules are not just descriptions of what people *usually* do, they are prescriptions for what people *should* do. However, these prescriptions are not laws of the universe; people can break rules and negotiate new rules.

Researchers have described the rules followed by conversants in a wide variety of situations. However, these rules tend to be local, idiosyncratic, and temporary. The primary contribution of this line of research has been to demonstrate that episodes have the characteristics of rule-following behavior rather than to result in a set of well-written specific rules.

Combine the notion of rules with Goffman's idea that frames are patterns. Goffman inadequately described the substance of these patterns. The rules perspective suggests that they are patterns of "felt moral obligation," that is, of deontic and practical logics.

Sometimes it seems as if individual communicators have formulated rules for themselves and set themselves to follow them. For example, in our study of unwanted repetitive patterns, the conversants' behavior was rigidly predictable, and most of them could articulate the sequence of contingent behavior (Cronen et al. 1979). To the extent that the conversants call these rules to their conscious attention, they can gain an insight into the predictable patterns of conversation that they get themselves into. In fact, several of the participants in our study of unwanted repetitive behaviors told us that the interview led them to illuminating discoveries of their own rules for meaning and action.

However, most of the time, whatever it is that we know that enables us to coordinate our actions with our conversants, it is *not* a long list of rules for meaning and action. More likely, it is a more flexible configuration of patterns of deontic and practical logics.

Some of these patterns are rigid—these can be described by precisely worded rules of the form: "If Jack is late, I will wait five minutes but no more." Other patterns are much more flexible and can be enacted in a wide variety of ways. A strike in baseball happens 1) if the batter swings, regardless of where the ball is pitched, 2) if the pitch is in the strike zone, regardless of whether the batter swings, and 3) if the ball is hit but goes outside the foul lines (unless the batter has two strikes already). In the same way, a fight can occur in a wide variety of ways. Communicators know the pattern "fight," but there may be an infinite number of specific ways in which this pattern can occur.

The rules perspective insists that the substance of our social worlds is moral; that is, it involves our sense of felt moral obligation. It offers a formulation for writing specific rules in instances in which the logic of meaning and action is sufficiently rigid and suggests more pliant forms of deontic and practical logics as ways of describing more elastic episodes.

Juggling Scripts, Goals, and Contingency

Conversants have to juggle several things as they work to achieve coordinated enactments of episodes. Among these are the cultural or social *scripts* that describe or prescribe how certain things should be done, their own *goals* for what episodes they want to achieve or want to prevent from occurring, and the *rules* that prescibe patterns of contingency between their acts and those of their interlocutors.

A good juggler can keep all the balls in the air at once; conversants sometimes have to choose which of these aspects are most important. The most interesting and challenging communication situations occur when the acts required by cultural scripts are incompatible with those required by the personal goals of the conversant or the contingency developed by the flow of the conversation. In these situations, how does the conversant respond?

Conversants do not always respond the same way, of course, nor do all conversants respond alike. Remembering to distrust simple categories, it is useful to use O'Keefe's (1988) description of three logics of message design (described in Chapter 3) to sensitize ourselves to some of the ways people handle these conflicting imperatives for their actions.

■ Conversants using a *conventional* logic would normally adhere to the cultural script and expect others to do the same. Predictable problems in producing coordinated episodes would arise when a conventional person is talking with a person using an expressive or rhetorical logic. We expect conventional people to offer accounts that justify their behavior by conforming to norms (e.g., "I had to do that because in *[situation]* that's just what you are supposed to do."). Conventional communicators would criticize others for not acting as expected and blame them for actions that deviate from the norms. Lutz's description of the emotion song seems a perfect example of how conventional conversants call each other to account and thus maintain the social order.

■ Conversants using *expressive* logics normally adhere to their own goals, dismissing cultural norms as irrelevant and the interaction contingency as unimportant in their virtuous expression of their own identity. Predictable problems emerge in conversations with interlocutors using conventional or rhetorical logics of message design. If the conversants have difficulty cooordinating their enactment of the episode, we would expect to hear accounts justifying the expressive interlocutors' behavior by linking their actions to the self. "I had to do that," we might be told, "because that is the way I think; anything else would have been dishonest. You wouldn't want me to be dishonest, would you?" Expressives will be sharply critical of interlocutors who appear "slippery" (i.e., those who use rhetorical tactics to facilitate the coordination of the interlocutors' lines of action) or who appear unduly respectful of traditional ways of action.

■ Conversants using a *rhetorical* logic of message design respond primarily to the contingencies of the interaction, looking for ways to make the episode compatible with cultural scripts and personal goals. They predict problems when dealing with conventional or expressive interlocutors and use a wide array of devices to get past those problems. These conversants may account for their behavior by saying "I had to do that because it made it possible for us to work together without fighting all the time."

Adapting to the contingencies of the interaction seems the most difficult of the three "balls" that conversants must juggle. Both scripts and goals are somehow outside of "real time." Scripts exist before any given conversation, and the conversant's task is to be a part of an episode that fits the pattern; goals exist in the imagination located in a future time, and the conversant's task is to be a part of an episode that causes that goal to occur. Responding to the contingency is done in the *now* of action; it responds to the immediate present and future. More than pattern matching, contingency calls for continual adaptation, a sense of the evolution of the logics of meaning and action, and an ability to steer a process that we can only influence, not control.

Responding to the contingency of an interaction requires good judgment and an assessment of the "openings," or opportunities, in the situation, not simply using well-rehearsed lines from other occasions. Here are four types of things that conversants do to facilitate their coordination with others.

Punctuate the Sequence of Events

Every culture develops signals that conversants use to tell each other that they want to end what they are doing, start something new, or change what is going on. Most of these signals are conventional; that is, some other signal could serve as well. They are meaningful only if they help the conversants coordinate. Let me call these signals to your attention by describing some research on three categories of them: greetings, turn taking, and leave taking.

The first five minutes of a conversation are the site of some important decisions, including the decision about whether to continue the conversation (Krivonos and Knapp 1975; Goffman 1971). Most conversations last for fewer than five minutes; however, if a conversation goes past the five-minute mark, it is likely to go much longer. These five minutes feature a ritualistic exchange of information and *greetings;* the nonverbal manner as well as the content of this information subtly cues other conversants as to whether the speaker wants to continue to talk or to end the conversation. For example, if I want to talk longer, I might answer the ritual question How are you? with something other than one of the usual responses; this gives my conversant the opportunity to ignore my unconventional response and end the conversation or to respond to it and open a space for a longer conversation.

Turn taking refers to the process by which we exchange the roles and responsibilities of speakers and listeners in conversations. There are complicated patterns of signals that allow us, for the most part, to have our chance to speak and to allow our interlocutors the same privilege (Duncan 1985).

Nofsinger (1975) coined the term *demand ticket* for conversational devices that people use to get a chance to speak. These include complex patterns of gaze, clearing one's throat, subtle shifts in posture (generally leaning forward), and facial expressions that others recognize as preparing to speak.

The opposite of a demand ticket is a *turn-yielding device*. These devices consist of cues that speakers use to signal that they are about finished speaking and would appreciate someone else taking a turn. Turn-yielding cues include rapid eye movements or a series of dysfluencies (such as "uh") with a slowing rate of speech.

In a conversation with more than two people, a speaker sometimes just gives up, allowing the others to compete for the next speaking turn. On other occasions, however, speakers designate the next speaker. One way of doing this is by *direct address:* after making a statement, the speaker adds, "Don't you agree, Tom?" Another turn-selection device is *third-person refer-ence.* After making a statement, the speaker addresses Mary but says, "and I'm quite sure of this because Tom agrees with me." These turn-selection devices are surprisingly powerful. Those conversants who ignore them are treated as if they have violated the deontic logic of conversation; that is, they have done something that they ought not to have done.

Coordinating the end of a conversation, or the end of an episode within an ongoing conversation, often requires a skillful performance. In a study of "The Rhetoric of Goodbye," Knapp et al. (1973) found that conversants try to accomplish three things when they end a conversation. First, they summa-rize the conversation, saying what has been done ("Well! We sure had fun! Thanks for the good company!"). Second, they signal the impending de-creased access between them ("I guess I won't see you again until next week."). Third, they signal supportiveness ("See you later!" "I'll give you a call this weekend!" or simply, "Good-bye!").

Like the research on rules discussed earlier, the most significant contri-bution of these studies is to show that we use a wide array of both subtle and blatant cues as a way of coordinating our punctuations of episodes. The specific array of cues used differ among cultures, generations, and social and occupational groups. You are best advised to use the research described here as a way to sensitize you to the cues used by the people with whom you communicate rather than as a list of what particular cues mean. Of course, the meaning of these cues is in how they are used, and uses vary and change.

Give Accounts

In Chapter 1, we used "accounts" as a way of describing the moral orders of our social worlds. They are also effective tools for negotiating what episode is occurring and for negotiating the meaning of particular acts within episodes. As Buttny (1990, p. 219) put it,

> *An account is an explanation offered to an accuser which attempts to change the potentially pejorative meanings of action. What is interesting about this is how a bit of talk in just the right place can transform what was initially seen as reproachable to something seen now as justifiable or at least understandable.*

Disclaimers.   Some accounts are offered *before* performing an act that might create a coordination problem (Hewitt and Stokes 1975). These are called *disclaimers,* and there are several types of disclaimers.

■ *Hedging*: "I'm not sure about this, but . . . ." "That surprises me, and I haven't given it much thought, but my first reaction would be . . . ." Hedging is an explicit statement that what follows is tentative. It signals others that the speaker is not willing to defend what follows; it offers a blatant opening for the other to persuade, inform, or disagree.

■ *Giving credentials*: "Don't get me wrong, I think your hair is lovely, but . . . ." "I'm not prejudiced, some of my best friends are . . . ." Giving credentials is a way of softening an anticipated negative reaction to what the speaker is about to say.

■ *Sin licenses*: "I know its not 'politically correct' to say this, but . . . ." "You will find this offensive, but . . . ." Sin licenses are statements that acknowledge that what is about to be said violates the script for appropriate behavior. By acknowledging that, the speaker answers the anticipated question, Don't you know any better than to say that? and claims that there must be substantial reasons for him or her to make the statement. If they work, sin licenses focus attention on the statement itself rather than on the speaker's propriety in making the statement.

■ *Cognitive accounts*: "I know this sounds crazy, but . . . ." "You may think this silly, but . . . ." Cognitive accounts give an answer to the anticipated challenge of whether the speaker has lost her or his mind. By showing that the speaker at least knows that the statement he or she is about to make strains the boundaries of rationality, the speaker hopes to be perceived as rational.

■ *Appeal for suspended judgment*: "Hear me out before you get angry . . ." "Will you listen to me first and then tell me I'm crazy?" These appeals for suspended judgment ask for an opportunity to explain the statement that is about to be made before being required to defend oneself or the statement from attack.

Excuses.   Accounts given *after* an act that threatens the ability to coordinate activities were summarized by Semin and Manstead (1983). They called these after-the-fact accounts *excuses.*

■ *Accidents:* Speakers deny their intention to threaten the coordinated episode ("I didn't mean to do it!")
■ *Mistakes:* Speakers deny volition by saying that others made them do the act ("I was coerced!"), that they were temporarily insane ("I just lost my head!"), or that they did not have the authority or power to do what needed to be done ("I tried, but failed!").
■ *Evasion:* Speakers deny agency by saying that it was not they who did the

dreadful deed, that they have amnesia ("I cannot recall having done that"), or that they did not act alone ("Others are equally guilty as I; since we cannot all be punished equally, I should not be punished at all").

■ *Appeals for sympathy:* Speakers appeal to mitigating circumstances ("It seemed like a good idea at the time" "I've had a rough life—what do you expect from me?").

■ *Appeals for absolution:* Speakers appeal to moral principles ("Yes, I did it, but it was in revenge for what he had done to me" "It was in self-defense" "If I had not spiked the tree, the logging company would have done a greater evil by cutting down the forest").

Standing alone, outside the flow of conversation, all of these accounts and excuses seem pretty lame. In the situations in which they occur, they may also seem disingenuous and self-serving, or they may work quite well to keep the coordinated production of the episode on track.

Metacommunicate

As Bateson defined it, metacommunication is the use of statements that comprise the relationship between the speakers. We can easily expand that definition to include explicit reference to the episode, or what the speakers are doing to and with each other.

The following account of an actual event illustrates both the need for, and difficulty we sometimes have in, achieving metacommunication. In some places, school teachers are legally required to report suspected child abuse. Social workers are then assigned to visit the home of the child and discuss the charge with the parents. If they determine that abuse is occurring, they are required to institute legal proceedings. One social worker realized, to her dismay, that she was assigned to investigate her best friend, with whom she often talked about their children. As friends, they had a well-developed script for talking about their families; as a social worker, she had a well-developed script for conducting an investigative interview for potential child abuse. Not surprisingly, the two scripts did not match. What was she to do?

When she arrived at the door, the social worker was welcomed. When she said, "I'm here to talk about your children," this was heard as the beginning of an episode in which friends talk about their families. It took her several attempts before her statement was heard as a metacommunication that explained that the episode that they would follow today would follow a very different script. Needless to say, the warmth of the initial welcome faded quickly.

Reconstruct the Context

Sometimes the problem in coordinating an episode goes beyond simply adjusting the conversants' lines of action so that they do not trip over each other. You may find yourself in an episode in which you do not want to participate. Whatever is happening, you do not want to be involved. For example, people are sometimes cruel. If a group of people are taunting a self-conscious teenager, they may offer you a part in their script that you do not want. How do you *avoid* participating in the unwanted episode?

■ *Exiting the situation:* One way to avoid participating in an unwanted episode is to leave it. ("Do what you will, but as for me, leave me out!")
■ *Blocking the performance of the episode:* Another way to avoid participating in an unwanted episode is to prevent it from occurring ("Anyone who wants to continue will do so over my dead body!").
■ *Reframing:* Reframing means the construction of a different episode. Recall the distinction between "stories told" and "stories lived" that was made in Chapter 1. Employing this distinction, we can discern two strategies of reframing.

Changing the story you *tell* yourself about the episode is one way of reframing. If you reframe the issue, you may find that you are not obligated to participate, or that the episode is not nearly as distasteful as you had thought. For example, how should you participate in episodes in which race relations are central? If you frame race relations as a question of who will exploit whom and punctuate the present moment as the extension of thousands of years of exploitation, then a battle to the finish is the only episode you can imagine. But if you reframe the issue as how we in the present can collectively achieve a nonexploitative relationship, then you have many more choices.

You have to change the pattern of coordinated action itself if you are to reframe stories *lived* (Branham and Pearce 1985). To do this, you have to perform an act that meets three conditions. First, the act must fit the existing, unfolding logic of meaning and action sufficiently well to be relevant. That is, the interlocutors have to take it into account. Second, it must differ from the existing, unfolding logic of meaning and action to such an extent that it necessitates a change in the frame. To use Goffman's terms, it introduces a new "key" for the interpretation of what is in the frame, what are the most important elements in the frame, and what the elements in the frame mean. Third, it must initiate a sequence of subsequent acts that make those changes in the frame real. That is, the new frame is "made" in the continued enactment of the episode.

A Final Word: How Do our Social Worlds Appear "Real" to Us?

The transmission model of communication would have us believe that the real world exists before and outside our social worlds. In this view, communication works by representing the objects of that world that include both an *outer* realm of things and raw happenings and an *inner* world of thoughts and mental images.

The social constructionist position sharply disagrees. Philosopher Richard Rorty (1989, p. 21) claimed that "we have no prelinguistic consciousness to which language needs to be adequate, no deep sense of how things are which it is the duty of philosophers to spell out in language. What is described as such a consciousness is simply a disposition to use the language of our ancestors, to worship the corpses of their metaphors." If we take Rorty at face value, he urges us to acknowledge our freedom to adopt new metaphors, and to live *in* them rather than try to look *through* them to some more basic level of reality.

Yeah, but . . . if our lives are *only* the metaphors we use and the stories we *tell*, why do we die when we get sick, and how is it that we get so caught up in our stories about who we are and what is right and beautiful that we will fight and suffer for them? I think Rorty overstates his case because he still thinks in terms of a dualism, with raw happenings on one side and mental stuff on the other. At least this passage is written as if one had to choose between stories and objects.

The social constructionist perspective does not make the dualistic assumption that you have to choose between mental and physical elements. To the contrary, when we *tell* a story, we are performing an *action*. That action is itself as much a part of the universe as a rock. Unlike a rock, actions are done in language and have properties that uninterpreted objects do not. When we *call* something by name, the calling and the name itself is part of reality, not simply a representation of it.

This perspective enables us to understand how the stories we tell enmesh us so deeply. Communication theorist John Shotter (1986, p. 213) started with the now-familiar observation that language is a means for doing things, for coordinating actions and for living a life, not an instrument that pictures some nonlinguistic world. He then noted that "people's everyday practical activities can be seen as constituting or creating in the course of their own conduct 'organized settings' for their own appropriate continuation." That is, every act that we do points toward an episode in which it has meaning. That episode, in turn, constrains the choice of our next act. The unfolding sequence of coordinated acts in a conversation "to imply, posit, or intimate *in their execution* a realm of next possible actions, a world of opportunities and barriers, of enabling-constraints, relative to the activity's continuation." (Shotter 1986, p. 213)

These contexts seem objectively real to us in part because they are created by the combination of our actions and those of our interlocutors. The context made real often does not resemble what any of us had in mind. Because it differs from our individual wishes and desires, the social world both is and appears to us to be objective, a reality "out there" that we have to take into account. "As a result," Shotter said, "in their everyday practical activities, rather than acting out of any 'ideas,' 'scripts,' 'plans,' or 'inner mental representation,' people can act in a seemingly thoughtless, 'natural,' or spontaneous way *into* settings that they themselves, all unaware, have to an extent themselves created." (Shotter 1986, p. 213)

Praxis

1. Coordinating the Meaning of Acts in Episodes

This activity requires you to make the distinction between game playing and game mastery as two forms of competence. If you need to, review the discussion of this distinction in Chapters 2 and 3.

If the only form of competence that we had was game playing, we would be stymied as soon as we encountered a problem coordinating our definitions of episodes with other conversants. However, game mastery suggests that we have the potential to go outside our scripts, rules, and interpretive schemas to find ways of coordinating with others. We can detect the differences between "our" rules and "their" rules for how to perform an episode, and we can do something about it.

But do what? As discussed in the "Narrative" section, we can 1) punctuate the episode, 2) give accounts, 3) metacommunicate, or 4) reconstruct the context. Review these concepts so that you can *do* these things in class and *recognize* them when others do them.

In the "Narrative" section, I described two cases of coordination problems in the enactment of episodes. One involved American servicemen and British women during World War II, the other, a young man who wanted to discuss some things with the Mayor.

Before class, working alone. Write the script of a conversation between a serviceman and a British woman as it might have happened if both communicated at the *game playing* level of competence. Now write the script of a conversation between the Mayor and the young man, again representing each as *game playing* within their own rules.

Write at least two variations of each script in which you portray the conversants using accounts, metacommunication, and reconstruction of the context as ways of coordinating the episode.

In class, working in groups. Simulate the conversations you wrote that include the *game mastery* strategies. Take turns trying out different punctuations, different accounts, different forms of metacommunication, and different ways of reconstructing the context. Be playful and creative, but as you run through a series of these conversations, discuss which seem to work and which do not, or what conditions must obtain if certain strategies are to work.

2. Identifying Cues Used to Punctuate Episodes

Station yourself where you can observe some naturally occurring conversations. A lounge or dining area on campus works well; any public place, such as a park or shopping mall, will serve.

Carefully attend to the first five minutes of conversations. What kinds of information gets talked about? How careful are speakers in exchanging turns? What are the differences between conversations that stop at or before the "five-minute barrier" and those that continue past it?

Make a list of turn-taking cues. Separate them into "demand tickets," "turn-yielding cues," and "turn-selecting devices." Pay particular attention to cues that do not resemble those described in the "Narrative." Can you identify different patterns of cues used by people from different cultures, occupations, genders, or socioeconomic status? What happens when someone refuses to honor one of these cues? Is this a violation of a logic of felt moral obligation? How are such violations dealt with?

Listen carefully for "accounts." What accounts are offered, demanded, and accepted? How are these accounts used to coordinate communication?

How do people end conversations? Give particular attention to ritualistic forms of speech and manner that signal that the conversation is over. Do these fit the pattern suggested in the "Narrative" section about the three things that people try to do when they say goodbye?

Before class. By making the observations suggested in the paragraphs above, you have been acting as a communication researcher. You have probably noted a lot of things, some of which reconfirmed your expectations and some of which surprised you. Prepare a brief report that you will present to the class. Describe what surprised you *most* and what surprised you *least* in your observations. (I suggest that you look at *interactions,* using the *conversational triplet* as your unit of observation.)

In class. Make your report and compare your findings with those of other people. Did you notice—and were you surprised by—the same things as other people? If not, what does this tell you about yourself and the other people in your class? Discuss this with them.

3. An Exercise in Coordination

Coordinating our actions with others is difficult, in part, because the others are trying to coordinate their actions with us! I was part of a group that went to a Central American country to work with some colleagues. Our first meeting ended in a great deal of laughter. We North Americans came to the meeting a few minutes late, with no set agenda, and were very "laid back." The Central Americans came to the meeting early, had a detailed agenda, and started the meeting by getting to work immediately. It became obvious to both groups that each of us had expended considerable effort to adapt to the working style of the other, so much so that we reproduced the familiar coordination problems experienced by "Gringos" and "Latinos" because we reversed the usual "scripts" for how the episode might unfold!

The interactional contingency in conversations consists of just this sort of "zigging" when the other is "zagging." To get a feel for how this works, the game *coordination* was developed (Pearce and Cronen 1980). It simulates interactional contingency in a sufficiently restricted setting so that some characteristics of the process can be made more obviously visible.

The game *coordination* uses a simple artificial language consisting of four "messages": circle, star, triangle, and square. In this language, any sequence that contains all four messages within six turns is considered eloquent, any sequence that continues for more than six turns without using all four messages is considered defective and boring, and those who produce such sequences are considered conversationally impaired. There are three additional "metarules" for using this language:

1. All conversations must begin with "circle."
2. Conversants must produce a message when it is their turn (i.e., you may not not communicate).
3. Anything not explicitly permitted is forbidden (i.e., conversants must follow the rules exactly).

Figure 4.4 contains the rules for three persons, Pat, Mike, and Ellswood.

This exercise works best if you divide into groups. Assign one person to write the conversation (on a chalkboard?) and assign two others to be "Pat" or "Mike" or "Ellswood." (As you go along, rotate assignments so that everyone gets a chance to participate in several positions).

Following the rules listed above, simulate a conversation between Pat and Mike in which Pat speaks first (by saying "circle" of course). Remember that your goal is to produce a sequence in which all four messages are contained in no more than six turns. Look at the conversation that Mike and Pat make. Is it elegant? How do Pat and Mike feel about each other? Look at the rules that Pat and Mike have to follow: are they complex, sophisticated communicators? What does this tell you about the relationship between the *conversation* and the abilities of *each conversant* viewed as an individual?

Now simulate a conversation between Pat and Ellswood, in which Pat speaks first (by saying "circle," of course). Compare this conversation with that between Pat and Mike. Which is more eloquent? What accounts for the difference? Because Pat is the same in both conversations, is Mike or Ellswood the more competent communicator? How useful is it to talk about how competent *individuals* are?

1. All conversations must begin with "
2. Each speaker must respond to the other;
3. Everything not explicitly permitted is forbidden;
4. For *Pat:*

if the other says:	*then Pat must say:*
○	□ or ★ or △
★	○ or △ or ★
△	○ or □ or ★ or △
□	

5. For *Mike:*

if the other says:	*then Mike must say:*
○	□
□	★ or □ or △
★	○ or △ or □
△	○ or □ or ★

6. For *Ellswood:*

if the other says:	*then Ellswood must say:*
○	○
□	○
★	△
△	□

Figure 4.4 *The game "coordination." This game allows you to experience the logic of meaning and action of a conversation from a first-person perspective.*

Next, have a conversation between Mike and Ellswood in which Mike speaks first (saying "circle," of course). Compare this conversation to the others. What accounts for the difference?

Finally, have a conversation between Pat and Mike in which Mike speaks first (saying "circle," of course). Compare this conversation to the others. Note how much difference so simple a thing as who speaks first can make in a conversation.

The conversations produced if you follow these directions are very different. As you probably noticed, the rules contain some tricks so that you could feel the frustrations and facilitations of interactional contingencies. Some of the conversations probably went very well, and others were frustrating. Notice that the problems you had in the "failed" episodes were not the problems of any of the individuals: all three are capable of participating in a coordinated enactment of the desired episode. Notice that the problems were not a simple function of the complexity of the rules or the amount of freedom of choice the conversants had: the "sophisticated" Pat and Mike were not always able to achieve their goals, and the "simple-minded" Ellswood was sometimes able to do quite well. When Pat and Mike were communicating, their ability to produce the desired outcome hinged on something as simple as who spoke first; when Ellswood was communicating with Pat or Mike, their ability to produce the desired outcome hinged on the particular ways that their rules "meshed" once a line of action was started.

Actual conversations differ from this simulation, of course, in that they use much more complicated languages, the rules the conversants follow are much more varied, and conversants do not always follow the rules. That having been noted, can you use the concept of interactional contingency to account for the way some conversations seem to go smoothly and others seem so frustrating?

Who do we thank or blame when things happen in conversation? Usually, when things go well we tend to take the credit; when things go badly, we blame other people. If you did not know the rules that Pat, Mike, or Ellswood were following and could base your perception of them only on their performance in the conversation, what would you think? Remember the conversation in which Pat and Mike could not produce the desired conversation but each could communicate "eloquently" with Ellswood. Pat is likely to perceive Mike as conversationally impaired and blame him for their failure, and vice versa, whereas each is likely to think, erroneously, that Ellswood is quite a sophisticated guy.

4. Unwanted Repetitive Patterns

How much control do people have over the episodes in which they participate? To what extent can they change episodes that are not going as they want? How successful are they in avoiding episodes they do not like and in finding ways of getting into those they prefer?

These questions open up some basic issues, among them autonomy, persuasion, and power. From this communication perspective, power can be defined in terms of your ability to involve yourself in desired episodes and to avoid involvement in unwanted episodes. The anatomy of oppression and exploitation, it seems to me, can be written in terms of those unwanted episodes in which you are compelled to participate and those desired episodes to which you have no access.

Do a self-inventory of your own power. To what episodes are you denied access? How is this access denied—is it that you do not have the required entry fee (e.g., there are restaurants at which I cannot eat because I simply cannot afford to) or ability (I cannot play basketball in the NBA because I cannot shoot or rebound sufficiently well). Or are you denied access on the basis of some personal characteristic, such as race, sex, age, or religion? What resources can you draw on to gain admittance to episodes in which you want to participate? Note that some episodes are fragile: you can force yourself in but only by doing such violence that the episode is not what you wanted it to be. For example, you cannot buy friendship or force yourself into a voluntary association. What communication strategies might you use to gain access to previously blocked episodes?

From this perspective, persuasion is the process of getting an interlocutor to align his or her actions so that they coordinate with your own preferred line of action.

Autonomy refers to the extent to which you are pushed and pulled by events as opposed to deciding and choosing for yourself what you will do. Psychologists have made a living arguing about whether we are autonomous agents who live and move as expressions of our "true selves" or whether our behavior is controlled by reinforcement schedules. The truth is probably a little of both, but one line of research disclosed a fascinating pattern of social interaction that we call *unwanted repetitive patterns* or "URPs" (Cronen et al. 1979). In an unwanted repetitive pattern, an autonomous agent acts as if she or he were controlled by the interaction contingency.

Two persons with whom I worked were all-too-predictable in having loud fights. We took this as an opportunity for research and found that these people sincerely did not want to fight with each other but found themselves "compelled" to act in ways that they knew would provoke and continue the fight. "When he said what he did," each reported, "I had no choice. I *had* to respond as I did." "What did you think that he would do next?" "Oh, I knew that we were getting into it again, but there was nothing else I could do."

As a matter of fact, there were many things that they could have done, but we interpreted their statement as a *valid description of their perceptions* even though it was *not an accurate representation of their options.* That is, they had become so enmeshed in the unfolding logic of the interactional contingency that they really could not think of anything else to do, or if they could think of it, doing anything else would have seemed a moral betrayal.

We interviewed a large number of other persons, and found that virtually all had particular relationships in which unwanted repetitive patterns occurred. Do you recognize yourself in this picture? Describe the circumstances in which you engage in repetitive patterns. Give particular attention to the feeling of being trapped or enmeshed in the interactional contingency. Who should you blame for being trapped in these unwanted repetitive patterns.

Before class. Choose at least one of the terms discussed above: autonomy, persuasion, and power. Describe some episode in your life in which you feel that you have an unusual amount or lack of autonomy, persuasiveness, or power. Write the script for this episode, and analyze it according to the Heyerdahl solution. How is this episode *made?* Use the concepts that you have learned, including the conversational triplet and the notion of interactional contingency. Write a short (one- or two-page) description of the episode and explanation of how you come to have so much or so little autonomy, persuasiveness, or power.

In class. Compare your report with those of other people. Look for common and unusual elements. Focus on the accounts given in the "explanations." Do they focus on *individuals* or do they describe *interactive patterns?* Which type of explanation do you find most convincing?

References

Abbott, Edwin. *Flatland: A Romance of Many Dimensions.* Princeton: Princeton University Press, 1991.

Argyle, Michael, and Beit-Hallahmi, B. *The Social Psychology of Religion.* London: Routledge and Kegan Paul, 1975.

Averill, James. *Anger and Aggression: An Essay on Emotion.* New York: Springer-Verlag, 1982.

Averill, James. *Voyages of the Heart: Living an Emotionally Creative Life.* New York: Free Press, 1992.

Bales, Robert Freed. *Interpersonal Process Analysis.* Cambridge: Addison-Wesley, 1950.

Bateson, Gregory. "A Theory of Play and Fantasy." In *Steps to an Ecology of Mind,* 177–193. New York: Ballantine, 1972.

Branham, Robert J., and Pearce, W. Barnett. "Between Text and Context: Toward a Rhetoric of Contextual Reconstruction." *Quarterly Journal of Speech* 71 (1985): 19–36.

Buttny, Richard. "Blame-Account Sequences in Therapy: The Negotiation of Relational Meanings." *Semiotica* 78 (1990): 219–247.

Cody, Michael and McLaughlin, Margaret. "The Situation as a Construct in Interpersonal Communication Research." In *The Handbook of Interpersonal Communication,* edited by Mark L. Knapp and Gerald R. Miller, 263–312. Beverly Hills, CA: Sage, 1985.

Cornelius, Randy. "The Interpersonal Logic of the Weeping Eye." Ph.D. dissertation, University of Massachusetts, 1981.

Cronen, Vernon E., Pearce, W. Barnett, and Snavely, Lonna. "A Theory of Rule Structure and Forms of Episodes, and a Study of Unwanted Repetitive Patterns (URPs)." In *Communication Yearbook III,* edited by Dan Nimmo, 225–240. New Brunswick: Transaction Press, 1979.

Cronen, Vernon E., Johnson, Kenneth, and Lannamann, John W. "Paradoxes, Double-binds, and Reflexive Loops: An Alternative Theoretical Perspective." *Family Process* 20 (1982): 91–112.

Cronen, Vernon E., Pearce, W. Barnett, and Tomm, Carl. "A Dialectical View of Personal Change." In *The Social Construction of the Person,* edited by Kenneth J. Gergen and Keith E. Davis, 203–224. New York: Springer-Verlag, 1985.

Duncan, Starkey. *Interaction Structure and Strategy.* New York: Cambridge University Press, 1985.

Forgas, Joseph. *Social Episodes: The Study of Interaction Routines.* London: Academic Press, 1979.

Forgas, Joseph P. "Episode Cognition and Personality: A Multidimensional Analysis." *Journal of Personality* 51 (1983): 34–48.

Gardner, Howard. *The Mind's New Science: A History of the Cognitive Revolution.* New York: Basic Books, 1985.

Goffman, Erving. *Relations in Public.* New York: Basic Books, 1971.

Goffman, Erving. *Frame Analysis.* Cambridge: Harvard University Press, 1974.

Grice, H. P. "Logic and Conversation." In *Syntax and Semantics: Volume 3: Speech Acts,* edited by P. Cole and J. L. Morgan. New York: Academic Press, 1975.

Gumperz, John J. "Introduction." In *Directions in Sociolinguistics,* edited by J. J. Gumperz and Del Hymes, 1–25. New York: Holt, Rinehart and Winston, 1972.

Hall, Edward T. *Beyond Culture.* Garden City: Anchor Press, 1977.

Harré, Rom. *Social Being.* Totowa: Littlefield, Adams, 1980.

Harris, Marvin. *Cows, Pigs, Wars, and Witches: The Riddles of Culture.* New York: Vintage, 1989.

Hewitt, Jack, and Stokes, Randall. "Disclaimers." *American Sociological Review* 40 (1975): 1–11.

Jones, E. E., and Gerard, H. B. *Foundations of Social Psychology.* New York: Wiley, 1967.

Keenan, Elaine. "The Universality of Conversational Postulates." *Language in Society* 5 (1975): 67–80.

Knapp, Mark L., Hart, Rodrick P., Friedrich, Gustav W., and Shulman, Gary M. "The Rhetoric of Goodbye: Verbal and Nonverbal Correlates of Human Leave-taking." *Speech Monographs* 40 (1973): 182–198.

Krivonos, P. D. and Knapp, Mark L. "Initiating Communication: What do you say when you say 'Hello'." *Central States Speech Journal* 26 (1975): 115–125.

LeGuin, Ursula. "Why are Americans Afraid of Dragons?" In *The Language of the Night: Essays on Fantasy and Science Fiction,* edited by Susan Wood, 39–46. New York: Putnam's Sons, 1972.

Lodge, David. *Nice Work: A Novel.* London: Secker and Warburg, 1988.

Lutz, Catherine. *Unnatural Emotions.* Chicago: University of Chicago Press, 1988.

Lutz, Catherine. "Morality, Domination, and Understandings of 'Justifiable Anger' among the Ifaluk." In *Everyday Understanding,* edited by Gunn R. Semin and Kenneth J. Gergen, 204–226. London: Sage, 1990.

McHugh, Peter. *Defining the Situation: The Organization of Meaning in Social Interaction.* Indianapolis: Bobbs-Merrill, 1968.

McLaughlin, Margaret L. *Conversation: How Talk is Organized.* Beverly Hills: Sage, 1984.

Milgram, Stanley. *Obedience to Authority.* New York: Harper and Row, 1974.

Miller, George E. *The Psychology of Communication: Seven Essays.* New York: Basic Books, 1967.

Nofsinger, Robert. "The Demand Ticket: A Conversational Device for Getting the Floor." *Speech Monographs,* 42 (1975): 1–9.

O'Keefe, Barbara, Delia, Jesse, and O'Keefe, Daniel. "Interaction Analysis and the Analysis of Interactional Organization." In *Studies in Symbolic Interaction,* vol. 3, 25–57. New York: JAI Press, 1980.

O'Keefe, Barbara. "The Logic of Message Design: Individual Differences in Reasoning abut Communication." *Communication Monographs* 55 (1988): 80–103.

Pearce, W. Barnett. *Communication and the Human Condition.* Carbondale: Southern Illinois University Press, 1989.

Pearce, W. Barnett and Cronen, Vernon E. *Communication, Action, and Meaning: The Creation of Social Realities.* New York: Praeger, 1980.

Pearce, W. Barnett, Cronen, Vernon E., and Conklin, Forrest. "On What to Look At When Studying Communication: A Hierarchical Model of Actors' Meanings." *Communication* 46 (1979): 195–220.

Rorty, Richard. *Contingency, Irony, and Solidarity.* New York: Cambridge, 1989.

Rosaldo, Renato. *Culture and Truth: The Remaking of Social Analysis.* Boston: Beacon Press, 1989.

Rosen, Lawrence. *Bargaining for Reality: The Construction of Social Relations in a Muslim Community.* Chicago: University of Chicago Press, 1984.

Scheflen, Albert E. *How Behavior Means.* New York: Gordon and Breach, 1973.

Semin, Gunn R., and Manstead, A. S. R. *The Accountability of Conduct: A Social Psychological Analysis.* London: Academic Press, 1983.

Shimanoff, Susan B. *Communication Rules: Theory and Research.* Beverly Hills, CA: Sage, 1980.

Shotter, John. "Speaking Practically: Whorf, the Formative Function of Comunication, and Knowing of the Third Kind." In *Contextualism and Understanding in Behavioral Science,* edited by Ralph L. Rosnow and Marianthi Georgoudi, 211–227. New York: Praeger, 1986.

Snow, Charles Percy. *The Two Cultures and the Scientific Revolution.* New York: Cambridge, 1959.

Watzlawick, Paul. *How Real is Real: An Anecdotal Introduction to Communication Theory.* New York: Vantage, 1974.

Zimbardo, P. G. "A Pirandellian Prison." *New York Times Sunday Magazine,* April 8, 1973, 38–60.

CHAPTER 5 *Relationships*

People's lives are fabricated in and by their relationships with other people. Our greatest moments of joy and sorrow are found in relationships.

Duck 1985, p. 655

[Relationships are the primary topic of language. The great evolutionary step in human communication was] the discovery of how to be specific about something other than relationships.

Bateson 1972, p. 367

We have an impoverished language of relatedness. We cannot ask whether a *relationship* hopes, fears, or wishes, nor can we understand how it is that a relationship could determine Bob's feelings and Sarah's thoughts rather than vice versa. It is as if we have thousands of terms to describe the individual pieces in a game of chess, and virtually none by which we can articulate the game itself.

Gergen 1991, p. 160

OUTLINE

Narrative

Relationships and Interpersonal Communication

Language Games and Relationships

Some Things We Know About Interpersonal Communication in Relationships

A Final Word: A Language Game for Relationships

Praxis

1. Conflict and Confusion in Multiple Relationships
2. Dealing with Confusion Competently
3. Stages in Relationship Development
4. Circular Questioning

OBJECTIVES

After reading this chapter, you will be able to

- Identify and deal with confusion in relationships more competently
- Be sensitive to changes and stability in relationships
- Understand relationships as the context in which selves are shaped
- Be able to use the techniques of "circular questioning"

KEY WORDS AND PHRASES

Some terms that will help you understand this chapter include

reflexivity, dialectical and ecological processes, relational stages, patterns of communication, and gender and communication

Narrative

To be human means to live a life immersed in social relationships. The first words that we speak name particular relationships, probably "Mama" or "Daddy." One of the first things we learned about our social worlds is that adults are differentiated by relationships. We have to learn that not all adult women are "mommies" and that conversational rules differ depending on whether your conversant is a member of the family. Ethnographers treat complex patterns of kinship relations as one of the very few "cultural universals." No matter how "advanced" or "primitive," all societies have elaborate, well-defined patterns of who is related to whom in what ways, each with its own implications for the kinds of conversations that can, must, and should occur.

Some strands of the common sense in our society treat relationships as if they were formed voluntarily by fully functioning, consenting adults. The shape and duration of these relationships are treated as if they are matters of volition; as long as all the participants in those relationships agree, then—so this perspective suggests—anything goes.

Counterpoint 5.1

Colin Turnbull's *The Human Cycle* (1983) is a fascinating comparison of the structure of relationships at five stages of life (childhood, adolescence, youth, adulthood, and old age) in three cultures (upper-class British, hunter-gatherer Mbuti, and orthodox Hindu). While insisting that "Nowhere is the world richer, more exciting, or more beautiful than it is in our own lives" (p. 15) and that, in one sense at least, "the very obvious differences between the diversity of cultures we have touched on are only skin-deep" (p. 266), Turnbull describes "the much more subtle and vital differences in our concepts of both self and society" (p. 267) that each institutionalizes. In my book, *Communication and the Human Condition* (1989), I took this argument one step further, claiming that those who live in different cultures experience fundamentally different ways of being human *because* they engage in different forms of communication. Turnbull's description of three cultures shows "alternative social systems at work, how other societies handle the business of living together, facing conflict and resolving it, ordering interpersonal and intergroup relationships into a comprehensible system that achieves the maximum advantages for the society as a whole while allowing the maximum possible freedom for each individual to develop his own way and make his own unique contribution to society." (p. 268)

Are our relationships "social contracts" freely entered into by fully functioning adults? Clearly, such relationships are possible. But is this the appropriate model for thinking about relationships? No, because such social contracts are the exception, not the norm.

Being in relationships is—to adopt the vocabulary of the new automobile showroom—a "standard feature" for human beings; it is not "optional equipment." Genetically and psychologically, human beings cannot not be in relationships with other people. The question is not *whether* we will have relations, but what kind, with whom, and with what understanding of what we are about in those relationships. We first enter into relationships before we are born; physically, we depend for our very lives on the umbilical connection to our mothers. Immediately after birth, we find our way into a complex set of relationships that we did not choose and on which we depend for physical, emotional, and social sustenance.

If I were to declare that there is little connection between interpersonal relationships and interpersonal communication, that statement would contradict every communication theorist who has ever lived as well as common sense. But having noted the obvious, that there is a close connection between conversations and relationships, the more difficult task is to determine just what that relationship is.

Relationships and Interpersonal Communication

Reflexivity is the technical term for the connection between conversations and relationships. This term requires a careful definition.

Let *conversations* be understood as forms of conjoint actions, that is, as makings and doings. (This should be a comfortable definition; it glosses over the difference between the first- and third-person definitions offered in Chapter 1 because here I just want to emphasize that conversations are something that is done.)

By *relationships,* I mean a whole series of hyphenated things, such as father-son, sister-brother, teacher-student, salesperson-customer, and aunt-nephew. However, for present purposes, I must insist on a rather unusual definition of what these familiar things are. Let relationships be understood as a set of patterned linkages in which two or more objects are constituted. (The reason for this unusual definition is discussed in the following section, "Language Games and Relationships.")

Reflexivity describes a pattern in which one thing affects another which then, in turn, affects the first. In this definition, conversations are forms of action that affect relationships, and those relationships in turn affect conversation.

To describe this process, you must think of spirals and circles, not straight lines. Although reflexivity has an inherent whiff of paradox about it, and hard-eyed prose is not necessarily the best medium for depicting it, there

Refrain 5.1

Reflexivity describes a pattern in which one thing affects another which then, in turn, affects the first.

Think of the image of a snake biting its tail or, in a more mammalian image, a puppy chasing its tail. The faster the puppy moves in pursuit, the faster the tail moves in "flight."

There are two notions of reflexivity in communication theory. One entered through cybernetics and is based on the image of a mirror: the person who is looking at the reflection is also the person reflected. The other concept entered through Wittgenstein's analysis of language and is based on the grammatical concept of reflexivity: an act performed by a person also acts upon the person who performed it.

This second, grammatical, notion of reflexivity is the one most relevant to the study of relationships and interpersonal communication.

is really nothing mysterious about it—it simply requires being careful about what language game you are using.

If Arthur and Seymour are fighting, Arthur may ask either linear or reflexive questions. Each is a part of a very different language game.

- *Linear questions:* In this fight, how can I defeat Seymour? How much will it cost me to defeat him? What resources do I have available to me? Is it in my best interest to risk these resources in order to beat him?
- *Reflexive questions:* What kind of person will I become if I win this fight with Seymour? Regardless of who wins, what kind of social world are we creating by fighting? What will it cost me if I defeat him? What will I miss most when the fight is over?

We can pull out three different aspects of this reflexive connection; all three combine to describe the reflexive connection.

Relationships Are Made in Conversations

Relationships are an important part of our social worlds, and like all other events and objects in our social worlds, are made in conversations. This means that we should apply the Heyerdahl solution if we want to understand a particular relationship. That is, if you want to understand your relationship with your favorite uncle *from a communication perspective,* you would look at how it is made in conversations.

Having looked at the characteristics of speech acts and episodes, however, you can think about some of the implications of applying the Heyerdahl

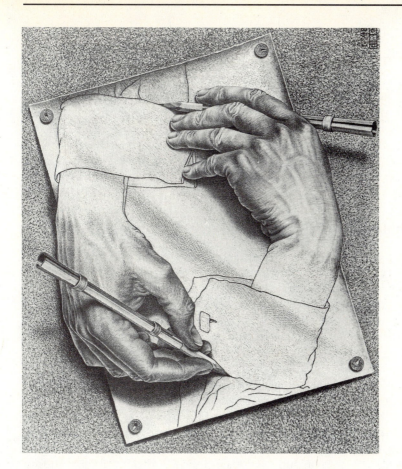

Counterpoint 5.2

Many people find that the etchings of M. C. Escher capture something important about reflexive social processes. Figure 5.1 shows a famous print of one hand drawing another hand, but that hand is drawing the first. The best way that I know to explain the statement that the conversations in which we make our relationships are also made by those relationships is to point to this picture and say that the patterns of connections are like that!

Remember the discussion of monologue and dialogue as two forms of communication. I believe that both forms of communication are reflexive, but whereas monologue shields itself from a recognition of reflexive effects, dialogue places them in the foreground.

solution. It is not just that relationships are made in conversations; it is that relationships bear in them the consequences of being made in a process having the specific characteristics of conversation. That is, the structural features of conversation are projected onto the relationships they make.

For instance, speech acts are inherently unfinished; their meaning emerges in the continuing sequence of actions. What implications does this unfinished process have in the construction on relationships? Again, episodes are transpersonal, durative processes of interaction in which neither conversant has total control over what is happening. What can we understand about relationships if we attend to this feature of the process by which they are made?

Relationships Are Made of Clusters of Conversations

Except in the most unusual circumstances, a single conversation does not comprise a relationship. Again, except in the most unusual circumstances, no relationship includes all of the conversations in which a person engages.

If we take the statements in the preceding paragraph as anchors, then the questions we must address include *which* conversations are "in" and which "outside of" a relationship, and *by what process* this punctuation is made.

A story is told of a traveler who stopped where a group of men were working. "What are you doing?" She asked the first man who walked by. "I'm carrying a lot of very heavy stones from one place to another!" he replied, complaining. Undeterred, she asked the next man, who was carrying load similar to that of the first man. "What are you doing?" "I'm building a magnificent temple!" he boasted.

This story focuses on punctuation, and the fact that it can serve equally well for understanding the meaning of episodes and for understanding relationships shows that the activity of punctuation is common to both. As an episode, the question is whether the workmen *punctuated* the act of carrying a lot of heavy stones as a part of "building a magnificent temple" or not. In much the same way, we have conversations that weigh as much as a ten-ton rock (although their weights are calibrated on different scales) and the question is, of which relationships are these a part? If they are part of relationships that are as lofty to the spirit as building a temple, then the conversation means something very different than if it is part of a relationship in which the workman is exploited or finds meaningless.

We are not always free to punctuate conversations into or out of relationships as we see fit. Let's distinguish three types of relationships. Some relationships are genetic: you are your parents' child and always will be. Other relationships are conventional, defined by law or custom. For example, marriages are conventional, as are partnerships and, to some extent, relationships among employees and employers. Finally, other relationships are purely voluntary, the result of the free choice of the participants.

These voluntary relationships are usefully described by the "social contract" concept with which I began this chapter. For example, when you initiate a same-sex friendship, you do not have to call your parents and friends and make a formal announcement, you seldom rent a church or meeting room and host a celebratory party, and you probably do not receive unsolicited advice from distant aunts and uncles about how to be a "good friend." Instead, your friendship may develop without any particular fanfare and may have characteristics that are unlike those of other friendships (Wright 1978). One reason why such friendships seem free, comfortable, and spontaneous is that they are comprised only by those conversations that you punctuate as "in" them. You do not have to explain to your friend where you were last night and why you did not call last week—unless you have specifically included such conversations in your friendship.

Conventional relationships, on the other hand, have imposed punctuations of what is included and excluded. For example, if you marry, there are some legally required conversations that you must punctuate within your relationship. These include sexual activities within the marriage and the necessity to account to your mate for any sexual activities that occur (or are thought to occur) outside the marriage. These conversations also include teamwork in confronting the Internal Revenue Service and shared responsibilities for the debts you accrue.

One of the reasons why conventional relationships sometimes seem difficult or oppressive is that the conversations punctuated as the boundary of the relationship are not comfortable. Bill knows that as a good husband, he should stay home with his wife more often and go to fewer sports events with the guys, but he does not want to. Mary knows that as a good wife, she should go to more sports events with Bill but she just does not enjoy them.

Counterpoint 5.3

By keeping in mind what is inside and what is outside of the boundaries that we make by punctuation, we can understand a great deal about our social worlds. The meaning of what we see depends on our perspective, that is, whether we see if from the inside or from the outside. For example, from the outside, the walls around a set of conversations punctuated as the boundaries of a relationship may seem restrictive and confining; from the inside of that relationship, however, those same boundaries may seem comforting and liberating.

As a thought exercise, imagine what geometry would be like if our only perspective was from inside the figures that we study. Clearly, geometry is almost always performed from outside the triangles, squares, and trapezoids that preoccupy the attention of geometers. Can you imagine what kind of knowledge geometers would develop if they could only see those shapes from inside them?

At the beginning of her novel *The Dispossessed,* Ursula LeGuin (1974, pp. 1–2) makes some highly relevant observations about a wall. As you read this passage, think of the boundaries around relationships as viewed from both sides.

> *There was a wall. It did not look important. It was built of uncut rocks roughly mortared. An adult could look right over it, and even a child could climb it. Where it crossed the roadway, instead of having a gate it degenerated into mere geometry, a line, an idea of boundary. But the idea was real. It was important. For seven generations there had been nothing in the world more important than that wall.*
>
> *Like all walls it was ambiguous, two-faced. What was inside it and what was outside it depended on which side of it you were on.*
>
> *Looked at from one side, the wall enclosed a barren 60-acre field called the Port of Anarres. On the field there were a couple of large gantry cranes, a rocket pad, three warehouses, a truck garage, and a dormitory. . . . It was in fact a quarantine. The wall shut in not only the landing field but also the ships that came down out of space, and the men that came on the ships, and the worlds they came from, and the rest of the universe. It enclosed the universe, leaving Anarres outside, free.*
>
> *Looked at from the other side, the wall enclosed Anarres: the whole planet was inside it, a great prison camp, cut off from other worlds and other men, in quarantine.*

If it is possible to *describe* a relationship as the cluster of conversations that are punctuated as in it and if it is possible to determine what conversations people *would like* to add or subtract from it, we can get an interesting picture of social worlds. The meaning of a particular relationship is determined by just those conversations that occur in it. For example, Bill and Mary may have a wonderful marriage that does not include a category of conversations involving spectator sports. John and Tonia may have just as good a marriage that involves both spectator and participant athletics but does not include a category of conversations involving entertaining friends that is a central feature of Bill and Mary's relationship. On the other hand, John and Tonia may have some real problems because John wants to compete in the national skydiving contest and Tonia not only refuses to participate but argues that needlessly risking his life is a failure to accept his responsibilities as husband and father.

Genetic relationships are those about which we have no choice. As the old adage says, "Home is where, when you have to go, they have to let you in!" Cultures differ, however, in the extent to which genetics is an important structuring device for relationships. In some societies, there is more opportunity for voluntary and conventional relationships; in others, genetic relationships are more important.

Relationships Are a Category of Contexts for Conversations

The reflexive connection occurs because the relationships made in conversation are simultaneously the context in which those conversations take place. As conversants, we act *into* contexts as well as out of them, and the contexts that we imagine, perceive, or invent structure the way we communicate.

Relationships are a part of our social worlds; they are embedded in the logics of meaning and action that govern the way we think and act. Well-established contexts function as reasons for our actions; we say that we *had* to act as we did because of our relationship.

As you have become tuned to hear accounts, you probably have heard relationships cited as the purposes or reasons for unusual acts. For example, you should have little difficulty putting whole conversations around these phrases: "Because she's my friend!" "So that I can be her friend!" "That's what fathers do!" "Because I'm your father!" "Not as long as you put your feet under my dinner table, you don't!" Each of these statements is a specific point in the powerful deontic and practical logics that constitute the substance of the speaker's social worlds.

Language Games and Relationships

Ironically, the harder social scientists have tried to develop a theory about relationships, the farther they have gotten from what they are studying. The reason for this progressive distancing has to do with the language games in which social scientists do research and theory building. To compound the irony, many social scientists recognized that their problem lay in their language, but the corrective steps they took were in precisely the wrong direction.

Following the lead of nineteenth century physicists (and frankly, envious of the successes those physicists enjoyed), social scientists assumed that ordinary language is slippery and ambiguous, a poor vehicle for describing objective, precise reality. As they studied interpersonal relationships, they believed that their first language of relationships was slippery and must be made more rigid, clear, and noncontradictory so that it could describe the objective world of raw happenings.

But what if the real world of raw happenings is itself slippery and ambiguous? If relationships are made in conversations and if conversations are made by the imperfect conjoint enactment of episodes and the unfinished performance of speech acts, then it seems reasonable to say that relationships are polysemic, polyphonic, and mutable themselves. If so, an overly precise language game is bound to distort them; what is needed is a sufficiently

Counterpoint 5.4

My criticism of the project that tried to clean up language so that it can more accurately describe an allegedly perfect world is based on my belief that there is absolutely no reason to assume that the world is anything other than messy, shape changing, and heteroglossic. Certainly, if we want to describe our social worlds, we have to use a language sufficiently flexible and complex to keep up with all of the devious, mysterious things that we do.

Duncan (1962, pp. 380, 384) discussed irony, not only as a figure of speech but as a form of action.

> *Irony holds belief, the tragic moment of truth, open to doubt. It exposes motives which the actors do not know or seek to hide. Roles shift and change. . . . The ironic actor withdraws from action to become an audience to other actors, and even to himself. He comments on the action in asides, or in soliloquy which audiences are allowed to overhear. . . .*
>
> *There is a kind of double-talk in irony where we say one thing, but really mean another. This is not simply an artistic trick, for when we act, we act before several audiences, and sometimes we must act before all of them at the same time.*

polyphonic language game to catch the many nuances of relationships. As Wheelwright (1962, p. 128) put it, "If reality is largely fluid and half paradoxical, then steel nets are not the best things with which to take samples of it." Unfortunately, some social scientists committed themselves to the task of repairing their steel nets by making them even more steely.

Other social theorists have identified the problem of our language for relationships more accurately. The problem stems from the fact that our language is overly precise, linear, and static; when used to describe events and objects that are uncertain, unfinished, and mutable within a heteroglossic, polysemic, and polyphonic social world, this language distorts by making relationships seem as if they are more stable than they are.

The remainder of this section describes four attempts to deal with the problem of language for relationships.

Schutz's Concept of Interpersonal Needs

Schutz (1958) suggested that human beings have three "interpersonal needs" that must be met, just as the needs for food, air, and water must be met. These needs are for inclusion (i.e., to be a part of social groups), affection (i.e., to have someone to love), and control (i.e., to be able to affect other people). Although there are many ways to name and explain the ways in which we relate to others, this one has some merits.

Think of the need for inclusion. To be a part of a group provides a kind of comfort and certainty that enables us to function better. Certainly loneliness—an emotion prompted by the insufficient quantity or quality of relationships—has prompted as many life-changing decisions in as many lives as any other emotion. In many societies, to be expelled from the community is equivalent to being dead and is used instead of capital punishment. For many young people in a highly mobile society such as ours, loneliness is a frightening possibility and one of the factors taken into consideration when choosing where to go to school, what job to take, and what forms of interpersonal relationships in which to participate. Members of urban gangs exhibit a pathological need for inclusion that is apparently not being met elsewhere. They are willing to perform criminal acts; they wear "colors" to identify themselves to each other; they fight and die in order to belong. The military services of all nations use the same motivations to build morale, particularly in elite units.

Think of the need for affection. Most of us find it hard to deal with being hated or disliked by persons whom we meet daily. One way that we deal with being hated is to hate back; there are well-known patterns in which we "demonize" the person who will not love us as a way of justifying to ourselves why we spend so much time and energy hating them. If Randy says that Bob is crazy, an immoral monster who fiendishly schemes to destroy all that is good and beautiful, you should explore the hypothesis that Bob does not like Randy, and that Randy perceives Bob in a manner that makes that dislike tolerable. (Of course, Randy obviously does not like Bob, and Bob will very probably perceive Randy as some sort of villain or fool . . . and so the pattern will escalate. This spiral of reciprocal protection from being disliked is at least one of the ways in which feuds and wars are made.)

Perhaps we can stand not being loved, but it is even harder for us not to have something to love. Deprive a human being of all loving social relationships and she or he will love a boat, a dress, an animal, a house, or something else. Far greater than our need to be loved is our need to love, and understanding this explains a great deal of human behavior.

The need for *control* is not necessarily a manipulative one. It refers to an ability to affect those with whom we are in relation, to be taken into account. We do not want to be invisible; even persecution or outright hatred is more acceptable than simply disappearing. People who are in wheelchairs or on crutches often report that they become "invisible" to others who simply ignore them. Members of discriminated groups are invisible as long as they are in their roles (generally, menial workers or servants) and embarrassingly visible when they are not (e.g., when walking through an upperclass neighborhood after dark), and this is one of the forms of violence inflicted by economic and social class structures and racial discrimination.

The well-known syndrome called the "malevolent transformation" indicates that what people need most is to be in relationship; this need is greater than the needs for love, affection, and inclusion (or whatever other specific needs might be listed).

Malevolent transformation describes a pattern in which a person acts in what seems to be a self-defeating and opposite manner to that which would satisfy his or her unmet interpersonal needs. Groucho Marx summarized the transformation most succinctly when, after having his application for membership in an exclusive country club rejected, he said, "Ha! I'd never join a club that would have me for a member!" On another occasion, he threatened, "I'm going to join a club and hit you with it!"

Hmm . . . What is a (country) club that it can be used to "hit" someone? In the context of the malevolent transformation, Marx makes sense. That might be reason to worry!

More conventional examples of the malevolent transformation include the delinquency of Little Johnny, who needed to be included in a group but was shunned. Johnny responded by acting in ways that will forever prevent him from being included. He burned down the group's playhouse. Ten years later, if Big John needs to love and be loved but is treated as if he is a social leper, he may act in the most unlovable and unloving manner possible by being the quintessential male chauvinist pig.

This transformation of the interpersonal needs suggests that the "opposite" of each need is not its antonym (that is, "hate" rather than "love") but apathy (literally, "without emotion"); being ignored. That is, it is better to be hated than ignored because hate is a relationship, even if it is not the desired relationship. The most intolerable thing of all is to be made irrelevant or invisible, that is, to be treated as if other people's conversations are not contingent on your actions.

Buber's Implicit Theory of Reflexivity

In Chapter 2, you learned Martin Buber's (1988) distinction between monologue and dialogue. Buber's sensitivity to these distinctions grew out of his concept of relationships as (although this is not quite his way of putting it) a set of connections in which two or more entities are constituted.

Recall Buber's statement that the "I" of "I-it" is not the same "I" as the "I" of "I-thou." If a running back limps back to the huddle, the quarterback may ask, "How's the leg?" This is an "I-it" relationship; the quarterback means, "Can you do your part in the next play? If not, get off the field and I'll bring on someone who can." After the game, the quarterback may ask, "How's the leg?" In this instance, this is an "I-thou" relationship; the quarterback means "I know it's painful; do you want some help or some companionship?" Any conversational analyst could see that the running back is being given a different place in the moral orders of these interactions; it took someone with Buber's intuitive sense for reflexivity to call our attention to the fact that the quarterback also inhabits a very different place in the moral order of these conversations. The "I" of "I-thou" is not the same as the "I" of "I-it."

Buber's aphorism captures the notion that the entity "I" (as well as the other entities involved) is not separate from the others, and that the relationship is not *between* autonomous entities. Rather, the relationship is a matrix of connections and the entities "I," "it," and "thou" are constituted by being in the matrix. This is hard to say in ordinary language, so let me use some special symbols.

Our common-sense notion of a relationship is that it is *between* two or more autonomous entities. We could symbolize this concept with a hyphen. For example, the relationship *between* a father and son would be written like this: "father [-] son." To the contrary, Buber suggests that the entities "father" and "son" themselves are *in* the relationship. That is, we should write the relationship like this: [father-son].

Notice that I generalized Buber's insight from pronouns to nouns. It makes sense: how can there be a "son" unless there is a "father"? A "leader" unless there are "followers"? A "lover" unless there is a "loved one"? In all these cases, what stands on one side of the hyphen is an impossible entity unless there is a corresponding entity on the other. Relationships are nonmathematical equations in which every entity is constituted in a set of connections that contains the other.

Buber's insight can be generalized to include verbs as well. For example, the typical way of thinking about relational verbs is that they are between people: "I [love] you"; "I [hate] you." However, this way of thinking does not acknowledge the reflexivity of relationships. "Hate" and "love" are part of the set of connections in which "I" and "you" are constituted. We should punctuate these emotions like this: [I hate you] or [I love you]. Said another way, I cannot hate or love without feeling the consequences myself. Love and hate are not something an autonomous "I" does to "you"; it is a relationship in which "I" as well as "you" are constituted. The worst thing about hateful people is that they enmesh me (and you) in hateful relationships, thus constituting us as "haters."

Counterpoint 5.5

Reflexivity is the antidote to reciprocity. Many of the moral codes that people use are variations on the formula for reciprocity that might be summarized as "to others as from others." (This formula is my way of lumping together the wide range of moral codes bounded by "an eye for an eye, a tooth for a tooth" on the one hand and "do unto others before they do unto you" on the other.)

If reflexivity were worked into a moral code, it might be phrased something like this: "To others as you would want to be." (This is not quite the same as the "Golden Rule" that specifies "do unto others as you would have them do unto you.")

The rationale for a reflexive relational ethic goes something like this. If you think of yourself as *outside* your relationships, you confer love or hate on the basis of the characteristics of the other person. That is, you hate hateful people and love loveable people. From this perspective, notions of unmerited love, altruism, or compassion seem very strange. On the other hand, if you think of yourself as *inside* the relationship, your decisions about loving and hating are at least in part determined by the kind of person you want to be and your calculations of the effects of your acts on yourself. From this perspective, the person who can love only loveable persons and feels duty bound to hate hateful persons has little autonomy; she or he is being *controlled* by the characteristics of other people.

Rawlins's Dialectical Perspective

Rawlins (1992, p. 7) suggested that relationships are shaped by a dialectical process between "antagonistic yet interdependent aspects of communication." To capture the dynamic nature of relationships, we cannot use any single term. He proposed using pairs of antonyms. For example, the dialectics of contexts can be expressed in the pairs "public" and "private," and "ideal" and "real."

In the movie "When Harry Met Sally," the young people were riding in a car together, talking. If you had to use a single set of terms to describe the context in which their conversation took place, you would say "private" and "real." And yet Sally's boyfriend and Harry's girlfriend (who was also a friend of Sally's) were part of the conversation even though they were not in the car. Not only were they part of what Sally and Harry talked about, but this conversation would soon be a part of those relationships. So the context is both "private" and "public."

Rawlins said that the "interactional dialectics" of actual conversations could be expressed in four pairs of antonyms: "dependence" and "independence;" "affection" and "instrumentality," "judgment" and "acceptance," and "expressiveness" and "protectiveness." That is, the unfolding pattern of each conversation can best be described using all four of these pairs of terms.

I think that Rawlins's notion of complementary terms and a dialectical process has much to commend it. They are a constant reminder that relationships are fluid and polysemous. They provide an alternative to single words that are too precise and too linear descriptions of the process of communication that are too simplistic. I return to Rawlins's work later in this chapter.

Refrain 5.2

Rawlins believes that relationships are inherently dialectical. As such, they cannot be captured within any single description; they consist of an ongoing, irreducible tension among opposite characteristics.

The four antonyms that he suggested as descriptions of relationships are

dependence vs. independence
affection vs. instrumentality
judgment vs. acceptance
expressiveness vs. protectiveness

As I understand it, relationships do not do well if they are fully described by any of the terms on one side of the antonym. That is, to keep a relationship healthy, the tensions between dependence and independence, e.g., must be accepted. The relationship is a continuing process of moving among these antithetical aspects.

Bateson's Ecological Analysis of Relationships

The notions of system and process are among the most important discoveries of the twentieth century. In virtually every discipline, from physics to psychology, theorists have had to replace notions of entities with systems, of linear relations with complex processes, and of temporally static models with those that move time to the foreground.

In the field of communication, Gregory Bateson (1972; 1980) is one of the people who focused most precisely on this task. In essence, Bateson argued that communication should be thought of in a language game more closely resembling that of biology (particularly evolutionary theory) rather than physics (particularly Newtonian mechanics). That is, instead of thinking of communication as objects and forces that are causally related, we should think of it as a system, but then, not just any kind of system. If we adopt the language game of biology, communication should not be thought of in terms used for physiology, organized around the terms "structure" and "function." Rather, we should employ terms like those used in evolutionary theory, such as *variability, selective pressures,* and *adaptedness* (Toulmin 1982, p. 207) and ecology, such as *coevolution, synergy,* and *systemic patterns.*

In Bateson's hands, this shift in language games directs our attention to a whole set of phenomena that would likely seem irrelevant or unimportant in other vocabularies. For example, Bateson observed that human beings are mammals, and that for us—as for all mammals—relationships are our primary form of existence. If you look at all the creatures that run, crawl, and fly on this planet, you notice that there are important differences among them. Generally speaking, reptiles do not have the same form of family life as mammals. This is not an ethical difference, in that neither you nor an alligator chose to be what you are, but it is a moral difference in that you live in a moral world very different from that of, for example, an alligator.

Alligators regularly eat their young, but this cannot be considered the *crime* of infanticide. Alligators simply do not have the instincts and nervous systems capable of recognizing maternal or paternal relationships. Human beings, on the other hand, could not live without a kind of parental relationship unknown among reptiles, and this biological fact intrudes into the social worlds that we create in interpersonal communication—including the invention of "laws" that define some actions as "crimes."

Bateson spent many years observing the communication patterns of animals. He concluded that the "discourse" of "preverbal mammals" is "primarily about the rules and the contingencies of relationship" (1972, pp. 366–367). Bateson offered as an example the behavior of a cat who is telling you to feed it. The cat will meow and rub itself against your leg, particularly if you are standing in front of the refrigerator. Bateson cautions against anthropomorphizing; the cat is *not* saying "feed me" or "milk!" because cats have no such language. What cats and all other mammals have is a complex language whose content is solely about relationships. What the cat is really saying, in Bateson's guess, is something equivalent to "Mama!" or, more articulately, "Dependency! dependency!"

The great evolutionary step in language, Bateson (1972, p. 367) argues, is the "discovery of how to be specific about something other than relationship." And even here, we have not abandoned the language of relationships; we have simply permeated it with ways of talking about other things as well. If your friend says, "I have to be at the dentist at three o'clock," this clearly articulates something other than relationship but simultaneously *may* have all sorts of relational meanings, which are your job to figure out and respond to. Is it the equivalent of the cat's meow? Is your friend saying "dependency!" and asking you to drive her to the dentist? Is it a way of saying "poor me" and asking you to engage in a relationship of care taking? Is it an excuse for not paying attention to what you are saying? Is it an indirect way of saying "Don't expect to see me at our usual place later today"?

The same ability that enables us to talk about events and objects reduces our ability to talk about relationship. Bateson (1972, p. 372) wryly concludes that animals such as cats "communicate about things, when they must" by using signals that are part of a language devoted entirely to relationships; "human beings use language, which is primarily oriented toward things, to discuss relationships."

Watzlawick et al. (1967) built on Bateson's thinking. They argued that all human communication occurs on two levels simultaneously, content and relationship (see Figure 5.2). For example, when Harry tells Sally that men

Wife: Honey, you really watch too much TV.	*While the content addresses a specific behavior, the relationship is saying: I wish you didn't have so many things which take time and attention away from me. TV is only one minor example which happened to strike me at the moment.*	**Figure 5.2** *"Content" and "relationship" meanings in a conversation. (From Knapp and Vangelisti, © 1992, pp. 4–5)*
Husband: I do not.	*The relationship message has been ignored completely and the husband prepares himself for the impending battle over TV watching.*	
Wife: C'mon, honey . . . you do too.	*The wife feels obligated to defend her initial statement. She cannot or will not verbalize the major problem with the relationship, but tries not to be too argumentative at this point. She is still hoping her husband will respond to her cues that reveal the relationship message—sitting on the arm of his chair with her arm around his shoulders.*	
Husband: All right, then. I won't watch any TV for a whole week, damn it!	*He is still trying to win on the content level. His kick-me-while-I'm-down strategy is clever because if she agrees, she is really a bitch—knowing what a sacrifice it would be. (The "damn it" dramatized the sacrifice.) Besides, if she agrees, he will still "win" because she will feel guilty for having caused him to be one-down—which, of course, puts him one-up.*	
Wife: Oh, just forget it. Do what you want.	*The wife sees the trap her husband has prepared on the content level. She gives up on the possibility of positive communication on the relationship level and removes herself from his chair and starts to leave the scene.*	
Husband: Forget it! How can I forget it? You come in here and make a big deal out of my TV habits. Then, to satisfy you, I agree to cut it out completely and you say, "forget it"! What's wrong with you, anyway?	*He realizes he has "won" on the content level and finally tunes in the relationship level—only to find negative cues. As if enjoying a relationship where he dominates, he tries to prolong his "winning" streak by urging continued argument—never realizing he is also prolonging his counterpart's losing streak.*	

cannot be friends with women, he is really communicating two things. The first is an opinion, suitable for being written as a thesis for debate. The other has something to do with their relationship. Just what this means is not so clear, but it suggests that Harry is interested only in a romantic relationship with Sally.

Second, Watzlawick et al. argued that the *relationship* level is the context for the *content* level of meaning. That is, the meaning of the *opinion* that Harry offered Sally, apparently as a topic for a debate, derives its meaning from the relationship level of the statement. In other words, Sally would be very foolish if she treated Harry's statement only as a dispassionate topic for *content* analysis; she should be on her guard and try to discern what relational meaning is being expressed.

If Watzlawick et al. (1987) are right, then content and relationship levels of meaning are present in every conversation and many of the problems we have in conversations stem from the conflicts between these levels.

Knapp and Vangelisti (1992) analyzed a short, troubling conversation in terms of the content and relationship levels. Their analysis shows that the statements we make in conversations often mean far more than the words say. (See Figure 5.2)

Finally, Watzlawick et al. suggested that the two levels of content use different types of codes. The content level of statements uses a "digital" code, in which the statement either says something or it does not. Digital codes are "on" or "off," with nothing in the middle. The relational level of statements uses an *analogic* code, in which there are endless shades of meaning. Returning to Sally and Harry driving through the night, Sally should not expect to be able to identify *precisely* what Harry is saying at the relationship level. There is probably something of his male ego, something of his ideal concept of romantic relationships, and something of his immediate state of physical arousal all wrapped up in a statement that must be polysemic.

Counterpoint 5.6

Watzlawick et al.'s (1967) application of Bateson's ideas to interpersonal communication shaped a great deal of communication theory and research for 20 years. However, we now can identify some of the limitations of their thought. For example, we now believe that they erred by limiting the polysemy of statements to two levels. There are surely far more levels of context than just these two. In addition, the relationship among the levels of hierarchical contexts is variable. That is, content affects the relationship as well as vice versa; the various levels of meaning are fully reflexive. Using more complex models of the hierarchical relations among actors' meanings, researchers have been endlessly entertained by the complex, shifting, and often paradoxical patterns they have found (Cronen et al. 1982).

Bateson's key idea is that something has gone wrong in the evolution of our species' language. Like any mammal's, our language is one of relationships, but we have forgotten that and started treating it as if its primary function was to represent the objects of a preverbal world. This idea agrees with Wittgenstein's about what is wrong with our use of language (i.e., that we think it works by representing the objects of a nonlinguistic world) but differs in a very interesting way about how language actually works. Bateson locates language within the evolutionary patterns of *homo sapiens* and sees it as an incomplete and, in some ways at least, dysfunctional evolution from a complex system for expressing relationships; Wittgenstein locates language within the complex patterns of conjoint activities in which people engage, identifying it with the way it is used in those language games.

These are not incommensurate perspectives, and both lead to some interesting conclusions. Bateson explained that he was outraged by the confounded patterns created by the "false epistemology" that results when we forget that we are *in* an ecological system.

> If you put God outside and set him vis-a-vis his creation and if you have the idea that you are created in his image, you will logically and naturally see yourself as outside and against the things around you. And as you arrogate all mind to yourself, you will see the world around you as mindless and therefore not entitled to moral or ethical consideration. The environment will seem to be yours to exploit. Your survival unit will be you and your folks or conspecifics against the environment of other social units, other races, and the brutes and vegetable.
>
> If this is your estimate of your relation to nature and you have an advanced technology, *your likelihood of survival will be that of a snowball in hell. You will die either of the toxic by-products of your own hate, or, simply, of over-population and overgrazing. The raw materials of the world are finite (Bateson 1972, p. 462).*

Wittgenstein had a similar "therapeutic" objective. Convinced that our misuse of language gets us into trouble, his project was to develop a method for making clear what we mean by what we say so that we could avoid the troubles that are built into our language.

The Missing Social Constructionist Alternative

The process of developing a language game that works well for understanding interpersonal communication in social relationships is far from finished. The approaches reviewed earlier all have some important strengths that commend them, and most of them can be extended far beyond where they are now.

I titled this subsection "The Missing Social Constructionist Alternative" because I believe that some very important work remains to be done in this area. There has been a great deal of work from the social constructionist perspective on episodes, selves, and cultures. For some reason, the social construction of relationships has been neglected.

Some Things We Know About Interpersonal Communication in Relationships

The "things we know" about interpersonal communication in relationships, or anything else for that matter, are "constructed." Remember Prigogine's comment about science being a conversation with nature. Nature, he said, always answers our questions but only in the terms in which we posed them.

When researchers have looked at relationships, what they found is structured by the language games they used to observe, describe, and report the phenomenon *and* by the language games of the conversations in which these findings have become a part. For example, a researcher who wants to publish some advice about relationships in a popular magazine must use a different language game than is required by scholarly journals. This process is particularly important when social scientists are dealing with aspects of experience that are familiar to us all. It is unlikely that any research project will disclose something that we did not already know. More common is the experience of bringing an aspect of common knowledge to the collective attention of a group of scholars who engage in sometimes heated debate in an attempt to determine its implications. That is, they negotiate about what language game is most useful for thinking about this part of our social worlds. In what episodes should we deal with this bit of information? How shall we punctuate this study?

Counterpoint 5.7

In the discussion of "what we know" about interpersonal communication, or anything else, I am referring to the fact that *knowledge* is socially constructed in processes of conversation, and that the content of knowledge is structured by the frames of those conversations. That is, one set of questions has to do with the "findings" of a particular research project. These questions will focus on the methodology used: were the measurements or observations reliable? Were they valid? How powerful were the statistical tests?

However, these questions all arise within a punctuated frame. (The technical name for such a frame in science is *paradigm*). We know that such frames are far from neutral. Whatever frame (or paradigm) comprises the social worlds in which "what we know" exists imposes its own biases. With the tools we have developed for conversational analysis, we can ask questions about the frame itself. Who is included and who excluded from these conversations? What language games are required (e.g., those that use terms like *reliability* and *validity*)? Which permitted, or forbidden (e.g., those in which the scientist says, "I have a hunch . . ." or "Your data are ugly")? What are the conversational triplets in which "findings" are made?

These questions are taken seriously within the scientific community. For example, if I attend a professional convention and report some of my activities during the previous year, what is the process that determines whether that report is casual conversation of interest only to my friends, a classic blunder that reduces the sum total of human knowledge by some appreciable amount, or a finding that all other researchers will have to take into account for years to come? LaTour and Woolgar (1986) found that the routine conversational practices in scientific laboratories construct some things as "knowledge" and other things as just markings on a piece of paper.

What does it take to be a communication theorist, sociologist, psychologist, historian, art critic, or anything else? Among other things, it means *talking* like communication theorists (or art historians or economists) do. That is, adopting their language games is part of the process by which you are initiated into membership of the club. But you know that language games are not neutral with respect to social power or to questions about what exists and what is the significance of what exists. A whole new subdiscipline has developed called the "rhetoric of science." It describes and critiques the language games of particular branches of science, pointing out what is useful and what is mystifying about the ways that, for example, economists talk like economists (Nelson et al. 1987).

In this section, I have punctuated "what we know" about interpersonal communication in relationships in three categories.

First, a good deal of research has posed the question What types of relationships are there? The results of these studies comprise taxonomies, or a set of categories into which all relationships can be indexed.

Second, many researchers have been motivated by the fact that relationships do not stand still. Not only is there something like a life-cycle of relationships, but there is a life-cycle of people in relationships. They ask Are there regular features in the changes that occur in relationships over time? Are these correlated with developmental changes in the human life cycle? This research focused on development stages.

Third, some researchers focus on patterns of communication themselves, wondering what are the relationships between certain kinds of conversations and the relationships in which they occur. These researchers ask What are some of the interesting patterns of communication that occur? In what kinds of relationships do they occur? What do they do to those relationships?

Types of Relationships

Are there underlying dimensions of interpersonal relationships? Boxes, houses, and bodies can be described precisely using the dimensions of height, width, depth, and weight; are there comparable dimensions for describing interpersonal relationships? Can we talk about relationships in the same way that we can talk about the size of a car or linebacker? Perhaps.

Let us first note that the scales for describing interpersonal relationships are not nearly as precise as those for measuring height. Instead of carefully calibrated scales and uniform measures, the best way of characterizing relationships derives from ordinary language. We have a rich array of vocabulary; we distinguish between loving someone, liking them, disliking them, hating them, and hardly knowing them. We expect each other to recognize and use subtle distinctions between "just friends," "friends," "boyfriends/girlfriends," "lovers," and people about whom we are "serious." Important conversations hinge on establishing just these differences, but ordinary language is notoriously imprecise. As we know, people use language in a wide variety of ways. If Tom is your friend and Bill is your friend, are your relationships to them the same? Clearly not, and a persistent attempt to get you to describe the differences among them with mathematical precision will make you very frustrated because ordinary language just does not work that way. But how can ordinary language be improved?

For about 20 years, a group of researchers tried to discern the underlying dimensions on which differences in interpersonal relationships were judged. The two most important factors emerging from these studies (as shown in Figure 5.3) are a continuum running from "friendly" to "hostile" relations, and a continuum from "dominant" to "submissive" behavior. These continuums are unrelated to each other, and thus can be represented as coordinates on a graph. That is, a relationship can be described by identifying the location

Figure 5.3
Two-dimensional model of interpersonal relationships. (From Knapp and Vangelisti © 1992 Allyn and Bacon.)

of each person. Bill and Sally may have a relationship identified as "friendly-dominant" and "friendly-submissive"; Jane and Glen a relationship as "hostile-dominant" and "hostile-dominant." As you would expect, Glen and Jane fight a lot (struggling over who is the dominant person in the relationship), but Sally and Bill get along well, having "agreed" that they are friendly and that Sally is the dominant person in the relationship.

Social psychologist Robert Carson (1969) noted that the dynamics of these two continuums are different. If we take each location in the matrix as simultaneously *expressing* a definition of the relationship and *requesting* the other to respond appropriately, then the rules are to respond with an *equal* degree of friendliness or hostility and an *opposite* degree of dominance and submissiveness.

■ *Complementary* relationships are stable because the participants "agree" about both dimensions of their relationship. Conversants in complementary relationships should be able to co-construct speech acts and episodes without great difficulty because they draw on compatible understandings of their relationship. In the same way, the conversations they produce are likely to reproduce the relationship in pretty much the same form as it was before their conversation. Using this system for description, there are two forms of complementary relations:

> Hostile-dominant–hostile-submissive
> Friendly-dominant–friendly-submissive

■ *Noncomplementary* relationships are unstable because the participants "agree" about one dimension of their relationship but not about the other. Conversants in noncomplementary relations are likely to have difficulty co-constructing speech acts and episodes consistent with their preferred lines of action; whatever is the ostensible *content* of the conversations, they are continuing to negotiate about the non–agreed-on dimension of their relationship. There are six forms of noncomplementary relationships:

> Hostile-dominant–hostile-dominant
> Hostile-submissive–hostile-submissive
> Friendly-dominant–friendly-dominant
> Friendly-submissive–friendly-submissive
> Hostile-dominant–friendly-submissive
> Friendly-dominant–hostile-submissive

If the conversants disagree about both dimensions of their relationship, the relationship is *anticomplementary*. These relationships are extremely unstable; there is hardly enough agreement to permit the participants to converse. They will have extreme difficulty in co-constructing coherent speech acts or episodes. There are only two forms of anticomplementary relationships:

Friendly-dominant–hostile-dominant
Friendly-submissive–hostile-submissive

Carson's two-dimensional model of relationships provides us with a vocabulary that seems more precise than ordinary language. To use the model to its fullest advantage, however, we have to remember the notions of continuums and find a way of including time.

The use of continuums in this model reminds us that there are distinctions in the amount of hostility and dominance being expressed. Perhaps most of our relational concerns are not *whether* our relationship falls in the "friendly" quadrant but *what extent* or *what type* of friendliness is involved. When the person you love asks if the two of you can be friends, this appears a comfortable, complementary relationship in the "friendly" end of the continuum, but it can break your heart.

This same issue reminds us of the importance of time. Relationships never stand still; sometimes they are reproduced in stable forms, but they are always in the process of being made. You can use Carson's matrix to map the changes in a relationship. Carson illustrated this use of the model by describing an exploitative episode that Eric Berne (1964) called, with new-wave explicitness, "Now I've Got You, You Son of a Bitch!" (Berne used the acronym NIGYSOB as an abbreviation [Figure 5.4].)

As the conversation begins, Joe acts friendly, slightly submissive; Gene responds appropriately: friendly, slightly dominant. A series of moves occur in which Joe acts increasingly submissive, "inviting" Gene to become more and more dominant, until finally Gene is acting in an untenably dominant manner. Joe then jumps to the hostile dominant quadrant, issuing an unanswerable challenge to Gene's dominance, forcing Gene to withdraw. Joe can then shout the name of the game. The conversation might go like this:

1. *Joe:* Can you help me choose a tie to go with this suit?
2. *Gene:* Sure, how about the blue one?
3. *Joe:* Really? Boy, I would not have picked that one.
4. *Gene:* Yes, well, my girlfriend says that I have good taste in color combinations.
5. *Joe:* I think color combinations are the most difficult part of men's fashions.
6. *Gene:* Not really. If you know something about physics, you know that there are only a few primary colors, and if you stick with them you won't get lost in all the funny shades that designers come up with. Trust me on this.
7. *Joe:* No, I don't think I will. I'm writing an article for *Gentleman's Quarterly,* you see, and I don't think the editor would be satisfied

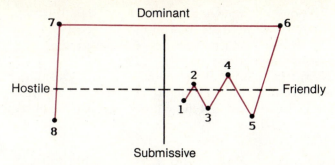

Figure 5.4 *Putting time into the two-dimensional model. This is a diagram of the episode NIGYSOB. The conversation itself is in the Narrative. Joe takes turns 1, 3, 5, and 7; Gene takes turns 2, 4, and 6. If the game is well played, Gene is left with no choice; the logic of meaning and action compels him to make a statement in turn #8 that will be diagrammed in the "hostile-submissive" quadrant.*

with such simple-minded advice as "stick to the primary colors." Do you think your girlfriend is trying to be polite when she compliments your fashion taste, or is she as dumb as you are?

I never said that Joe was a nice guy, but the structure of this episode is perhaps all too common. A similar structure can be imposed on the "friendly-hostile" continuum, showing how someone can invite another person to become increasingly friendly (or hostile) until they take an untenable position, then the first jumps to the other side, exposing the other to ridicule.

Other researchers have found a four-dimensional model underlying judgments of relationships. Perhaps the most respected of these is the study by Wish et al. (1976). It requires the ability to visualize in four-dimensional space. That's easy for computers to do, but very difficult to write about in words, which stand in straight lines and move from left to right one space at a time. Imagine four continuums, joined at the middle, each at right angles to all of the others. The continuums are:

- Cooperative-friendly–competitive-hostile
- Equal-unequal
- Intense-superficial
- Socioemotional-informal–task-oriented–formal

Wish et al.'s four-factor model does not contradict Carson's simpler two-factor model but adds some further distinctions. Their data indicate that most of the differentiations that human beings make in their perceptions of relationships can be accounted for by arraying them along these four dimensions.

How many distinctions are enough? If we shift from a third-person perspective (i.e., asking What accounts for most of the variance in the way *they* perceive their relationships?) to a first-person perspective (i.e., asking How can I best understand the relationship in which I am now acting?), we may get no single answer to the question of the optimal number of categories. In one situation, I may need only one dimension of judgment to know that my best relational move is "away, fast." In others, I may need all the subtlety I can get.

Developmental Stages in Relationships

In an introduction to one of his films, Woody Allen says that "Relationships are like sharks; they must keep moving or die." In his lectures about interpersonal communication, Jim Applegate notes that Allen is a poor guide to ichthyology. Biologists have found that, according to this criterion, not even sharks are like sharks: at least some sharks rest comfortably without moving. Relationships are always in the process of being remade, but one of the remarkable things about relationships is that they are so stable. Allen's comment notwithstanding, the most difficult task that we sometimes face is to introduce change in relationships.

This is not to say that change does not occur. It is to note that change is the exception rather than the rule, and that change, when it occurs, is likely to follow well-worn paths rather than generate something unique. In the next paragraphs, I want to focus on some of the normal phases of relational change. To further limit the discussion, I will focus on *voluntary* relationships, simply noting here that genetic and social relationships change, too.

In contemporary Western culture, one of the most pressing tasks for young adults is to develop a *voluntary* relationship that will be the basis of their family. (In other cultures and at other times, this task did not exist: parents would arrange marriages; the young adults' task was simply to show up and make the best of it.) The difficulty of this task is evidenced by the amount of energy it consumes and the amount of money that is devoted to it. (Think it through: how much time and money is spent on learning the social skills necessary to impress a future mate, being at the right spot to meet him or her, fantasizing about and planning for the relationship, listening to love songs, watching romantic movies, reading magazines, and all the rest?)

Knapp and Vangelisti (1992) developed a general model of interaction stages in relationships (Figure 5.5). This model divides the process into two halves, "coming together" and "coming apart." Each of these halves is further divided into five "stages," which are the reciprocals of each other. That is, the first stage of "coming together" is "initiating" and the last stage of "coming apart" is "terminating." This follows the rule that the first thing that you do in a relationship is the last thing that you undo.

The crucial parts of the model are in the middle stages. Assume that

Process	Stage	Representative Dialogue
Coming Together	Initiating	"Hi, how ya doin'?" "Fine. You?"
	Experimenting	"Oh, so you like to ski . . . so do I." "You do?! Great. Where do you go?"
	Intensifying	"I . . . I think I love you." "I love you too."
	Integrating	"I feel so much a part of you." "Yeah, we are like one person. What happens to you happens to me."
	Bonding	"I want to be with you always." "Let's get married."
Coming Apart	Differentiating	"I just don't like big social gatherings." "Sometimes I don't understand you. This is one area where I'm certainly not like you at all."
	Circumscribing	"Did you have a good time on your trip?" "What time will dinner be ready?"
	Stagnating	"What's there to talk about?" "Right. I know what you're going to say and you know what I'm going to say."
	Avoiding	"I'm so busy. I just don't know when I'll be able to see you." "If I'm not around when you try, you'll understand."
	Terminating	"I'm leaving you . . . and don't bother trying to contact me." "Don't worry."

Figure 5.5
A model of interactional stages. (From Knapp and Vangelisti, 1992, p. 33)

you have formed a relationship. Some important skills are required to determine the extent to which you achieve and maintain "integration" and "bonding." A continual negotiation during the course of the relationship will construct a logic of interaction that constitutes "integrating" on one hand and "circumscribing" on the other; that constitutes "bonding" on one hand and "differentiating" on the other.

Knapp and Vangelisti take care to warn that this model of interaction stages does not assume a mechanical progression. They recognize that the process is not necessarily linear—that is, a one-way movement through the stages—although it may be. Sometimes people skip stages, as in a "one-night stand" of sexual intimacy with someone in whose life you are not at all "integrated." However, Knapp and Vangelisti (1992, p. 53) believe that most people develop relationships in something like the sequence described in the model. Further, they believe that things are done in each stage that prepare for the next. "Skipping steps is a gamble," they say, because the relational partners do not have the information they need to take the next step or to decide whether they want to take the next step. "Some social norms even help to inhibit skipping steps" (1992, p. 53).

Although relationships are "never at rest, continually moving and in flux" (1992, p. 52), Knapp and Vangelisti insist that the development of relationships is irreversible. "Once something has been worked through," they said (p. 55), "it is different. Once communicators have achieved a certain level of interaction, they can never go back to 'the way we were.' " Even if they move "backward" to a previous stage of the relationship, it will be colored by their history; even if they stay within a particular stage (Knapp and Vangelisti say "stagnate"), to continue a relationship of a certain sort is not the same as to achieve that stage in a relationship. In the curious physics of interpersonal relationships, even the perceived *lack* of change can be the "cause" of change in relationships.

Knapp and Vangelisti did not distinguish among men and women in their description of relational patterns. However, there is quite a bit of work showing that men and women communicate differently (we have already explored that topic in Chapter 1), *and* that men and women have different relational styles at various points in their lives.

Earlier in this chapter, you were introduced to Rawlins's (1992) work on friendship. Recall that he treated friendship (and conversation itself) as shaped by a dialectical tension between opposing forces (e.g., the public and the private). Rawlins is particularly sensitive to the human life cycle, noting that although friendships are important at all stages of life, some of the dialectical tensions are more pressing in some stages than in others.

The "young adult" stage consists of the ages from the late teens to the early 30s. This is "a pivotal stage for exploring the roles that friendships will play in adult life, constrained by the demands of work, love relationships, and/ or family. Friends may provide crucial input regarding one's self-conceptions, career options, mate selection, community involvement, and recreational activities" (Rawlins, 1992, p. 103). Often, these years involve physical separation from one's family of origin and a change in the network of one's peers as a result of leaving high school for college or work. As a result, despite the fact that they typically have more opportunity to meet people than any other age group, young adults report more loneliness than any other age group.

There are some clear differences between the way young adult men and women form friendships. These differences explain some reasons why men and women misunderstand each other so often.

Young adult women tend to form same-sex friendships that mix the dialectic between affection and instrumentality; in these friendships, care and utility are interwoven in complex relationships. These relationships are marked by their volatility: some are uplifting and functional, whereas others are emotionally draining and burdensome. Young adult women's same-sex friendships often feature considerable psychological flux as well as transformational potential.

On the other hand, young adult men tend to stress instrumental values in their same-sex friendships. These relationships are built around shared activities rather than expressions of intimacy or affection. Compared with women's same-sex friendships, men's are stable and within a restricted array of feelings. Women, more than men, are likely to confront their same-sex friends about things they do not like about them or problems in their relationships; men—either because they are more accepting of their friends or simply because their friendships are more shallow—are less likely to discuss or confront problematic issues in their relationships. "Female friendships manifest considerable expressiveness; male friendships exhibit much more protectiveness . . . women tend to confront their friends, even at the risk of severing the bond, whereas men are inclined to skirt threatening issues. In addition, women share more emotional concerns, personal feelings, and values, and support for the other" (Rawlins 1992, pp. 109–110).

Counterpoint 5.8

Gender is one of the "hot topics" in interpersonal communication, and I think research about it has already provided information that helps us understand recurring difficulties in communication between men and women and that helps us understand women and men as inhabiting distinct "places" in the moral orders of our society. That having been said, I think more remains to be learned. Specifically, as a male, I find the descriptions of gender-inflected styles a bit foreign. It is as if the male style of same-sex friendship, for example, is being described as "lacking" something in comparison with the female style.

Of course, this is just what many women have been saying all along about research on communication style, personality, and organizational behavior! They rightly point out that women were described as being just like men, only lacking something or not acting like a man well enough! Their observation is certainly correct, and "feminist" research (whether done by women or men) is a long-overdue corrective. However, in the belief that two wrongs do not make a right, let me plunge ahead.

My own experience is that male same-sex friendships include a coordinated support of each other's autonomy and competence. Much of what is described as the shallowness or lack of self-disclosure or intimacy in male friendship is, in my judgment, interpretable as a competence-giving collaboration.

If this interpretation is correct, and I admit that I have only my own experience and non-systematic observations to vouch for it, then certain features of cross-sex friendships are interpretable. Women often act in ways that they interpret as showing intimacy and support (in Knapp and Vangelisti's terms, "integrating" and "bonding"), but their male partners interpret these actions as intrusive, controlling, and nagging. Men often act in ways that they interpret as giving sufficient space for autonomous acts within the confines of a supportive relationship (where is this in Knapp and Vangelisti's model?), but their female partners interpret these actions as withdrawing, unsupportive, uncommunicative, and uncaring (in Knapp and Vangelisti's terms, "differentiating" and "stagnating").

This interpretation can be placed over the familiar "nag-withdraw" syndrome so familiar to family therapists. In addition to different punctuations of who does what "because" the other did whatever first, men and women may interpret what is being done differently. In the most common and stereotypical pattern, "he" thinks that he is collaborating with her in a way that respects both of their autonomy and "she" thinks that she is maintaining the intimacy and caring upon which their relationship is built. However, "he" thinks that she is intruding, threatening his autonomy, trying to live his life for him. At the same time, "she" thinks that he is cold, callous, and uncaring, treating his work or the Monday Night Football game as more important than their relationship.

At least, I *think* so. Rethinking descriptions of what is going on in our social worlds is an important game that any number can play! Try your hand at explaining the different communication and friendship patterns of men and women. You might start by giving an alternative interpretation of the conversation in Figure 5.2.

Young adult men and women differ in their patterns of cross-sex friendships as well. Men sharply distinguish between same- and cross-sex friendships but make few distinctions among their relationships with women. Few of young adult men's same-sex friendships are particularly intimate or involving on the basis of care. Cross-sex friendships offer the opportunity for self-disclosure, intimacy, and emotional involvement, and these are all seen as precursors for romance. "Males, experiencing limited intimacy with other males, may therefore look to females as potentially loyal, caring and supportive partners. But, informed by the socially conditioned alternatives of either friendship or romance, they often enact their cross-sex friendships as incipient love affairs" (Rawlins 1992, p. 111).

Young adult women, on the other hand, do not distinguish so sharply between their male and female friends but do make more distinctions among their cross-sex friends. "They are able to form close relationships with females and males. And they clearly distinguish between males they consider friends and those they regard romantically" (Rawlins, 1992, p. 111).

Significant Patterns of Communication

Knapp and Vangelisti (1992) described a long list of "potentially destructive" patterns of communication. These lead to rapid movements into and through the "coming apart" stages of a relationship. Although no pattern of communication is necessarily, in all cases, unconditionally bad or harmful, some are dangerous. When they occur, you should raise a "red flag" of warning. Here are two of these patterns.

Helpful-critical patterns. What looks like an attempt to be helpful or to offer constructive criticism can be done in a manner that undercuts the rights and duties—that is, the personhood—of the other.

Mind reading occurs when one person predicts or describes what another person is feeling or thinking, how he or she will react, or what his or her motivations are. In the best of situations, mind reading indicates an empathic sensitivity; in the worst cases, it is done inappropriately or incorrectly. If inappropriate, Mary speaks for Bill, embarrassing him or not allowing him the right to decide what and how to present his thinking. If incorrect, the mind reader disqualifies Bill's rejection by attributing a perverse or pathological motivation.

> *Mary:* Oh, thanks anyway, but Bill does not like to go sailing.
> *Bill:* Yes I do, I just don't get a chance to do much of it.
> *Mary:* Now, Bill, these are our friends. You do not have to pretend to be "macho" with them. It's O.K. if you are afraid of large bodies of water.
> *Bill:* But I like sailing!
> *Mary:* I just don't know what to say. This isn't like you.

A fallacious or unsuccessfully enacted offer of help is destructive of a relationship. The episodic sequence might go like this: 1) Joan presents herself as willing to be helpful; 2) Tomas asks her to discuss a personal problem and help him decide what to do; 3) Joan agrees, assuring Tomas of her support; 4) Tomas describes his problem; 5) Joan recoils, expresses her shock and condemns Tomas; 6) Tomas reacts angrily, his self-confidence shattered; 7) Joan condemns Tomas for his anger, justifying herself as "trying to help" a person incapable of gratitude.

Critical comments may destroy relationships if they are too critical or too frequent. The most dangerous types of critical statements are those that undercut the other's rights and duties as a person, particularly the right to make statements, own feelings, and make choices. The long history of racial and sexual politics is replete with examples of this type of criticism, in which no idea is good if it comes from a woman or person of an oppressed minority. Supply your own examples of racist and sexist talk; you will encounter many of them without looking too far.

Confusing patterns.   Confusion is not always bad, but there are times and types of confusion that pose great dangers to relationships. One pattern forms a conversational triplet like this: 1) person *A* makes a statement that has two inconsistent meanings (e.g., different meanings at the *content* and *relational* level or a verbal message that might be an innocent comment or a sexually explicit remark); 2) person *B* responds to one part of person *A's* statement, ignoring the other; and 3) person *A* criticizes person *B* for not noticing or responding to the other part of the message.

For example, if Jack *says* that he and Eloise should think about their work while *nonverbally* suggesting that they become more physically intimate, he has given an inconsistent message. No matter how Eloise responds—by becoming more physically intimate or by attending to their work—she is vulnerable to a kind of attack that is very dangerous. Jack can act offended, criticize her, and claim moral justification for acting atrociously by citing the part of the message to which she did not respond.

A well-known tactic is to position oneself as deserving special attention while defining anything that the other does as insufficient. "Go ahead, have a good time. Don't let the fact that I am staying here, miserable and alone, keep you from having a good time. I want you to have a good time!" Now: how do you respond to that in such a way that it co-constructs a speech act that you can live with?

Yet another destructively confusing tactic is to get into a "who's the most sensitive" competition. If Robyn claims that she is offended because Ron said something offensive, she has cast Ron into the role of insensitive brute in such a way that he cannot extricate himself. This pattern constructs a conversational triplet in which the first turn is Robyn's accusation (perhaps enacted with a slight sob or gasp at the brutishness of her interlocutor). The second turn is Ron's "defense." However, whatever he says will be capable of being interpreted in either of two ways, both of which show him to be guilty as charged. If he *denies* that his previous actions are brutish, he thereby displays that he is so insensitive that he cannot even understand the offensiveness of his actions. On the other hand, if he *acknowledges* his guilt, he has confessed to the crime. In the third turn in this triplet, Robyn can select one of these interpretations and use it as a club with which to beat Ron.

(No conversations occur out of context, of course, and the interesting thing about the "who's more sensitive" contest is that it works only with interlocutors whose logics of meaning and action make them feel that they *ought* to be sensitive. For real insensitive brutes, this game does not work at all!)

Many people used to believe that relational confusion was always danger-ous, that paradoxes produced psychopathologies. We now know better: even the most healthy relationships contain confusion. The difference between healthy and pathological relationships is not so much the *presence* of confusion as it is the way people in those relationships *deal with* it.

Paul Watzlawick (1976, pp. 18–19) described four types of confusion in interpersonal relationships.

1. A person in a high-power position (e.g., parent or employer) punishes those in lower-power positions (e.g., children or employees) for correctly perceiving the outside world or themselves. For example, an alcoholic father demands that his children perceive him as gentle and loving even though he frequently comes home drunk and abuses them violently. Such children or employees are likely to distrust their own perceptions, spending an inordinate amount of time trying to figure out how they "should" perceive reality. Seen out of the context of the relationship, this behavior looks like schizophrenia.

2. The significant others of a particular individual expect him or her to have feelings different from those he or she actually experiences. This person is likely to feel guilty for being unable to feel what he or she "ought" to feel. Completing the reflexive loop, this guilt itself can then become one of the feelings that the person ought *not* to experience. For example, if a woman's parents have sacrificed in order for her to have a particular career, and she finds that she does not like that career, she may feel guilty for disliking her job, which is, of course, much worse than just disliking her job. Seen out of the context of this relationship, her behavior may seem like depression.

3. A person may receive simultaneous, contradictory injunctions by a significant other. These injunctions may compel the person both to act and not act. The prototypical paradox is conveyed in different channels, one of which is verbal and the other behavioral. For example, parents may tell their children: "Do what I tell you to do, not what I really want you to do" if they repeatedly *say* "Be careful" but reward daredevilish behavior. Another example is the parent or employer who says both "Win at any cost" *and* "Always act ethically." Examined out of the context of this relationship, the person may act in ways that would be considered "delinquent" or "criminal."

4. There is a class of injunctions that are paradoxical because there is no way to fulfill them without simultaneously failing to fulfill them. For example, it is very possible to act spontaneously but *not* by complying with the command "Be spontaneous!" A wife may tell her husband that she is disappointed that he did not bring her flowers. The next day, he arrives with a beautiful bouquet of roses, only to discover that they do not "count" as a valid gift because he did not bring them spontaneously. Clearly, once his wife says "Bring me flowers" he cannot bring them without having been instructed to do so. Considered outside the context of this relationship, paradoxical messages like these lead to behaviors that appear paralyzed and incompetent.

One of the most interesting effects of Watzlawick's analysis is that it locates confusion in the relationship, not the person. In later paragraphs, I use the term "the confused person." Note that I am not describing some intrapsychic, mental state of the person as "confused"; rather, I am describing the person as located in a confused relationship. To say that "he is confused" normally implies that "he"—an autonomous person—has some trait or is in some state that is disoriented. From the communication perspective, however, to say that "he is confused" is to refer to his location in relation to other people. The significance of this difference lies in the moral order invoked by the phrase "he is confused." In the first instance, it is a moral order of sickness or blame of an individual; in the second, it is a moral order that describes patterns of relationships.

Among other things, the focus on patterns of relationships helps individuals cope with the circumstances in which they find themselves. If we use a language game that defines persons as confused, our grammar points us in the direction of treating the confused persons as lacking something necessary to orient themselves to the world; with the best of intentions, we advise them to subordinate their own judgment to that of some "expert." On the other hand, if we use a language game that defines relationships as often confused, and individuals as usually acting appropriately in those relationships, our grammar helps us to respond with empathy rather than blame. We are naturally led to advise the confused person to act confidently as a game master in extricating himself or herself from the situation or changing that situation.

Watzlawick described how these forms of confusion can produce unfortunate patterns of behavior in those who are competent as game players. He suggested rather dire consequences: schizophrenia, depression, delinquency, and behavioral paralysis. However, confusion is not always bad. In fact, there are certain benefits to confusion:

> *After the initial shock, confusion triggers off an immediate search for meaning or order to reduce the anxiety inherent in any uncertain situation. The result is an unusual increase in attention, coupled with a readiness to assume causal connections even where such connections may appear to be quite nonsensical. While the search can be extended to include such small details or such remote possibilities that it leads to further confusion, it can equally well lead to fresh and creative ways of conceptualizing reality." (Watzlawick 1976, pp. 27–28)*

The interactional view. A group of therapists at the Mental Research Institute in Palo Alto, California, worked out some of the implications of Bateson's theory of communication. They integrated two of Bateson's assumptions. First, they took seriously Bateson's suggestion that our first language is relational, and we have superimposed a *content* language on top of it. They treated every utterance as if it had both *content* and *relational* meanings and that the relational meaning functioned as a context for the content meaning. Thinking of relational meanings in terms of power—that is, the meaning of each relational message has to do with dominance—they employed a vocabulary for relational messages that included three terms. Always with respect to the person addressed in the message, "one-up" messages expressed a high-power, dominating position; "one-down" messages expressed a low-power, subordinate position; and "one-across" messages expressed a neutral or medium-power, egalitarian position.

The second of Bateson's assumptions that the Palo Alto group incorporated is the notion that all communicative acts occur in contexts of relationships. That is, they adopted Bateson's social ecological frame for thinking about any particular act, person, episode, or relationship.

When these two ideas were integrated, it quickly became clear that the meaning of any message had to be determined from its place in a cluster of messages. The Palo Alto group focused on two-turn sequences, or "interactions." A one-up message, for example, means something very different if it follows another one-up message than it does if it follows a one-down message. The sequence

> one-up;
> > one-down;
> one-up

is "complementary;" whereas the sequence

> one-up;
> > one-up;
> one-up

is "symmetrical" (Sluzki and Beavin 1977). Complementary relationships tend to be stable; symmetrical relationships tend to be unstable. In fact, symmetrical relationships tend to "escalate," with each successive act being more "up" than the previous, until one person cannot sustain the escalation any more. That is, people tend to fight until one backs down.

As therapists, the Palo Alto group were particularly interested in communication patterns that caused problems. Both complementary and symmetrical patterns can cause problems, of course, but recognizing which pattern troubles the family gives the therapists direction for their intervention. If the problem was a symmetrical escalation, then any attempt by the therapists to force them to do anything—that is, if the therapist performs a one-up act—simply adds energy to the pattern. For example:

> *John:* Mary, do what I say!
> *Mary:* No, John, you do what I say!
> *Therapist:* Let me tell you both what to do!

The family might tell the therapist, "Welcome to the family!" In this case the therapist is acting, in Italian systemic therapist Gianfranco Cecchin's terms, as "Dr. Homeostat." The therapist's behavior reinforces the symmetrical pattern, which now has three participants, not just two.

However, the therapist could have offered a complimentary response:

> *Therapist:* I'm impressed! Both of you know exactly what the other should do. I'm not so sure, myself. There are some things that trouble me. Can you help me?

Will this solve John and Mary's problem? Probably not, but it does give them an invitation to participate in a conversational pattern that has a different (complementary) structure—and this tactic may open up some opportunities for them to deal with each other differently.

Another opportunity for the therapists is to engage in a paradoxical injunction. These interventions do not oppose or contradict the pattern occurring in the family. To the contrary, it joins with and extends that pattern to the point at which it is no longer functional. For example, a client who suffers from insomnia will be told to stay awake for a week. When the week is over, the client will be asked how she or he did. When the reply, "I fell asleep," is given, the therapist expresses sympathetic disappointment and sends the client off with the injunction "try harder to stay awake." After awhile, so it is reported, the problem of insomnia goes away. In the case of John and Mary, who are locked in a symmetrical escalation, the therapist might instruct them to tell each other what to do and how to do it in every area of their life; they should give detailed instructions for such tasks as brushing teeth, combing hair, and dressing. This takes the symmetrical pattern, extends it by prescribing the symptom, and in so doing reduces it to an absurdity, thereby provoking a behavioral change.

Circular questioning. Gregory Bateson's "systemic" theory of communication was brilliantly articulated as a set of practices for family therapists by Mara Silvini-Palazzoli et al. (1978; 1980). Because their Center for the Study of the Family is located Milan, Italy, they have become known as the Milan group and their work is referred to as the Milan approach in systemic therapy. Perhaps their most important contribution is "circular questioning," a remarkably powerful and adaptable way of moving around in relationships (Tomm 1985). Although designed for therapists as an interview protocol, circular questioning can be used as a means of thinking through your own relationships, as a research strategy for discerning the social structures around you (although if you ask the questions to other people, those structures will very likely change), and as a means of communicating very effectively with those with whom you are in relationship.

This form of conversation is "circular" in several ways. First, it explores circular rather than linear connections within relationships. Second, the questioning itself, as practiced in clinical settings, circulates around all the people in the group. The therapists ask first one and then another person for their

Counterpoint 5.9

Bateson noted that human communication is a very special kind of thing because it exists in a world of information, not of energy or substance. Communication, he said, is a matter of "difference."

> But what is a difference? A difference is a very peculiar and obscure concept. It is certainly not a thing or an event. This piece of paper is different from the wood of this lectern. . . . But if we start to ask about the localization of those differences, we get into trouble. Obviously the difference between the paper and the wood is not in the paper; it is obviously not in the wood; it is obviously not in the space between them, and it is obviously not in the time between them. . . .
>
> A difference, then, is an abstract matter.
>
> In the hard sciences, effects are, in general, caused by rather concrete conditions or events—impacts, forces, and so forth. But when you enter the world of communication . . . you leave behind that whole world in which effects are brought about by forces and impacts and energy exchange. You enter a world in which "effects"—and I am not sure one should still use the same word—are brought about by differences. . . .
>
> In the world of mind, nothing—that which is not—can be a cause. In the hard sciences, we ask for causes and we expect them to exist and be "real." But remember that zero is different from one, and because zero is different from one, zero can be a cause in the psychological world, the world of communication. The letter which you do not write can get an angry reply; and the income tax form which you do not fill in can trigger the Internal Revenue boys into energetic action . . . (Bateson 1972, p. 452)

perspective on the same issue. Finally, the questioning often seeks to produce "gossiping in the presence of the other." One person is asked how a second person thinks about a third; this line of questioning makes visible the circular connections among relationships.

The Milan group focused on Bateson's observation that human communication occurs in a domain of information, not energy, and that information is based on the perception of "difference." Circular questions target perceptions of difference, not "facts." For example, if John describes Father as impatient, these questions focus on "difference":

- When did he become so impatient? (asking John to compare "then" and "now")
- Other than Father, who is the next most impatient member of your

family? Who is the least impatient? (asking John to compare Father and others)

Bateson's social ecological concepts led the Milan group to insist that whole families come to therapy sessions. Using the Milan style, therapists ask one person in a family to comment, in the presence of the others, about how a second perceives a third. They usually start with the youngest member of the family or the least powerful person in a group. If the family came to therapy because the oldest daughter is bulimic, the therapist might ask each member of the family in turn, starting with the youngest:

- Who was the first to notice Sister's bulimia? Who was the last? (differentiating among relationships with Sister, from the perspective of the respondent)
- Who suffers most because Sister has bulimia?
- To whom does Sister show her condition most? To whom does she show it least?
- How does your Mother explain Sister's condition to your Father? How does your Father explain Sister's condition to your Brother?
- In your family, who blames whom the most for Sister's condition?

Communication systems are structured by reflexive loops rather than linear causal sequences; they evolve as wholes rather than just one part affecting another. Circular questioning seeks to discover some of the ways these evolutionary loops are perceived by the members of the group. Because this is all in the realm of information, the Milan group found ways of cleverly implanting suggestions about alternative ways of punctuating these loops. For example,

- To whom does Mother show her depression? (suggesting that "depression" is something "shown" in the interpersonal world of episodes rather than something "possessed by" or that "happens to" a person)
- If Mother were no longer depressed, who would miss it the most? Who would miss it the least? (suggesting that Mother's depression, whatever else it is and does, serves certain evolutionary functions within the system)
- How depressed will Mother get before she starts to be more happy? (suggesting that depression is in process and that there will be a "bottom point" and recovery?)
- Who will be the first to notice when Mother is no longer depressed? Who will be the last to notice? (suggesting that others in the family bear some role in the social construction of depression)
- When Mother is no longer depressed and you all look back on this time, what will Mother miss most about being depressed? (suggesting that there will be a time when the problem is history and showing that Mother can view her depression from perspectives other than that of a victim).

Finally, the Milan group were well aware that interviews are not neutral. In fact, they view themselves as joining with the family in cocreating the episode of therapy. As such, they cannot act as neutral "experts" dispensing advice because they tend to cocreate their clients in the shape of their own hypotheses about them; nor can they be analysts making evaluative judgments because they are participants in the process of enacting the interviews. Boscolo and Cecchin (Boscolo et al. 1987) have adapted what is called "second-order cybernetics"—that is, the analysis of systems that make observations—into circular questioning. The system includes the interviewer as well as the person or family interviewed. Instead of believing that *the system creates the problem* that brings the family to therapy (and hence that the system must be changed), the Milan approach suggests that *the problem creates the system,* which includes the family and the therapist.

One corollary to this observation is that anything the therapist does is likely to function homeostatically (i.e., reproducing the existing pattern in the system). If the family comes to the therapist for a diagnosis, any diagnosis that the therapist gives is likely to reinforce just those problems they are meant to change. "As soon as a treating professional agrees that something is wrong—as soon as he or she even agrees to let a family in the door—even more of the family's energies are apt to get sidetracked into forms of protection, often called resistance by the clinician" (Boscolo et al. 1987, p. 15).

In practice, this means that circular questioning never criticizes or even agrees that there is a problem. In fact, the Milan group is famous for giving "positive connotations" to their clients, such as praising them for being such a strong family to have developed such complex problems! In addition, circular questioning never offers an expert diagnosis. To the contrary, the questioning is driven by curiosity rather than by expert knowledge. There are very few *why* questions asked or implicitly answered; most of the questions have in them (remember the Heyerdahl solution) the issue of *how* things happen.

- If you were to drop out of school, how would your Mother's relation to your Father change? (among other things, focusing on the pattern of adjustments brought about by the threatened act)
- How does your Mother show depression? In what situations does she show depression? To whom? (By eliciting descriptions of episodes, the focus is on how depression is made in conversations rather than treating it as a thing).

Circular questioning can be distinguished by four characteristics: 1) its focus on discovering the differences in the information within a system, 2) its focus on individuals in relation to others, 3) its delight in exploring and posing alternatives to the evolutionary loops within a system, and 4) its preoccupation with *how* things are made in social interaction.

A Final Word: A Language Game for Relationships

If relationships were *between* people, then they would be relatively easy to understand within the powerful language games that are used to measure objects. However, because relationships are reflexive—that is, sets of connections in which entities are constituted—then we must use a language game capable of describing complex loops within mutable patterns of actions.

In my judgment, such a language game has not yet been developed. Relationships continue to mystify us because we frame them in language games that do not fit. One of the places where communication scholars need to make significant advances is right here.

In the meantime, what we know about interpersonal communication in relationships is very helpful in sensitizing us to some of the dynamics of relationships and in providing us with some ways of joining in patterns of communication.

Praxis

1. Conflict and Confusion in Multiple Relationships

Before class. Make a list of some of the important voluntary relationships that you have (or want to have). Use your own names for these relationships; my list would include "friends," "coauthors," "sailing partners," and "basketball teammates." Now articulate the most important rights and duties that stem from each relationship. Remember to include the rights you extend to the other as well as those you claim for yourself, and the duties for each. (These are not exotic: my "duty" to "acquaintances" is to speak to them if I encounter them on the street; failing to do so sends a "relational message" that denies our acquaintance.)

In class. Compare the lists you have made with those of other people in your class. First, note whether you and the others have the same names for relationships. More important than the labels themselves, check whether you make the same number of distinctions among relationships. It is possible that you differentiate two or three types of friendship where someone else does not.

Now compare your list of duties and obligations that stem from particular relationships with those made by the others. Are there differences?

To get a feel for the implications of these differences, use these lists of "rights and duties" as if they were the rules for the simulated conversation in Figure 5.2. Improvise conversations with your classmates who listed different "rights and duties" for particular relationships. What kinds of conversations are made when your rules mesh with theirs?

After doing several improvisations, discuss with others in your group what specific rules or rights and duties that you claim or offer to others are particularly dangerous or difficult. What rules are particularly helpful?

Using the concepts of *punctuation, accounts, metacommunication,* and *reconstructing the context* discussed in Chapter 4, what "repairs" can you suggest that would make the conversations better?

2. Dealing with Confusion Competently

In the "Narrative" section, Watzlawick's work summarizing four types of confusion was described. In each case, Watzlawick suggested that a person who followed the rules of that kind of situation—that is, whose competence is in *game playing*—would appear to have significant psychological problems. How would persons whose competence is in *game mastery* fare? How might they act so as to avoid the negative consequences of confused relationships and achieve what Watzlawick called the "benefits of confusion"?

Working in groups in class.

1. Take each of Watzlawick's examples of confused relationships described in the Narrative. Write two scripts of an episode that might be produced in each of the examples. In one script, portray the confused person acting as a game player, behaving in ways appropriately described as schizophrenic, depressed, delinquent, and paralyzed. In the other script, portray the confused person acting as a game master, behaving in ways that allow him or her to be perceived as sane, responsible, and effective.

2. Try your hand as a playwright again. Take the first set of scripts that you wrote for #1 (in which the confused person acted as a game player rather than a game master). It is unfair to blame the victim for being placed in a confusing relationship, and unfair to expect the victim to do all the work in untangling such relationships. Write another variation of each episode, this time changing the behavior of the higher-powered person: what can she or he do to minimize or dispel the confusion?

3. In a final role as author, introduce a compassionate, skillful third party to the episode. This third party might be a friend, a family member, or a professional therapist. What might such an intervener do that would dispel the confusion or enable the confused person to act with game-mastery competence? What does this third party have to know? What are some of the useful and some of the dangerous things this person might do?

3. Stages in Relationship Development

How "general" is the model of interactional stages developed by Knapp and Vangelisti shown in Figure 5.5? Note that it is a *descriptive* model, not a *prescriptive* one; that is, it claims only that these are the stages that relationships go through, not that these are the stages that relationships *should* go through. So let's evaluate the model on its own terms: *which* relationships among *what persons* go through these stages?

I have a hunch that this model is most accurate in describing romantic relationships among adolescents and young adults in contemporary Western societies or those influenced by Western societies.

Test the model by seeing if it fits other kinds of relationships.

■ Working in pairs or small groups, take turns interviewing each other about your nonvoluntary, nonromantic relationships, such as with your parents or siblings. Do these relationships follow the model? Is the model limited to romantic relationships?

■ Working alone or in small groups, interview people from cultures other than Western or eurocentric about their romantic relationships. For example, compare the experience of Native Americans, Africans, Far East Asians, and West Asians. Be sure to include people from different religious traditions, including Christianity, Islam, Judaism, Buddhism, Hinduism, and Shinto. To what extent do these relationships resemble each other? Do they follow the model? Is the model limited to Western eurocentric culture?

I think Knapp and Vangelisti's model is interesting and useful, but I do not think that it is universally applicable. If it is not universal, what should we think or do? Does that make it useless? Of course not; it simply means that we must specify those relationships for which it is useful. Should we develop other models for other relationships? Perhaps. Should we develop a healthy skepticism about any such model? Certainly.

Part of this healthy skepticism is a willingness to be playful. If the model is limited to romantic relationships, perhaps we should inquire about the defining characteristic of these relationships. Let me offer as a modest suggestion that we rethink the whole basis of romantic relationships: "love."

The romantic notion is that love is something that happens to a person and that it is located *inside* an individual. But what if "love" is co-constructed in the same way as "anger"; that is, as Averill described anger, what if love is a transitory social role that is enacted in episodes?

If love is a transitory social role rather than some "thing" inside the afflicted party, then we should explain love by looking at the interactional contingencies in the episodes co-constructed by interlocutors rather than, on the one hand, identifying the loveable attributes of the beloved or the personality of the lover. What would be the practical effect of this reconceptualization? Would we love more wisely? Would we be better lovers?

For the minute, assume that love is a transitory social role. Bring to class the lyrics of one of your favorite romantic songs or romantic poems. Working in small groups, rewrite the lyrics or poetry to make it consistent with Averill's concept of love as a transitory social role.

When you finish, you probably will find the product not nearly as romantic as the original. But before you throw your new lyric or poem away, compare what is lost and what is gained in your revision.

Also bring to class some nonromantic writings about love. For example, in the Christian Bible, First Corinthians Chapter 13 describes love. You can find other texts that talk about love for a family member or love of one's country. In the same small group, rewrite these texts in ways that incorporate Averill's notion of love as a transitory social role and the notion of reflexivity that you learned in this chapter. Incorporate as much as possible of the other concepts about interpersonal communication that you have learned.

4. Circular Questioning

Working in groups of four, practice posing circular questions. Let two people simulate a relationship (e.g., friends, family, or thief or victim). Let the other two work as a team, using circular questions. Each interviewer should help the other pose the questions in proper form. Switch roles and continue until you have a good feel for asking questions in this manner.

Now practice using this interviewing technique in a wide variety of contexts. What would be gained and lost if journalists were to use circular questioning in interviewing politicians? What would you discover if you were to pose circular questions to yourself about the reasons why you took this course (When did you first get the idea that this course would be a good one to take? To whom do you show your interest in this course? How do you show your involvement in this course? Who would be the first to notice if you were not really interested in this course?) Would your relationships with your friends and family change if you were to participate in circular questioning of each other? In what way? How would these changes take place?

References

Bateson, Gregory. *Steps to an Ecology of Mind*. New York: Ballantine, 1972.

Bateson, Gregory. *Mind and Nature: A Necessary Unity*. New York: Bantam, 1980.

Berne, Eric. *Games People Play: The Psychology of Human Relationships*. New York: Grove, 1964.

Boscolo, Luigi, Cecchin, Gianfranco, Hoffman, Lynn, and Penn, Peggy. *Milan Systemic Family Therapy: Conversations in Theory and Practice*. New York: Basic Books, 1987.

Buber, Martin. *I and Thou*. New York: Macmillan, 1988.

Carson, Robert. *Interaction Concepts of Personality*. Chicago: Aldine, 1969.

Cronen, Vernon E., Johnson, Kenneth, and Lannamann, John W. "Paradoxes, Double-binds, and Reflexive Loops: An Alternative Theoretical Perspective." *Family Process* 20 (1982): 91–112.

Duck, Steve. "Social and Personal Relationships." In *Handbook of Interpersonal Communication*, edited by Mark L. Knapp and Gerald R. Miller, 655–686. Beverly Hills: Sage, 1985.

Duncan, Hugh Dalziel. *Communication and Social Order*. New York: Oxford University Press, 1962.

Gergen, Kenneth. *The Saturated Self: Dilemmas of Identity in Contemporary Life*. New York: Basic Books, 1991.

Knapp, Mark L., and Vangelisti, Anita L. *Interpersonal Communication and Human Relationships*, 2nd ed. Boston: Allyn and Bacon, 1992.

LaTour, Bruno, and Woolgar, Steve. *Laboratory Life: The Construction of Scientific Facts*. Princeton: Princeton University Press, 1986.

LeGuin, Ursula. *The Dispossessed*. New York: Harper and Row, 1974.

Nelson, John S., McGill, Allan, and McCloskey, Donald N. *The Rhetoric of the Human Sciences: Language and Argument in Scholarship and Public Affairs*. Madison: University of Wisconsin Press, 1987.

Pearce, W. Barnett. *Communication and the Human Condition*. Carbondale: University of Southern Illinois Press, 1989.

Rawlins, Bill. *Friendship Matters*. New York: Aldine de Gruyter, 1992.

Schutz, W. C. *FIRO: A Three-Dimensional Theory of Interpersonal Behavior*. New York: Holt, Rinehart and Winston, 1958.

Silvini-Palazzoli, Mara, Prata, Guiliana, Boscolo, Luigi, and Cecchin, Gianfranco. *Paradox and Counterparadox: A New Model in the Therapy of the Family in Schizophrenic Transaction*. New York: Jason Aronson, 1978.

Silvini-Palazzoli, Mara, Prata, Guiliana, Boscolo, Luigi, and Cecchin, Gianfranco. "Hypothesizing-Circularity-Neutrality: Three Guidelines for the Conductor of the Session." *Family Process* 19 (1980): 2–13.

Sluzki, Carlos, and Beavin, Janet. "Symmetry and Complementarity: An Operational Definition and Typology of Dyads." In *The Interactional View*, edited by Paul Watzlawick and John Weakland, 71–87. New York: Norton, 1977.

Tomm, Carl. "Circular Interviewing: A Multifaceted Clinical Tool." In *Applications of Systemic Family Therapy*, edited by Roz Draper and David Campbell. London: Grune and Statton, 1985.

Toulmin, Stephen. *The Return to Cosmology: Postmodern Science and the Theology of Nature*. Berkeley: University of California Press, 1982.

Turnbull, Colin. *The Human Cycle*. New York: Simon and Schuster, 1983.

Watzlawick, Paul. *How Real is Real? An Anecdotal Introduction to Communication Theory*. New York: Vintage, 1976.

Watzlawick, Paul, Beavin, Janet, and Jackson, Don. *Pragmatics of Human Communication*. New York: Norton, 1967.

Wheelwright, Philip. *Metaphor and Reality*. Bloomington: Indiana University Press, 1962.

Wish, M., Deutsch, M., and Kaplan, S. J. "Perceived Dimensions of Interpersonal Relations." *Journal of Personality and Social Psychology* 33 (1976): 409–420.

Wright, Paul H. "Toward a Theory of Friendship Based on a Conception of Self." *Human Communication Research* 18 (1978): 196–207.

CHAPTER
6 *Self*

Know thyself.

The Oracle at Delphi

I am what I am and that's all that I am.

Popeye

Traditional assumptions about the nature of identity
are now in jeopardy. It is not simply that the present
turn of events has altered the emphasis placed on rationality, the emotions, and the like, or that it adds new concepts to the traditional vernacular. Rather . . . the very
idea of individual selves—in possession of mental
qualities—is now threatened with eradication.

Gergen 1991, p. x

OBJECTIVES

After reading this chapter, you will be able to

- Understand the ways in which people are empowered and disempowered in conversation
- Analyze the "identity crisis" and other psychological maladies as social constructions
- Differentiate between the self as a physical-moral entity and as a moral agent
- Understand popular culture and the fashion industry as part of postmodernity
- Take a more deliberate role in socially constructing your own self

KEY WORDS AND PHRASES

Some terms that will help you understand this chapter include

languages of self, self as moral agent and as moral-physical entity, multiphrenia, enlightenment and postmodernity

Narrative

Bill sat staring into space.

"What's wrong?" Jane asked.

"Nothing, really, but . . ." Bill replied. "Sometimes I just don't understand myself. I worked hard to get to college, and I'm working two part-time jobs to pay for it, and now that I'm here, I'm not sure that I should be."

"Are you having trouble with your studies?"

"No, that's not it. I'm doing well in my courses, and I'm very interested in learning, but I feel myself changing. I'm not the same person who left home two years ago. The person who made the decision to come to college seems naive and uninformed to me now, and I don't know if I should remain committed to the decisions that person made. I don't know if I *like* the person I am becoming—frankly, it scares me sometimes. Who am I? Who will I be five years from now? Right now, I want to major in physics. Five years from now, will I want to be a physicist or will I want to write poetry? How can I plan for my future if my self is so volatile? I love you . . . but what happens to our relationship if I change? Do I have to hope that you change, too? And that you change in the same directions and at the same rate that I do? Is that fair? Would you love a penniless poet as much as a world-famous physicist?"

How should we think about Bill? How should Jane reply to him? Should she circumscribe their relationship so that she does not get hurt by Bill's ambivalence and hesitance? Or should she bond with him in this episode of exploration and growth? Her response, like ours, depends on what we think about the self and how it is related to interpersonal communication.

If Bill *has* a self, and that self is an object that can be known and described, then we are likely to be short-tempered with him. He fails what might be called the "Popeye test" of clear-minded identity. Bill does *not* know what he is and probably is pretending to be something other than what he is.

From Popeye's perspective, we ask What's wrong with Bill? He has a problem, and the possibilities are exhausted by two alternatives: either he does not know who he is or he knows but cannot express it. If he does not know his self, then he is confused or has defective analytical powers; if he cannot express his self, then he is incompetent in basic communication skills. If Jane thinks like Popeye, she might drop Bill for a more clear-minded boyfriend.

On the other hand if Bill *is* a self, and if that self is constructed in patterns of conversations, then we are likely to congratulate him on his perceptiveness. That is, Bill has passed what we might call the "Gergen test" of self-reflective vacillation.

From Gergen's perspective, we note that Bill lives in a society in which there are many incommensurate language games for identity, and that he is

Does Bill flunk the "Pop-eye test" of clear-minded self-awareness? Or is Bill experiencing the kind of situation that Gergen described? Does Bill have a self that he simply does not know? Or is Bill a self who is sufficiently self-aware that he can detect changes and alternatives? How should Jane feel about being in a relationship with Bill?

aware of how his experiences with them affect him. Rather than a sign of his inarticulateness, if Jane thinks like Gergen, she might see Bill's stammering as a way of *doing* something, not as a failed attempt to *describe* something.

But what might Bill be doing in this kind of soliloquy? Well, he might be trying on various languages for being a self in contemporary society and deciding which ones fit.

> *When we are searching for ways to express "who we are" and are finding the process to be difficult, it is not [necessarily] because we are having trouble expressing the real identity within. Rather, we are in the process of developing the ability to identify ourselves under particular conditions. It is part of the process of learning to have an identity—further specifying and changing it. The stumbling efforts we all at times make when we are trying to say who we are seem to us as more akin to a child's fumbling efforts to throw a ball than to a process of representing mental phenomena in language. (Cronen and Pearce 1991/1992, p. 58)*

Bill has made an important discovery: his "self" is not a natural object, immutable and outside the hurly-burly processes of communication. In fact, the self—like episodes and relationships—both *shape* and *are shaped by* the conversations in which we make our social worlds.

Contemporary society contains many language games for personal identity, and there are some important contradictions between, and ambiguities within, these language games. If you use some of the concepts presented in this chapter, you will be better able to identify and move among these language games for identity. After reading this chapter, you should be better equipped to handle the questions of identity that contemporary society poses.

Self as a Part of Your Social Worlds

William James described our *sensations* (i.e., the raw stimulations of our nervous system) as a "big, buzzing, booming confusion." Of course, we do not *perceive* our social worlds this way; we pick out clusters of the flood of stimulations that inundate us, perceive them as meaningful units, and then organize them into our social worlds. Every normal human being identifies a portion of their social worlds as "myself"; we all learn to use various personal pronouns that punctuate differences between me/my/I and you/yours. "The terms available for making our personalities intelligible—terms of emotion, motivation, thought, values, opinions, and the like—place important constraints over our forms of action" (Gergen 1991, p. 5). Romantic relationships depend on particular vocabularies of identity and emotion that differentiate a cad from a former lover. Jurisprudence requires a well-developed vocabulary of intentions and extenuating circumstances that differentiate a felon from a victim of tragic circumstance. Democracy itself derives from certain vocabularies of personal rights, abilities, and responsibilities.

As *physical entities,* we live in a world of "raw happenings" that do not come prepackaged and labeled for our use. The collective "we"—all of us, conversing as a society—have both the right and the obligation to transmute these raw happenings into events. We use the alchemy of naming to label and thus locate within our social worlds the nameless objects that we bump up against as we live. In addition, because we are powerful parts of the physical world, we produce raw happenings ourselves by moving around and making things. In both of these ways, we are participants in the continuing creation of the universe at the level of entities with temporal and spacial dimensions.

However, the situation is somewhat different from our perspective of ourselves as *moral persons.* Each of us is born into a pre-existing moral world in which the raw happenings of life *are* prepackaged and prelabeled for our use by other people. In fact, our selves are "given" to us by our society. We are assigned a name, a Social Security number, and a place in the economic structure; we are expected to act within a cluster of rights and responsibilities deriving from our parents' position within the social structure, the community in which we live, and the pattern of conversations in which we are able or required to participate.

This social process of conferring an identity as moral persons is so powerful that it is usually invisible. However, those of us who study such things for a living have come to believe that this is a far more complicated and fateful process than it seems.

Viewed from a communication perspective, our selves are part of the

Counterpoint 6.1

Wittgenstein frequently engaged in imaginative exercises in which he envisioned societies that never existed. For example, what language games would develop in a society in which all its people lacked the sense of hearing or seeing? Wittgenstein said that these would be very different forms of life than the ones that we know, and there is good reason to believe that he was correct.

> *The study of the deaf shows us that much of what is distinctively human in us—our capacities for language, for thought, for communication, and culture—do not develop automatically in us, are not just biological functions, but are, equally, social and historical in origin; that they are a gift—the most wonderful of gifts—from one generation to another . . .*
>
> *The existence of a visual language, sign, and of the striking enhancements of perception and visual intelligence that go with its acquisition, shows us that the brain is rich in potentials we would scarcely have guessed of, shows us the almost unlimited plasticity and resource of the nervous system, the human organism, when it is faced with the new and must adapt. If this subject shows us the vulnerabilities, the ways in which (often unwittingly) we may harm ourselves, it shows us, equally, our unknown and unexpected strengths, the infinite resources for survival and transcendence which Nature and Culture, together, have given us (Sacks 1991, p. xiii).*

In much the same way, Davies and Harré (1990) envisioned a society that did not have (and that had no memory of or experience with) the personal pronouns "I" and "me." The "selves" in that society, they suggested, would be very different from those that we take for granted. Can "I" be "myself" only if the language and conversational structures of my society provide "places" or "resources" for "me"?

One of the earliest science fiction books explored just this idea. Zimiatin (1924) envisioned a society that tried to stamp out individualism by eliminating the first person singular pronoun "I". Any self-reference in the language had to use "we."

Listen carefully to the discourse around you for the use of personal pronouns. Who would be the first to notice if you did not use the first person singular "I"? In what conversations would you be most helped or hindered if you had no concept of "me"?

---

process by which we make our social worlds. Patterns of conversations with our parents, brothers and sisters, teachers and classmates, and government officials *produce* the "self" that we know ourselves to be. That self has a name ("Barnett"), it is defined in contrast with other selves ("intelligent, kind, tall . . ."), it has a history ("I went camping in the White Mountains") and abilities ("I can sew but cannot weave"). This self then shapes our participation in conversations ("A person like me must . . .") and thus is a causal factor in the making of our social worlds as well as being a product of those social worlds.

If we are looking to explain how particular conversations occur, we must include an account of our identities. People will often say that they acted in a certain way *because* that was the only thing "a person like me" could do. In fact, studies of unwanted repetitive patterns (Cronen et al. 1979) have found that self-concept is one of the primary reasons subjects performed actions that they did not like and knew would lead to unwanted consequences. They *had* to act as they did, so they told us, because "a person like me" *could not* act otherwise.

In addition, people often act as they do *to become* the self that they want to be. The dynamics of peer pressure among adolescents and young adults often prominently feature identity. People do things that they know are not right or pleasant to sustain a particular social identity or to avoid an unwanted identity. They feel great pressure to act in certain ways to avoid being classified as nerds, geeks, jocks, and so on. (If these terms seem out of date, that simply attests to the rapidity with which elaborate vocabularies of types of persons are developed and changed. Because I am no longer a native in the culture of adolescents, I may be an adequate guide to the existence of such vocabularies but a poor guide to their content.)

Counterpoint 6.2

If you read the discussion of unwanted repetitive patterns carefully, you should be able to discern the deontic logic and practical syllogism as the unmentioned structure of the explanation of how "self" causes people to do things that they do not want to do and know will turn out badly. This sentence is typical of what our subjects told us: "In a situation like that, when he does what he did, a person like me has to act like I act, regardless of the consequences."

Pull the sentence apart like this:

- "a situation like that" refers to the episode
- "he does what he did" refers to the preceding act in a conversational triplet
- "a person like me" refers to the self
- "regardless of the consequences" may refer to the subsequent act in a conversational triplet or to how the completed episode will be punctuated.

We found that "felt enmeshment" in unwanted repetitive patterns occurred when subjects perceived a strong obligatory connection between their actions and their perception of the episode, the preceding act in the conversational triplet, and their self-concept, *and* a strong "irrelevant" connection between their actions and the consequences. That is, unwanted repetitive patterns occur when there is a certain, very strong configuration of the deontic logic of meaning and action and an absence of reasoning following the structure of the practical syllogism.

This model of deontic logic provides some tools for your imagination. What kinds of episodes occur when there are other configurations of deontic logic? What other configurations are possible? What happens if there is a strong "obligatory" relationship between self and a particular act, but an equally strong "prohibitive" relationship between episode and the same act?

Some Events Make Us Mindful of Our Selves

Most of the time, most of us are more like Popeye than we are like Kenneth Gergen or Bill. That is, we are quite confident that we know who and what we are. We find that the Delphic Oracle's advice makes good sense but is unnecessary—we already know ourselves!

In his studies of persuasion, psychologist Milton Rokeach (1960) found that our beliefs about our identity were the more resistant to change than beliefs about anything else. Ordinary persuasive attempts simply cannot touch our knowledge about who we are and what we are like. But events do happen that call into question our basic beliefs of who we are.

Normally, the self is reconstructed in conversations as if the self that we are is "natural"; the self usually functions as an invisible "frame" within which we act normally. However, things happen that make this frame visible. Sometimes these things make us ask, as an existential question, Who am I? We become a little less like Popeye and a little more like Gergen when

■ traumatic events threaten our sense of who we are. These events may be either "positive" or "negative." When you graduate from school and become a professional, your identity changes. For example, the "self" of a Doctor making life-and-death decisions about your patients is not quite the same as the "self" of a medical student cramming for an anatomy exam; when you marry and have a child, your "self" as parent is not the same as your "self" as single young adult or even as newlywed. An athlete suffering a career-ending injury, a family whose home is destroyed by war or tornado, a factory production worker whose job is eliminated by the automation of the factory, an elderly person who is moved into a foreign culture and a strange place: all of these people are likely to lose some of the Popeye-ish confidence in their identity. What events can you imagine that would have this kind of effect on you?

■ The near-mandatory "identity crises" of young adulthood and the "midlife crises" experienced by middle-aged adults are periods when the question Who am I? suddenly seems both relevant and fascinating. There are any number of movies, plays, and short stories as well as social scientific research about these experiences. In what vocabularies are the answers to the question Who am I? offered? What vocabulary would you think is the best for addressing such questions?

■ People who have any of the wide range of characteristics that are treated as stigmas have a lifelong project of managing their identities. Some people are born with the sexual characteristics of both males and females ("intersexed") but have to live in a society that differentiates between "males" and "females." What resources does our society provide for developing a coherent identity for those who do not fit the conventional categories? Geertz (1983, p. 81) says that "Intersexuality is more than an empirical surprise; it is a cultural challenge," and describes strikingly different ways in which three societies deal with it. How do you think of yourself and present yourself to others if you are HIV positive? Would you raise questions about your identity if you had a child with a prominent birth-defect? Whatever your race, religion, or national origin, there is some place on earth where you would be part of a minority and considered "inferior" or "strange." If you were to live in such a place, would your awareness of your self be increased? How would you handle the daily perceptions that others think of you in terms of an unwanted or unrespected category?

■ Sometimes we meet a stranger whose world is so different from ours that we begin to question our own. When we engage in dialogue with someone from another culture or economic class, we can get a glimpse of what our culture, class, or our selves look like from the perspective of that other person. This is always a humbling experience; it shows that many of the things we have taken for granted are arbitrary and that others have consequences that we never realized. When this happens, two types of changes occur. The "inward" change is to call into question our concept of self; the "outward" change is to restructure our political beliefs and practices.

Counterpoint 6.3

In the discussion of experiences that call our "selves" into question, I am trying to express the concept of the self as made in processes of conversation and avoid talking as if your self was a thing, buried somewhere in your mind. Perhaps the effort of my struggle with language shows!

You have heard people use expressions like "part of me wants to go to the party tonight, but another part of me realizes that I need to study." It is not hard to discern what is meant by statements like this, but they contain a grammar that can cause us problems. Not only does this grammar invite the silly questions about "what parts are those, pray tell?" and "which of those parts is the larger, I wonder?", but it creates an interesting philosophical problem. Who is this speaker who divides "me" up? Is the "I" who speaks in a coalition with one part of "me" against the other?

Clifford Geertz wrestled with the same problem in his studies of what it means to be a person in various cultures. He warned that he was never going to discern "persons" per se; he could only see, hear, touch, and smell what persons *do*. But even that is not enough, because he was always going to perceive something different from what the people he was studying perceived. "The trick is not to get yourself into some inner correspondence of spirit with your informants. . . . The trick is to figure out what the devil they think they are up to" (Geertz 1983, p. 58). And even this is at a distance. In our natural state, we use "experience-near" concepts for our own experience. We use them

> *spontaneously, unself-consciously, as it were colloquially; [we] do not, except fleetingly and on occasion, recognize that there are any "concepts" involved at all. That is what "experience-near" means— that ideas and the realities they inform are naturally and indissolubly bound up together. What else could you call a hippopotamus? Of course the gods are powerful, why else would we fear them? The ethnographer does not . . . perceive what his informants perceive. What he perceives, and that uncertainly enough, is what they perceive "with"—or "by means of," or "through . . ."* (Geertz 1983, p. 58, emphasis added).

What Geertz said about ethnographers is true about Bill's own reflections about himself. When we start wondering Who am I? we will never find an "object" that we can describe. What we can achieve—and it is a very important achievement—is a discovery of what we perceive ourselves "with" or "by means of" or "through." That is, we can place the languages of identity in the foreground of our thoughts and in so doing discover not only who we are but also what options we have.

Concepts of Self Develop Historically

The concept of self in your common sense has not always been treated as the norm, and in all probability, there will come a time when it is no longer taken as a norm. That is, you should locate your concept of what a self is within the history of ideas.

According to the *Oxford English Dictionary*, the term *self* was first used in English in 1595. Based on his analysis of diaries and travelogues, John Lyons (1978) said that the modern concept of self was "invented" in the eighteenth century—with tongue firmly in cheek, he suggested the year 1750. Will some future edition of the *Oxford English Dictionary* describe the term "self" as first used in English in 1595, last used in 2156? What kind of events might lead to this term's growing old and dying?

Concepts of Self Develop Culturally

Just as you "historicized" your concept of self, locate it within a particular culture. Geertz characterized the dominant Western concept of self this way:

> *a bounded, unique, more or less integrated motivational and cognitive universe, a dynamic center of awareness, emotion, judgment, and action organized into a distinctive whole and set contrastively both against other such wholes and against a social and natural background. (Geertz 1975, p. 48)*

In this language game, striving for self-actualization and turning to one's inner self for strength, definition, and guidance in dealing with others makes sense. This language game also encourages you to differentiate your inner, or private, self from the public self you present to other people, to quantify the amount of this inner self that you disclose to others, and to ask if what you disclose is consistent with your inner self.

This concept, which seems natural to people in industrialized nations with European heritages, seems unnatural to people in other forms of life and with different cultural traditions. In traditional, non-Western cultures, Bill Gudykunst and Stella Ting-Toomey (1988, p. 82) noted, the "self" is not differentiated from the nexus of social relationships in which the individual participates. Were this textbook written by a Chinese scholar for Chinese students, there would probably not be a chapter on the self, and if such a textbook did have a section on self, it would likely use a language game that stresses contextual appropriateness rather than transcontextual consistency (Chang 1987). That is, it would focus on the extent to which one responds appropriately or dutifully in the relationships that define the self rather than, like Shakespeare, on urging one to be "true" to one's inner self.

Counterpoint 6.4

I make no apology for asking you to think about yourself as enculturated and differentiating your culture from others. There are two reasons for my insistence on this point.

First, the social, economic, and environmental realities of contemporary society require us to be aware of other cultures. What we do affects and is affected by them whether we are conscious of it or not, and it makes sense to be alert to the larger conversations of which we are a part.

Second, my purpose is to call to your attention the materials by, with, or through which you perceive your self, and the best way of doing this is by comparison and contrast. The concepts of self in various cultures differ markedly, and you can gain an appreciation for what you take for granted by exploring what other cultures use to understand themselves.

There is something very important in the perspective that comes from being aware of the materials (e.g., conversations, language, social structures, array of accounts) that your culture provides. It is hard to say just *what* is so important, however. Geertz (1983, p. 16) called it "a fugitive truth" and said

> To see ourselves as others see us can be eye-opening. To see others as sharing a nature with ourselves is the merest decency. But it is from the far more difficult achievement of seeing ourselves amongst others, as a local example of the forms human life has locally taken, a case among cases, a world among worlds, that the largeness of mind, without which objectivity is self-congratulation and tolerance a sham, comes.

Communication theorist Donal Carbaugh (1990, p. 127) contrasted the contemporary American concept of self ("individualistic, self-reflexive, and loquacious") with those of several other cultures that have different notions of the relationship between speech and self. Some think of the self more as a silent thinker than a speaker of opinion. Others view self as a player of public roles in which individuality and uniqueness is foreign, or as a purveyor of harmonious relations in which self is downplayed or depreciated. In other cultures, self is identified with social rank; only some social ranks are allowed to engage in significant speech. Each of these cultural concepts structures different ways of thinking about the self and envisions whole different vocabularies in which to answer the question Who am I?

Multiple Languages of Self

In the preceding section, you located your concept of self as, first, within a matrix of your own experience; second, within a continuing process of historical development; and third, within a particular cultural tradition. In those discussions, I sometimes wrote as if there was only one concept of self in the contemporary world. Of course, that's not true; there are many. The present section will help you identify some of the major languages of self in contemporary American culture.

Englightenment and Poststructural Languages of Self

Davies and Harré (1991/1992, p. 2) noted that people in contemporary society have "access to many ways of talking about oneself and one's activities." One of these "ways of talking," they said, is an inheritance from the "Enlightenment" (i.e, the philosophical and scientific tradition that flowered between the seventeenth and nineteenth centuries in Europe and the United States). This "E-model" of the self "presents as an ideal a rational person leading a rational life in a rational universe in which contradictions must always be eliminated" (Davies and Harré 1991/1992, p. 6). To be considered fully functioning adults, people must show how their activities are consistent across time and across situations.

This "way of talking" about the self sharply contrasts with a "post-structural" discourse (or "P-model"). Poststructuralism names a cluster of intellectual developments that presume that the social world is produced through talk; it uses the method of deconstruction to expose how various structures in the social world were made. The P-model of the self "presents a human individual as caught in a number of discursive nets" (Davies and Harré 1991/1992, p. 7). That is, the normal condition of human beings is to live in contradictions. Rightly understood, a self that understands itself within the P-model can say "with enthusiasm, 'so this is how I get to be all of these things. And having understood this I now see how I can begin to change them' " (Davies and Harré 1991/1992, p. 9).

There is an intransitive relationship between these two ways of talking about self. The P-model says that one of the many inconsistent languages of the self is the E-model. Further, from the P-model, the E-model seems curiously circumscribed because it denies the validity of any other way of talking about the self. On the other hand, the way of talking about the self

---

Refrain 6.1

Davies and Harré differentiate the "enlightenment" and "poststructural" models of self. (They call these the "E-model" and "P-model" of the self.)

These models are seldom formally stated, of course. They do, however, comprise the background assumptions that we use when we take "who I am" and "who you are" into account as we converse.

According to the *E-model of self*, persons are rational agents in a rational world; their personalities are (or, more to the point, *should be*) consistent and coherent; and they should be capable of giving explanations for their actions.

According to the *P-model of self*, persons are moral agents in a world comprised of multiple, sometimes contradictory discourses; their personalities are always plural and mutable; they are (or, more to the point, *should be*) inconsistent and flexible, adapting to changing circumstances.

identified as the E-model recognizes the existence of other ways of talking but thinks that they are immature or fallacious.

Bill's musings about his self, described at the beginning of this chapter, appear very different depending on whether one understands him as speaking in an E- or P-model of self.

Romantic, Modernist, and Postmodern Languages of Self

Gergen's book, *The Saturated Self: Dilemmas of Identity in Contemporary Life* (1991), presents a major study of the languages of self in a society structured by the new technologies of communication. Gergen found three major languages of self, romantic, modernist, and postmodern, intertwined in contemporary society. Each of these languages is grounded in particular historical moments and prefigures certain kinds of conversations.

The romanticist language of self attributes to each person characteristics of personal depth: passion, soul, creativity, and moral fiber. The modernist language of self focuses on our ability to reason: it emphasizes beliefs, opinions, and conscious intentions, and it values predictability, honesty, and sincerity. The postmodern language constructs a "multiphrenic" self in which values and reason are compromised and in which the self is increasingly portrayed as inadequate.

The romantic vocabulary of self.   Originating in the eighteenth and nineteenth centuries, the romantic view of the self may be seen as a protest against blind faith in human reason—or, more precisely, against the reduction of human worth and experience to rational values (i.e., it is at least in part a reaction against the E-model of the self identified by Davies and Harré).

Romanticism uses a vocabulary of passion, purpose, and personal depths that can never be fully plumbed. It puts love at the forefront of human endeavors; those who abandon merely functional or useful activities for the purposes of passion, style, or even a beautiful gesture are praiseworthy. "For many, the loss of such a vocabulary would essentially be the collapse of anything meaningful in life. If love as intimate communion, intrinsic worth, creative inspiration, moral values, and passionate expression were all scratched from our vocabularies, life for many would be a pallid affair indeed" (Gergen 1991, p. 27).

This language of self is, like the others, sufficiently rich that those who live within it can craft a life of dignity and honor. It is sufficiently robust that they can answer relevant questions efficiently and confidently. And yet it looks thoroughly wrong-headed to those whose self is constructed in the language of modernity.

The modernist language of self.   Languages do not "die"; they just simply pass out of popular usage. And they are usually not discarded totally

or everywhere or all at once; other vocabularies simply start being used for important functions. This is what happened to the romanticist vocabulary. It has not gone away: it lives in splendor on the soap operas, in movies, in testimonials to perfumes and credit cards, and in a hundred other places. However, since the beginning of the twentieth century, the modernist language of the self has usurped many of the functions that might otherwise have used the romantic language.

In the modernist language, the self is constituted as a fixed and knowable entity. Instead of celebrating the mysterious, passionate, never fully finished identity created in the romanticist vocabulary, those using the modernist language prize people who are open and consistent. Modernist literature discloses how persons come to be the individuals that they truly are, or probes past the trappings of an ostensibly positive identity to discern the discreditable character really lurking behind the facade. In this vocabulary, precise measurements of self are possible. A whole industry has developed around personality "inventories," measures of "self-esteem," and even scholastic aptitude and achievement.

In the modernist vocabulary, the self is produced from experience. This perception contrasts with the romanticist emphasis on genetics, in which genius, inspiration, and passion were considered inherent to the individual. For modernists, human beings are something like machines, capable of functioning well but susceptible to damage by the environment. As a result, modernists look to behavioral modification as the way to solve problems and to modifications of the environment as a way to avoid their occurrence.

Autonomy and reliability are equated with health in the modernist vocabulary of self. Just as a well-designed machine resists deterioration, so a properly molded self is "self-directing," "solid," "trustworthy," and "consistent." "The modernist man is genuine rather than phony, principled rather than craven, and stable rather than wavering" (Gergen 1991, p. 44).

In summary, although the romantic individual was forever a mystery, the modernist self is

> *knowable, present in the here and now, just slightly below the surface of his actions. He is not likely to be transported by sudden inspiration, be smitten by some great passion, or give way to a rush of suicidal urges. Rather, he is reliable and trustworthy. His work today is good tomorrow and the next. The modernist self is not likely to have his reason clouded by intense emotional dramas; his reasons guide his actions and his voice is clear and honest. And we must not await the arrival of some naturally gifted, inspired, or insightful man to lead our nation or our institutions. Everyone is created equal, and it is up to us as parents and good citizens to mold the young. With proper molding, and the help of science, we create the future of our dreams. (Gergen 1991, p. 47)*

This description of the selves constructed in the modernist language bears a striking resemblance to the profile of a good worker in a factory, a good soldier, and a good citizen. This correlation is no accident.

The multiple languages of self in postmodern society.   Since World War I, and accelerating in the second half of the twentieth century, intellectual and social movements have exposed the foundations of many systems of beliefs, forms of practice, and social institutions. The tools of analysis, criti-

---

Refrain 6.2

Like Davies and Harré, Gergen believes that there are several, different concepts of self in contemporary society. Also like Davies and Harré, he identifies them with particular historical periods.

Unlike Davies and Harré, Gergen locates these concepts of self in specific "vocabularies" that we speak.

(In doing this, is Gergen expressing an E-model or a P-model of self? Hmm. I think it is a clear P-model.)

The *romantic vocabulary of self* focuses on passion, purpose, and mystery. Persons cannot ever be fully known; what counts most are actions done on the basis of strong, pure emotions; mere logic is a pale substitute for feeling. Who you are is determined by your "inner nature."

The *modernist vocabulary of self* envisions the self as a fixed and knowable entity. Actions that are open, honest, consistent, and dependable are prized; passion and emotions are threats to clear thinking and responsible performance. Healthy persons are autonomous and clearly known to themselves. Who you are is determined by the experience that you have had.

The *contemporary, "postmodern" period* contains multiple languages of the self. In this context, contemporary selves are characterized by *multiphrenia*, in which there is:

A vertigo of the valued: the disorientation of what is good and important;
The expansion of inadequacy: a pervasive feeling that you fail to measure up to some standard; and,
Rationality in recession: an inability to depend on reason because there are so many potential interlocutors who do not share the same standards for rationality.

(Gergen's characterization of "multiphrenia" is, of course, from a particular perspective. In which language, romantic or modernist, does he describe "multiphrenia"? I think he *uses* the modernist vocabulary— which prizes rationality, takes "inadequacy" seriously, locates values outside the individual, and treats the self as shaped by experiences rather than its own "inner nature"—to describe the postmodern condition. Do you agree?)

cism, and inquiry developed by these movements are sufficiently powerful to "deconstruct" virtually any certitude, tradition, or social structure. Perhaps the clearest description of the result of these movements is the principle that there is no grand narrative for society, that no such overarching story can be developed, and further, that the attempt to construct such a totalizing and inclusive frame is morally wrong as well as practically misguided.

Postmodernity has profound implications for self. "Under postmodern conditions," Gergen (1991, pp. 5–6) said, "persons exist in a state of continuous construction and reconstruction; it is a world where anything goes that can be negotiated. Each reality of self gives way to reflexive questioning, irony, and ultimately the playful probing of yet another reality. The center fails to hold." He called this condition *multiphrenia*.

There is no single vocabulary in the postmodern language of the self; instead, there are multiple vocabularies including the romantic and the modern. Consistent with Davies and Harré's notion of the P-model of the self, the defining characteristic of the postmodern language is that whatever vocabulary is used, there are other, contradictory vocabularies that are simultaneously relevant.

Gergen (1991, p. 6) attributes this condition to the new communication technologies that have "saturated" us. The strength of Gergen's analysis lies in what he means by saturation. He is not referring to information overload caused by too many stimuli. Rather, he clearly has in mind too many "connections" within the webs of relations. To get a sense of what he means, picture the atomic model of communication (Fig. 1.5). Now imagine a conversational triplet at the nexus of 50 or 100 contexts.

The new media of communication are the infrastructure for a qualitative change in the social worlds in which we live. They make possible such a radical increase in the number of conversations possible that they create a different ecology in which the self is constituted. By altering the meaning of time and distance and by creating the possibility for a vastly increased number of conversations, even those people struggling to hold onto a romantic or modern concept of self find themselves at the nexus of a vastly increased number of conversations, with access to people all over the world by telephone, electronic mail, or jet airplane. In those conversations, we are expected to know current events from all around the world because we have access to multichannel, round-the-clock news sources, and, if we are "good" people, we will react responsibly to the famines, floods, wars, and shipwrecks around the world.

If we think of ourselves at a particular point within our social worlds, the new media of communication have increased the density of the social structures in which we live. Our abilities have far outstripped our capabilities. That is, the array of conversations in which we might participate is far greater than the number in which we can actually participate. How many people do you know well enough to call on the telephone and have a conversation? Surely far more than you have time to call. How many channels of "information" can

Counterpoint 6.5

I agree with Gergen's description that the postmodern language of the self is really not a language. It is best described as a motley of languages, a cacophony of disparate voices, and a heteroglossia.

This is not to say that the postmodern language of the self is chaotic. If you snatch it from lived experience and view it everywhere all at once as if it were a timeless text, it would appear without form and void. However, selves are not constructed in timeless space; they are found in specific instances of conversation with particular interlocutors within episodes whose framing is mutable but not infinitely so. The apparent chaos of postmodernity lies within stories told; when we remember that we are inextricably enmeshed in stories lived, we have nonarbitrary limits on the array of selves that we can be.

Like the languages of morality, the languages of self

in our discourse are many, and they have remarkably diverse historical origins, but they do not float in free air, and their name is not chaos. They are embedded in specific social practices and institutions—religious, political, artistic, scientific, athletic, economic, and so on. We need many different moral concepts because there are many different linguistic threads woven into any fabric of practices and institutions as rich as ours. It is a motley; not a building in need of new foundations but a coat of many colors, one constantly in need of mending and patching, sometimes even recutting and restyling. (Stout 1988, pp. 291–292)

But Bakhtin (1986) said that heteroglossia is the first and natural state of human society. If he is right, and I believe that he is, what then is unique about postmodernity?

Postmodernity has two unique features. First, the enabling infrastructure of communication—that is, the media—have undergone unprecedented changes. None of us has a morally valid excuse not to be in conversation with (or at least knowledgeable about) anyone else on earth. If the Kurds are being attacked by the Iraqis, the Somalis are starving, or a shipwrecked freighter is leaking oil in the North Atlantic, we have no *moral* reason for not caring, being informed, and taking appropriate action *because the enabling infrastructure is in place.* To put it succinctly: maybe the world has always been heteroglossic, but we never had the infrastructure in place before so that we *could* and in some ways *have to* deal with all of it, all at once, and all of the time.

Second, the postmodern period is unique because there is no grand narrative. In the Soviet Union during Bakhtin's life, Marxist-Leninism provided the grand narrative that organized all of the other language games. Of course, many people resisted, did not believe in, or hardly paid attention to the official state dogma, but they were defined in relationship to that dogma. In the contemporary period, there are many dogmas that

give guidance and sustaining structure to people, but none of these has
the status of a grand narrative such that the others are defined in relationship
to it. To put it bluntly, we are all heretics now because there is no orthodoxy
(Lyotard 1979; Berger 1979).

I do not believe that this situation can or will long continue. I think that
a new language of the self must be developed, and that it will in many
ways be unlike those that it replaces, not just a cacophony of them.
Chapters 9 and 10 of *Communication and the Human Condition*
(Pearce 1989) is devoted to an exploration of some of the characteristics
of such a language. When it comes, I believe that it will be the result of
"bricolage," a process of picking up bits and pieces of leftover languages
and integrating them into a new language. Technically, a new language
developed in this way is called a *creole,* and I believe that a postmodern
language of the self, when it is developed, will be such a creole.

> *Our task, like Thomas Aquinas's, Thomas Jefferson's, or Martin Luther
> King's, is to take the many parts of a complicated social and concep-
> tual inheritance and stitch them together into a pattern that meets the
> needs of the moment. It has never been otherwise. The creative intellectual
> task of every generation, in other words, involves moral bricolage. It
> is no accident that Aquinas, Jefferson, and King were as eclectic
> as they were in using moral languages—and no shame either. (Stout
> 1988, p. 292)*

you get on your television? Far more than you can possibly watch. Because
we are overfilled with conversational opportunities, we have a

> *multiplicity of incoherent and unrelated languages of the self. For
> everything we "know to be true" about ourselves, other voices within
> respond with doubt and even derision. This fragmentation of self-
> conceptions corresponds to a multiplicity of incoherent and discon-
> nected relationships. These relationships pull us in myriad directions,
> inviting us to play such a variety of roles that the very concept of
> an "authentic self" with knowable characteristics recedes from view.
> (Gergen 1991, pp. 6–7)*

Not everyone submits willingly to this postmodern condition, of course.
For many, this kind of life seems immoral, crazy, and unrelated to their daily
concerns of raising a family, paying the bills, and striving to achieve their
goals without being overtaken by those who would ensnare them in unwanted
obligations. To counteract these effects of the new communication media,
some people become very selective users of the media; they watch some
television shows and not others; they become very adept in their travels and
use of telephone and computer services so that they avoid conversations that
would challenge their vocabularies of self. Others deliberately embrace a

particular vocabulary of self that contradicts Gergen's description of postmodernity. Some are determined modernists, others romantics, and still others
use a vocabulary from a religious, ethnic, or philosophical tradition.

Of course, the fact that different people select among all these ways of
coping with the new communication media, and that the new communication
media provide common places, such as newspapers or television programs,
in which these people can meet or learn of each other, simply increases the
heteroglossia in which we live.

Multiphrenia

However, the multiple languages of the self in postmodern society prefigures
the development of a condition that Gergen called "multiphrenia." If *schizophrenia* means having multiple personalities; *multiphrenia* must mean the
same thing except that it is perceived as "normal," perhaps even "laudable."
Multiphrenia has three distinctive features.

Vertigo of the valued.   Vertigo of the valued is the ironic result of being
relieved of too many restrictions and presented with too many opportunities.
The new media of communication—including transportation—allow us to
overcome time and space, the factors that have traditionally restricted the
development of relationships. With the restrictions gone, we are "free" to
make commitments and then discover that each commitment exacts its costs.

> *If two persons become close friends, for example, each acquires certain
> rights, duties, and privileges. Most relationships of any significance
> carry with them a range of obligations—for communication, joint
> activities, preparing for the other's pleasure, rendering appropriate
> congratulations, and so on. Thus, as relations accumulate and ex-
> pand over time, there is a steadily increasing range of phone calls
> to make and answer, greeting cards to address, visits or activities to
> arrange, meals to prepare, preparations to be made, clothes to buy,
> makeup to apply. . . . Liberation becomes a swirling vertigo of
> demands. (Gergen 1991, p. 75)*

The multiphrenic self thus invents ways to avoid conversations and relationships with others. Some use their telephone answering machines as ways to
discover who is calling before deciding whether to answer; others prize long
walks and solitary hobbies. Relationships become shallower; people begin to
resent the "demands" of what should be joyous occasions and relationships.

The expansion of inadequacy.   The expansion of inadequacy refers to
the feeling that one is not measuring up to the expectations of others. The
problem is not necessarily with the one being measured; in the new age of

telecommunications, the standards against which one is measured have become much more diverse—to the point where no one can possibly feel "okay."

The mass media expose us to a concentrated barrage of standards for self-evaluation. Are you sufficiently clean, deodorized, adventurous, well traveled, well read, low in cholesterol, slim, fit, skilled in cooking, groomed, insured, and protected from car trouble by using the right motor oil? These comparisons are driven by the force of the marketplace; those who seek to make you feel inadequate really want to take money out of your pocket in a capitalist drama of sin and redemption. Nonetheless, a steady diet of well-produced messages setting up standards for self-assessment leads to a "seeping of self-doubt into everyday consciousness, a subtle feeling of inadequacy that smothers one's activities with an uneasy sense of impending emptiness" (Gergen 1991, p. 76).

In addition to the mass media, interpersonal relations can set up an impossible standard for self-evaluation. The new communication media make it possible to expand the array of our friends, to maintain relationships started at very different points of our lives, and to sustain relationships with people who live in very different material circumstances. Each of these relationships sets up a standard: Are you as physically fit as your friend from Ohio? As relaxed and content as your friend the beach bum in southern California? As

Contemporary society treats identity as something of a problem. Evidence of our fascination with who we are (and who we might be) can be found all around us. What does this tell us about ourselves?

industrious as your friend who works 12 hours a day in Chicago? As spiritual as your friend the Zen monk in New York? As well traveled and cosmopolitan as your friend the international news correspondent now stationed in Cairo (or is it Delhi?)?

> *All the voices at odds with one's current conduct thus stand as internal critics, scolding, ridiculing, and robbing action of its potential for fulfillment. One settles in front of the television for enjoyment, and the chorus begins: "twelve-year-old," "couch potato," "lazy," "irresponsible". . . . One sits down with a good book, and again, "sedentary," "antisocial," "inefficient," "fantasist". . . . Join friends for a game of tennis and "skin cancer," "shirker of household duties," "underexercised," "overly competitive" come up. Work late and it is "workaholic," "heart attack prone," "overly ambitious," "irresponsible family member." Each moment is enveloped in the guilt born of all that was possible but now foreclosed. (Gergen 1991, p. 77)*

Counterpoint 6.6

Gergen's claim about the "expansion of inadequacy" seems a little thin. If the situation is defined as multiple languages of the self, then "the chorus" that begins whenever you do something ought to contain as many phrases of praise as it does of criticism. That is, if you work late, you should hear the cheers: industrious, good provider for your family, and serious-minded.

Unfortunately, it does not quite work out that way. In the last century, numerous new words have been invented that describe the self; virtually all are terms of "mental deficit." For example, here are some words that have come into common usage: low self-esteem, depressed, stressed, obsessive-compulsive, sadomasochistic, identity crisis, self-alienated, authoritarian, repressed, paranoid, bulimic, midlife crisis, anxious, anoretic, kleptomaniac, and homophobic. "These words discredit the individual, drawing attention to problems, shortcomings, or incapacities. To put it more broadly, the vocabulary of human deficit has undergone enormous expansion within the present century. We have countless ways of locating faults within ourselves and others that were unavailable to even our great-grandfathers." (Gergen 1991, pp. 13–14)

Gergen describes a "spiraling cycle of enfeeblement" that is far from neutral politically or economically. The spiral is set into motion by the invention by the scientific establishment of a new term for some human dysfunction or failure. The cycle goes like this:

1. Physicians or psychologists invent a new term that labels an unhealthy condition or pattern of undesirable behavior. This labeling is often

driven by the needs of the health profession to provide specific diagnoses so that insurance companies can determine whether and for how much medical costs the patient is covered. The dynamic of this process is a tension between the medical profession's desire to expand the number and severity of treatable problems, and the insurance industry's desire to reduce the number of problems for which they will pay and the cost of the treatments.

2. These new labels (and descriptions of the symptoms) are disseminated to the general public. For example, the films of Alfred Hitchcock and Woody Allen have popularized psychoanalytic vocabulary until it has become part of common sense.

3. As people learn the new vocabulary, they come to see themselves and others in these terms. The terms are not only labels, of course, but part of logics of meaning and action. "How much can you trust an *addictive personality,* how much devotion does a *manic-depressive* merit, should you hire a *bulimic,* can you cherish a *hysteric*?" (Gergen 1991, p. 15).

4. The public begins to believe that professionals are essential for a "cure" for these problems. Seeing a therapist is considered the appropriate answer for life's problems; a doctor's opinion is necessary for making life choices.

5. As more and more people come to professionals with a wider array of symptoms and complaints, the professional community tries to meet their needs by developing a still larger, more differentiated vocabulary, which starts the cycle all over again.

Rationality in recession.   Rationality in recession refers to the problem of thinking, arguing, and deciding within a wider sphere. Rationality is a description of a way of thinking or talking; it is used when one acts consistently with the beliefs of a community. However, the new media of communication—by reducing the impediments of time and space—have enlarged the array of others who have to be taken into account and thus included people who do not share the same judgments of what is rational and what is not.

Conversations in contemporary society often include statements from very different vocabularies of self. For example:

> *Bill*: The figures are clear. If we want to preserve our profits we must lay off half of the workers at the Akron plant.
> *Marsha*: No. It would simply be too heartless to do that to our employees. I'm not going to do it.

Bill's statement is framed in the vocabulary of modernity, and it seems powerfully rational from that perspective. Marsha's statement is framed in the vocabulary of romanticism. From the perspective of modernity, Marsha seems irrational, an irritating impediment to progress. From the perspective of romanticism, however, Marsha's statement is clearly rational and praiseworthy, whereas Bill's is a leaden-eyed bean counter's way of working.

From our perspective as an observer, it is clear that there are two rationalities at work here. But what is it like from Bill and Marsha's perspective? Specifically, what do they feel after they have gone through some hundreds of repetitions of conversations like this? Let's assume that each is aware that the other is using a different rationality. Does this plurality of rationalities make rational choices easier or more difficult? Gergen (1991, p. 79) fears the worst: "as social saturation steadily expands the population of the self . . . we approach a condition in which the very idea of 'rational choice' becomes meaningless."

Some Concepts for Making Sense of Self

Gergen's description of the multiphrenic self sounds pretty horrible. However, even Gergen believes that the prospects for selves in contemporary society are not as bad as they might seem. We find ourselves in a period between stable eras; the old languages of the self have not gone away, but none has established itself as a grand narrative. Like Lyotard (1979), I do not believe that a new grand narrative is going to develop. The new language of the self will be something different, a *creole* created within a radically altered infrastructure for social worlds.

In the meantime, however, until the new language of self is developed, there are some concepts that will serve us well in sorting through the questions of identity, community, and morality that confront us.

First- and Third-Person Perspectives

Earlier in this book, you learned to distinguish these perspectives. We will use them again in the following section, this time in combination with some other ideas, but I want to add the idea that person perspectives are associated with different rights and responsibilities.

The moral order in which we are located as selves consists of clusters of rights and responsibilities. If we think of this moral order as a terrain, it is not a level plain; a somewhat different set of rights and responsibilities are attached to each specific location. For each self, performing some speech acts is easy; they roll "down-hill." However, other speech acts are difficult (like moving "up-hill") or impossible (like jumping over a mountain).

One way we reference our location in this moral order is by citing our roles. For example, to say "I am a student" does far more than simply to attach a label to the way you spend your days; it is to lay claim to a particular set of rights and duties that contrast sharply to those invoked by the statement "I'm a doctor" or "I'm a ditchdigger." A friend of mine keeps a sign that says "PRESS" in his automobile and puts it on the dashboard when he parks illegally. By this means, he locates himself as having responsibilities that transcend normal parking rules and claims the right to park illegally with impunity.

Far more than we usually realize, our conversations consist of claims and negotiations about the rights and duties of the conversants. Even the pronouns we use index different positions within the moral order. If "I" say "I'm hungry," it makes little sense for you to ask me How do you know? In the moral geography of the first person, "I's" have the right to avow their hunger—and a large class of other things. On the other hand, if "I" say "she is hungry," it makes very good sense for you to ask me How do you know? I might respond by talking about my observations of her stomach growling, the incidence of food metaphors in her talk, the quick glances first to her watch and then to the nearby restaurant, and my punctuation of all this as having started just when the odor of fresh baked bread from the nearby bakery started to fill the room. But no matter how well supported is my ascription of her hunger, I do not have the right to just assert it; I have the responsibility of providing an account if one is requested.

Take this one step further. If she says, "I'm hungry," and I reply, "No, you are not," my statement is not even primarily a description of a state of affairs; it is a clear denial of her claim to have the rights that go with the first person. On the other hand, if I tell her that she must decide for herself whether to cut class to help a sick roommate or attend class and prepare for the exam, I am insisting that she accept the rights and responsibilities that go with the first-person position.

Our sensitivity to the way we index our selves in the moral order makes possible some profoundly liberating moves. For example, I was told this story as the transcript of the shortest psychological therapy session on record:

> *Therapist:* Why have you come to see me?
> *Patient:* Doctor, I have a personality problem.
> *Therapist:* No, you have a personality characteristic. Let's talk about it
> and see whether it is a problem or not.
> *(Pause)*
> *Patient:* Thank you very much, Doctor. Goodbye.

As I understand this story, the patient was taking a third-person perspective relative to his "problem." The therapist's question located the patient in a first-person perspective, and in so doing helped the patient claim a different set of rights and responsibilities in dealing with the "characteristic." Viewed from this perspective, he had no problem and did not need any further therapy.

Self as Physical Entity and Self as Moral Agent

Clarifying the differences between the first- and third-person perspectives is very helpful, but there is a further ambiguity within the grammar of the first-person pronoun. Do the two forms of the pronoun "I" and "me" refer to the same thing? For that matter, does "I" always mean the same thing?

Consider the statement "I am confused." There seems to be no trouble with it, and the meaning of "I" is clear. However, what if the same person made this statement: "I think that I am confused." In this second sentence, the first-person pronoun is used twice. Does it refer to the same self? Is the "I" that thinks the same as the "I" that is confused? The ambiguity within the grammar of the first-person pronoun is illumined even more in this sentence: "I'm *certain* that I'm confused." Clearly, a grammar in which an "I" can be both certain and confused at the same time contains an ambiguity.

Let's shift the illustration from confusion to morality. If I say that I want to do good but I find that I in fact do evil, and that I do not want to do evil but I do it anyway, what should you think about me? Who is the "I" that wants to do good, and how is that "I" related to the "I" that does evil? And who is the "I" that paraphrases St. Paul so poorly?

In a series of lectures given at Oxford University in Spring, 1989, Harré suggested that there is a "double indexicality" in the first-person pronoun. That is, when we say "I" or "me," we are referring to ourselves *both* as physical entities and as moral agents. These aspects of ourselves are quite different.

As physical entities, we are embodied beings, "objects" located within material conditions, including ongoing, unfinished speech acts, relationships, and episodes. In this sense, my self is identical to the corporal being that I recognize when I look in a mirror; "I" am the cluster of abilities and molecules that opens doors, reads books, and runs to catch the bus.

As moral agents, we are responsible, decision-making, moral entities located within a nexus of rights and duties. That is, my self is identified with the roles I play in the various relationships that constitute me; "I" am that dense node of expectations and attributions that comprise a story—a biography—within the social world.

In the troublesome phrase "I think I'm confused; no, I'm certain that I'm confused!" all the "I's" are alike in that they refer to the same physically embodied being. In this sense, the first person pronoun simply picks out the speaker from the other bodies in the room at the time. At the same time, all the "I's" work together to locate the person in a very difficult spot with respect to rights and duties. To be thoughtful, certain, and confused all at once is contradictory, but such contradictions are the stuff of the moral orders in which we live.

As a moral agent, I can certainly bewail my actions as a physical entity or be certain that the physical entity that is "me" is confused. The fact that the same first-person pronoun is used for myself both as physical entity and as moral agent embeds ambiguity in our language that can be avoided by making this distinction.

The confusion is nowhere more evident than in the second turn in this conversational triplet:

"Why did you do that?"

"I could not help myself."

"Well, you should not have done it."

The second turn says that the self as moral agent is not responsible for the actions of the self as physical entity (or is it the other way around?). Of course, many a scoundrel can hide behind this grammatical ambiguity, but a more resourceful interlocutor might have insisted on clarifying the relationship between the self as moral agent and as physical entity.

George Herbert Mead (1934, p. 178) said that "self" is a dialectical process involving both the "I" and the "me." Struggling with ways of making a distinction not distinguished in the language he was using, he described the self as "essentially a social process going on with these two distinguishable phases. If it did not have these two phases there could not be conscious responsibility, and there would be nothing novel in experience."

Mead's view is not quite the same as Harré's. In Mead's language, the "I" is the self perceived as a "subject": acting as an agent, capable of having motives, accounting for actions, taking initiatives, and deciding among alternatives. The "me" is the self perceived as an "object": acted on rather than acting, seeing itself as perceived by others, and affected by the decisions of others. Both are, in different ways, moral agents; neither is quite what Harré called a physical entity. Using Harré's terms for Mead's concepts: the "I" is a moral agent; the "me" is a moral (not physical) entity (not agent).

In Mead's description, the "I" is the moral agent who acts; the "me" is what we remember ourselves to be. However, the "me" that we remember was an "I" at the time, and we can remember it as an "I."

The "I" of this moment is present in the "me" of the next moment. There again I cannot turn around quick enough to catch myself. I become a "me" in so far as I remember what I said. . . . The "I" can be given, however, this functional relationship. It is because of the "I" that we say that we are never fully aware of what we are, that we surprise ourselves by our own action. It is as we act that we are aware of ourselves. It is in memory that the "I" is constantly present in experience. . . . If you ask, then, where directly in your own experience the "I" comes in, the answer is that it comes in as a historical figure. It is what you were a second ago that is the "I" of the "me." (Mead 1934, p. 174)

Counterpoint 6.7

I hope you see that this examination of the grammatical ambiguity of the first-person pronoun is far more than just word play. It has far-reaching, life-and-death implications.

For example, many people abuse alcohol, drugs, or both. Which is at fault, the abuser as moral agent or as physical entity? If substance abuse is a physical problem, then we should feel great sympathy for the moral agent who is tragically trapped within the body of a "sick" physical entity. On the other hand, if substance abuse is a moral problem, then we should hold the abuser accountable for all the things she or he does "while under the influence." For example, I was told of a judge who would not accept a defendant's plea that his actions were not criminal because he was drunk when he performed them. "Did anyone hold a gun to your head and make you drink?" the judge asked. "No, your Honor, but . . ." "Did anyone hold you down and force the liquor down your throat?" "No, your Honor, but . . ." "You mean that you put yourself in that condition of your own free will? Three hundred dollars and 30 days in the county jail! Next case!"

But maybe the preceding paragraph posed the question too simplistically. Perhaps self is not one or the other, either a moral agent or a physical entity. Surely the two are inter-related in some complex manner. But how? Where does the ability of moral agents to control their selves as physical entities start and end? To what extent are our moral selves the verbal expressions of the state of our hormones?

Once we disambiguate the first-person pronoun, we are able to pose— I think more clearly than otherwise—many of the most vexing problems of ethics, law, and self-development.

Mead's ability to write passable English has never been in question, but when he tried to *use* English to make distinctions that are not *in* English, he wound up stuttering and stammering.

The interaction between the "I" (moral agent) and the "me" (moral object) are the stuff of those "internal conversations" that comprise our thinking, worrying, deliberating, and planning. Hewitt (1984, p. 90) gave the example of

> *when we feel caught between what we want to do and what others want us to do. Suppose one has been invited to a party, but would really prefer to spend a quiet evening at home. "If I go," one might say to herself, "I won't have a good time, because I'm tired and I don't feel like partying. But if I don't go, I'll hurt his feelings.*

Well, maybe he'll understand if I explain that I'm tired. No, he'll remember I also refused an invitation last week. Perhaps I can go but not stay long. But that would also hurt his feelings, or perhaps make him angry." In this internal dialogue, we see the alternation between "I" and "me" that is self as process.

Is it too much to suggest that the quality of these internal conversations determines the extent to which we are ethical, careful, judicious, spontaneous, or deliberate? If so, it is well worth our while to make sure that both our "I" and "me" are well developed, skillful conversants.

The Locus of Identity

The communication theory called the "coordinated management of meaning" (Cronen and Pearce 1991/1992, pp. 54–56) treats the ambiguities within the grammars of personal pronouns as a resource, not a problem. That is, because we can use the first-person pronoun to reference ourselves as moral agent, moral object, and physical entity all at once, we have room to move around in our conversations. This flexibility enables wit, creativity, and the game mastery type of competence as well as providing the raw materials for making confusion.

Cronen and Pearce use the term *locus of identity* to refer to the perspective from which a person acts. This perspective is expressed in the paired terms for self and other; that is, "I-You," "I-They," or "We-you" (singular).

The distinctive feature of this theory is the extent to which it describes these perspectives as *made* in actual conversations rather than just *found* in the structure of the grammar. In a debate with philosopher Josiah Royce at Cambridge, John Dewey was confronted with the tangle of identity with which I began this section: "How can 'A' identify 'A'?" Dewey's answer is that there is no confusion between the two "A's" because one is performing an action, "identify*ing*," that the other is not (Farrell et al. 1959). This substitution of the gerund identifying embeds the locus of identity within the actions of a specific person in a specific context, not in the resources available to us all.

> *There is no deep philosophical mystery about identifying oneself in a particular situation. . . . From experience persons come to know discursive patterns that can be coherently organized around various loci of identity. There are, for example, ways to talk as a representative of a group that are different than the way to coherently talk as a personal friend or as a third-person detached observer. (Cronen and Pearce 1991/1992, p. 57)*

Some useful concepts can be gleaned from these attempts to wrestle with the limitations of the languages of the self. The distinction between first- and third-person perspectives keeps us in good stead, but Harré and Mead point out that the first-person perspective must be further disambiguated. Let us call the two aspects of the first-person perspective the self as moral agent versus the self as moral or physical entity. And finally, we remember to take these positions as made in particular conversations.

The Self in Interpersonal Communication

If Gergen (1991) is right about the state of contemporary society, it is characterized by the simultaneous presence of many languages of self, none of which can sustain its claim to be the dominant idiom, or grand narrative. Because researchers are persons, too, their work is done within these language games, and the questions they pose as well as the answers they get are prefigured in those languages.

Some teachers and researchers are deeply enmeshed in the romantic language game; their work shows you how to express and discover the eternal mystery of-yourself and the selves of other people. Others are predominantly modernist, conducting carefully controlled studies that define the causal connections between the social environment and your behavior. Some are postmodernist; their language game features metalanguage. Postmodernist criticism and instruction focuses on how patterns of language use construct the selves that we know ourselves to be. It is not too difficult to identify which of these languages is drawn on by this book!

In the review of literature that follows, I have not tried to reduce the heteroglossia of communication research about the self in interpersonal communication because the diversity of research mirrors the heteroglossia of contemporary society. However, by using the concepts that we gleaned from the preceding section, we can sort through the diversity and distinguish among perspectives. In what follows, I categorize approaches to this topic in terms of whether it takes a first- or third-person perspective, and whether it views the self as a moral agent or a physical or moral entity.

A reasonable question is Which of these accounts of the self is the right one? As it turns out, although reasonable, this is not the right question to ask, at least not without specifying what you want to *do* with the information.

The locus of identity results from how actions are situated. That is, your identity *in your relationship with Mike* results from the how Mike (as moral agent) positions both himself and you (as moral entities) and how you respond to those positioning. In other words, your identities result from the co-constructed act of identify*ing*.

Therefore, if you want to position yourself or Mike as an object viewed from the third-person perspective, then the information generated by studies within that language for the self is the most directly relevant. On the other hand, if you want to construct yourself or the self of those with whom you communicate as moral agents, you need information developed from within a different language of self.

Remember that selves are co-constructed, and that "information" is not neutral. If you discern that Mike is using information developed within the language of the self viewed as a third person treated as an object, you can infer that he is viewing you as a third person (and what position does that claim for him? The first-person perspective of self as moral agent, I think) and as a physical or moral entity rather than an agent (i.e., you are controlled by some factors that he has constructed for you). For example, if Mike says, "You are an aggressive person; aggressive people like to be in charge of others; so I am going to appoint you to the Student Government Task Force on School Spirit!" you are being constructed as a moral entity.

Differentiating among these languages of the self is crucial to understanding what to do with the information developed by various research traditions. Dialogue requires a different language of self than monologue; it occurs in languages that take a first-person perspective and treat the selves of both or all conversants as moral agents, not entities. In addition, *theoria* speaks a language of the self as physical-moral entities, usually from the third-person perspective; *praxis* requires a first-person language of the self as a moral agent who makes decisions, takes into account and is affected by the consequences of those decisions, and—in this process—creates social worlds that could have been other than what they are. The language that is "right" is the one that serves the purposes for which you use it.

Self as Moral-Physical Entity from a Third-Person Perspective: Personality Traits

Perhaps the single largest group of studies have been done in the modernist language of self; they focus on the relationship between personality traits and forms of communication. The common element in these studies is that they view the self as a physical or moral entity from a third-person perspective (i.e., they tell us what *he, she, or it* or *they* do in communication). By using impressive research designs and careful observations, these researchers claim the right to tell "us" that our personality traits (which they will measure for us, even if we deny having them) cause us to communicate in particular ways. In addition, these studies tend to treat us as objects, comprised by the perceptions of others and acted on by forces outside our knowledge or control.

Researchers who take this position believe that the differences among individuals account for much of the variety of ways in which we communicate. For example, Dean Hewes and Sally Planalp (1987, p. 172) claimed that "An understanding of the individual's knowledge, cognitive capacities and emotion is the necessary point of departure for building adequate theories of communication. That is the place of the individual in a science of communication." Thomas Steinfatt (1987) listed some of the personality traits most often associated with communication. One cluster of traits includes authoritarianism, dogmatism, rigidity, and intolerance of ambiguity. Another cluster includes *Machiavellianism* (i.e., the extent to which a person's behavior resembles the old Italian's advice to political leaders to be unscrupulous and tyrannical) and whether their "locus of control" is "internal" or "external."

Each of these research traditions tells us something but at the cost of not being able to tell us something else. These studies tell us a good bit about "them"; it tells us something about "me," but nothing about "I" or the possibilities of internal conversations between the "I" and the "me."

Counterpoint 6.8

One of the strongest criticisms of the "third person/self as moral/physical entity" research project comes from the application of the Heyerdahl solution with a twist. The twist consists of asking What *will be* made by a particular pattern of actions? rather than How was this object made?

Specifically, if we look at the practice of social science that uses a modernistic language of the self as a part of the larger societal conversation about what selves are possible, then we see this form of social science (like any other) as participating in the creation of the social worlds in which we live, move, and find our selves. That is, the application of this scientific process is not only a way of describing our social worlds, it is a way of *making* those social worlds. And if it makes our social worlds, it will make them in terms of the language that it uses.

Critics of the application of this form of "science" warn that if this language is accorded the role of "expertise" and implemented in parental behavior toward children, curricular development in the schools, and political decisions about gun control and compulsory military service, then we will *become* those kinds of selves that these scientists think that they are *discovering* are already there.

Self as a Moral-Physical Entity from a First-Person Perspective: Social Identity

Another group of researchers have asked how we achieve identification with a particular group of people—our social identity. That is, how do "I" know that I am an American, middle-aged, white male? How do I act in conversations so that other people respond to me as having that identity?

Donal Carbaugh (1990) asked, "How do contemporary Americans develop "selves" that are recognized as 'American'?" He focused on conversations that occurred in the nationally televised program named for its host, Phil Donahue, arguing that this was a place where Americans recognize themselves in the forms of talk that occur.

Carbaugh characterized this talk by writing four rules, each of which has these properties: 1) the participants in the show could "report" these rules in their own talk; 2) the rules described "repeated" features of the talk in the shows; 3) the rules were "intelligible" to the participants as sensible guides to action; and 4) the rules were invoked as "repair mechanisms" when problems occurred in the discussions on the show.

Here are the rules that met these requirements:

Rule #1: In the conversations of *Donahue,* a) the presentation of self is the preferred communication activity, and b) statements of personal opinions count as proper self presentations.

Each participant on the show is assumed to have a unique self that only he or she can access and about which he or she can—and should—talk. Presenting this self in talk—"standing up and speaking out for yourself"—is a highly valued activity. The structure of the show itself, particularly the actions of its host, constitutes a helpful scene for such a presentation, and these presentations in turn make the show interesting and profitable.

Rule #2: Interlocutors must grant speakers the moral "right" to present self through opinions.

As enacted in practice, this rule guarantees both the moral capacity of self to speak and the availability of a public forum for being heard, no matter how outlandish or trivial the content of the speech might be.

Rule #3: The presentation of self through opinions should be "respected," that is, tolerated as a rightful expression.

This rule, as enacted in practice, creates a tone that Carbaugh calls "rightful tolerance," a scene in which it is right and proper to tolerate various viewpoints. "Respect" in this case entails avoiding evaluation but does not imply "agreement" with the opinions expressed.

Rule #4: Asserting standards that are explicitly transindividual, or societal, is discouraged because such assertions are believed a) to unduly constrain the preferred presentations of self, b) to infringe on the "rights" of others, and c) to violate the code of proper "respect."

That is, every self is entitled to his or her own *personal* opinion as long as that opinion does not infringe on the right of every other self to have alternative opinions.

Carbaugh says that conversations following these rules construct a particular kind of person. Specifically, this "model person" is "realized through free expression, is responsible for and tolerant of a degree of dissensus, and speaks the virtues of individual 'choice' over majority standards." (p. 137)

Lawrence Wieder and Steven Pratt (1990) did the same kind of analysis of a minority group in contemporary American culture. Identity for Native Americans—in this case, they called themselves "Indians"—has several aspects. The Bureau of Indian Affairs (an agency of the federal government) has a precise, unambiguous way for determining who is a "real Indian" based on genetics. If someone is identified by this process as an Indian, they have certain rights and responsibilities under law, including access to land set aside for them by the federal government.

However, identity is also a social issue. "Being a visible and recognizable . . . real Indian for other real Indians is a continuous, ongoing, contingent achievement involving both the doings of the person who would be a real Indian and the doings of those real Indians with whom he or she interacts" (p. 50). To be treated as an Indian by other Indians means to be admitted to certain activities, extended certain courtesies, and granted certain respect within the community. This is not done on the basis of genetics or physical features; it is accomplished by participating in certain ways in conversations with other Indians.

Wieder and Pratt describe eight characteristics of communication behavior that help "real Indians" recognize each other. One of these is "reticence." In the Anglo world, reticence is conceived as a communication "problem" that people should be helped to overcome. From the perspective of "real Indians," Anglos talk far too much and too personally in public and with strangers. When "real Indians" meet, they are silent. This silence is *not* a lack of communication; to the contrary, "it communicates that the one who is silent is a real Indian" (p. 51). In other contexts, however, "real Indians" engage in a distinctive form of verbal sparring described as "razzing." This form of conversation involves humor, skill, and displays virtuosity in the cultural form. One must know how, when, about what, and with whom to "razz" (pp. 53–54).

This is a very interesting language of self that focuses directly on what Mead called the "me" (or, more precisely, the "us" that is the plural of "me"). Reading these descriptions gives a sense of how each of us engages in conversations that construct our identity. Each group offers us a series of tests that we have to pass if we are to be treated as a full-fledged member of the group.

Counterpoint 6.9

The discussion of the research that treats "self as physical-moral entity from the first-person perspective" raises some questions for me.

The absence of the data that treat "self as moral agent" strikes me as significant. I wonder if, for example, Native Americans have, in Hewitt's (1984) terms, "internal conversations" between the "I" and the "me" about social identity? If so, in what languages of self do they occur? Is the quality of these conversations related to the differences between Native Americans who have more or less difficulty finding their selves in the society in which they live?

I also wonder about the relationship between social support in developing an identity as a moral *entity* (that is, in Wieder and Pratt's terms, a "real Indian") and developing an identity as a moral *agent*. Can conversations designed to help someone develop an identity as an entity have the unwanted consequence of impeding the development of identity as an agent?

These questions are one reason why I am so interested in Carbaugh's work that focuses on the social identity of the "dominant" group in contemporary American culture: middle-class whites. Even though their identities are more problematic, it is easy to see the processes by which non–middle-class nonwhites' identities are constructed. And, I believe, the view from the margins of society are always clearer than from the center.

But how do middle-class whites learn about their selves? Carbaugh's *Talking American* (1988) provides one set of answers; Terry's *For Whites Only* (1970) provides another. The key to both is that the members of the dominant groups in any culture do not see themselves as a group. For them, the social world in which they live—even though it contains explicitly racist or classist beliefs and institutions—appears normal because they experience no resistance in their movements through it.

Hardiman (1979) presented a theory of *white identity development* that addresses these issues. Putting her ideas in the terms used in this chapter, she says that whites in the United States have exactly the opposite problem from that confronted by Indians in Wieder and Pratt's account; they have an overdeveloped social identity as an entity. Specific events or experiences must occur to challenge that identity and permit the development of self as a moral agent.

Self as Moral Agent from a Third-Person Perspective

The contributors to this body of research proudly display their modernist concept of the self. Calling their work "cognitive" because it deals with the knowledge and beliefs of the people they observe (hence approximating a sense of moral agency), they take a third-person perspective on the mental states of the people they study.

Charles Berger's (Berger and Calabrese 1975; Berger et al. 1976) "uncertainty reduction" approach is the clearest example of this perspective. Berger imagined conversants as primarily motivated to reduce two forms of uncertainty. First, they want to increase their ability to predict their own and others' beliefs and attitudes. This phenomenon is referred to as "cognitive uncertainty." Second, they want to increase their ability to predict their own and others' behavior in given situations. This is referred to as "behavioral uncertainty." The reduction of uncertainty in conversations, then, involves the creation of proactive predictions and retroactive explanations about our own and others' behavior, beliefs, and attitudes.

I confess to being puzzled by this approach. It reproduces the confusion in the grammar of the first-person pronoun by treating the people studied *both* as entities that are described from a third-person perspective and agents who have purposes, make predictions, dislike uncertainty, and so on. The problem is that these two senses of the self are not distinguished; they are all jumbled together.

Can moral agents be engaged in conversation when treated as third persons? Can "I's" be understood in a vocabulary of "he, she, it"? The explanation offered here is that people want to reduce uncertainty. That looks like the first premise of the practical syllogism leading to action, not the first premise of an alethic syllogism leading to a statement purporting to be true. However, the research design produces statements—empirical generalizations about how people usually act—a kind of knowledge that fits *theoria* rather than *praxis*.

The best use of this information is as a warning. Be wary when people treat you as a third person (i.e., as a physical or moral entity) but try to describe what you do as a moral agent! Your interests are not being served by such a confused language of self.

Self as Moral Agent from a First-Person Perspective

This information is the most useful for people who live in a society containing multiple languages of self and for those of us interested in *praxis* rather than *theoria*. Fortunately, there have been several major contributions to understand self from this perspective. In the following paragraphs, I will distinguish them in terms of whether their emphasis is on the first person singular (i.e., my self located in a social context) or the first person plural (i.e., on "face"—our selves as they are co-constructed in conversation).

First person singular: "my self."   As you might expect, this is the approach of those who take a psychological interest in selves.

"Persons in conversation," noted Rom Harré (1984, pp. 15, 58) are the primary human reality. As participants in this undifferentiated experience, we become selves by individually appropriating—and perhaps idiosyncratically transforming—certain features of the conversations in which we participate.

Our selves consist of three features, all appropriated from our social worlds: consciousness, agency, and identity. Consciousness consists of perceiving ourselves as located within the social world, that is, having a first-person position within our experience. Perceiving ourselves as agents involves accepting responsibility for certain aspects of our experience as the results of our own choices. Finally, our identity consists of an autobiography, that is, an organization of our experience into a story of who we are (Harré 1984, p. 20).

Harré is deliberately interested in developing a better language of self than currently exists; he is not content simply to work within conventional vocabularies. If we believe the social constructionist position, he says, then the language we use is part of the process by which we *make* the selves that we study, that we are, and that we have to live with in communities. It behooves us, he argues, to be proactive in our use of language so that we can make a "better psychology" of identity. Part of his explanation of this better psychology is a sustained analogy between physical and social worlds, in which conversations are the creative or causal factors in the social world just as the laws of motion or energy function in the physical world.

I take the array of persons as a primary human reality. I take the conversations in which those persons are engaged as completing the primary structure, bringing into being social and psychological real-

*ity. Conversation is to be thought of as creating a social world just
as causality generates a physical one. (Harré 1984, pp. 64–65)*

The *social* reality created by conversations has two parts. One is *work,*
or the practical domain where we collectively produce the means of life; it
includes farming and manufacturing, buying and selling, hunting and gather-
ing, and sewing and chopping firewood. The second domain is *expressive.* It
consists of the moral orders in which we negotiate virtues and vices, where
we sin and achieve honor, and where we preen and prance for the notice and
approval of others.

The *psychological* reality consists of human minds. Minds should not be
confused with brains. Brains are physical organs that can be weighed, bruised,
and—perhaps someday—transplanted. Minds are, in part, theories of themselves, clusters of beliefs that give rise to certain powers of action that produce
a recognition that, yes, "that is me."

Continuing the analogy between social and physical worlds, Harré notes
that one of the things we do when we converse is locate ourselves. Maps of
a campus or a ski slope may be useless to you no matter how well they
represent what they depict unless they contain some sort of marker that says
"you are HERE." In the physical world, we have elaborate ways of locating
ourselves "here" and "now" as we move about. In the social world, pronouns
serve this function. "I" and "we" are equivalent to "here" and "now." These
pronouns do not so much function to represent or depict who we are as they
do to locate our position within the moral worlds in which we live (Harré
1984, p. 60).

Without a sufficiently rich array of markers of location in the moral
order, or if those markers identify an insufficiently wide range of possible
locations, our selves are diminished. In this process, Harré finds the mechanism by which discriminatory social structures are made. For example, Harré
noted, in the old radio version of "The Lone Ranger," "Tonto" was portrayed
as less of a human being than his Anglo colleague. The Lone Ranger's lines
included many first-person pronoun self-references: "I'm not sure what we
should do, Tonto." Tonto, on the other hand, never referred to himself with
the first-person pronoun, but always by using his name: "Tonto confused,
Kemo Sabe." In this use of language, Harré found the mechanism for reproducing the social structure that separated Anglos from Indians. Is there a
difference between Tonto's saying "I'm confused" and "Tonto [is] confused"? Yes: "Tonto was the name of a public person. There was a pretty
clear implication that while the Lone Ranger had a rich and diversified personal
psychic life, the simple Indian," Harré criticized the script writers, "had no
need for the niceties of reference to personal psychic unities. His public or
social being would do" (1984, p. 67).

The emphasis on the self from the first-person pronoun does not imply
forgetting about social process. Harré argues for a fully reflexive relationship
between the personal and the social: "people and their modes of talk are

made by and for social orders, and social orders are people in conversation," he said (Harré 1984, p. 65) and described the process by which this reflexive relationship occurs like this:

> *We express ourselves in public performances, and the quality of these performances impress other people, who express their perceptions in ways that impress us . . . and so on. From this circular, reflexive process we develop our personal skills, our beliefs, and our implicit theory of who we are that is our "personality." (1980, pp. 4–5)*

Gergen (1991) presents a model of the development of the *multiphrenic* personality that presumes the multiple languages of self in the contemporary world. In his view, the task that each of us face is, to use Harré's term, appropriate from the world that which we need to act effectively and with integrity.

You probably noticed that Gergen writes as if we are in a radically new era, different from any that has gone before. The unique demands of being a self in contemporary society involve an usually keen sense of self as moral agent without forgetting our placement within co-constructed social worlds.

The multiphrenic personality is developed in a sequence of three stages. The first is *strategic manipulator*. The modernist self finds itself playing a series of roles designed to achieve certain social objectives. For example, I embrace my friends from South America when I meet them but do not embrace my friends from Northern Europe. In each case, I am acting politely according to my friends' cultures . . . but where am "I" in all of this? What is *my* cultural norm? Is my deontic logic mute with regard to hugging, consisting only of the requirement to adapt to the expectations of others? If you spend all your life flattering your boss so that you can be promoted to a sufficiently high position in which you can express your *own* personality, what has happened to your personality in the process? "No actions remain sincere, simple explosions of spontaneous impulse; all are instrumental," Gergen (1991, p. 149) mused.

The second stage in the development of a healthy multiphrenia is the *pastiche personality*. If we no longer believe in a prelinguistic "real" self, then we are free to be "social chameleons," adapting without guilt or shame to the requisites of the situation in which we find ourselves. The pastiche personality "constantly borrow[s] bits and pieces of identity from whatever sources are available and construct[s] them as useful or desirable in a given situation" (Gergen 1991, p. 150). The primary social skill needed by the pastiche personality is "self-monitoring."

There is reason to believe that pastiche personalities thrive in contemporary America. Snyder (1979) found that people who are better at strategic self-presentation, sensitive to their public image and to situational cues of appropriateness, and able to control or modify their appearance are generally more successful in contemporary social settings. That is, they like others, are less shy, less upset by inconsistencies, better at remembering information about others, more emotionally expressive, and more influential. Gergen (1991, p. 151) notes that a modernist would condemn such self-monitoring as incoherent, superficial, and deceitful. However, Snyder works in a postmodern vocabulary of self and praises it for giving the individual the flexibility to cope quickly and effectively with the shifting demands of social life.

The third stage in the development of an authentic self within the postmodern vocabulary requires relinquishing the notion of the self as autonomous, separated from others. Gergen calls this the *relational self.* It finds one's authentic role as a participant in a social process that includes more than one's own self. Self is identified not with a singular, autonomous "I" or "me" but as the nexus of a cluster of relationships, each of which is an "us."

At the moment, there is no well developed vocabulary for this *relational self,* although fragments of it occur in the recognition that there can be no leader without people who are led; no victor without people who are losers; no person who is attractive without those who are attracted. We need to

Counterpoint 6.10

"Popular culture" and fashion seem to be areas in which *pastiche* personalities function best. At least this is one interpretation of the fad of identifying with a musical group, sports team, or celebrity. Take a look at the insignia on t-shirts, hats, and jackets and ask yourself what is being made by wearing them. Why do people need to be "with it" in styles of clothing, haircuts, backpacks, athletic shoes, and all the rest?

> For the pastiche personality, there is no self outside of that which can be constructed with a social context. Clothing thus becomes a central means of creating the self. With proper clothing, one becomes the part. And if the clothing is orchestrated properly, it may also influence the very definition of the situation itself. In this context, the replacement of the department-store-reliable clothing by the remarkable array of apparel served up by "unique" boutiques becomes intelligible. Each international (meaning both exotic and universally acceptable) label promises a new and different statement of the self. And because making the same clothing statement season after season would be a mere repetition of the same old stories, the fashions must change. . . . It is not the world of fashion that drives the customer into a costly parade of continuous renewal, but the postmodern customer who seeks means of "being" in an ever-shifting multiplicity of social contexts. (Gergen 1991, pp. 154, 155)

develop a vocabulary that focuses on the coordinated actions of persons in conversations, not just on individuals—and our supply of such terms, at the moment, is limited. We have a better vocabulary for talking about Sarah's feelings for Ken than we do for the various forms of relationships among them. We particularly lack terms that indicate that the relationship between Sarah and Ken may be something other than the sum or average of each of their feelings or beliefs about the other.

First person plural: "our selves."   One attempt to develop a better vocabulary for dealing with *relational selves* is to focus less on selves and more on *relationships,* that is, to take what is co-constructed in conversations as the primary substance of our social worlds.

Our ability to participate in relationships and episodes depends on our location in the moral order. Some locations (the prosecuting attorney in a murder trial, your mother and father) include the right to demand that others describe what they were doing on the night of August 31; most do not. Most locations include the right to choose with whom and about what we will converse; some (patients in a psychiatric ward, prisoners of war) do not. The clarification and maintenance of our location in—to use Harré's terms—the productive and expressive orders is not simply a matter of self-gratification; it is a matter of power, the ability to participate in the speech acts that involve you.

Brown and Levinson (1979) noted that the concept of "face" is used in many cultures as a nontechnical description of a self's location within the moral order. If the best athlete in your high school can't make the team in college, he or she has "lost face" by being unable to prevent himself or herself from moving to a less desirable location in the moral order of your social worlds. On the other hand, when your professor stops you on the street when you are showing your parents around and praises your term paper, you have "gained face."

Face work, Brown and Levinson (1979, p. 62) suggest, is remarkably consistent in all cultures. They developed a rigorous, tightly focused model that assumes that all people want to have autonomy (i.e., to be unimpeded in their actions and movements) and approval (i.e., they want both positive feedback and to avoid too much negative feedback from others). Further, they assume that we are all rational—in a specific sense—about the ways of achieving autonomy and approval. That is, although we may not know any formal logic, we are all rather skilled at reasoning how to accomplish our goals. On the basis of these assumptions, and grounded in careful analysis of conversations in three cultures—the Tzeltal (a Mayan language spoken in Mexico), Tamil (spoken in south India), and English—Brown and Levinson developed a very useful model for understanding the way people coordinate in the mutual maintenance of face.

Adult conversants assume that all conversants have—and know each other to have—face and certain rational capacities. In this sense, "positive face" refers to autonomy, and "negative face" refers to the desire not to be disapproved of by others. Rationality refers to the expectation that each of us is responsible for linking our behavior to certain goals. That is, if you buy a new suit just before an important job interview, all of us who are hoping that the interview goes well for you will infer that your new sartorial elegance is *in order to* impress the interviewer. On the other hand, you will lose face if you select torn jeans and t-shirt for the interview; you will surely lose our approval because we will infer that something is wrong with you, and in some cases, you will lose autonomy because we will drag you back to your closet and force you to change clothes.

Some speech acts threaten the face of one or more conversants by creating a condition that restricts their autonomy or reduces their approval. Brown and Levinson call these by their acronym, FTAs, or "face-threatening acts." For example, an expression of disapproval is more than just a representation of the speakers' evaluation; it is an *act* that threatens the face of the other. In the same way, the command "get over here, you!" is not just an expression of a desired state of affairs, it is a threat to the autonomy of the person being ordered about.

The face of a conversant is not always vulnerable. In the military, privileges of rank allow acts that otherwise would be FTAs, for example, direct commands, to occur without threatening the face of either conversant, and, conversely, make other acts, normally quite benign, into serious FTAs. For example, the face of the officer is seriously threatened if enlisted personnel disagree with a suggestion and offer better alternatives. In psychological therapy sessions or in the conversations between a client and lawyer, certain definitions of the situation are created so that one person may speak freely about things that otherwise would threaten his or her face to admit.

When the faces of all conversants are reciprocally vulnerable to the acts of the others, any rational agent will seek to avoid FTAs or will employ certain strategies to minimize the threat they pose. Much of the value of Brown and Levinson's analysis comes from the taxonomy they developed of ways of doing FTAs without really destroying one's own or the other's face. First, they distinguish between doing acts "on" and "off record." This has to do with the clarity of the intention of the act. To do the act *on record* is to make it clear that the act threatens the face of one or the other conversant: "Smedley, I'm placing an official reprimand in your personnel file!" *Off record* means that there could be several interpretations, at least some of which are not threats to face. For example, if I say, "Oh, no! I forgot to go to the bank and have no money," this may or may not be a request for you to lend me enough to cover my lunch. At least, I can plausibly deny that was my intent and thus save face if you say, "don't look at me, buddy, I am not going to lend you money—again." Although my response is weak, I can say, "No, I was not asking for a loan."

An FTA may be done "with redress" or in ways that give face and thus counteract the potential damage of the act. A redressive act may be focused on either autonomy or approval. That is, it may anoint the face of the other person by going on record that the other person has autonomy or approval. For example, Bill may tell Tom, "Look, you may not like hearing this, but I know that you'd do the same for me . . ."

Many communication theorists have found the phrase "bald on record" useful. This describes an utterance that contains an FTA that is on record and is done "baldly"—that is, without redress. "In your face!" when shouted by one basketball player who has just dunked the ball over the other's failed attempt at defense is "bald on record" as an FTA.

Brown and Levinson offer some interesting observations about the rational use of FTAs, the conditions under which it makes sense to be on or off record, and when FTAs should be done with redress. For our purposes, the details of this analysis are less important than the fact that a great deal of our conversational behavior consists of the mutual care and construction of our public selves.

A Final Word: Second Thoughts About a Postmodern Sensibility

Gergen's description of the contemporary world as "postmodern" seems right to me. But this description is disturbing because there really is no "postmodern language of self." Instead, there are many different languages of the self that coexist in doubtful harmony, and there is a heightened sense of the importance of the process of communication itself. We have taken on board the postmodern sensibility if we understand that our selves are constructed in conversations, and, once constructed, those selves are contexts for the conversations in which we participate.

This postmodern sensibility requires us to give up several ways of talking or at least rethink what they mean. For example, "Know thyself!" does not mean to engage in introspective navel gazing but to do an analysis of the conversations in which you engage and the language you use in them. Circular questioning is an excellent technique for knowing thyself, although I suspect that the Oracle at Delphi had something else in mind when she made that cryptic remark. In addition, expressions like "to thine own self be true" do not make much sense without extensive qualification.

I have a lot of sympathy for Popeye's "I am what I am." I hear it as a romantic protest against the modern language of the self; it is an exclamation that no matter how many people converse with and about him in a language that treats him as a third-person entity, he remains a moral agent. However, if the statement quoted here is a sample of his competence in negotiating about languages of the self, I'm not sanguine about Popeye's ability to maintain face as a moral agent when he encounters the bean counters and actuarial tables of modern society.

When and if a postmodern language of the self is developed, it will necessarily focus on the ongoing tension between the self as a moral agent and as an entity constructed in social patterns of communication. The development of such a language is not inevitable, but it is needed as a resource for all of us who live in a world in which the languages of self comprise a cacophonous motley.

Praxis

1. Power, Oppression, and Liberation

The second half of this century has witnessed a concerted effort to institutionalize human rights. One part of this movement involves changing the identities of oppressed people.

If oppression is successful, it is invisible to the oppressed. The poor feel that they deserve their poverty and cannot imagine themselves well off; the victims of discrimination feel that they deserve to be treated less well than others (Frieri 1982). On the other hand, those who are wealthy believe that the gap between them and the poor is inevitable if not justified and may be completely oblivious to the conversational patterns by which they participate in discrimination.

Anecdotes have been used as one of the most powerful tools in restructuring the identities of oppressed peoples. Here are three such anecdotes.

1. Gandhi helped the citizens of his country to overcome the degradations of their experience as strangers in their own land during British colonial rule. He told them that "there is no shame in having been a slave. There is great shame in having been a slave-owner."

Working in groups of four, construct an explanation of why this statement is so effective. Assign two of you to use Harré's notion of being a moral agent rather than an entity and the idea of different rights and responsibilities stemming from the first- and third-person position within the moral order. Assign the other two to use Brown and Levinson's notions of face. Whose face was being given and whose lost in Gandhi's statement? Was this statement "bald on record" or was it done "with redress"?

2. During the civil rights movement of the 1960s, numerous stories were told by African Americans to other African Americans to foster both

resentment and pride. One of the most powerful stories had to do with a great fair held in Atlanta for whites only. The speaker described how his daughter saw the advertisement for the fair on television. She told him about the clowns, elephants and tigers, and exciting rides. "Can we go, Daddy? Please, Daddy, take me!" Turning to the audience, the storyteller said, "How do you tell your daughter, your darling daughter, whom you love almost as much as if she were white, that she can't go to the fair because she's a nigger?" As you might imagine, this anecdote was particularly effective for whites sympathetic to the civil rights movement.

Working in groups of four, develop an explanation of why this anecdote was effective. In what vocabulary of self is it located: romantic, modernist, or postmodern? What person-perspective does the speaker take for himself? What person-perspective does he invite the audience to take? Does he treat himself as moral agent or moral entity?

If sympathetic whites were powerfully affected by this story, what about racist whites? How do you think they would respond to the speaker telling this story? Write a conversation between the black civil rights activist and a white supremacist in which this story is the first turn. What languages of self are used in this conversation? How would the conversation differ if a different language of self were used?

When you are finished, compare your explanations with those of other groups.

3. In the continuing feminist movement of the 1990s, the story is told of three persons—a black woman, a white woman, and a white man—who were asked to look into a mirror and tell what they saw. The first said, "I see a black woman." The second said, "I see a woman." The third said, "I see a person."

The point of this story, of course, is that one's own race and gender are invisible to members of the dominant group, but that the gender and racial inflections of society are very obvious to those who are among the others. These inflections become part of their very identities in a way that being a white male would not.

Working in groups of four, take the role of a task force whose purpose is to help males become sensitive to the gender inflections of conversations in which they participate, and to help white males and females become more sensitive to the racial inflections of their conversations. Do a bit of research about how this is done, and assess these strategies in terms of how *effective* and how *ethical* you think they are. When you are finished, select the most and least effective, and most and least ethical strategy and describe them to the other groups.

2. The Identity Crisis

Psychologist Erik Erikson said that young adults confront an "identity crisis." A combination of social structures and genetic maturation make the late teens and early twenties a period in which the question Who am I? becomes a central concern. According to Erikson, much of the behavior of young adults can be understood as various ways of answering this question.

But is this question equally relevant and equally difficult for everyone? Slugoski and Ginsberg (1989) suggested that this question is more poignant for males than for females, and more common among relatively affluent or upwardly mobile members of modern, Western society than among those from a more traditional society or those with fewer choices. In fact, they suggest that the identity crisis is not a part of objective reality at all; it is a "culturally appropriated mode of discourse in which individuals imbue their actions with rationality and warrantability" (p. 37). That is, to have an identity crisis is *not* to have a physiological state that is different from those who do not experience the crisis; rather, it is to engage in a particular language game that *names* a set of experiences as a crisis, *initiates* a script for how the person and his or her significant others should converse, and *confers* a specific set of rights and responsibilities on the person suffering the crisis.

To have an identity crisis is to treat "identity" as if it were the achievement of the person, and thus to define the person as exercising personal freedom, self-efficacy, and responsibility. These are positively valued traits in contemporary American society, and the identity crisis may be seen as a means of laying claim to these virtues. By the same token, those who do not have an identity crisis are seen as exercising less freedom, efficacy, and responsibility. What's wrong with you? is the implicit question. Why aren't you having a crisis?

Working in groups of three or four, answer these questions. What language of self are Slugoski and Ginsburg using to think about the identity crisis? In what language of self did Erikson originally pose the description? Assign one person to simulate or role-play an identity crisis (something like Bill's with which the Narrative began, or worse), assign another to respond, and a third to monitor their use of languages of self. Exchange roles and change languages of self. Start with romantic, then modern, and then use the postmodern sensibility to the plurality of languages about the self. Keep track of the person positions that you use and whether the self is treated as a moral agent or as an entity.

3. The Spiraling Cycle of Enfeeblement

The "spiraling cycle of enfeeblement" was described at some length in Counterpoint 6.6. If Gergen is right, we have created a new growth industry in this country: the creation and dissemination of new labels for patterns of "mental deficit. They discredit the individual, drawing attention to problems, shortcomings, or incapacities" (Gergen 1991, p. 13).

Surely this is a game that any number can play! Working in groups of five, think up some new enfeebling labels and start using them. For example, you may judge someone to be pun impaired (the dreaded condition of not being able to appreciate your puns), or rose phobic (someone who does not like red-headed people), or suffering from post-dining syndrome (a cluster of symptoms that occur after you have had a big meal in which food does not seem interesting to you and you are a bit sleepy). Help each other invent these labels, unless the other group members are numero-phobic (i.e., they do not like to work with large numbers of other people). You may find a thesaurus or an etymological dictionary a great help in this project.

For fun, compare your most interesting creations with those of other groups. More seriously, think about the consequences that would follow if you were highly respected professionals who had the power to pass laws, distribute rewards and punishment, administer medication, and influence public opinion about these people.

4. Popular Culture and Fashion

The *pastiche personality* seems particularly attracted to popular culture and fashion. Working in groups of four, assign yourselves to watch television, listen to radio, read popular magazines, and watch some movies. As you do, carefully note the languages of the self that are used. When you have answered the following questions, discuss your findings with the other groups in the class.

1. Identify words and phrases that seem particularly associated with the romantic, modernist, and postmodern vocabularies of self.

2. Identify conversations that have mixed vocabularies. What kinds of communication problems occur?

3. Are the various vocabularies of self associated with particular forms of popular culture? For example, is romanticism really the dominant vocabulary in country and western music and on soap operas or telenovellas? Is modernistic vocabulary the predominant vocabulary in science fiction movies and popular science magazines? Does "Star Trek: The Next Generation" reflect a postmodern sensibility?

4. Based on this project, what is the mix of vocabularies of self in popular culture?

5. Do you agree with Gergen's comment about an impoverished vocabulary for the "relational self"? What instances of this vocabulary did you find? Where do you think this vocabulary will be developed?

5. *Constructing Your Self in Conversations*

In the section "The Self in Interpersonal Communication," I alluded to the fact that your self is co-constructed in conversations with many other people, and that these people speak in numerous different languages of self. The language that they use when speaking to you is not neutral with respect to the kind of self they want or want you to be.

You should not assume that everyone who speaks to you is *deliberately* trying to construct your self in one way or another because most people are only dimly aware of their language or the process of the social construction of selves. However, the fact that they speak a particular language of self from habit or ignorance probably means that they are even more confined by what its grammar prefigures than if they had deliberately chosen to use it.

The question I want to pose is how *you* should deal with *their* languages of self. At the very least, you should be aware of the languages of self that you use and that the people with whom you converse use. In the following activities, you should draw some conclusions about the kinds of languages of self that you feel most comfortable with in particular relationships and particular situations, and perhaps practice some game mastery skills in negotiating for changing your conversations to those languages.

Working in groups of three or four, identify some familiar episodes and relationships, such as basic training in the military; taking a standardized achievement test, such as the Scholastic Aptitude Test; or interviewing for a job. Using the notions of person-perspective and the distinction between self as moral agent or as physical-moral entity, identify what language of the self is used in these situations. Continue to think of situations until you have an example of all the ones discussed in the "Narrative" section. Write down just enough about each of these situations to hold them in your memories.

Try using Gergen's notion of romantic, modernistic, and postmodern language of the self. Can you associate these situations with these types of languages? What would be different if basic training in the military were to assume the postmodern concept that there are multiple languages, none of which is the grand narrative? What would happen if the SAT exam were conducted and scored in the romantic language of self?

Assigning roles to the members of your group, do impromptu skits of the situations you identified. Assign one person to act within the language of the self that you described as usually occurring in this setting; assign another person to try to change that language. Use all that you know about game mastery as ways of changing the frame in which selves are usually constructed in this situation. Assign the other member(s) of the group as critics and referees, carefully observing the skit and noting what works and what does not, and helping the change-agent to detect openings for game mastery.

References

Bakhtin, Mikhail. *Speech Genres and Other Late Essays.* Translated by Vern W. McGee. Austin: University of Texas Press, 1986.

Berger, Charles R., and Calabrese, R. J. "Some Explorations in Initial Interactions and Beyond: Toward a Developmental Theory of Interpersonal Communication." *Human Communication Research* 1 (1975): 99–112.

Berger, Charles R., Gardner, R., Parks, M., Schulman, L., and Miller, G. "Interpersonal Epistemology and Interpersonal Understanding." In *Explorations in Interpersonal Communication,* edited by Gerald R. Miller. Beverly Hills: Sage, 1976.

Berger, Peter L. *The Heretical Imperative: Contemporary Possibilities of Religious Affirmation.* Garden City: Anchor, 1979.

Brown, Penelope, and Levinson, Stephen. "Universals in Language Usage: Politeness Phenomenon." In *Questions and Politeness,* edited by E. N. Goody, 56–209. New York: Cambridge University Press, 1979.

Carbaugh, Donal. *Talking American: Cultural Discourses on "Donahue."* Norwood: Ablex, 1988.

Carbaugh, Donal. "Communication Rules in 'Donahue' Discourse." In *Cultural Communication and Intercultural Contact,* edited by Donal Carbaugh, 119–149. Hillsboro: Erlbaum, 1990.

Chang, Chung-Ying. "Chinese Philosophy and Contemporary Human Communication Theory." In *Communication Theory: Eastern and Western Perspectives,* edited by Lawrence Kincaid, 23–43. New York: Academic Press, 1987.

Cronen, Vernon E., and Pearce, W. Barnett. "Grammars of Identity and Their Implications for Discursive Practices In and Out of Academe: A Comparison of Davies and Harré's Views to Coordinated Management of Meaning Theory." *Research on Language and Social Interaction* 25 (1991/1992): 37–66.

Cronen, Vernon E., Pearce, W. Barnett, and Snavely, Lonna. "A Theory of Rule Structure and Forms of Episodes, and a Study of Unwanted Repetitive Patterns (URPs)." In *Communication Yearbook III,* edited by Dan Nimmo, 225–240. New Brunswick: Transaction Press, 1979.

Davies, Bronwyn, and Harré, Rom. "Positioning: The Discursive Production of Selves." *Journal for the Theory of Social Behaviour* 20 (1990): 43–64.

Davies, Bronwyn, and Harré, Rom. "Contradiction in Lived and Told Narratives." *Research on Language and Social Interaction* 25 (1991/1992), 1–36.

Farrell, J., Gutmann, J., Johnson, A., Kallen, H., Laidler, H., Lamont, C., Nagel, E., Randall Jr., J., Schneider, H., Taylor, H., and Thomas, M. *Dialogue on Dewey.* New York: Horizon Press, 1959.

Frieri, Paulo. *Pedagogy of the Oppressed.* Translated by Myra Bergman Ramos. New York: Continuum, 1982.

Geertz, Clifford. "On the Nature of Anthropological Understanding." *American Scientist* 63 (1975): 43–57.

Geertz, Clifford. *Local Knowledge: Further Essays in Interpretive Anthropology.* New York: Basic Books, 1983.

Gergen, Kenneth J. *The Saturated Self: Dilemmas of Identity in Contemporary Life.* New York: Basic Books, 1991.

Gudykunst, William, and Ting-Toomey, Stella. *Culture and Interpersonal Communication.* Newbury Park: Sage, 1988.

Hardiman, Rita. "White Identity Development Theory." New Perspectives, 1979.

Harré, Rom. *Social Being: A Theory for Social Psychology.* Totowa: Littlefield, Adams & Company, 1980.

Harré, Rom. *Personal Being: A Theory for Individual Psychology.* Cambridge: Harvard University Press, 1984.

Hewes, Dean, and Planalp, Sally. "The Individual's Place in Communication Science." In *Handbook of Communication Science,* edited by Charles R. Berger and Steve H. Chaffee, 146–184, Newbury Park: Sage, 1987.

Hewitt, John P. *Self and Society: A Symbolic Interactionist Social Psychology,* 3rd ed. Boston: Allyn and Bacon, 1984.

Lyons, John. *The Invention of the Self.* Carbondale: Southern Illinois University Press, 1978.

Lyotard, J. P. *The Postmodern Condition: A Report on Knowledge.* Minneapolis: University of Minnesota Press, 1979.

Mead, George Herbert. *Mind, Self, and Society: From the Standpoint of a Social Behaviorist.* Chicago: University of Chicago Press, 1934.

Pearce, W. Barnett. *Communication and the Human Condition.* Carbondale: Southern Illinois University Press, 1989.

Rokeach, Milton. *Beliefs, Attitudes, and Values: A Theory of Organization and Change.* San Francisco: Jossey-Bass, 1968.

Sacks, Oliver. *Seeing Voices.* London: Pan Books, 1991.

Slugoski, B. R. and Ginsburg, G. P. "Ego Identity and Explanatory Speech." In *Texts of Identity,* edited by John Shotter and Kenneth J. Gergen, 36–55. Newbury Park: Sage, 1989.

Snyder, Mark. "Self-Monitoring Process." In *Advances in Experimental Social Psychology,* vol. 12, edited by Leonard Berkowitz. New York: Academic Press, 1979.

Steinfatt, Thomas M. "Personality and Communication: Classical Approaches." In *Personality and Interpersonal Communication,* edited by James C. McCroskey and John A. Daly, 42–126. Newbury Park: Sage, 1987.

Stout, Jeffrey. *Ethics After Babel: The Languages of Morals and the Discontents.* Boston: Beacon Press, 1988.

Terry, Robert W. *For Whites Only.* Grand Rapids: Eerdman, 1970.

Wieder, D. Lawrence, and Pratt, Steven. "On Being a Recognizable Indian Among Indians." In *Cultural Communication and Intercultural Contact,* edited by Donal Carbaugh, 45–64. Hillsdale: Erlbaum, 1990.

Zimiatin, Evgenii Ivanovich. *We.* New York: Dutton, 1924.

CHAPTER
7 *Culture*

Culture is communication and communication is culture.

Hall 1959, p. 169

Culture is interpersonal communication "frozen"; interpersonal communication is culture "in process."

Pearce 1994

Communication and culture reciprocally influence each other. The culture from which individuals come affects the way they communicate, and the way individuals communicate can change the culture they share. Most analyses of interpersonal communication, however, virtually ignore this relationship and study communication in a cultural vacuum.

Gudykunst and Ting-Toomey 1988, p. 17

OBJECTIVES

After reading this chapter, you will be able to

- Differentiate between rhetorical sensitivity and exoticism as ways of relating to other cultures

- Differentiate between conversations that are intercultural from those that are deeply enmeshed in a single culture

- Compare various patterns of family communication

- Avoid linguistic tyranny when you are communicating with people from other cultures

- Assess three suggestions for living in postmodern society

KEY WORDS AND PHRASES

Some terms that will help you understand this chapter include

intercultural communication; communication in the family; limits, boundaries, and horizons; pidgin and creole; *bricolage*

Narrative

> *Rosa:* Hi! I'm Rosa. Who are you?
>
> *Robert:* I'm Robert. I'm a freshman and I come from Ohio. How about you?
>
> *Rosa:* I'm a senior communication major. I grew up here in Chicago. What's your major?
>
> *Robert:* I haven't decided yet. I want to take some courses in several areas that I don't know about before I decide.
>
> *Rosa:* That's a good idea. I changed majors three times before settling on communication! Do you live on campus?

For many people, this conversation is so mundane that they can practically "lip-synch" the lines. As I wrote it, I tried to typify the culture shared by Rosa and Robert. If I was successful as a playwright, this conversation required little thought on either of their parts; they acted spontaneously (i.e., following cultural scripts that they have learned so well that they have forgotten that they exist). If asked later, "Did you meet anyone interesting today?" each is likely to name the other. If Robert is asked to describe Rosa, he might say "she's friendly, helpful, and open minded." "How do you know that?" his querulous communication professor might ask persistently, until Robert finally says "Well, I just know! That's how she seemed to me"—or, in other words, by *intuition*.

The spontaneity of conversations such as this derives from the fact that their structure and the rules for who does what when and in what manner are deeply embedded in the culture of the conversants. Because Robert and Rosa are enmeshed in that culture, they are able to grasp almost instantaneously logical connections, moral evaluations, and aesthetic appeals that may resist even their most determined attempt to articulate, and they are able to act in the conversation without giving it any overt thought.

Careful analysis shows that far more than what Robert and Rosa are aware of is going on in this conversation. By their spontaneous ability to put together a pleasant conversation, they have identified each other as sharing a common culture. (This sets them apart from the aforementioned pesky querulous communication professors who ask "How do you know?") They have exchanged what their cultural script defines as the appropriate information on which to base further decisions about whether to continue the conversation or establish a relationship.

However natural this conversation may seem to Rosa and Robert, its coherence derives from a specific cultural context. There are many other cultures in the world with different scripts, frames, and rules. If this conversation were to occur elsewhere and at a different time, the conversation would appear deviant, perhaps shocking, but certainly not as bland as I intended for you to find it. Some of its distinctive features "fit" its specific cultural context.

1. The woman, Rosa, took the initiative in starting a conversation with a man that she did not know. Further, the man, Robert, treated this as normal; he did not take offense or show surprise. In some cultures, Rosa's assertiveness would be unusual, unseemly, and understood as evidence that she is an immoral person.

2. The whole conversation took place without identifying the conversants' families. In fact, Rosa and Robert consistently used only their first names—a practice considered shockingly familiar for a first conversation in some cultures and cripplingly uninformative in others.

3. The conversation assumed that Rosa and Robert were social equals, suitable for any relationship they chose to develop. In many cultures, whether this conversation itself would have occurred depends on their membership in appropriate social or economic categories, and if these were not known from the way they dressed or some such sign, they would certainly seek to discover it in the conversation.

4. Certain things did not occur in the conversation and would probably be considered inappropriate if they did. For example, Rosa did *not* ask: "Are you married?" "What's your gradepoint average?" "How much money do your parents make?" "What's your religion?"

Counterpoint 7.1

American researchers have focused on "initial interactions" as a particularly significant form of conversation. To what extent is this limited to the culture of the researchers?

One study compared Taiwanese and American college students. They found that it is impossible to compare the two conversations directly. The social structure of the United States makes meeting people a frequent and important event; in Taiwan, the most significant meetings are accomplished when both people are introduced by a third person.

Compared with college students in the United States, Taiwanese give relatively little information about themselves. Americans are garrulous and tend to talk freely in the initial conversation about topics that Chinese college students think of as "private" or "too intimate."

However, simple counts of bits of information given in these first encounters is misleading. Because of the social structure, when a Taiwanese is told the other's home town and high school, they know far more about the other than a similarly informed American (Alexander et al. 1986).

As I created them for the sake of this example, Rosa and Robert would find these questions unusual in a conversation with a newly met acquaintance. However, there are cultures in which these questions are normal parts of such conversations. It is not the content of the questions per se, but only their fit into culturally specific patterns of felt moral obligation that make them seem foreign to Robert and Rosa.

If Rosa or Robert had asked each other any of these questions, they would have revealed that they did not share a common culture (or that at least one of them chose not to follow the prescribed patterns for the culture that they shared). This would have produced a very different conversation and a very different response by each of them to the inquisitive communication professor's questions about "What happened in your conversation?" and "How do you know that he or she has those characteristics?"

A Concept of Culture for Interpersonal Communication

Culture is a part of our social worlds. Like other events and objects of our social worlds, it is simultaneously the context of the conversations in which we participate and the product of those conversations.

Culture is depicted in the "atomic model" as one of the multiple contexts for what we do and say in interpersonal communication. Along with speech acts, episodes, relationships, and the self, it frames each successive moment of action in interpersonal communication, imposing elaborate matrices of deontic logics within which we act and evaluate our actions.

The term *culture* is not easy to define precisely. It is used in a family of language games and has no single best definition. Gudykunst and Ting-Toomay (1988, pp. 27–30) took four pages to review various attempts to harness the concept into an acceptable verbal formula, and their own offering is not likely to be taken as definitive. "Culture," they say (p. 30), "is a script or a schema shared by a large group of people. The 'group' on which we focus throughout the book is the nation or society."

The various definitions of culture can be sorted into three groups, depending on whether the definer focuses on cultural artifacts (stone axes, Doric columns, Roman arches, Gothic cathedrals, or modern skyscrapers); collective beliefs (Islam, Christianity, animism, or democracy); or recurring, distinctive scripts or practices (college homecoming celebrations, elections, Thanksgiving, or human sacrifice).

I have come to believe that there *should not be* a definitive definition of culture. Culture is not a "thing" to be defined but something similar to a relationship or a "difference." That is, maybe it is best to think of culture as something like an eddy or a current or "dark." The "dark" is all too visible when you are trying to find your way on a steep hill on a cloudy night, but it disappears as soon as you shine a flashlight on it. Questions like How dark is it? and Where does the dark end and the light begin? are best answered indirectly because the dark shrinks away from the glare of too-intense scrutiny.

Culture is something like that. We learn culture by participating in it, not by studying it. That is, as infants, we are given roles in a particular set of relationships (but not others), are allowed or forced to act in a particular set of episodes (but not others), and are enveloped in a particular set of languages with which to name and comprehend all of this. As infants, we begin to feel our way around in the complex texture of social worlds; after a while, we don't bump into sharp edges quite so frequently—we learn what to expect and are less often surprised (and perhaps less often delighted!), and we begin to take more and more for granted. Culture is precisely this "taken-for-granted" aspect of our social worlds that surround the relationships, identities, or speech acts that we think about.

More useful than a definition is a description of when and why the term *culture* is used. In the preceding chapters, you learned to think of your social worlds as a terrain of conversations, and of yourself as locations within that terrain. To come to grips with culture, now take an Olympian view of this terrain *as if* you were outside it.

This fictitious, privileged perspective is possible because you can watch ethnographic films that depict social worlds in which you cannot participate, you can imagine worlds that have not and will never exist, you can travel and observe conversations in which you have no role, and you can develop the powers of empathy so that you see that even the conversations in which you participate are different if they are experienced from locations that you cannot be in. The first and most important value of these "travelers' tales" is that there are conversations beyond the array of those that you can participate in, that your social worlds have an *end* but that there are social worlds on the *other side* (Pearce and Kang 1988). In other words, your own social worlds are a part of a much larger set of social worlds, some of which you do not know about and many of which you could not enter no matter how hard you tried.

Almost a century ago, an ecologist named von Uexkull (1909) introduced a way of thinking that is useful for dealing with culture. He used the German word *umwelt* to name that part of the physical world that is available as a living space to the members of a species. For example, the sea is part of the *umwelt* of a seal but not that of a wolf, and neither can use the air like a bird. I suspect that neither the seal nor the wolf thinks much about the fact that one of them swims and the other does not, but that fact structures their lives in many ways, not the least of which is that fish are a prime food source for one but pretty much excluded from the diet of the other.

Culture is to social worlds as the *umwelt* is to the material world. Culture is that part of the sum total of humanity's social worlds that are available to groups of conversants as a living space. We know and can move around in our culture; what is outside is unknown and unavailable to us. Culture *sur-*

Refrain 7.1

Two Definitions of Culture

From a third-person perspective: Culture is that part of our social worlds in which we live and can move; that array of conversations in which we know how to participate.

From a first-person perspective: Culture is that part of our social worlds in which we live and can move but of which we are usually unaware; the "frame" for those events and objects that we focus on as the content of our social worlds.

rounds the events and objects on which we focus our attention; it is the context of the contexts in which we find ourselves and into which we act; it is the usually-taken-for-granted background, or *frame*, of our actions.

You are already familiar with Wittgenstein's (1922) statement that "the limits of my language make the limits of my world." But what kind of limits are these? Pearce and Kang (1988) distinguished between "horizons" and "boundaries." Horizons are the natural limits of sight; they mark the end of what can be seen but with no sense of confinement or impediment. That is, they are not *visible* as limits. Boundaries are imposed restrictions; the bars on a cage that mark off distinctions within the array of what we know between where we can go and where we cannot.

The natural state of human beings is to be limited within cultural horizons. We can feel fully free if we can move unimpeded within these horizons because, to put it simplistically, we do not know what we do not know. Horizons are the limits of our social *umwelt*. However, human beings have the ability to expand their social *umwelt* by peeking over those horizons (or, to change the metaphor, to deconstruct their symbols, empathically take the roles of others, imagine other worlds, etc.). When we do, we find ourselves thrust into social worlds for which we are unprepared or aware of social worlds into which we cannot gain admittance. Thus, horizons become boundaries.

Wittgenstein's project was to convert horizons into boundaries, thus freeing us from limits built into our language of which we were unaware. Thus freed, we can avoid repeating old mistakes and develop new ways of acting. In a strange way, the events of the twentieth century have done on a larger scale what Wittgenstein was trying to do for professional philosophers. The tragic wars of the first half of the century created an unprecedented economic and political interdependence among cultures once nearly separated by tradition, mutual choice, and geography. The development of the technologies of moving messages and people easily around the world have created an infrastructure for conversations in which we regularly confront things from

Counterpoint 7.2

In the description of culture as a social *umwelt,* I made extensive use of geographic and spacial metaphors. Treat these as metaphors, that is, sense what they are being used to do without taking them literally. The point I am making is fairly clear within the structure of the metaphor: your "life space" is smaller than the sum total of the past, present, and future life spaces of all human beings. You simply cannot live all the lives that have been lived.

The metaphor breaks down if you treat it literally. What is this notion of *the sum total* of all human life spaces? Who says that our social worlds are best represented spatially? I'm particularly suspicious of the notion implicit in the spacial metaphor that all points in the space are equivalent. In the discussion of heteroglossia and polysemy, I expressed my belief that—to mix metaphors—every *point* in the space of our social worlds is a part of many *dimensions* and that these dimensions are, at least potentially, incommensurate.

Perhaps there are better metaphors. Geertz (1983, p. 30) said that the three major metaphors for culture currently in use are "game," "drama," and "text."

> As "life is a game" proponents tend to gravitate toward face-to-face interaction, courtship and cocktail parties as the most fertile ground for their sort of analysis, and "life is a stage" proponents are attracted toward collective intensities, carnivals and insurrections for the same reason, so "life is a text" proponents incline toward the examination of imaginative forms: jokes, proverbs, popular arts. There is nothing either surprising or reprehensible in this; one naturally tries one's analogies out where they seem most likely to work. But their long-run fates surely rest on their capacity to move beyond their easier initial successes to hard and less predictable ones—of the game idea to make sense of worship, the drama idea to explicate humor, or the text idea to clarify war. (Geertz 1983, p. 33)

Joseph Campbell (1972) said that the events of the twentieth century both require and provide the opportunity for the development of new metaphors by which we can understand ourselves (he cited psychoanalysis as the turn "inward" and the exploration of space as the turn "outward").

I have no interest in defending my use of one of these metaphors instead of another; instead, I invite you to think with whatever metaphor works best for you.

However, the spacial metaphor works well to make the distinction between *boundaries* and *horizons.* For example:

> We are writing at the end of a long New England winter. If we knew only the geography of New England, the "margins" set by the Atlantic to the east, New York City to the south, the Berkshires to the

> west, and the St. Lawrence River to the north would appear to be the
> [horizons] of the world. We would feel free if we could travel unrestricted
> within this area. The idea of "leaving" would never occur to us because
> we do not know of—or believe in—anything outside it. Travelers who
> tell us of warm sun on white beaches with sparkling blue water
> even in the winter (sigh!) seem to us to be telling fairy tales. If they
> insist on being taken literally, we may accuse them of being mali-
> cious or deluded. On the other hand, if we learn that there is a world
> outside New England, with deserts and rain forests and warm
> beaches and coral reefs, then the margins of the region function as
> [boundaries] rather than [horizons]. Our sense of freedom vanishes unless
> we can travel outside the limits. Unrestricted regional travel, which
> gives us freedom within [horizons], is frustrating confinement within
> [boundaries]. (Pearce and Kang 1988, p. 22)

beyond our cultural horizons. In the process, those horizons are transmuted
into boundaries, and we have to decide whether to be content within our
cages or to expand our social *umwelt*. Either choice has important consequences, and the decision warrants a consideration of the role of culture in
interpersonal communication.

Culture Is Normally Invisible

By definition, what is prefigured by our culture appears "normal" to us.
Culture consists of those resources that we use to "normalize" our perceptions
and our actions. *Other people's cultures* are visible. *They* eat strange foods with
funny utensils, laugh at jokes that we don't understand, and miss the point
of our clever witticisms. *They* show up at the wrong time for appointments
without even the decency to apologize. On the other hand, *our* actions are
"natural," "normal," and "decent." (Curiously, they say the same thing
about us!)

In the quotation with which I began this chapter, Gudykunst and Ting-
Toomay reported that researchers usually study communication in "a cultural
vacuum." Although their point is clear, their metaphor is not the best. Neither
interpersonal communication nor research about it can occur in a cultural
vacuum; in fact, I cannot imagine what a cultural vacuum might be. What
Gudykunst and Ting-Toomay *meant* to say, I think, is that most researchers
do not specify the cultural context in which interpersonal communication
occurs; like the people they study, researchers think, act, and write in the
context of cultural patterns of which they are unaware and which they do
not focus on in their descriptions. Most interpersonal communication (and
most research about it) occurs within unnoticed and hence unremarked cultural frames that tacitly determine its shape.

Two Ways of Discovering Culture

An educated person (as opposed to one who has extensive "training") is distinguished, among other things, by an awareness of the sources and limitations of what he or she knows. One part of this quality is an awareness that we have cultural horizons. At least the awareness that, for example, not everyone observes the same religious or national holidays that we do or share a fondness for the same cultural symbols as we do facilitates communicating with people who have different cultural parameters than ours. Even if we are going to communicate primarily with people who share our culture, if we are going to engage in *game mastery*, we need to know what the rules are so that we can change them. With an awareness of our cultural horizons, we can seek out and converse with those who are not like us and glean the benefits of new perspectives on our own form of life and opening up new vistas for our amusement, edification, and aesthetic pleasure.

But *how* can we discover our cultural horizons? They are the most elusive parts of our social worlds. There are two proven ways.

By contrast.   In contrasting our culture with others, we hold our own taken-for-granted perception up against some other, and in the process we gain a sudden, vivid, and sometimes transforming awareness of the particularities of our culture. This discovery of our own culture breaks us out of "normalcy"; it is as if a wolf suddenly realized that his evolution of pelt and paws barred him from swimming in the sea like a seal, or if a seal were suddenly to see how the evolution of flippers forever prevented him from running miles in the woods like a wolf.

We have experiences like these when we discover the differences between our culture and those of other people. In my culture, being late for a meeting is considered rude—it requires an apology and an explanation. The extent to which my culture is structured by the mechanical computation of time is a discovery I made while working with people from other cultures in which promptness is not a virtue and minutes or hours are not the primary measure for activities. This lead to a greater discovery that my culture has a particular sense of time that is strikingly different from some others: it views time as linear, moving from one place to another, and as a commodity that is to be "spent" and not "wasted." No matter how natural this concept of time is to me, it is certainly not universal.

There are many ways to discover your own culture by contrast. Take a long, overseas vacation in which you live and work with people from other cultures. If you do not have the resources to do this, make friends with people from a different national, ethnic, or religious heritage than your own. In addition, take courses in cultural anthropology or "area studies" courses about parts of the world about which you know very little. Make a point to watch foreign movies; watch ethnographic films; and read books about and by authors from cultures different from your own. As you do, you get a double education. First, you learn about other people, places, and things. Second, by contrasting your own culture with theirs, you learn about your own.

By experiencing cultural change.   You do not have to travel to exotic places to contrast your culture with that of another. The dynamic forces in contemporary society are sufficiently powerful that they create cultural change rapidly, that is, within a normal lifespan.

Perhaps there was a time when only immigrants enlarged their cultural horizons. However, the pace of change is now so rapid that modernity makes immigrants of us all; all that you have to do to experience cultural change is wait for a bit.

I have no idea of what cultural changes you have experienced and will experience in your life, but I feel very confident in predicting that you have adapted or will have to adapt to a culture that has changed around you.

Counterpoint 7.3

"Progress" is one of the central beliefs in Western culture. Nisbett (1980, p. 8) wrote

The history of all that is greatest in the West . . . is grounded deeply in the belief that what one does in one's own time is at once tribute to the greatness and indispensability of the past, and confidence in an ever more golden future. . . . I remain convinced that this idea has done more good over a 2500-year period, led to more creativeness in more spheres, and given more strength to human hope and to individual desire for improvement than any other single idea in Western history.

After such a valedictory, we are dashed to read Nisbett's (1980, p. 9) dire observation that "Everything now suggests, however, that Western faith in the dogma of progress is waning rapidly . . ."

When the belief in progress is coupled with the powerful instruments of social change as they have been since the industrial revolution, the rate of change is increased. If we use a human life span as the measure, then the rate of change is rapid; that is, human beings may reasonably expect to see a new product, idea, or fashion come into being (as something "new"), mature (become something "old"), and be replaced by something else that is celebrated as being "new."

Pearce (1989, p. 145) described this pattern as the "strange loop of modernity." If you follow the arrows in Figure 7.1, you trace the cycle of novelty, obsolescence, and replacement. The length of time that it takes for something to go through this whole cycle is its "period." If the periods are sufficiently short, even the most committed modernists begin to recognize that they have gone around this path before.

Truth is rational

Change counts as progress

Self-worth is achieved by being the agent of change

The strange loop of modernity.

Figure 7.1
*The strange loop of
modernity (From
Pearce, 1989, p. 145)*

One of the consequences of the strange loop of modernity is that values are destroyed. That is, the value of any object has to do with its novelty; "old" is bad, and "new" is good. But novelty does not adhere in the object, only in its placement within a time sequence. As a result, no thing (and I think the play on words—nothing—is appropriate) has value other than that derived from its place within the strange loop.

The following description of the culture of people who write interpersonal communication textbooks may give you an analogy that you can use to understand your own experiences.

Gudykunst and Ting-Toomay's (1988, p. 17) description of the cultural vacuum in which books about interpersonal communication have been written is an accurate assessment. Until recently, the scholarly literature about interpersonal communication has said very little about culture. More specifically, it has silently assumed and thus unwittingly reproduced the cultural assumptions of the culture of those who wrote it: they are mostly male, predominantly white, upper-lower or middle class, and almost exclusively enmeshed in the culture of middle and late twentieth century United States.

History has a way of playing jokes at the expense of those who grow too comfortable within their cultural horizons, and so it has been in the study of interpersonal communication. We have not so much "discovered" culture as we have had it forced on our attention by the not-so-gentle blows of social and political events.

Thirty years ago, the analysis of Rosa and Robert's initial interaction would not have extended so far as to implicate their culture. For example, Watzlawick et al.'s (1967) concept that there were *two* levels of meaning in conversations—*content* and *relationship*—was a major and controversial innovation. However, as more research was done, we discovered that conversants' ability to participate in conversations like these is specific to their cultures. This became obvious, in part, because the white, male, United States culture was undergoing radical changes that showed up both in the practices of our subjects and in those of the researchers.

Take 1962 as a bench mark year for comparison with the present. It was in this year that Rosa Parks, a tired African-American woman riding home from work, refused to stand in the back of the bus so that white passengers could sit in the front. Sadly, if you had a "state-of-the-art" education in interpersonal communication in 1962 and wanted to do an analysis of this event from a communication perspective, you would probably not get to the issues that would have sensitized you to the civil rights movement and the rest of the cultural revolution of the 1960s.

Prior to 1962, interpersonal communication textbooks and research—like the society in which they existed—could be characterized like this.

1. They assumed a culturally homogeneous society. That society was white, Anglo-Saxon, and Protestant; they spoke English as their only language. Of course, non-WASPS and non-English speakers existed, but they did so as "others." They were identified by their differences from the norm and left to find their own way of getting around in society. For example, traffic signs, high school classrooms, and public announcements were made only in English, and minority groups were "acceptable" based on how closely they approximated the characteristics of the "stories told" by WASPs about themselves.

2. They assumed that everyone shared a common rationality. That is, that there is one "right" way of reasoning, and anyone who does not draw the same conclusions from the same evidence is either a knave or a fool. Students were taught what counted as persuasive evidence, making no allowance for cultural difference in what counts as "evidence," much less what counts as "persuasion." That is, everyone was expected to perform the same conversational implications, to use the same array of accounts, to punctuate episodes similarly, and to do "face-work" in the same manner.

3. They assumed that the contexts in which people acted were stable. That is, particular acts could be evaluated on the basis of how well they fit the requirements of specific situations, and those situations were not expected to change. Etiquette books as well as manuals on how to win friends and influence people prescribed how to dress, speak, and think "properly" and "effectively." This assumption was institutionalized in a particular form of deontic logic that paralleled the categorical syllogism. That is, if the actions of particular individuals did not fit what was prefigured by the established contexts of relationships, episodes, and selves, the individuals—not the contexts—were at fault. The goals of discipline, law and order, education, and therapy were to help wayward individuals fit into established contexts.

4. They assumed that the locus of social action was the individual, and that individuals (each of us, separately) are autonomous, cognitive entities who possess certain rights and live in an objective world of events and objects.

The obvious tension between this assumption of radical individualism and the strong contextualism in #3 earlier was bridged by an ethic of responsibility. It was considered the moral responsibility of individuals to discern the common rationality (#2) within the horizons of a common culture (#1) so that each person would hold themselves responsible for "fitting in" to the established contexts. Individuals who did not fit in were not considered as evidence that might call the first, second, or third assumptions into question, but as morally irresponsible persons who should be admonished.

Around 30 years later, American culture has changed and so have interpersonal textbooks and research. Both are far more aware of culture, and are sensitive to their specific cultural patterns as well as to their horizons. In addition to being more aware of culture, contemporary American culture includes a set of assumptions that specifically deny each of those listed earlier, and these are prominently featured in interpersonal communication textbooks. Specifically:

1. We live in a culturally diverse society in which "we" are many different things. When thought of all together, we are a "collage" or "motley" rather than either a single cultural group or a homogeneous intercultural group. This statement simply recognizes that we Americans come from many different cultural backgrounds and that the "melting pot" is a poor metaphor for our cultural experience in this country. In addition, we live in an increasingly interdependent world in which military, economic, and political alliances, as well as our mutual participation in the ecology, prevent us from constructing sharp boundaries around any homogeneous notion of who "we" are.

2. There are many rationalities and sets of values that cannot be reduced to some common denominator or forced to fit, or agree, with one another. As people communicate with each other within these rationalities, they produce many mutually exclusive stories, each of which contain powerful ethical imperatives for action, which surround any given situation. For example, the five hundredth anniversary of the arrival of the Europeans in the Americas is no longer an unchallenged celebration of the discovery of a "new world" by the inhabitants of Europe. Native Americans say that they discovered Columbus, not the other way around. (That is, *he* was lost, not them!) African Americans and Hispanics find little place for themselves in the sacred story of the Pilgrims who fled England for Massachusetts to escape religious persecution—their story has a different plot with different heroes, villains, and motives. In 1992, Columbus's journey was remembered in many communities during "commemorations" (rather than "celebrations") of the encounter between two worlds (rather than the discovery of one by the other).

3. The situations in which conversations occur are not only not stable, they are inherently open ended. We have become sufficiently experienced with change to realize that even the most sincere efforts to replicate the status

quo may bring about a transformation in the episodes, relationships, and identities that comprise our social worlds. We now regularly think not only of how our actions fit existing situations but how they will create new ones. We even have access to a set of evaluative terms that criticize people who "fit in" to situations in which they should not. These include being "co-opted," "oppressed," and "mystified," as well as "copping-out."

4. The locus of action is seen as interpersonal systems that co-construct reality. In business, we look at the economic system as well as individual virtues as the explanation of success or failure. Clusters of conversations are seen as the substance of families and organizations, and the characteristics of those conversations as the difference between better or worse performances. We are at least beginning to develop a vocabulary that permits us to describe co-constructed entities and actions—although we have a long way to go.

This comparison shows that American culture has changed in some important ways in the past 30 years. One result of these changes is an increased awareness of culture per se that is reflected in interpersonal communication textbooks. You will certainly experience cultural changes that will sensitize you to specific features of your culture and will require you to adopt new ways of conversing.

Counterpoint 7.4

Newspaper columnist William Pfaff (1992, p. 3) noted that the 1992 Presidential elections contrasted two "worlds." President Bush came of age in an America that

> *was white, provincial in its attitudes, Protestant and closely attached to a rural past. . . . The norms of society were Protestant, and this was taken for granted by the rest, who usually tried to assimilate themselves to the majority, internalizing the discrimination, proudly putting forward their successes—their ballplayers, boxers, Medal of Honor winners, etc., as evidence that Catholics and Jews could be "good" Americans too . . .*

Bill Clinton was a generation younger and came to age in a very different world. The cultural frame that his age cohort brought into conversations about the draft, "character," "family values," and the role of the government in dealing with the economy differed greatly from that of President Bush's age group. This is not to say that all the "baby boomers" agreed with Clinton or that all of the World War II veterans agreed with or voted for Bush, but it does show that within the lifetime of people who went to the polls in November 1992, there had been a major cultural change, and that one part of that cultural change is an explicit recognition of cultural diversity.

> *The United States in which Bill Clinton came of age was by contrast one of the deepest doubts: about a particular war, and foreign relationships and threats in general; about the credibility of the nation's democracy, the justice of relations between races and classes at home . . .*

Pfaff noted that the "integrative forces" of this "new country" are those of "popular communication and entertainment rather than conscious instruction, or felt family or community continuities." Like many thoughtful observers, he wondered if these integrative forces are sufficient to establish a nation's "dynamic center, its integrative culture and tradition," but it is, he notes, the new reality with which we have to deal.

Communication and the Family: A Case Study of Cultural Change

The patterns of conversations within families are, some argue, the most important in our social worlds. They comprise the matrix of conversations into which we were born and nurtured as infants, in which our children will find themselves and their deontic logics of action and meaning, and in which many of the most important decisions of our lives will be made. However, all families are not alike, and in the United States, there has been a great deal of change.

In the 1992 Republican National Convention, the phrase "family values" was suggested as a political rallying cry. It quickly became apparent that there was little consensus on what values were included under that banner; even the definition of what comprised a family seemed controversial.

Let's rejoin Rosa and Robert some time after their first meeting.

> *Robert:* Rosa, let's get married and have a family.
> *Rosa:* That's an interesting suggestion, Robert. What kind of family do you have in mind?
> *Robert (stunned):* What? A *family!* You know, me, you, some kids.
> *Rosa (determined):* No. Before I agree to marry you, I want to know what I am getting into. Will this be a traditional family, an extended family, a companionate family, a professional family, or a dual career family?
> *Robert:* Rosa, what have you been reading?

Although this is an unlikely conversation, it makes the point that contemporary U.S. society includes various types of families, and that they place very different conversational and relational demands on their members.

Six types of families were identified by Dizard and Gadlin (1984). Like the languages of self, these types of families arose within particular historical and material conditions; Dizard and Gadlin interpret them as responding to particular patterns of work, production, and consumption—that is, "the marketplace."

Traditional families are large and complex; the husband-wife-children node are intermeshed within a dense network of kinship relations. The family is the site of most of the work by which it produces its livelihood—think of the "family farm," in which the workplace and the home are the same. The needs and desires of individuals, and even the relationship between husband and wife, are routinely subordinated to the economic and social necessities of the larger family. From a communication perspective, such families are comprised of interlocking conversations in which decisions are made by the elders, in which solidarity prevails over individuality or creativity, and in which the horizons of the culture are firmly held in place by a resolute determination to ward off "threats." A contemporary example of traditional family structure may be found in Minnesota among the Mennonites, or in Pennsylvania, among the Amish.

The development of an urban, industrial society changed the circumstances in which families existed. In more and more families, the workplace is separate from the home. People leave the family to "go to work," exchange work for goods, and return with them to the family.

According to Dizard and Gadlin (pp. 288, 289), the *expanded family* was created by poverty in a modern economy. "Like the traditional family, relations with kin are intense and extensive, often competing directly with ties between spouses. Unlike the traditional family, however, marriages tend to be quite unstable, largely because under modern, urban, industrial conditions the male head of household is a problematic figure. Stripped of the capacity to earn a living, males tend to become peripheral and females tend to dominate the family network." The stability—and "whatever comfort, joy, and strength there is to be found among the poor in our society" (Dizard and Gadlin, 1984, p. 189)—in extended families come from conversations among kin rather than from the husband-wife bonding.

The *companionate family* is characterized by its relative autonomy from kin; its primary relationship is between spouses, who are supposed to be "best friends" and share activities and feelings. Parents seek to become companions to their children. "Ties to relatives are present and strong, especially to immediate relatives, but unlike the traditional and the expanded families, households are decidedly not permeable: the home is for the nuclear family. Relatives can visit but are not expected to remain. Children are rarely moved from one household to another as personal circumstances and economic exigencies change" (Dizard and Gadlin 1984, p. 290).

The communication demands in the companionate family are quite strong. The primary dyad—wife and husband—must provide for each other the mutuality and support that was supplied by a diverse set of kinfolk in traditional families. Moreover, each family member must balance the rival demands of work outside the home and relational demands or opportunities inside the home. "For the companionship to flourish, especially after the first romantic blushes have faded" (whatever that might mean!), Dizard and Gadlin (1984, p. 190) observed, "at least two conditions must be met: the couple must be able to spend considerable time together and husband and wife must see one another as substantively equal . . . both conditions are difficult to sustain over time, making the companionate family less stable than it might otherwise be."

The tensions in the companionate family lead to various responses. Think of the familiar conversations that construct each of these responses (and note how many soap opera plot lines are contained in this brief list!):

> *Some families drift back toward an involvement with kin, back toward an assertion of traditional patterns. Others strive for even greater involvement in the marketplace, making a virtue of the separation of husband and wife roles. Others find themselves in tumultuous relationships. Still others hang on and make do, maintaining respectability and suffering stoically the absence of involvement and affection that follows the decline of companionship. (Dizard and Gadlin 1984, p. 291)*

The *professional family* is one way of resolving the tension between kin and marketplace. "The professionalized family looks like the companionate family with one crucial difference: it is largely organized around the principal task of maintaining the husband's high level of occupational commitment" (Dizard and Gadlin 1984, p. 291). Professional families are mobile, with shallow roots in communities, and its ties to kin are subordinate to career contingencies.

Women were not likely to be long satisfied with the role offered them in the professional family, and, Dizard and Gadlin argue, their dissatisfaction led to the women's movement and to the development of yet another type of family, the *dual-career family*. In addition, the children in such families provided much of the energy behind the "counter-culture" movement of the 1960s and 1970s.

Dual-career families are highly mobile and stress the autonomy of the people in them. As a result, they are often terminated in divorce. Deeply enmeshed in the marketplace, members of these families often feel that the demands of family life outweigh the rewards.

The deliberate weighing of the costs and rewards of relationships in the context of a materialistic, affluent society has produced yet another kind of "family": *singles*. Many singles have children, networks of friends, and careers. This family has been most prominently portrayed on the television show "Murphy Brown," where it served as an example of what former Vice President Dan Quayle saw as the deterioration of "family values."

Intercultural Communication: A Special Case of Interpersonal Communication

All interpersonal communication occurs within the context of culture. However, in most conversations, the cultural context is invisible; the limits of the conversants' social *umwelt* are treated as horizons rather than as boundaries. Let *"intercultural communication"* refer to conversations in which the "limits" of the conversants' social *umwelt are* visible, in which they are treated as boundaries.

Intercultural communication is not necessarily exotic; these conversations do not have to involve folks with strange customs or different skin colors. When Columbus splashed ashore on that Caribbean island and encountered the people who lived there, their conversation was clearly intercultural—their *umwelt* included different material cultures, different ideological cultures, different routinized practices, and even different languages. However, intercultural communication can occur among people who look alike and speak the "same" language.

The more common definition of intercultural communication focuses on the background of the interlocutors. In this way of thinking, intercultural communication occurs when a Kenyan converses with a Briton. In my way of thinking, we do not know whether the conversation between the Kenyan and the Briton is intercultural simply on the basis of their background. Kenyans and Britons can talk for years without becoming aware of their cultural limits—that is, without converting their cultural horizons into cultural boundaries. For example, if both continue to act according to the script for how one should speak to the other, they can coordinate their conversations without learning much about the other or anything about themselves. On the other hand, intercultural communication can occur in a conversation between neighbors or even siblings if they do encounter their horizons as boundaries.

Think with me about a conversation between Ann Swidler and Barry Palmer (Bellah et al. 1985). I believe that this was an asymmetric conversation in which Palmer communicated interculturally but Swidler did not. This conversation was presented as part of the "data" on which some important conclusions about contemporary American life were based. Swidler and her colleagues argued that contemporary Americans' first moral language is "individualism," and that this moral language is incapable of sustaining the public order (pp. 20, 161, 163). They urged a renewal of "biblical" and "civic republican" moral languages as a way of keeping individualism in check, trusting that individualism will limit the tendencies of these languages to sanction discrimination and oppression. Both the conclusions and the evidence on which they are based have elicited quite a bit of attention.

The research included a series of semistructured interviews with ordinary Americans. Of course, "research interviews" are just a form of conversation, and we can understand them as we would any other conversation.

Counterpoint 7.5

When Columbus crossed the Atlantic, he started a long conversation among the cultures of different continents. Robert M. Pirsig (1991, p. 46) claimed that the "character" of the American cowboy is a rendition of Native American values, and that American culture is a mixture of European and Native American values. In making this claim, Pirsig underestimates the influence of African and, more recently, Asian values in order to stress the distinctive and, in his judgment, usually disregarded effect of Native American culture. Perhaps because European languages and material culture have dominated, we often ignore how much the European cultures learned from, and were changed by, their contacts with Native American cultures.

Columbus in India primo appellens, magnis excipitur muneribus ab Incolis. IX.

Intercultural communication. Columbus discovers America and confronts the "Indians." Or is it that the Native Americans discover Columbus? Either way, this meeting brought a new level of consciousness about both cultures.

Refrain 7.2

Cultural communication: conversations in which the participants are not aware of their cultural horizons; these conversations almost always repeat normal patterns and reproduce the social worlds in which they occur.

Intercultural communication: conversations in which the participants are aware of their cultural horizons; these conversations are usually perceived as rupturing the taken-for-granted surroundings of the social worlds in which they occur.

The interviews focused on moral choices that people made: Why do you work? Why did you change jobs? Why did you marry and start a family? The researchers "did not seek to impose our ideas on those with whom we talked" but they "did attempt to uncover assumptions, to make explicit what the person we were talking to might rather have left implicit. The interview as we employed it was active, Socratic" (p. 304).

The researchers believed that the interviews revealed the horizons of the respondents' cultures. They found that the ordinary Americans with whom they talked were soon rendered unable to articulate good reasons why they made the moral choices that determined the course of their lives.

Ann Swidler was "trying to get Brian Palmer to clarify the basis of his moral judgments." Mr. Palmer had said that "lying is one of the things I want to regulate."

Swidler: Why?

Palmer: Well, it's a kind of thing that is a habit you get into. Kind of self-perpetuating. It's like digging a hole. You just keep digging and digging.

Swidler: So why is it wrong?

Palmer: Why is integrity important and lying bad? I don't know. It just is. It's just so basic. I don't want to be bothered with challenging that. It's part of me. I don't know where it came from, but it's very important.

Swidler: When you think about what's right and what's wrong, are things bad because they are bad for people, or are they right or wrong in themselves, and if so how do you know?

Palmer: Well, some things are bad because . . . I guess I feel like everybody on this planet is entitled to have a little bit of space, and things that detract from other people's space are kind of bad . . . (Bellah et al. 1985, pp. 304, 305).

Swidler and the others interpreted this conversation as showing that Brian Palmer lacked a sufficiently powerful moral language; that when confronted by a "Socratic" interlocutor, he was quickly reduced to incoherent babbling ("I don't know. It just is." "I guess I feel that everyone on this planet is entitled to have a little bit of space . . ."). They characterized Palmer as using the moral language of individualism that they believe is rampant in the popular culture of the United States but is philosophically defective.

In his analysis of Swidler's report of this conversation, Stout (1988, p. 194) suggested that the Socratic interview method is not necessarily the best tool for uncovering people's reasons. At its best, the Socratic method engages both interviewer and the interviewed in a conversation that leads to unexpected self-understandings. At its worse, the persistent queries *Why?* or How do you know that? can be a tool for intellectual bullying; it relentlessly continues until the person interviewed "either becomes confused or starts sounding suspiciously like a philosopher." Stout (1988, pp. 35, 36) warned that

> *there are many propositions that we are justified in believing but wouldn't know how to justify. Anything we could say on behalf of such a proposition seems less certain that the proposition itself. By now, it is hard to debate with flat-earthers. What real doubt do they have that can be addressed with justifying reasons? . . .* we ought to be suspicious of people who want reasons even when they can't supply reasonable doubts *(emphasis added)*.

This is what happened to Brian Palmer. "When Brian says that the wrongness of lying is basic," Stout (1988, p. 195) suggested, what he means is that "he can't think of anything more certain than the wrongness of lying that might be introduced to support the idea that lying is wrong. He'd rather not be bothered with the sort of challenge that the question implies. . . . But his interviewer won't stop."

Because our social worlds are heteroglossic, *all* conversations are *potentially* "intercultural." The cultural *umwelt* of different interlocutors is never completely identical; if the conversation continues long enough or if they probe each other's background understandings deeply enough, they will reach the horizons of their culture. Differences in our social worlds are very apparent when one conversant is from a different country or ethnicity than the other, but none of us could ever find ourselves in precisely the same nexus of social worlds as anyone else. Most of the time, these cultural differences are not important for the purposes of conducting the conversation, and we communicate in ways described here as "deeply enmeshed in our culture." We assume that our interlocutor shares the same cultural surroundings for the conversation that we do, and often this assumption is good enough. However, in some instances, we come to the horizon of the culture of one or more conversants—that is what happened in the conversation between Swidler and

Palmer. Swidler's Socratic questioning pushed Palmer to the limit of his culture and demanded that he respond.

Intercultural communication can be fun, frustrating, and illuminating. In this instance, it was an oppressive use of *linguistic tyranny*. In effect, Swidler was demanding that Palmer give her—in *her* own language, not *his*—reasons that *she* would find acceptable for *him* believing that lying is bad. This is altogether a different thing from finding out in *his* language the reason that *he* finds acceptable for his beliefs.

The meaning of Palmer's explanation of why lying is bad—"I don't know. It just is."—depends on the concept of communication that we use to interpret it. If we assume that communication is a means of representing Palmer's "intrapsychic state" (that is, meanings inside his head), then we should understand him as saying that his head is empty. This seems rather unlikely: Palmer is a middle-aged man who has been successful in business, whose first marriage failed but who has remarried and is thoughtfully restructuring his life to make sure that his second marriage succeeds—hardly the history of an empty mind. On the other hand, if we understand communication as a way of making and doing something, then Palmer's statement describes his present location within his social worlds; it locates him at a particular point in a matrix of rights and responsibilities. It says that, for him, now, this is the commitment that he has made. Stout (p. 195) muses, "Evidently . . . Brian doesn't know how to answer questions that aren't connected to real doubts . . . he can't think of anything more certain than the wrongness of lying that might be introduced to support the idea that lying is wrong."

Palmer's answer does not satisfy Swidler, and she pursues him, demanding that he respond within her language game. Her language game uses the pattern of the categorical syllogism as the frame to reconstruct his logic: give me an abstract statement of a principle by which we can judge lying to be wrong, she insists, and Palmer gamely tried: "I guess I feel that everyone on this planet . . ."

Palmer's *first* response to Swidler's challenge to justify his judgment that integrity is good and lying is bad was to say, "It just is. It's just so basic. I don't want to be bothered with challenging that. It's part of me." Deeply enmeshed in the culture of the Aristotelian philosophical tradition, Swidler did not even hear this as an answer. However, as Stout (pp. 195, 196) noted, Palmer's answer is quite satisfactory—even an eloquent moral statement—in the culture shaped by the philosophic tradition of Wittgenstein and the American pragmatists. Unlike the cultural assumptions surrounding Swidler's Socratic method, this tradition is content grounding moral certainty in the experience of the speaker rather than in abstract principles suitable for writing on God's Own Chalkboard in the Sky. In fact, when Palmer is describing his experience without Swidler's relentless Socratic probing, he uses a moral vocabulary of reciprocity, involvement, shared goals, and mutual respect. The lame individualism expressed in his *second* attempt to satisfy his interrogator,

Stout (p. 196) concluded, is certainly not his "first moral language" but "his language of last resort—a set of slogans he reaches for (with obvious reluctance) when somebody won't take storytelling or unprincipled talk of habit and happiness as sufficient for the purposes of justification."

Swidler bullied Palmer by means of *linguistic tyranny*. She demanded that he describe his morality in her terms, and then she judged his performance according to her standards. What horizons of her own culture prevented her from hearing and accepting Palmer's clear statement that he did not "want to be bothered with challenging" his judgments that "integrity [is] important and lying bad"? Why did this conversation not confront her with these aspects of her own culture?

After the interview, Swidler changed from interlocutor to author; in this role, she took over Palmer's voice and, in a widely read book, said

> *His description of his reasons for changing his life and of his current happiness seems to come down mainly to a shift in his notions of what would make him happy. His new goal—devotion to marriage and children—seems as arbitrary and unexamined as his earlier pursuit of material success. Both are justified as idiosyncratic prefer- ence rather than as representing a larger sense of the purpose of life.* (Bellah et al., p. 6)

Swidler demanded that any moral language must give *reasons* that represent a larger sense of the purpose of life, that is, moral principles that have the form "One ought always to . . ." Instead, Palmer offered a *narrative* of his own life, saying in effect, I have lived in two ways, the first made me unhappy, and I responded by changing my form of life (e.g., by trying to take control of lying), and the second form of life makes me happy. For him, that is a sufficient answer unless Swidler—or the slings and arrows of outrageous fortune—bring him reasons to doubt what he is experiencing.

Counterpoint 7.6

Regardless of what Swidler intended to do in her conversation with Palmer, there came a point where his voice ended and hers took over. When she and her colleagues wrote *Habits of the Heart,* they did to Palmer what I am now doing to both: putting *their* words into *my contexts* of interpretation and presentation. Whatever else that does, it drastically reduces their ability to "speak back" and to "speak for themselves." How will Swidler answer my interpretation of this conversation to you? To whom and in what context will Palmer articulate his side of what happened?

One of the most fascinating issues in social science is that of saying something useful about other people and other cultures without disempowering them. Social scientists have become very sensitive to the dangers of *linguistic tyranny,* recognizing that when "we" put what "they" are up to in "our ways of putting things," we have imposed our interpretive and evaluative criteria and thus changed what we are describing.

This isn't a new discovery, of course. Almost anyone who has been quoted in a newspaper story understands that what was said (in the context in which it was said, in the tone of voice in which it was uttered) is different from what was quoted (in a different context, in cold impersonal print).

Forget about "accuracy." There is no way in which "we" can ever "accurately" reproduce what occurred because we would have to reproduce the whole context of the original event, including the fact that it was the original event and not a retelling of it. It can't be done.

In many conversations, you will be asked to—or will want to—describe what happened in a particular time or place, or recount what someone said. How can you do this in a manner that respects the other person? Those who have wrestled with this have come up with three ways: quotation, translation, and interlocution.

Quotation involves saying just what the other person said. However, there is no way to reproduce it exactly. If I *write* the words that you *said,* I have distorted them tremendously. If I play an audio or video tape recording of what you said, I am still playing it into a context other than the one in which you spoke.

Translation "is not a simple recasting of others' ways of putting things in terms of our own ways of putting them (i.e., the kind in which things get lost), but displaying the logic of their ways of putting them in the locutions of ours; a conception which . . . brings it rather closer to what a critic does to illumine a poem than what an astronomer does to account for a star" (Geertz 1983, p. 10). Translations may consist of a paraphrase or a description. "Experience-near" descriptions are close accounts of what happened, giving as much as possible a feeling of being a participant; "experience-distant" descriptions are much more abstract, using the most powerful words in our vocabulary to establish an interpretive frame. A hand-held camera showing what an exotic ritual (such as professional football) looks like from the perspective of a player is an "experience-near" translation; a scholarly treatise on ritualized sublimated aggression as manifested in football is an "experience-distant" translation.

Interlocution involves engaging in conversation with the person whose voice is being appropriated. For example, an ethnography that uses interlocution will record conversations between the ethnographer and the people being studied, including the subjects' reactions to what the ethnographer wrote about them.

Swidler first quoted Palmer, then gave an experience-distant translation of his moral language ("individualism"). An interlocution would have included Palmer's reaction to what Swidler wrote about him.

We are constantly representing what other people said and did. Make a record of these events, and identify whether the representation was a quotation, translation, or interlocution. Which of these modes of representation gives the person represented most power? Which gives the least? Which is the most frequently used?

This conversation resulted in Palmer's being bullied into saying some foolish things. It was an asymmetric intercultural conversation because Palmer, but not Swidler, was forced to confront the horizons of his culture. We can only wonder how Palmer felt when he read Swidler's account of the moral poverty of his successful and happy marriage, and of the decisions that he made to restructure his life.

Fortunately, not all instances of intercultural communication come out so badly. Often the experience of being brought to the horizons of your culture is the means of self-discovery, an opportunity for the exercise of curiosity, the occasion of the pleasures of exploration, and, simply put, fun.

Culture and Interpersonal Communication

Recall Gergen's (1991) description of "postmodern" society in which there are many different languages of self. Now we are in a position to see that Gergen was right as far as he went, but that the plurality of logics of meaning and action extend beyond languages of self. They include all aspects of culture, such as speech acts, episodes, and relationships.

Living a life, establishing relationships, moving effectively in the social settings that we encounter, and simply having a conversation is made more challenging by the plurality of cultures. Geertz (1986, p. 122) characterized the social and material conditions at the end of the twentieth century as a "collage" and argued that life in a collage requires special skills. To live in a collage, he argued, requires special skills.

> One must in the first place render oneself capable of sorting out its elements, determining what they are (which usually involves determining where they come from and what they amounted to when they were there) and how, practically, they relate to one another, without at the same time blurring one's own sense of one's own location and one's own identity within it.

The combination of these skills avoids the twin dangers of losing one's self in the pluralism of multiple cultures (what Geertz calls "cosmopolitanism without content") and of treating one's own culture as if all others were inferior ("parochialism without tears").

When we do encounter the horizons of our own culture (from the inside, of course), we have several options. One is to shore up the boundaries of our culture, marking the limits of our social worlds and remaining in them. A second option is to import materials from "outside," enriching who we are and what we know. A third is to extend those boundaries. Geertz (1986, pp. 113, 114) noted that

> *the reach of our minds, the range of signs we can manage somehow to interpret, is what defines the intellectual, emotional and moral space within which we live. The greater that is, the greater we can make it become by trying to understand what flat earthers or the Reverend Jim Jones . . . are all about . . . the clearer we become to ourselves. . . .*
>
> *It is the asymmetries . . . between what we believe or feel and what others do, that make it possible to locate where we now are in the world, how it feels to be there, and where we might or might not want to go. To obscure those gaps and those asymmetries by relegating them to a realm of repressible or ignorable difference, mere unlikeness . . . is to cut us off from such knowledge and such possibility: the possibility of quite literally, and quite thoroughly, changing our minds.*

Interpersonal communication in a culturally diverse society is rich with both promise and peril. It means that every conversation may become intercultural—that is, that we might at any moment be brought unexpectedly to the horizon of our culture. It means that we must find a way of dealing with people whose cultural horizons differ from ours when we attempt to decide whether to raise taxes or reduce services, or whether to build new highways or invest in public transit systems. Moreover, it means that we risk running into the limits of our languages when we talk about such mundane matters as the responsibilities a son has to his father (clearly different in different kinds of families), the ways in which men and women communicate, or the assessment of responsibility in an urban riot.

What communication skills enable us to converse within a culturally diverse society? How do these skills differ from those that suffice for conversations that are "deeply enmeshed" in a stable culture? Here are four observations—two "negative" and two "positive"—about intercultural communication.

Distrust Intuition

Most of our conversations find us "mindless," simply acting naturally and spontaneously. If pressed to explain how we know, for example, that our interlocutor is telling the truth or lying, we say that we know it "intuitively," or we protest that "everybody" knows what we have perceived.

Counterpoint 7.7

We make judgments about important things on the basis of our intuitions. These judgments consist of the application of a great deal of cultural knowledge to specific cases. Your decision that this man is trustworthy is based on many subtle observations of his nonverbal cues as well as a series of stereotypes that you have developed. This knowledge looks foolish when it is expressed in sentences. For example, "All men with little beady eyes are devious and cannot be trusted" seems silly. However, such intuitive judgments are absolutely essential (we cannot explore the full personality of every person we meet on the street) and important (if we misjudge, we may lose our lunch, our fortunes, or our lives).

Is this man telling the truth?

What does "intuitively" mean? I do not believe that intuition is a separate means of perception, but at the same time I believe that there is a phenomenon that we sometimes label *intuition*. We know something intuitively when we think with the taken-for-granted parts of our culture that surround the event in which we are participating. Such thinking is very fast and does not leave traces of the steps that it follows; we may be completely unable to retrace the steps that we took in arriving at our judgment or to articulate good reasons for the decision we made. You just feel that it is right, for example, to break off a relationship with Joe, even though you cannot explain why—to yourself, to Joe, or to your mutual friends. You *intuitively* trust Sam and let him use your car.

Intuitive judgments have three characteristics: 1) they are often impossible to explain or justify; 2) we have great confidence that they are "correct" decisions or accurate judgments; they seem obviously right, effortless, and overwhelmingly powerful; and 3) they are often wrong. We frequently trust people who are unreliable or who are deliberately manipulating us—if it were not so, the used car industry would not prosper as much as it does. Intuitive judgments are particularly suspect when you are conversing with someone from a different culture.

In intercultural communication, you cannot act "naturally." That is, your intuition or ability to act spontaneously is always a guide for you to act appropriately within your own culture; it guides you poorly in conversations in which you encounter the horizons of that culture and must adapt to another. Ann Swidler acted naturally and oppressed Brian Palmer.

One of the great moral maxims of Western culture is the "Golden Rule": "Do unto others as you would have them do unto you." This ethical principle adds anticipation to reciprocity: it admonishes us to do good to others *before* they have had a chance to act toward us. A careful analysis of this maxim, however, shows that it works best in monocultural social settings. What if the other person does not want to be treated as you want to be treated?

For example, some people feel that brutal honesty is the best policy in conversations; others feel that social sensitivity requires much more "face work." Assume that you are among the latter, and you meet someone who acts according to both the Golden Rule and the strategy of always being "bald on record." Think through the way the conversation might go; feel yourself being pushed around against your will by the self-righteous virtues of the other person. If you confront your interlocutor with a demand for an account (Why are you always telling me things that I don't want to know? Why do you ask me to tell you things that I don't want to tell you?), you are likely to be told that *you* are in the wrong because 1) you are not sufficiently "honest"; or 2) your interlocutor is simply treating you as he or she would like to be treated. Your response should be, with whatever level of emotional intensity you care to deliver it, that your culture differs from that of your insensitive interlocutor and that he or she should kindly and quickly stop acting in such an ethnocentric manner.

Differentiate "Knowing About" Other Cultures from "Knowing How" to Converse with Them

Knowing *about* another culture is an insufficient guide for knowing how to converse with people in other cultures. What you know about another culture gives you the ability to describe and understand people in them, but not necessarily the ability to join them in the process of co-creating speech acts in a coherent conversation. Knowing about other cultures can be simply an idle fascination with the exotic, in which nuggets of information are displayed in conversation as a way of ornamenting the speaker. Let me contrast *exoticism,* or knowing *about* another culture, with *rhetorical sensitivity,* or knowing *how* to communicate with another people from other cultures.

Exoticism: knowing about other cultures.   There are many resources now for learning about the artifacts of other cultures: you can visit a museum or take a packaged tourist tour of the temples and villages of exotic cultures. There are also many resources for learning about the beliefs of various cultures: courses in comparative religions are offered at most universities, and anthropologists have developed a wonderful literature about the histories, customs, folk ways, and myths of many human cultures. Documentary films provide an accessible way to engage the routinized practices of the mundane forms of life of people in cultures different from your own.

All of these resources produce what Jack Bilmes (1986, p. 189) called "the level of sociological explanation of human action." He explained

> *The discursive sociologist, like the linguist, deals not with individual choice but with systemic constraints on choice and systemic resources for action. He asks: What does it take for behavior, within a particular context, to be meaningful, what are the bases of intelligibility within a cultural group, and how does the requirement of intelligibility limit what members can do or how they can react within particular situations? . . . The object is not to strictly predict members' behavior, but to demonstrate the constraints on members and the resources available to them in creating effects, to show the possibilities inherent in the system and how those possibilities are effectuated. Broadly speaking, the concern is with system and structure, not with statistical outcomes, on the one hand, or individual choices, on the other.*

If we *stop* our inquiry with a "sociological level of explanation," we have done the equivalent of putting other people and their cultural artifacts into glass cases in museums. Although this may quench our taste for exoticism, it is more likely to confirm our enmeshment in our own culture (what Geertz called "parochialism without tears") by reinforcing the line between "us" (who visit museums and watch or make ethnographic movies about bizarre customs) and "them" (who are the subjects of ethnographic films, museum displays, and ethnic shows).

Rhetorical sensitivity: knowing how to communicate with other cultures.   To be able to *participate* in intercultural communication, we need a different kind of knowledge. This kind of knowledge is *praxis;* it is the "practical wisdom" of making good judgments that if I say *this* at this particular moment in the conversation, it will direct the conversation in *that* way. More specifically, intercultural conversations require a rhetorical sensitivity to "openings."

Praxis consists of a particular form of reasoning that might be expressed in the question What acts can I perform that will become the cause of the effect that I want? In intercultural communication, this reasoning uses what Bilmes' called "sociological explanation" for the purposes of engaging with those whose cultures are not the same as ours. Unlike Bilmes' model, *praxis* deals not only with individuals but also with individuals situated at particular moments in the unfolding of a conversation. As a part of the practical wisdom required to communicate well, rhetorical sensitivity consists of a fascinated awareness of what is happening in the conversation and the ability to sense and seize opportunities to influence the direction in which it unfolds.

Rhetorical sensitivity requires a good deal of self-awareness and, sometimes, creativity. If we have never encountered the horizons of our culture, then we do not know where they are; we do not know how far we can stretch or how wide an array of conversations can fit into our social worlds without having to make an adjustment. If deeply enculturated conversations are the only ones that we have experienced, we will give a trivial recitation of the obvious as answer to the question What acts can I perform in this conversation? Experience in intercultural communication gives a sense of where those horizons are, and this way increases our rhetorical sensitivity to what we are able and willing to do.

There is a kind of awkwardness when people first encounter the horizons of their culture. Think of the first time you had to beg on the street for money for food, or the first time you encountered a beggar; think of the first time you realized that the family with whom you were visiting has very different rules for meaning and action than the family in which you grew up. This awkwardness contrasts with the much more sophisticated conversational behavior of a person who has learned—and learned to be comfortable with—the horizons of his or her own culture.

Rhetorical sensitivity requires an ability to assess the contingencies of actions, that is, to anticipate your interlocutor's responses to your own actions. This cannot be an exact science because people are not automatons; however, by using all that you know and your keen observations of the other you may be able to make good judgments about these responses.

Conversants who are rhetorically *in*sensitive act "naturally," not realizing or taking into account the situation in which they find themselves or the way their acts intermesh with those of other people. If you were visiting in the home of a family who remove their shoes at the front door, how long would it take for you to notice that you were the only one who walked into the house with shoes on? I have seen people blissfully unaware that they were the only shod person during a whole evening; others quickly notice what is going on and either remove their shoes or make a conscious decision not to.

The difference between noticing what is going on and not noticing is rhetorical sensitivity.

Finally, rhetorical sensitivity requires an ability to sense "openings" in the logic of the conversation. "Openings" are words, phrases, actions, or "props" that allow you to influence what is going on. Openings are very important in conversations in a culturally diverse society because differences in gender, economic class, race, religion, and ethnic heritage mean that we will frequently engage in conversations in which "acting naturally" is insufficient. We will need to manage our conversations, to steer them into mutually productive and satisfactory patterns.

There can be no complete list of such openings because each is specific to the situation; however, there can be a trained sensitivity to them. The basic structure of an opening is that there is something *shared* among the conversants that permits something else to be *contrasted*.

One form of opening is a shared activity. By participating in a common activity, whether it be sewing or basketball, dancing or chopping down a tree, the conversants establish the first part of an opening—they create something shared. On this basis, they then can compare and contrast other elements of their experience. For example, what does sewing mean in each culture? Is it an economic means of producing commodities for sale, a neutral activity enabling intense social interaction (e.g., gossip, storytelling, or enforcement of group norms)? Is it a site of artistic expression? Is it a gender-specific activity designed to create a space in which the other gender will not or cannot intrude?

Another form of opening deals with language. In oral conversation, 1) the words that we speak are built around some metaphor, 2) they describe

Counterpoint 7.8

The concepts of *rhetorical sensitivity* and *game mastery* as forms of competence are related but not identical. As I see it, *game mastery* requires rhetorical sensitivity but includes something else as well: the ability to imagine alternatives to the cultural scripts and the ability to anticipate the success of performing according to these alternatives.

The term *rhetorical sensitivity* focuses attention on the ability to spot openings for game mastery. This ability is similar to teamwork in various activities requiring closely coordinated movements, such as dance and martial arts. I think that rhetorical sensitivity can be learned but not taught. Practice listening for openings in the conversations you participate in or overhear; imagine what the conversant might have said other than what she or he did, and what would have been the outcome.

a pattern of belief, feeling, or both, and 3) they arc comprised physically of a set of sounds, gestures, and movements. If we "match" our interlocutor on any two of these three, we can introduce a contrast in the third as an *opening* that we have created.

For example, if we use the same *metaphor* and *nonverbal cues* as our interlocutor does, we can introduce a different set of beliefs or values about what is being talked about. If we match our interlocutor's *beliefs* and *nonverbal cues,* we can propose a different metaphor with some hope that it will be adopted.

Finally, use of humor, parody, metacommunication, and the presentation of exotic artifacts constitutes openings. Each of these forms of communication builds multiple levels of meaning into the conversation, permitting a "matching" on one level while acknowledging a difference on another.

Developing a Pidgin as a Means of Achieving Coordination

The first "positive" observation about conversation in a culturally diverse society is that we can achieve it relatively easily—*if* all that we aspire to is minimal coordination. There is a long history of cultures that have rubbed together, usually in the marketplace, and have developed a special kind of language called *pidgin* to communicate.

A pidgin is not really a language; it is a created substitute for a language that has a small vocabulary, a rudimentary grammar, and is not the "native" or "first" language of anyone who uses it. Although it is impossible to express great thoughts, deep emotions, or complex ideas in pidgin, it is possible to negotiate terms for buying and selling and for giving and taking orders between "masters" and "servants."

Contemporary pidgins include the stereotypical ways in which we often think and talk about members of minority groups or those with stigmatic conditions. As soon as we start treating "those people" as if they were all alike, and as soon as we start using easy phrases quoted from the culture around us, we are using a kind of moral pidgin that allows us to deal with people of other cultures without coming into contact with our own cultural horizons.

In contemporary society, there will be conversations among people with very different cultures. These conversations are not likely to be intercultural communication as I have defined it here if it is confined to various sorts of pidgin.

Developing a Creole for Intercultural Communication

If we are committed to understanding each other, not just skating around each other without bumping too painfully, pidgins can develop into creoles. A creole is a new language born out of the interaction among people with dissimilar cultures. It is the first language of the participants (or at least it might be), and it has a sufficiently rich vocabulary and grammar to permit the expression of the whole realm of human emotions and thoughts. It is sufficiently powerful that those who use it can develop rhetorical sensitivity and encounter their own cultural horizons. Creole contains sufficient resources to enable perspicuous contrasts between other moral languages.

Bricolage: a means of developing creole. The term *bricolage* was introduced by Claude Levi-Strauss; a *bricoleur* takes stock of the problems that confront him or her and proceeds by sorting out, reordering, packaging, weighing, and filling in the materials available until a solution is reached. Think of making a shelter from a storm in a deserted field. All you have available are some dead branches, some large rocks, and the blanket you brought with you. Of course! Using the branches as a frame and securing the blanket with rocks—you take what is available and put it to novel uses— this is bricolage. Stout (1988, p. 75) said that all creativity involves bricolage.

Pidgins become creoles as human beings confront the need (a "problem") to express something that their language does not permit. They take stock of the various resources—my language, your language, linguistic items that we might make up—and assemble them together. If we do it well, other people take it up, finding that we have provided them with the resources they need to meet a similar (but never quite identical) need, and so on. The fact that dictionaries get longer every edition, and that every edition has a substantial number of new words and phrases indicates that even English is still the site of considerable *bricolage*.

Dialogue: a means of developing creole. A second way in which creoles are developed is by dialogue. Not every conversation is a dialogue, of course. In dialogue, the conversation is constructed in such a manner as to allow the individual participants to speak in their own voices, and these voices are woven together into a tapestry in which each has its place.

> *The question is not whether you agree with what I say, and certainly not with the imperfect way that I am saying it; rather, whether you see some of the things that I see and am trying to point to and am offering a vocabulary to talk about and whether you see other things of this ilk that I have not seen, and can point them out to me. And finally, of course, the question is whether those things that various ones of us have seen are indeed there. The purpose is that we may all live enriched . . . (Smith 1988, 11)*

Dialogue is dangerous. The attempt to interweave *your* voice with that of someone else makes you vulnerable, particularly if they have no interest in, or ability to, weave. Your voice may be suppressed in the conversation; worse, you may be perceived as "uppity," "heretical," or sharing the crime for which

Socrates was killed, "corrupting the young." The danger is the other side of the opportunity because the distinguishing characteristic of humankind is, in the final analysis, the ability to participate in critical self-consciousness, and the conversational structure in which this ability is best developed and best practiced is dialogue.

A Final Word: New Communication Skills Are Needed

The social and material conditions of contemporary society require us to communicate in a culturally diverse world. This means that new conversational skills, not needed (or at least not so conspicuously needed) in a smaller, more stable, more homogeneous world, are the difference between communicating well and communicating poorly.

A practiced ease in dialogue, a certain knack of bricolage, and a well-developed rhetorical sensitivity will give you resources on which to draw in conversations in which you encounter the horizons of your culture. In such conversations, distrust your intuitions, interpret vertigo as information about your cultural horizons, and look for openings.

These special skills for conversations in a culturally diverse society will help you avoid the twin dangers of which Clifford Geertz warned: a sterile exoticism ("cosmopolitanism without content") and an inability to reach beyond the limits of your own culture ("parochialism without tears"). You will be open to the possibility of genuine dialogue with others who are not like you; you will know the many pleasures of exploring new reaches in your social worlds.

> *To see ourselves as others see us can be eye-opening. To see others as sharing a nature with ourselves is the merest decency. But it is from the far more difficult achievement of seeing ourselves amongst others, as a local example of the forms human life has locally taken, a case among cases, a world among worlds, that the largeness of mind, without which objectivity is self-congratulation and tolerance a sham, comes. (Geertz 1983, p. 16).*

Praxis

1. Improving Intercultural Communication

I do not for a minute believe that Ann Swidler set out to bully Brian Palmer. I suspect that she thought that the conversation on page 316 was deeply enculturated and that she and Palmer were located at similar places within comparable social worlds. As a result, she trusted her intuitive judgments about what to say and how to say it, oblivious to the fact that her Socratic questioning brought Brian Palmer up against the horizon of his cultural *umwelt* and forced him to make a decision about how to continue the conversation. When Swidler rejected his statement that "That's just the way it is," he chose to try to speak in her moral language and wound up saying things that she could use in her book. Trying to invent a universal moral principle that makes integrity good and lying bad, he uttered the philosophical equivalent of baby talk.

What else might he have done?

1. He might have decided to help Swidler discover her own cultural horizons. One way of doing this is to use *circular questioning* (see Chapter 5, "Relationships").

Take turns re-enacting the conversation, first as Palmer and then as Swidler. In the role of Palmer, avoid the trap of offering universal moral principles. Instead, ask the person playing the role of Swidler circular questions. For example, Palmer might ask Swidler

- Who would be most affected if I were to come up with a universal principle about the morality of integrity and lying? Would it change my life more than yours or someone else's?
- What would be different in my life if I were to articulate such a universal principle? Would I be more ethical? Happier? Richer? More handsome?
- If I were to start lying and were not concerned with personal integrity, who would be the first to notice? What would be different in my work? My family?
- What would it cost you to give up the notion that statements of moral principles are the only way to justify one's morality? Who would lose respect for you? What could you no longer do that you think is important? To whom would you have to explain yourself?

Be relaxed, inventive, and creative in these conversations. Do not try so hard to ask the "right" questions that you cannot ask anything, and enjoy making up the answers.

Carefully observe the effect of these questions on the person playing the role of Swidler. What brings him or her to the point of confrontation with his or her own cultural horizons? How does the conversation change after that point?

2. Brian Palmer might have used some of the techniques for managing the interactional contingency that were discussed in Chapter 4, "Episodes." Again role-play the conversation between Palmer and Swidler. This time, make it a contest: when you are Swidler, keep asking some variation of *why*

until you can extract some sort of moral principle from Palmer that you can use in your book; when you have the role of Palmer, try to avoid giving a universal ethical principle by

■ Giving accounts (e.g., "I've had a hard life, and you can't expect me to talk like a philosopher").

■ Metacommunicate (e.g., "I know that you expect me to say something silly like 'all people on earth have the right to their own space' but I don't work that way, and I resent your pushing me to fit into your language game").

■ Reconstruct the context (e.g., "I think you have crossed over some kind of line here; you aren't asking this as part of your research, are you? You are looking for some help in your personal life. Are the concepts of integrity and lying disturbing to you? What have you done that makes you so vulnerable to the simple idea that lying is bad and integrity is good?").

2. Family Communication Patterns

In the 1992 Presidential campaign, the Republican Party attempted to make "family values" a central issue. As it turned out, this was not a particularly successful strategy.

Before class: Gather some of the news coverage of the 1992 Republican National Convention. I suggest the major national newpapers, such as the *New York Times* and the *Washington Post,* and the national newsweeklies, such as *Time, Newsweek,* and *U.S. News and World Report.* If you can get videotapes of some of the most important speeches, this would be very useful. Look also at some of the "alternative" or nonmainstream press, such as the *Christian Science Monitor.*

In class. Using Dizard and Gadlin's typology, just which kind of "family" did the speakers have in mind when they spoke of "family values"?

In the "Narrative" section, I described an episode in which Robert asked Rosa to marry him, and she made her answer conditional on their agreeing about what kind of family they would have.

Form groups of three or four, including at least one man and one woman. Assign two people to take the roles of Rosa and Robert and continue the conversation; assign the other(s) to make sure that the first two act consistently with the various types of families described by Dizard and Gadlin. Repeat these conversations until you have worked out various images of your wedded bliss.

In your conversations, decide whether either or both of you will have a "bachelor's party" with exotic dancers, what kind of wedding you will have, who will earn the money you need, whether anyone other than yourselves will live with you in your house, whether you expect your spouse to enjoy the same recreations that you do, where you will spend Thanksgiving and religious holidays, and who will keep track of the family's finances. Focus not only on the decisions you reach but also the process by which these decisions are made.

3. Common Sense and Intercultural Communication

Geertz (1983, p. 91) proved that the *content* of what "everybody knows" differs among cultures, but that the *form* of common sense is pretty much everywhere the same. "Common sense . . . represents the world as a familiar world, one everyone can, and should, recognize, and within which everyone stands, or should, on his own feet."

Intercultural communication as described in this chapter is the natural enemy of common sense. It is the foregrounding of the taken for granted; it is the deliberate contemplation of the fact that our social worlds contain much in them that is not familiar; and it runs the risk of vertigo.

Outside class. Expose yourself to another culture in whatever way is available to you. Pay particular attention to what the other culture treats as "common sense" that yours does not. Look for cultural assumptions that are so deeply enculturated that they probably will not be marked as significant events; they will not be the object of "accounts" because they will be taken for granted.

Compare these cultural assumptions with those of your own culture. By observing your own common sense, note that it is *artificial*—that is, it is *made* in recurring patterns of conversation just like the common sense of the other culture.

In class. Working in groups of three or four, compare your observations. Discuss how your conversations would be different if you substituted the content of the *other* common sense for your own. What accounts would you give, demand, and accept that you take for granted now? What would you accept that you now demand accounts for? What accounts would you accept that you do not now?

These comparisons of cultural assumptions comprise the openings that you should sense as part of your rhetorical sensitivity. They identify the places where you can create the preconditions for successful communication among people from different cultures.

Look again at the conversation between Ann Swidler and Brian Palmer. What openings are there? If you were to advise them about improving their conversation, what would you suggest?

4. Recipes for Living in Postmodern Society

In Chapter 6, Gergen's suggestion of three stages in the development of a healthy multiphrenic personality were summarized. In this chapter, Geertz was described as naming two skills and two dangers of life in a cultural collage, and I described four characteristics of intercultural communication. How do these various prescriptions fit together? How much confidence do you have in them?

Working in three teams, explore whether Geertz', Gergen's, and my "solutions" are sufficiently powerful to solve the problems that Gergen and Geertz described. First, identify those problems. Second, make sure you understand what Geertz, Gergen, and I have suggested. Then, stage a debate between your three teams. Assign each team to argue that one of these solutions is better than the other two.

When you finish the debate, compare your results with other groups. Which of these sets of solutions fared the best in your debates? How much confidence do you have in any of them?

References

Alexander, Alison, Cronen, Vernon E., Kang, Kyung-wha, Tsou, Benny, and Banks, Jane. "Patterns of Topic Sequencing and Information Gain: A Comparative Study of Relationship Development in Chinese and American Cultures." *Communication Quarterly* 43: (1986): 66–78.

Bellah, Robert, et al. *Habits of the Heart: Individualism and Commitment in American Life.* Berkeley: University of California Press, 1985.

Bilmes, Jack. *Discourse and Behavior.* New York: Plenum Press, 1986.

Campbell, Joseph. *Metaphors to Live By.* New York: Viking, 1972.

Dizard, Jan, and Gadlin, Howard. "Family Life and the Marketplace: Diversity and Change in the American Family." In *Historical Social Psychology,* edited by Kenneth J. Gergen and Mary M. Gergen, 281–302. Hillsdale: Erlbaum, 1984.

Hall, Edward T. *The Silent Language.* New York: Doubleday, 1959.

Geertz, Clifford. *Local Knowledge: Further Essays in Interpretive Anthropology.* New York: Basic Books, 1983.

Geertz, Clifford. "The Uses of Diversity." *Michigan Quarterly Review* 25 (1986): 106–123.

Gergen, Kenneth J. *The Saturated Self: Dilemmas of Identity in Contemporary Life.* New York: Basic Books, 1991.

Gudykunst, William B., and Ting-Toomay, Stella, with Chua, Elizabeth. *Culture and Interpersonal Communication.* Newbury Park: Sage, 1988.

Nisbett, Robert. *History of the Idea of Progress.* New York: Basic Books, 1980.

Pearce, W. Barnett. *Communication and the Human Condition.* Carbondale: Southern Illinois Press, 1989.

Pearce, W. Barnett. *Interpersonal Communication: Making Social Worlds.* New York: HarperCollins, 1994.

Pearce, W. Barnett, and Kang, Kyung-wha. "Conceptual Migrations: Understanding 'Traveller's Tales' for Cross-Cultural Adaptation." In *Cross-Cultural Adaptation: Current Approaches,* edited by Young Yum Kim and William B. Gudykunst, 20–41. Newbury Park: Sage, 1988.

Pirsig, Robert M. *Lila: An Inquiry into Morals.* New York: Bantam, 1991.

Pfaff, William. *Chicago Tribune.* Sunday, November 8, 1992, Section 4, p. 3.

Smith, W. C. "Transcendence." *Harvard Divinity Bulletin*. 18 (1988): 10–15.

Stout, Jeffrey. *Ethics After Babel: The Languages of Morals and Their Discontents.* Boston: Beacon Press, 1988.

von Uexkull, J. *Umwelt and Innenwelt der Tiere*. Berlin: Springer, 1909.

Watzlawick, Paul, Beavin, Janet, and Jackson, Don. *Pragmatics of Human Communication*. New York: Norton, 1967.

Wittgenstein, Ludwig. *Tractatus Logico-Philosophicus*. Translated by C. K. Ogden. London: Routledge & Kegan Paul, 1922.

PART THREE

Recapitulation

. . . think of social life as a kind of conversation. All our actions . . . are creating a kind of conversation, an endless conversation into which individuals enter, make their contribution to the common discourse, and eventually fall silent, though some may go on contributing to the conversations of mankind long after they are dead, by writing books, becoming legendary, and so on. Babies are immersed in this conversation. . . . We construct our worlds in talk of various kinds. Every exchanging of symbolic objects is a kind of extension of that conversation, I believe. So we have . . . to look at the properties of talk, the form of conversations, if we want really to get to the heart of what it is to be a human being, engaging with other people in constructing a social world.

Rom Harré (in Jonathan Miller, States of Mind. *New York: Pantheon, 1983, p. 159)*

The physical world is elegant in design, predictable in action, and fixed in purpose. The social world, the world we have made, is vastly inelegant, unpredictable, and unfixed. Made of ambiguity and ambivalence, contradiction and conflict, it is a clown in the temple. It can change as you look at it. Sometimes, it changes because you are looking at it. It requires alertness, curiosity, impatience, courage, and skepticism.

Warren Bennis, Why Leaders Can't Lead: The Unconscious Conspiracy Continues. *San Francisco: Jossey-Bass, 1990, p. 48.*

CHAPTER

8 *Putting It All Together*

Of all affairs, communication is the most wonderful.
That things should be able to pass from the plan of external
pushing and pulling to that of revealing themselves to
man, and thereby to themselves; and that the fruit
of communication should be participation, sharing, is
a wonder. . . . When communication occurs, all
natural events are subject to reconsideration and revision; they are re-adapted to meet the requirements
of conversation, whether it be public discourse or that
preliminary discourse termed thinking. Events turn
into objects, things with a meaning.

Dewey 1958, p. 166.

OUTLINE	OBJECTIVES	KEY WORDS AND PHRASES

Narrative

Two Metaphors for "Putting It All Together"

Relations Among Aspects of our Social Worlds

Patterns of Interpersonal Communication

Three Final Words

Praxis

1. Racism, Sexism, and Classism

2. Developing Healthy Self-Concepts

3. Interviewing

After reading this chapter, you will be able to

- Analyze the way racism, sexism, and classicism are socially constructed

- Identify forms of communication that promote psychological and social health

- Choose among several styles of interviewing

Some terms that will help you understand this chapter include

language, paradox, enabling, healthy self-concepts, interviewing, reflexivity, "good communication"

Narrative

Kyle and Shirley work together in the office of a law firm. Kyle noticed that Shirley is often late for work on Mondays and after most holidays. At work, her moods often shifted abruptly. In one minute, she would be high spirited and gregarious; in the next, sullen and withdrawn. The quality of her work became inconsistent; she sometimes made mistakes that were far below her competence.

Concerned and wanting to be helpful, Kyle quietly began to check Shirley's work before she turned it in, correcting the most obvious mistakes. He became very sensitive to her moods, and tried to fit in with them. He talked freely when she was happy and avoided her when she was depressed. When their supervisor questioned her tardiness, he sometimes lied, saying that she was running an errand for the company. He sometimes did her work for her so that her moodiness and tardiness would not be noticed by their supervisor.

What should we think about Kyle's behavior? From one perspective, he appears kind, generous, and caring. From another, his actions fit the classic profile of a person who—to use the technical term—"enables" someone else to continue to abuse alcohol or other drugs without confronting the consequences of their condition.

Like all of us at one time or another, Kyle is involved in a conversation that requires him to act in the context of contradictory demands. In this case, if he wants to maintain a "normal" relationship with Shirley, he must cooperate with her in the mutual production of her "face." This means that he help her provide accounts for her poor work and tardiness; that he not call attention to the fact that her failures are increasing his work load. On the other hand, if he wants to help her confront the fact that her performance at work is poor—or simply get her to do her share of the work at the office— he will have to confront her in a way that is very different from their current patterns of communication.

Let's assume that Kyle is very competent in all of the particular areas of interpersonal communication that we have discussed: he knows about the co-construction of speech acts, he is skilled at punctuating the stream of events into coherent episodes, he is sensitive to the relationships that he acts into and out of, and he is even able to make his own cultural frames visible. With all of this, he still does not know what to do in his conversations with Shirley.

Situations such as this one confronting Kyle pose the strongest tests of our practical wisdom (i.e., *phronesis*) because they require good judgment among the various things that we know how to do. Kyle knows that whatever he does will have far-reaching implications for his relationship with Shirley, for the episode of their working together, and for the array of speech acts that will characterize the office in the future.

Kyle's decision involves putting together the various strands of the logic of meaning and action in which he finds himself. This "putting it all together" is something that you do in *all* your conversations. Usually, you do not find yourself in a predicament as difficult as Kyle's; most of the time you find ways to integrate the various contexts of conversations so that they are coherent, pleasant, and effective.

However, it is not always easy, and in some cases, not always possible to have such a happy outcome. In previous chapters, you learned that these logics are often confused; the subject of this chapter is what to do about the tangles and jumbles that occur in our social worlds.

Two Metaphors for "Putting It All Together"

But what does it mean to put it all together? Who does this "putting"? Just what is "put"? How does it fit "together"? Remember that communication is a process of making and doing: in what way do we "put" episodes and relationships together? If our self-concept and our culture are contradictory, how do we put them together so that we can act in the "now" of a conversation?

Two images help me understand the process of putting the various aspects of conversation together: juggling and weaving.

Juggling

Like jugglers, communicators pick up various objects that we find in our social worlds and start throwing them back and forth, in this way making them into the substance of the conversations in which we live. This is inherently a social process, and our own skills must be matched with those of the persons who catch what we throw and throw what we catch.

Every conversation always includes all of these: speech acts, self, relationship, episode, and culture. Within each of these, there can be competing definitions of relationships, conflicting pressures from episodic scripts and our goals for the episode, and uncertainty about the speech act that is being performed. All of this makes *juggling* necessary.

Just like juggling balls or clubs, conversational juggling requires certain skills. Unlike juggling, which only a few people learn to do, every "normal" human being learns how to juggle the events and objects of their social world to make coherent conversations.

Even the most skillful juggler can be overwhelmed if he or she has to keep too many balls in the air. Are five "aspects" of communication too many? Conversational juggling is possible because 1) in each conversation some things are more relevant than others; 2) in most conversations, the actions we take in making speech acts, self, relationships, episode, and culture are compatible; and 3) in most conversations, we can rely on intuition for much of what we do.

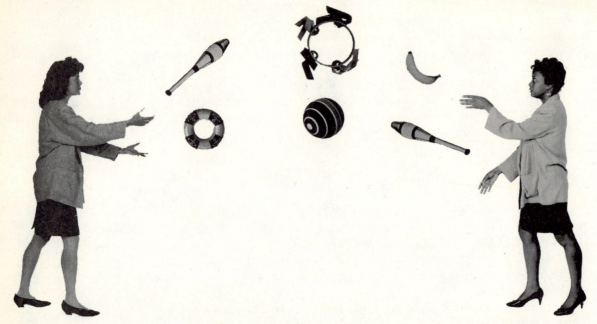

Communicators "put it all together" by juggling the events and objects of their social worlds to make a specific conversation.

Counterpoint 8.1

In the text, I said that "every 'normal' human being learns how to juggle. . . . " This statement begs the question of what "normal" means, of course.

I am content to use a circular argument here: normal human beings are those who can participate in normal conversations with other people. Although this circular argument gives no help in identifying the attributes that distinguish *normal* from *abnormal* people, it does locate the *site* in which such attributes are noticed. That site is, of course, the conversations that we have with other people.

Most of us have a keen sense of when things go slightly wrong in conversation. If your interlocutors do not juggle episode and relationship well—that is, they talk in ways that are appropriate for your relationship but not in this particular setting—you quickly note it and wonder what is wrong with them.

Any metaphor can be pushed too far and should not be taken literally. The image of juggling distorts what conversants do when they put it all together because it implies that the events and objects "tossed" back and forth are discrete entities, unrelated to each other, and not significantly changed by the process of being thrown around. In interpersonal communication, however, the creation of our social worlds is continuous, and our selves, speech acts, cultures, episodes, and relationships change as we "juggle" them. The self that we "throw" to the other person in the first act of a conversational triplet is not quite the same self that she "throws" back in the second act, or that we "throw" yet again in the third act. Those changes in our self affect our relationship to those with whom we are juggling, which in turn affects the episode in which we are acting, and so on, in a continuous, fluid, and reflexive process.

Counterpoint 8.2

I had been trying to describe the continuing creation of our social worlds in class. As usual, I had waved my arms a lot, mostly in circular patterns, and spoken in run-on sentences. I left the classroom with a sense of frustration, and met one of my students at the head of the stairs.

"Just a minute, Prof," he said. "Do you mean to say that *nothing* stands still in conversation? That everything rotates around everything else?"

"Yes!" I cried. "That's *exactly* what I am trying to say."

"Wow . . . I'm going to have to think about that," he replied.

As you can see, *I* am still thinking about this brief conversation. I wondered at my student's trouble in visualizing a fluid, reflexive process, and his amazement when he "got the picture." He acted as if I were teaching something new, highly radical, and perhaps slightly subversive. But although this view of our social worlds may be unusual, it really is neither new nor original.

Our Western intellectual heritage has taught us to think in terms of unchanging entities (e.g., atoms) that fit together in relatively simple ways (e.g, Newton's three laws of motion). Even people who are not physicists have been deeply affected by this cosmology; they apply this schema to the events and objects in their social *umwelt.* But physicists have known for nearly a century that the universe is far more complex than this, that things that are "as old as the hills" are very young, that the "fixed" stars are not only in motion but are in a process of evolution, that we are surrounded by swirling forces that reciprocally influence each other in complex patterns. I believe that my student would have been less amazed by—and would have had less difficulty understanding—the social constructionist notion of communication if he had understood the cosmology taught in contemporary physics and astronomy classes.

"Putting it all together" in conversation is like weaving together the events and objects of our social worlds.

Weaving

The metaphor of weaving is in some ways a better metaphor for conversation than is juggling because in the hands of an accomplished weaver, the individual strands of fabric are less important than the pattern that they construct. Many strands of materials can be braided into complex patterns; a skillful weaver can choose which of the strands will give the dominant texture or color to the whole pattern. A less skilled or less gifted weaver ties ugly, rough knots that have unpredictable or boring, repetitive colors or textures. When I am talking with a skillful conversationalist, I am reminded of a master weaver who takes the strands of both my self-concept and his, our relationship, the episode in which we are participating, the speech acts we are performing, and our cultural horizons and braids them into a pattern sufficiently familiar so that I can recognize it and sufficiently unpredictable so that it is interesting. This is an art form whose beauty is enhanced by understanding the complexity of the process by which it is accomplished.

Relations Among Aspects of our Social Worlds

Whether we weave or juggle, we have to organize the speech acts, episode, relationships, self, and culture that are being made in the conversation. These organizational patterns may be described with two terms: compatibility and hierarchy.

Compatibility

If you have only two eggs, and you are trying to make *both* a two-egg omelette and a two-egg cake, then the performance demands of your recipes are incompatible: you cannot juggle them so that you can follow both recipes as they are written. The best that you can do is to have either the omelette or the cake (but the decision about *which* is more preferable is not found in the recipes themselves) or you might decide to cook a single fried egg and a one-egg cake (but that would be a form of *game mastery* in which you adapt the recipes to the necessity of your juggling).

Because communication is a process of making and doing, compatibility refers to what we are to do in a specific instance. Each of the aspects of conversation is like a recipe; certain acts are required if we are to maintain *face,* others, if we are to co-construct a mutually satisfactory relationship, and still others, if we are to pull off the performance of a particular episode. The analogy of a recipe breaks down, of course, because *most* performance demands in conversations include many ways of achieving the same goal. However, the necessity to juggle the performance demands of speech acts, self, episode, culture, and relationship *simultaneously* means that there are many instances in which our skills as game players are stressed.

Let the term *compatible* refer to instances in which what we are required to do, for example, by the *episode* in which we are participating, is the same as that which we are required to do, for example, by our *relationships* with other people. Let the term *incompatible* refer to instances in which we cannot do *both* what is required by the episode and by our relationships.

Incompatibility is not a cognitive problem (i.e., *knowing* what to do) as much as it is one of being able to *perform* all that we must do. For example, if you are a witness to a traffic accident involving a friend, you may be sworn to give truthful testimony in court that would convict your friend of criminal negligence. In this case, what do you do—lie and face charges of perjury or tell the truth and lose a friendship? If you are starving and homeless during a blizzard, the performance demands of your self ("honesty") may conflict with those of your relationship to your children ("parental responsibility"). Without trying to resolve the question of what you would do in that situation, clearly the actions required by each aspect of the situation are incompatible. No matter which you choose—virtuously watching your children freeze while you starve or stealing firewood and two eggs and build a guilty fire for warmth and to cook an omelette and a cake—you will have to live with the consequences of having to choose between incompatible requirements.

Often, we can resolve incompatible demands by stepping out of this particular instant in time. For example, we can do first one thing and then another, or we can call into being things that have not happened yet.

A dramatic instance of both of these ways of playing with time occurred in Maine. Some young people were shipwrecked on an island in one of the tidal rivers. Because the tides in that part of the world rise and fall over ten feet and have a current of over four knots that reverse direction twice a day, it is a dangerous area for navigation, and because the water is always cold, these teen-agers were in a life-threatening situation. They managed to get to shore and found that there was one house on the island, closed for the winter.

They broke into the house, burned the owner's firewood, ate the owner's food, took dry clothing from the closets, and dripped all over the floors. Before leaving, they left a long letter for the owner, whom they did not know, explaining the circumstances, apologizing for the damage, and promising to repay. According to local legend, that incident was the beginning of a long friendship, but it might have turned out otherwise if the shipwrecked sailors had not been so careful to punctuate their violence to the house and locate it as one part of a longer episode. They *made* their entry to the house compatible with their own sense of dignity by proposing it as a part of an as-yet-unrealized friendship; within the context of that friendship, the owner would welcome the damage to his house in exchange for keeping them from freezing after their close escape from the river. As it turned out, the owner accepted this definition of the events, acknowledging a particularly deft bit of conversational juggling or weaving.

Hierarchy

Kyle was juggling with incompatible performance demands in his conversations with Shirley. When she came in late, he had to act either as a coworker ("Shirley, this has got to stop! You are making me do your work as well as mine") or as a co-conspirator ("Shirley, I told your boss that you were at the mail room sending out a special delivery letter"). Whether wisely or not, he was letting the performance demands of his relationship with her (co-conspirators, helpful, friendly) take precedence over the performance demands of the episode (coworkers). That is, *relationship* was the context for *episode*.

Let *hierarchy* describe the pattern of relationships among the various aspects of communication that we are continuously juggling. One way of understanding this relationship is as a series of concentric circles or boxes inside each other (see Figure 8.1). In each case, the larger circle or box is the one that predominates.

Another way of representing the hierarchy is to use the atomic model presented in Figure 1.5 that shows you at each moment during a conversation at the nexus of social worlds. In this case, you are simultaneously performing a speech act, co-constructing an episode, reproducing a social relationship, enacting your self concept, and moving inside your culture. As shown in Figure 8.2, you have juggled this complicated set of relationships by making the episode the most important context (as shown by the darkest lines) and your concept of self the least important (as shown by the lightest lines).

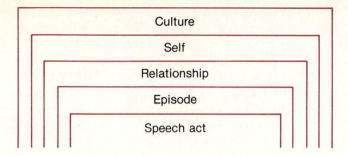

Figure 8.1
The hierarchy of contexts. (From Pearce et al. 1979)

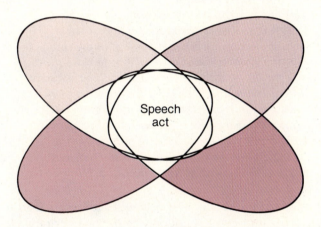

Figure 8.2
The hierarchical relations among aspects of communication (another representation).

The hierarchical relationship among the various aspects of conversation are invisible if their performance demands are compatible. The hierarchical relationship—that is, which event is the context for which—is revealed when the performance demands are incompatible. If your culture requires you to act in a manner incompatible with the requirements of your relationship with your interlocutor, you will act consistently with the one that is the context for the other.

For example, many cultures are racist. In the contemporary world, many young people work or study in cultures far from their homes. In so doing, they meet other young people and sometimes form close friendships with them. It is only to be expected that they will invite each other to visit them in their homes when they return to their native countries; it is likely that some of them will fall in love and want to marry. However, when their *relationships* to their friends encounter the cultural patterns of racism and the *relationships* with their parents and siblings, incompatible performance demands result. In fact, most cultures even provide *scripts* for how such problems are to be dealt with.

In his remarkably candid book, *The Human Cycle*, anthropologist Colin Turnbull (1984, p. 205) describes the efforts he and Kumari, "an Indian girl from a good Hindu family," made to juggle or weave the incompatible demands of their relationship and the culture of upper-class England.

Their plan to marry was opposed by both families, who cited both racial and religious reasons. Undaunted, Turnbull and Kumari attempted to overcome the social barriers to an inter-racial relationship that were erected by society. Their efforts included attending together the social events staged by Turnbull's social class for couples planning to marry.

> *I escorted her to the Flower Ball in London, where she was considered not quite proper, the reason given being that the then Princesses Elizabeth and Margaret were also attending. Now social considerations at the widest national extension were impinging. To be a responsible, patriotic adult it was evidently necessary to be a racist. There was much more furor, however, when I brought Kumari into that south country hunting territory and escorted her to the ball given at Arundel Castle for the coming out of the Duke of Norfolk's daughter. Kumari fled to India and I to Africa. Between us we first established our own economic marker for a joint adulthood, and as soon as I could support her we were to get married. But when with my first job in hand I wrote a formal letter of proposal, it was delayed in the Indian mails and she received it months later, just two weeks after she had finally succumbed and married a Hindu.*

If *relationship* is the context for *culture*, you may well act in ways that are considered inappropriate for your culture, not only by having inter-racial friendships or marriages, but in the manner in which you present this situation to your parents and siblings. If *culture* is the context for *relationships*, you may act in ways that preclude you from making friends with your classmates or co-workers who are from other races. In fact, you might develop a conversational style that functions to shield you from the possibility of getting to know and like someone from another race or social class.

There is no universal pattern of hierarchical relationships. For example, relationship can be the context for episode or vice versa. In fact, much of the dynamism in our social worlds is caused by changes in what is the context for what. Consider a couple who meet at a party and begin to date each other. They probably evaluate their relationship on the basis of the episodes they co-create: "I must like her," he tells himself, "because we have so much fun together." Sometime later, they realize that something has changed. The common word for this is "commitment;" in the terms I am using here, it is that *relationship* has become the context for *episode*. That is, now they are willing to co-construct episodes that are not necessarily much fun because they are part of their relationship.

After many years of marriage, a woman may realize that it has been a

(while dating)	(while engaged)	(after years of marriage)
"Episode" is the context for "Relationship"	"Relationship" is the context for "Episodes"	"Self" is the context for "Relationship"

Figure 8.3
Hierarchical patterns of relationships at different times in a person's life.

long time since she has participated in an episode that she enjoyed. She feels that she has been foolish, that her life has not turned out as she wanted or expected; she tells herself that she is "trapped" by her relationship to her husband and demands that he join her in a systematic process of restructuring their relationship. At this point in time, her *self* is the context for her *relationship*. (Figure 8.3 shows these three patterns that occur at different times in her life.)

Patterns of Interpersonal Communication

Using the concepts of hierarchy and compatibility, we can look at some specific forms of communication and see how the conversants juggle or weave speech acts, episodes, relationships, self-concept, and culture.

Enabling

Enabling is a term used to describe conversations between a person who has a problem with alcohol or other drugs and those people who are sincerely but naively trying to help them. By definition, a person who has a problem with alcohol or other drugs acts in ways that are harmful to self and others.

To decide that someone with whom you work or play is abusing drugs is no small matter. Among other things, it means that you have decided to revoke their moral right to avow their own competency; you have decided for them that they have a problem and that they need help for which they have not asked and that they may well not want. However, the alternative is to *enable* them to continue in their abusive or dependent patterns.

Enabling as an aspect of deontic logic and practical reasoning.   There are several reasons why people fall into *enabling* patterns of conversation. Some people feel that they "must" or "ought" to act in ways that are "helpful." When Kyle saw that Shirley had difficulties, he tried to protect her. Perhaps Kyle was absolutely sincere in his attempts to help, but what he did was to shield Shirley from the need to seek help.

In this case, it is not clear how to punctuate the episodes that Kyle and Shirley co-construct. The performance demands of the episode are not clear. One plausible framing of the episode includes a script in which the speech act of "covering" for the other counts as "keeping her from being fired"

Counterpoint 8.3

Those who work with alcohol and drug-related problems have developed some standard terms.

Use: This term describes use that is not harmful for the user or others.

Misuse: This term describes behavior that is similar to "abuse" but is less regular in occurrence. For example, someone who regularly uses alcohol to relax without trying to reduce the cause of stress or relieve stress by other means could be described as misusing alcohol because they may be beginning a habit of use that will harm them in the future.

Abuse: This term describes use of chemicals in ways that harm the individual or others. For example, a drunk driver returning from a wedding has abused alcohol. This term also describes the beginning of dependent behavior. Abusive users are usually regular users who still have some control over their use patterns, but changing their behavior is getting more and more difficult.

Dependency: The term describes persons who cannot control their use of alcohol or other drugs. They are damaging their health, ruining their personal relationships, and destroying their opinions of themselves as capable, productive people. When they refrain from using the addictive substance they will suffer physical and/or psychological withdrawal pains. They find ways to justify their behavior and insist that they are in control.

Enabling: This term describes behaviors that unwittingly allow or encourage alcohol and other drug problems to continue or worsen by preventing the abuser from experiencing the consequences of his or her condition.

---

and is thus "being helpful." Another plausible framing of the episode includes a script in which the same acts count as "shielding her from the consequences of her acts" and is thus not only not helpful, but in fact has become part of the drug-dependent person's problem.

Enabling as an aspect of relationships.   Enablers do not want to jeopardize their relationship with the drug-dependent person. Perhaps Kyle valued his friendship with Shirley—or hoped to develop a romantic relationship with her—and felt that he would lose both if he confronted her about her behavior. Of course, there is the potential for many levels of exploitation in such a relationship: with whatever degree of sincerity or cynicism, Shirley might offer Kyle a relationship as part of a bargain for him to continue covering for her at work, or Kyle might, with whatever degree of sincerity or callousness, propose such a bargain.

Enabling as an aspect of self.   Enablers sometimes feel good by helping the chemically dependent person. In this case, the self-concept of the enabler "needs" someone who is not functioning well so that he or she can act as a "helper." If this pattern escalates, it can produce very bizarre forms of behavior in which one person is required (by the logic of the relationship) to display ever-greater extremes of capability and the other, to display ever-greater extremes of incompetence. As the relationship goes on, the conversations become more and more asymmetric, with the helper (Kyle) acting as if he is more and more the intelligent, competent, and caring partner, and the helped (Shirley) acting if she is increasingly dependent and incompetent.

Of course, we should not interpret this or any other relationship without suspecting that it is more complex than it may appear. For example, if we were to watch Kyle and Shirley over a period of time, we might find that Shirley is more competent as a communicator than Kyle. Assume that Kyle has moved in with Shirley so that he can take care of her. I believe that any social worker or therapist would recognize the following hypothetical scenario.

Shirley skillfully enticed Kyle into a relationship in which he is her protector. She used all sorts of conversational devices, including nonverbal cues and the careful construction of episodes that offer him the role of protector, to structure this relationship; now that it is established, she counts on the logical force to bind him to it.

Kyle does not quite know how he got into this situation and would like to break it off. However, every time he tries to act autonomously (e.g., going out for an evening by himself or with other friends), Shirley responds with an act of spectacular dependency (e.g., abusing drugs or being taken to a hospital, her life barely saved). Shirley's "inability" to take care of herself, of course, is part of a conversational triplet that redefines Kyle's "autonomous" evening out as a "irresponsible shirking" of his responsibility to take care of Shirley.

It is possible to construct other plausible scenarios, of course. Here is one in which Kyle is the more competent communicator, managing to bring about coordinated actions that meet his needs more than hers. Again, I believe that any experienced social worker will recognize this pattern.

Kyle carefully constructed a set of conversations in which Shirley was forced to acknowledge that he is more capable than she. The relationship that develops makes it legitimate for him to point out every fault and failure of hers and requires her to present herself as less competent than he (e.g., by deferring to his judgment or asking his opinion about virtually every matter of judgment).

Shirley is not quite sure how she became enmeshed in this relationship but finds it impossible to leave it. Kyle cleverly blocks her attempts to prove herself as autonomous and competent. For example, if Shirley acts autonomously by going out for an evening by herself, Kyle will find some aspect of her performance (she forgot her housekeys, she went to a dangerous part of town, she had a couple of drinks—"and what might have happened?!") that he can use to convince them both that she needs his presence and help on every issue.

In any case, the surface pattern of enabling is not necessarily the same as the relationship that emerges if we take a longer and closer look at the conversations. Enabling may be a pattern carefully woven by two conversationalists, both of whom are happy with the results, but it may also be a one-sided pattern. Think of two weavers working on the same tapestry in which one is more skillful than another. Every time the less skilled tries to bring out his pattern, the other weaves his strands of fabric in such a way as to make a different pattern.

Enabling as an aspect of episodic scripts.   Some enablers have unresolved issues of alcohol or drug abuse in their own families. For them, enabling is part of their culture; it is the form of social relationships that they learned as children. Sharon's father was an alcoholic, and she is married to an alcoholic. When her husband has a hangover, she calls his office and tells them that he is sick; when he has abrupt mood changes, she tells the children to excuse him because he had a hard day at the office. She literally cannot imagine herself acting otherwise; this is the only pattern of behavior within her cultural horizons. What odds would you give that her children will be alcoholics or enablers, too?

Refrain 8.1

The principle that all communication occurs in context reminds us that it is very difficult to discern what *pattern* is produced by any single communicative *act*. Nowhere is this more clear than in the comparison between "enabling" and "supporting."

"Enabling" consists of those patterns of interaction that allow a person with a problem, such as substance abuse, to continue behaving in the problematic manner without confronting the consequences. "Supporting" consists of those patterns of interaction that allow a person to overcome or avoid problems by providing a certain set of consequences to the other's actions. These consequences include feeling included, recognized, responded to, and appreciated.

Some specific actions taken in the context of "enabling" may resemble those taken in the context of "supporting." What is important is the "whole" pattern.

Supporting Healthy Self-Concepts

If "putting it all together" in conversations is like weaving, then some of the strands of fabric are the self-concepts of the interlocutors. The discussion of enabling shows how the concept of self as *helper* or *helped* can be woven into a destructive pattern of relationship. However, conversations are also the site of the processes by which healthy self-concepts are developed. By observing patterns of communication in families and organizations, we have developed a good bit of sophistication about conversational styles in which healthy self-concepts emerge.

The list of (what I call, with tongue firmly in cheek) the "Nine Commandments" in Figure 8.4 are typical of many ways of summarizing this information. If you look at the commandments closely, you will see that they are predicated on several basic assumptions.

The co-construction of healthy self-concepts.

These commandments assume that self-concepts are co-constructed in conversations with other people. By acting in the ways commanded here, you do not "give" the other person a healthy self-concept or "cause" him or her to have one, but you do establish the preconditions for the development of a healthy self-concept. That is, you provide the social *umwelt* in which healthy self-concepts can emerge.

Like the concept of "normal" people introduced earlier in this chapter, these commandments do not seem very precise about what makes a self-concept "healthy." However, on closer reading, some features of a "healthy" self-concept are clearly implied. Shame, doubts about one's worth, and embarrassment are *not* the components of or ways of producing a *healthy* self-concept; on the other hand, some sense of success, of feeling wanted and belonging, and an ability to be proud of oneself is a part of *health*. Finally,

Thou shalt
1. Make a person feel that he or she belongs, that he or she is wanted.
2. Try to help each person achieve some success every day.
3. Recognize the effort the person makes.
4. Do not cause the person to doubt his or her worth; do not shame or embarrass him or her.
5. Answer each person's questions openly, honestly, attentively, and immediately when possible.
6. Compliment sincerely new clothes, hair styles, neat work, any improvement in school work, homework, etc.
7. Encourage the person to speak of himself or herself proudly and often.
8. Meet the person's eyes when he or she is talking to you.
9. Listen closely and attentively.

Figure 8.4
Nine commandments for helping others have a healthy self-concept.

interacting contingently with other people is both the way of producing a healthy self-concept and of acting as a person with a healthy self-concept. That is, you are to recognize the other's effort, acknowledge changes (particularly "improvements"), make nonverbal contact, and listen well to other people.

Health as an ability.   These nine commandments actually do have a precise definition of what it means to be a healthy person, but the definition is not what you might have expected. *Health* is not the possession (or absence) of particular attributes; it is the *ability* to engage in a particular kind of activity. Specifically, the ability to enter into symmetrically contingent conversations with others is the substance of a healthy self-concept.

Reflexivity in healthy self-concepts.   Finally, this list of commandments about how to help *others* have a healthy self-concept has a hidden reflexivity. What kind of person do *you* become if you engage in "symmetrically contingent conversations with others" as a way of helping *them*? Of course, you, too, find these co-constructed conversations the social *umwelt* in which your self-concept can emerge "healthy" as well. Helping, like anything else, is reflexive. One of the great discoveries is that helping others is the best way of helping yourself. There is nothing mystical about this observation: we live in the patterns of communication that we co-construct with other people; these conversations are the ecology in which our selves, relationships, cultures, and episodes exist. If we create ugly, spiteful, garbage-filled conversations, then those are the *umwelt* in which we live; but if we create beauty, caring, truthfulness, and honesty, then we can live in those environments. It should not surprise us that those who hurt others bear the scars of those hurts, or that those who help others are "healthy."

Persuasive Interviewing

Interviewing consists of a wide array of conversations that have a certain asymmetry as their common feature. In an interview, one person will do most of the asking and the other most of the answering of questions; one person (the interviewer) is usually the more skilled or practiced of the interlocutors, and the interviewer usually has a specific idea in mind for what the interviewed person will say or do during or after the interview.

The development of news, the new genre of "infotainment," and talk shows on television have given us a wide array of models for interviews. These public interviews can be arrayed along a continuum from Bill Moyers on one end to Sam Donaldson on the other. Bill Moyers uses a great deal of preparation and skill to create a conversation in which the person interviewed *can* say what she or he wants to say as well as possible; Sam Donaldson uses an equivalent amount of preparation and skill to create a conversation in which the person interviewed *must* say something that he or she does not want to say.

There is a hidden reflexivity in conversations. We live in the patterns of communication that we co-construct with others. If we create ugly, spiteful conversations, then that is what we live in and what we become. But if we create beauty, caring, truthfulness, and honesty, then that is what we live in and what we become.

For all their diversity, these public interviews pale in comparison with those done in private. A similar continuum can be constructed between "therapeutic interviews" (using circular questioning or some other technique) and "interrogations" (using bright lights and threats, or some other coercive technique).

One form of interview consists of persuading a person to do something that he or she feels should be done but is reluctant to do. For example, how do investigative reporters convince people to allow themselves to be televised saying things that will cost them their jobs?

I interviewed veteran investigative reporter Michael Lyons, who described his technique for persuading reluctant witnesses to agree to a televised interview. (Hmm . . . In this interview, did I function more as Bill Moyers or as Sam Donaldson?) The reporter described an instance in which he had to persuade a man who worked for a defense contractor to appear on "Sixty Minutes" to expose corruption and waste in the Navy. They met in a hotel restaurant. The facts of corruption and waste were not the issue; the question was whether this man would risk his job—and perhaps set himself up for less sophisticated retaliation—by appearing on television.

According to Lyons, his interview technique has three stages: bonding, exalting, and closing. In the *bonding* phase, the interviewer "echoes" what the interviewed person says: "Yes, I know how you feel." "I'm outraged about that, too." "You're right, this is an important step that you are taking." In the *exalting* phase, the interviewer connects what the person is being asked to do with some of the well-known but seldom used "power words" in the person's vocabulary. For example, the interviewer may say, "It takes real *courage* for you to testify." The repetition of this power word empowers the

Refrain 8.2

There are many forms of interviewing, and very different communication episodes can be performed using the same "question and answer" format. In the Narrative, I contrast "persuasive interviewing" with "circular questioning." The former is designed to elicit compliance with the questioner's intentions; the latter is designed to help the answerer discover and act according to his or her own intentions.

These two forms do not exhaust the range of interviews. "Interrogations" including torture or threats are the most monologic; the form of interview associated with Carl Roger's "Client-Centered Therapy" (in which the questioner simply restates as a question what the answerer says) is perhaps the most dialogic.

person to make a risky decision. Finally, the *closing* consists of actually bringing the person to allow himself to be recorded.

Call this a "persuasive interview." It exemplifies the process of weaving the various strands of our social worlds into a braid that allows the journalist to get his or her story. The power words (I read this as part of the "culture") are *conditionally* connected to the *relationship* with the journalist and to the *self* of the interviewee; these power words apply if and only if the person engages in the *episode* of going on television and testifying against the miscreants.

This conversational pattern can be contrasted with other ways of braiding strands of social reality. For example, paying the informant for the information (a bribe, by any name, costs the same) consists of linking performance in the episode to a desired consequence (more money). This braid is much thinner and less "noble" than that intertwining self, culture, and episode.

Living Comfortably with Paradox

Paradoxes are states of affairs in which mutually contradictory things are both true. Logicians and rhetoricians have long been aware of paradoxes, because they seem to strain our very ability to comprehend the world. One of the oldest paradoxes involves the charming man from the Mediterranean island of Crete who starts to tell you about his culture. "All Cretans are liars," he says. "But aren't you a Cretan?" you ask. "Yes, of course. I am very proud to be from Crete," he replies. "But," you stammer as he smiles inscrutably, "if you say that all Cretans are liars, and you are from Crete, then you must be lying about all Cretans being liars, but if you are lying, then not all Cretans are liars and maybe you are telling the truth and all Cretans are liars . . ."

Ways of understanding paradoxes.   Paradoxes are confusing, but they are also very useful. In the hands of mathematicians and logicians, they are tools that test the consistency of formal symbolic systems. The term itself comes from two Greek words: *para* ("beyond") and *doxos* ("belief"). If you believe two things to be true, but they are contradictory, you have encountered a paradox; the paradox is at least a signal that something is wrong with your beliefs. Nicolas Falletta (1983, p. xvii) said that the best definition of a paradox is "truth standing on its head to attract attention."

> *Paradoxes have played a dramatic part in intellectual history, often foreshadowing revolutionary developments in science, mathematics, and logic. Whenever, in any discipline, we discover a problem that cannot be solved within the conceptual framework that supposedly should apply, we experience shock. The shock may compel us to discard the old framework and adopt a new one. It is to this process of intellectual molting that we owe the birth of many of the major*

ideas in mathematics and science. (Rappoport 1967, quoted in Falletta, 1983, p. xviii)

Paradoxes in the realm of action are more difficult to deal with than paradoxes in the semantic realm. Ordinary people have little trouble affirming their beliefs in inconsistent, mutually exclusive propositions—a fact that says something important about the difference between "believing" something and "affirming belief in a proposition." However, if people feel morally committed to performing mutually exclusive acts in a particular setting, this can be very troubling. What do you do when you "must" lie and tell the truth simultaneously?

At the beginning of the twentieth century, British philosopher Bertrand Russell proposed what he called the "theory of logical types" as a way of instructing us how to use language without encountering paradoxes. The theory forbade "classes" to be members of themselves—that is, your Cretan friend and his statement that "all Cretans are liars" cannot *both* describe the class of all Cretans and their lies *and* be a member of that class. His solution to the problem of paradox is perhaps less interesting than the fact that he understood the potential for encountering paradoxes to be a problem and warned us to try to avoid them. This sentiment persisted, and extended even to people who had not read his snappily titled *Principia Mathematica*.

In the middle of the twentieth century, Gregory Bateson and others noted that schizophrenics were enmeshed in paradoxical conversational structures with their families. That is, they were simultaneously required to act in mutually contradictory ways, they were prohibited from talking about the problem, and they were unable to leave the family system. Bateson and his colleagues developed this as the theory of "double binds" and argued that such patterns were the context in which schizophrenia develops.

The concept of double binds was enormously exciting to communication theorists and psychologists. If we could teach people to prevent the development of double binds, we could reduce the occurrence of schizophrenia. Unfortunately, it did not work out quite so simply. Further research showed that families that did not have schizophrenic members had just as many double binds as those who did. Apparently, the experience of double binds is not, at least in itself, a sufficient cause of severe psychological trouble.

Ways of dealing with pragmatic paradoxes. We have come now to realize that *pragmatic paradoxes*, that is, the requirement to act at any one time in a mutually exclusive way, are a normal feature of our social worlds, and that they do not usually cause us great problems. Some of the ways that we deal with pragmatic paradoxes are these:

1. Clarify the hierarchical relation among the paradoxical demands. That is, we decide that one of the mutually exclusive things that we must do is more important than the other, so we deliberately break the paradox by

not doing one of the things that we *must* do. For example, if your mother fell and broke her leg and needed you to drive her to the hospital and your professor expected you to come by his office to pick up an assignment sheet, you are in a pragmatic paradox. Few of us would agonize over the decision about what to do, however, and most of us would find ourselves at the hospital emergency room.

2. Reconstruct the context. Mutually exclusive requirements always occur in a context that holds them in their relationship. If you can reconstruct the context, what once seemed mutually exclusive is no longer paradoxical. For example, this is often presented as a paradox:

> all statements in this box are false

If the statement truly describes all statements in the box, it must be one of the false statements that it truly describes, and thus must be both true and false simultaneously.

Note that this statement is paradoxical *only* in a context in which some statements are considered "true" and others "false." Some schools of Buddhism hold that the nature of the world is such and the nature of language is such that all statements, whether in boxes or not, are false. In this Buddhist context, the boxed statement that all boxed statements are false is not particularly interesting and certainly not "true."

Bertrand Russell showed a different way of reconstructing the context. His "theory of logical types" forbids us to put statements *about* the box *into* the box, so he would have us take the statement out of the box and thus eliminate the paradox.

Counterpoint 8.4

If our social worlds are heteroglossic and polyphonic and if every utterance we make is polysemic, then we should make friends with paradox and contradiction because we will have close acquaintance with them both. Those of us whose thinking is structured by print media are often paralyzed by contradiction and paradox. To avoid any such paralysis, look at two classic ways of dealing with paradox.

This is a classic paradox:

> All statements in this box are false.

On closer inspection, the paradoxicality of this statement depends on two assumptions, not usually articulated. The first consists of a belief about "truth" and "falsity," specifically, that some statements are false and others are true. The second assumption is that the statement is— or can be —"in" the box.

Russell's solution to the paradox is to deny the second assumption. His "law of logical types" states that no statement about a class can also be a member of the class. In other words:

All statements in this box are false.   →   [   ]

Russell's solution "protects" statements from paradoxicality, making them falsifiable by empirical test of, for example, the statements in the box.

The other solution, which I associate with Buddhism, denies the first assumption. To the extent that language represents the world, this philosophy teaches, it distorts it; therefore, *all* statements are false, whether they are in a box or not. That is:

All statements are false

> All statements in this box are false

The Buddhist solution subtly redefines the meaning of truth and falsity, such that the falsity of the self-referential statement in the box is not really very interesting. "Of course, they are false!" we say, "so are all other statements."

This all leads to a much more tolerant treatment of language and communicative acts than is implied in Russell's way of thinking or in the original paradox. That is, polysemy is a fact of life: everything we say means more than what we meant by it, and some of these meanings are quite different than what we intended.

In *Communication and the Human Condition* (Pearce 1989, p. 84), I argued that *mystery* (along with coherence and coordination) is an inherent, universal feature of human life.

> *Mystery comprises recognition of the limits of the stories in which we are enmeshed. These limits are not taken as confining boundaries, but the surest sign that there exists something beyond them. Mystery is a quality of experience of the human world, characterized by rapt attention, open-mindedness, a sense of wonder, perhaps even awe . . . it is a way of treating words and language as "friends" instead of either "masters" or "slaves."*

There is an irony in mystery that must be accepted, not dispelled: "The problem is words. Only with words can man become conscious; only with words learned from another can man learn how to talk to himself. Only through getting the better of words does it become possible for some, a little of the time, to transcend the verbal context and to become, for brief instants, free" (Shands 1971, pp. 19, 20).

If we extend this "friendship" with language to others and claim it for ourselves, we have room in which to deal with contradictions and paradoxes without making them into problems.

3. Use humor, irony, or sarcasm. Ordinary language seldom has the precision or single mindedness of scientific or logical talk. Instead, it is filled with metaphors, allusions, and other ways in which we *can* do multiple things all at the same time. For example, if we are required to be true to our own self and to obey the commands of the sergeant, we can find ways of doing what we are required to do in a manner that clearly allows us to maintain our own principles. The comic strip "Beetle Bailey" has demonstrated how this is done for dozens of years.

Recall the problem confronting Colin Turnbull. On the one hand, he had a (romantic) relationship with Kumari that he wanted to turn into marriage (i.e., into a relationship with romantic, familial, and economic aspects). On the other hand, he had a complex set of economic relationships with the institutions of his society that would cut him off from funds if he acted too bizarrely—for example, by marrying someone who could not be taken to formal social events that he was expected to attend because she was of the "wrong" race. Finally, both he and Kumari had familial relationships with their parents, both sets of whom opposed the relationship.

Colin Turnbull and Kumari were in a situation that might well be called a pragmatic paradox. They tried to resolve the paradox by doing something like Russell suggested: to leave the box (in this case, England) so that their relationship would not be in contact with those parts of their social worlds with which it conflicted. Sadly, it did not quite work, and thus the tragic experience of their relationship is a final cautionary tale for us. Juggling and weaving are arts requiring skill, good judgment and—for lack of a better word—luck. It does not always work out as it should.

Three Final Words

In this final "final" section, I want to weave together several strands of what I have written, highlighting themes that are subtexts stretched throughout the book.

Robinson's Laws of Shared Pain and Joy

Spider Robinson (1981, p. 71) declared that two laws govern our social worlds: "shared pain is lessened, and shared joy is increased." By "sharing," he means being talked about with a caring interlocutor—that is, someone who follows the nine commandments in Figure 8.4.

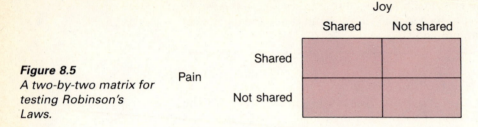

Figure 8.5
A two-by-two matrix for testing Robinson's Laws.

How should we think about these laws?

Robinson writes fiction, but I believe these statements to be true. Specifically, I believe that if you were to do a survey of all experiences of pain and joy, and were to divide each into two types, shared and not shared, thus making a two-by-two table (Figure 8.5), what the statisticians call an *interactive* effect would be seen. That is, the *amount* of joy would be greatest in the *shared* cell, but the *amount* of pain would be lowest in the *shared* cell.

This proposed empirical test is silly, of course, not least because pain and joy are not easily converted to amounts that can be statistically analyzed. (Which hurts the most? A broken arm, being rejected by the man or woman you love, or the death of your parents? Of course these are different *kinds* of pain that cannot be reasonably compared—that's my point.)

What is *not* silly is thinking about the reason why there is something "true" about Robinson's statements. Let me call attention to two things: the perils of quantification and the location of the events and objects of our social worlds.

Numbers are a vocabulary, and statistics is a syntax. The apparent clarity and precision of mathematics makes it seem that it is a better representation of "the world" than our subjective, flexible, corrigible perceptions. For example, the terms "lessened" and "increased" *appear* to have a precise meaning if the quantity of some variable can be measured. But if we think about what is being talked about, it quickly becomes clear that "more" and "less"—in this context, at least—are metaphors.

Sharing does not mean transporting some of my pain or joy to someone else, nor does it mean creating in someone else's mind the same experience as in mine. Rather, it is a rather vague term indexing a particular type of conversation in which my emotion is acknowledged, I do not feel shame or embarrassment, and you and I act in ways that are symmetrically contingent. That is, sharing is a way of coping with (reducing) pain and of enhancing (increasing) joy.

Implicit in the discussion of whether pain and joy can be usefully measured is a struggle with language that runs throughout this book. Language is at once the great facilitator: we would not have human worlds without it. But at the same time, the very *capacities* that language gives us are *snares*. By enabling us to do some things, it makes it harder to do others (see Pearce

Counterpoint 8.5

In this chapter, I contrasted two forms of conversation, *enabling* and *supporting*. Perhaps you noticed that the term "help" was used in both, and that it was not used in the same way.

Determine some of the differences between these two uses of "help." As you do, remember to identify the perspective from which you are describing what help means. From a third-person perspective, the help provided by an enabler may be quite different from what it appears to be from the perspective of the enabler or the drug-dependent person being enabled.

At least one of the distinctions has to do with the concept of communication that is implicitly understood in each use of the term. If you do not push the distinction too hard, it seems that to *help* in enabling is to create a conversational context in which the enabled person can continue a specific form of actions; to *help* in supporting is to create a conversational context in which the supported person can choose among a wider array of actions. In *enabling*, the helper finds himself or herself more deeply enmeshed in a particular, unhealthy relationship with the person being enabled; in *supporting*, the helper finds himself or herself freer to develop many relationships or many kinds of relationships with the person being supported. From the perspective of an observer, enablers seem to be working within a *transmission* concept of communication; that is, they see themselves as doing something *for* or *to* the other person in a one-way, linear process. From the same perspective, supporters seem to be working within a *social constructionist* concept of communication; that is, they see themselves as engaged in a co-construction of a social *umwelt* in which both they and the other can live and develop "healthily."

1989, Chapter 3). Specifically, the language into which most of us were born and must use if we are to understand and be understood by our fellows is *not* well adapted to a social constructionist perspective.

If pain and joy, like the other events and objects of our social worlds, exist in conversations, if conversations comprise the objective reality of social worlds, and if conversations are co-constructed, unfinished, polyphonic, reflexive, and all the other things discussed in this book, then we need to develop a language that directs our attention toward those features rather than to other things. Such a language would indicate that the stuff of our social worlds does not lie just or even primarily either "in our heads" or in physical place outside our actions. Rather, pain and joy are created and continually recreated in the continuing, recursive crucible of conversation. We should look there for those things that enrich or degrade our lives, and the form, or configuration, of those conversations constitutes our social worlds.

Stability and Change in our Social Worlds

The arguments among the pre-Socratic Greek philosophers are one of the foundations of Western culture. Among other things, they heatedly debated the question of whether the physical universe was comprised of change or stability. They sometimes posed the question quite prosaically: can you put your foot in the same river twice?

Leaving the philosophers and physicists to continue this discussion about the physical world, the nature of our social worlds is quite clear: they are indeterminant, changing, and with multiple meanings at any one point. In Chapter 2, you learned the terms heteroglossia, polyphony, and polysemy as labels for various aspects of the continuing process of the creation of social worlds. In Chapter 3, the conversational triplet provided a model for understanding the unfolding nature of the creation of the events and objects of the social world. Clearly, you cannot say the same thing twice even if you quote yourself or replay a videotape of what you said yesterday or five minutes ago. And because we live *in* communication, the fact that you cannot have the same conversation twice means that you are not quite the same person in any two conversations.

I am suggesting a picture of our social worlds as formless, seething, and in constant change—a picture strikingly different from ordinary life as most of us know it most of the time. Most of us live within "local" conditions of stability and structure. These local conditions can be as broad as a culture and can last far longer than a human lifetime. If so, then what's the point of worrying about the underlying flux?

Two important implications derive from the awareness of the fluidity of our social worlds. One has to do with our sensitivity to what is going on around us, the second, with competence.

Sensitivity to forces that create stability.
Which is the natural order, stability or change? The understanding of interpersonal communication presented in this book argues for *change*. This does not deny the existence of stability, but it implies that stability is *achieved* rather than *found*. If you find yourself within a social world that appears stable, permanent, and structured, these features should claim your attention. By applying the Heyerdahl solution, you should look for patterns of conversations that have produced a local condition of *monoglossia* (i.e., in which there is only one language), *monophonia* (i.e., in which only one voice—no matter how many speakers use that voice—is heard), and *monosemy* (i.e., words mean just what they say and only what they say). How is such an orderly, tidy space within social worlds made? Who makes it? What patterns of power are prefigured in it?

We have a tendency to take *clarity* and *order* in our social worlds as givens; we seek explanations for change. The analysis of interpersonal communication in this book suggests reversing that presumption: the fact of change is natural and needs no further explanation, the direction of change is a fruitful topic for exploration, and pockets of local stability and order should strike us as intensely unusual and excite our curiosity.

Situational differences in what competence means.   The second implication of recognizing that the substance of our social worlds is flux has to do with competence. In Chapter 2, you learned that *game playing* and *game mastery* are different depending on whether they occurred in situations that were clear and stable or ambiguous and changing. Specifically, game mastery in clear and stable situations means achieving coordination in ways that differ from the established scripts, goals, and rules of the context. On the other hand, game mastery in ambiguous and changing situations involves creating order where there is none, achieving coordination by establishing scripts, goals, and rules when such structures are missing, confused, or jumbled.

If nothing else, Chapters 4, 5, 6, and 7 suggested that contemporary society *as a whole* is better described as ambiguous and changing than clear and stable. There are many local areas of clarity and stability, of course, but these are the results of powerful processes of structure making. If you are to live a life of dignity and honor, to develop sustaining relationships and a healthy identity, and to cope with the various strangers you will meet, you will need to be able to use both kinds of competence—*game mastery* and *game playing*—in both kinds of situations.

When your social worlds seem comfortable and stable, you will be happy to play out the established scripts as a game player; but at other times, you may need to be creative and find alternatives to those scripts by exercising your game mastery. When your social worlds seem chaotic and unstable, you will enjoy the opportunities of polysemy and improvise as a game player; but at other times, you will want to act as a game master and impose order on fluctuating impermanence and create clarity in the midst of confusion.

That is to say, the conditions of contemporary society require an unusual awareness of interpersonal communication: its contexts, its processes, and its potentials. What is lost is a certain kind of innocence; what is gained is a certain kind of sophistication that Aristotle called *phronesis*.

What "Good" Communication Means

Earlier in the book, I contrasted two concepts of communication. I compared the answers they give to three questions: What is communication? How does it work? and What work does it do? The rest of this book can be seen as an extended discussion of the *social constructionist* answer to those questions.

However, a fourth question has never been far from the surface: What is "good" communication?

The *transmission/representation* model of communication focuses on the accuracy with which messages *represent* reality and the fidelity with which they are transmitted. Because this model has an affinity for the modernist vocabulary of self, "good" communication *from this perspective* occurs when the mental pictures or images in your head resemble those in mine, and both resemble the events and objects of the real world. We have communicated well when we agree with or understand each other in this sense.

By now, the description of good communication in the preceding paragraph should seem very strange. From a social constructionist perspective, good communication occurs when you and others are able to coordinate your actions sufficiently well that your conversations comprise social worlds in which you and they can live well—that is, with dignity, honor, joy and love.

Praxis

1. Racism, Sexism, and Classism

Why do people tell racist or sexist jokes? Why do they repeat so many times the same ethnic stereotypes in conversations with people unlikely to challenge or correct those derogatory simplifications? What are people doing when they laugh at or make fun of the characteristics of people who are richer or poorer than they?

There are probably many reasons, but this one may be more often important than it would seem: By communicating in ways that are offensive to selected groups of people, racists and sexists protect themselves from the frightening possibility of developing friendly relationships with those they put down. Try this as an explanation the next time someone refers to you in ways that classify you as a member of some unliked group: interpret their comment as an unimaginative way of protecting them from getting to know and like you. How does this change the way you think about them? Practice interpreting racist, sexist, and classist remarks with this interpretation; look for *openings* in what is said that would allow you to reconstruct the context in which the remarks are made.

Of course, the situation is more complicated than this. The preceding paragraph locates the racist, sexist, or classist remark in the *first* position of the conversational triplet, and suggests that you reply (in the *second* position) in such a way that the *third* utterance is something other than the first. But if we locate the racist, sexist, or classist comment in the *second* position, the structure of the conversational triplet directs our attention to the comments preceding as well as following it.

Before class. Listen carefully for racist, sexist, and classist comments. In each case, note what was said and done immediately before and after the comment. How are these linked in terms of the interpersonal needs of inclusion, affection, and autonomy? As I have done this exercise, I hear derogatory remarks made *after* someone has talked about how "they" do not like "us" (thus threatening our need for affection), how "they" are out to get us (thus threatening our need for inclusion), or how "they" are taking away "our" resources or ability to do what we choose (thus threatening our need for autonomy). The comments *following* the sexist or racist remark are even more illuminating.

If this interpretation is at all accurate, it suggests that at least some of the problem of racism, sexism, or classism is part of a spiraling process in which a perceived threat elicits a response from us that increases the likelihood of the thing that we fear is actually happening. The first part of this process has been called the *malevolent transformation* (when affection is denied, the person responds in a hateful manner as if to say "I did not want your affection anyway!"); the second part of the process is a self-fulfilling prophecy (an action that predicts that something will come true and, by predicting it, makes it so).

In class. Form groups of three or four people; include as much gender, racial, and economic diversity within your group as possible. Compare your notes of sexist, racist, and classist comments that you heard, noting their position (first, second, or third *turns*) within conversational triplets. Try the hypothesis that at least one function of such comments is to preclude the possibility of establishing a personal relationship or engaging in dialogue with a member of the group being put down. What else is being made and done by these comments? What do you think that the speaker intended to be heard as saying?

Discuss your conclusions with other groups.

2. Developing Healthy Self-Concepts

In the first part of this chapter, I spent some time describing an unhealthy pattern of conversations between Kyle and Shirley. Later in the chapter, I gave a list of nine "commandments" that produce a more healthy pattern of conversations.

Divide into groups of three persons. Let one person play Kyle, one Shirley, and one an observer. In this project, Kyle and Shirley will alternate between the unhealthy pattern of *enabling* and the healthy pattern of *supporting*. The observer will coach both Kyle and Shirley to make sure that they stay in character.

As you repeat the process, make notes of the skills needed to bring off each type of conversation. What did Kyle and Shirley try? What worked and what did not work? What conversational ploys and performances are appropriate for enabling that are not for supporting, and vice versa?

After finishing the exercise, compare your notes with those of other groups. Can you come up with a recipe for *enabling*? How would you change the list of nine commandments for being *supportive*? With which conversational skills do you feel that you have most experience and competence? With which do you feel you have least experience and competence?

3. Interviewing

Compare and contrast two forms of interviews: *circular questioning* and the *persuasive interview* described in this chapter.

Work in groups of three, exchanging roles frequently. For each round, one person is the interviewer, one the interviewed, and the third is a consultant helping the others stay in character and to use the appropriate interview technique.

Pick a topic involving corruption, waste, mismanagement, larceny, or some other horrendous crime. The person being interviewed is not the criminal but has first-hand knowledge of what happened, sufficient to convict the culprit if she or he were to testify but is in some relationship with the culprit so that it would be dangerous or at least inconvenient to testify. Work together to create a scenario in sufficient detail that you can improvise in the interview.

First, practice the *persuasive interview*. Let the interviewer work through the stages of bonding, exalting, and closing. Let the interviewed person alternate resisting and complying with the technique.

Second, practice *circular questioning* about the same topic.

After several improvisations in each style, discuss the similarities and differences in them. What did it feel like to be interviewed in the two styles? What did it feel like to be the interviewer in the two styles? Which did you like best? Which made you feel more in control? What differences between the conversations in these two styles did you notice when you were in the third-person role? How do these styles of interviews compare with the nine commandments for supporting a healthy personality in Figure 8.4? How do these styles of interviews fit into the distinction between monologue and dialogue?

When you finish, compare your observations with those made by the members of other groups.

References

Dewey, John. *Experience and Nature*, 2nd ed. New York: Dover, 1958.

Falletta, Nicolas. *The Paradoxicon*. Garden City: Doubleday, 1983.

Pearce, W. Barnett. *Communication and the Human Condition*. Carbondale: Southern Illinois Press, 1989.

Pearce, W. Barnett, Cronen, Vernon E., and Conklin, R. Forrest. "On What to Look At When Studying Communication: A Hierarchical Model of Actors' Meanings." *Communication* 4 (1979): 195–220.

Rappoport, Anatol. "Escape from Paradox." *Scientific American* 217 (1967): 50–56.

Robinson, Spider. *Time Travelers Strictly Cash.* New York: Ace Books, 1981.

Shands, Harley Cecil. *The War with Words: Structure and Transcendence.* The Hague: Mouton, 1971.

Turnbull, Colin. *The Human Cycle.* New York: Simon & Schuster, 1984.

PHOTO CREDITS

NAME INDEX

SUBJECT INDEX